loading...

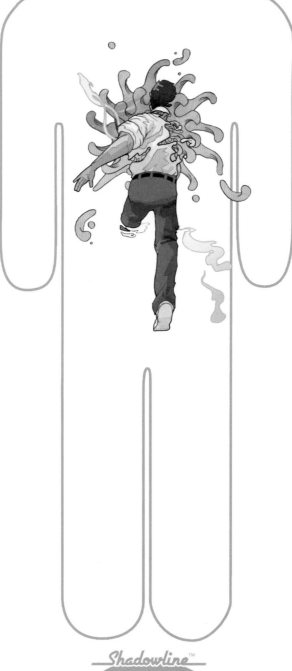

image

shadowlineonline.com

THE INFINITE VACATION

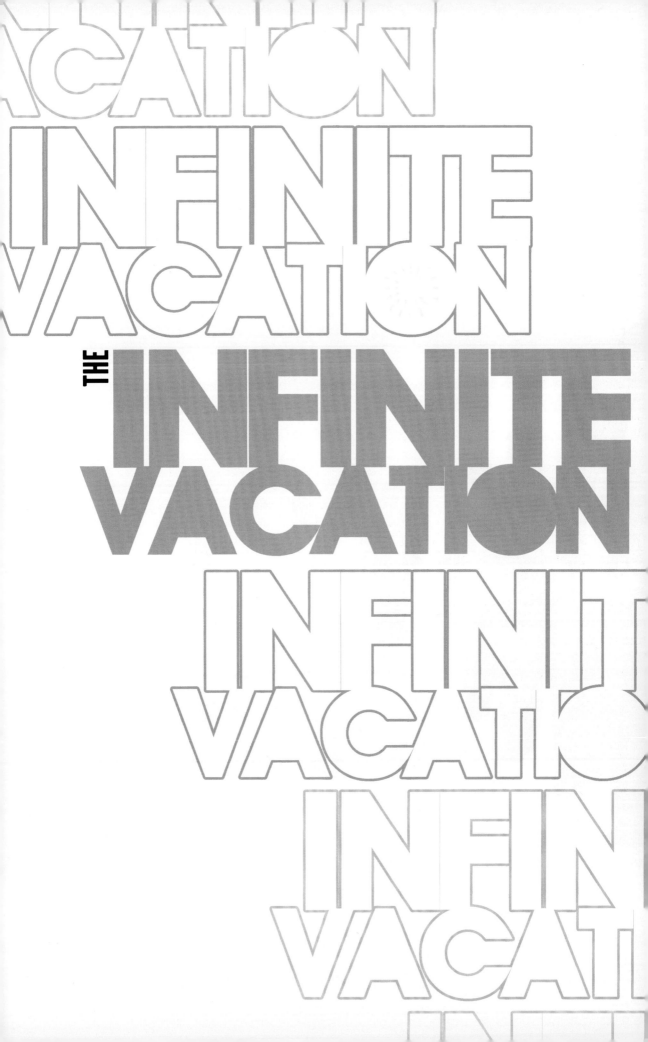

INFINITE VACATION, MAY, 2013, FIRST PRINTING.
Published by Image Comics, Inc. Office of
publication: 2001 Center St. Sixth Floor,
Berkeley, CA 94704. Copyright © 2013 NICK
SPENCER & CHRISTIAN WARD. Originally pub-
lished in single magazine form as INFINITE
VACATION #1-5 All rights reserved. INFINITE
VACATION (including all prominent characters
featured herein), its logo and all character
likenesses are trademarks of NICK SPENCER
& CHRISTIAN WARD, unless otherwise noted.
Image Comics® and its logos are registered
trademarks of Image Comics, Inc. Shadowline
and its logos are ™ and © 2013 Jim Valentino.

InternationalRights/ForeignLicensing
foreignlicensing@imagecomics.com

ISBN: 978-1-60706-721-4

IMAGE COMICS PRESENTS
A
Shadowline™
PRODUCTION

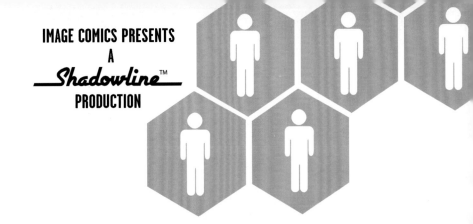

STORY BY NICK SPENCER & CHRISTIAN WARD

THE **INFINITE VACATION**

loading...

SCRIPT BY NICK SPENCER
ART BY CHRISTIAN WARD

LETTERS BY JEFF POWELL
PHOTOGRAPHY BY KENDALL BRUNS
DESIGN BY TIM DANIEL

EDITS BY JADE DODGE (ORIGINAL SERIES ISSUES 1-4)
PUBLISHER JIM VALENTINO

IMAGE COMICS, INC.
Robert Kirkman - chief operating officer   Erik Larsen - chief financial officer   Todd McFarlane - president
Marc Silvestri - chief executive officer   Jim Valentino - vice-president   Eric Stephenson - publisher   Ron Richards - director of business development
Jennifer de Guzman - pr & marketing director   Branwyn Bigglestone - accounts manager   Emily Miller - accounting assistant
Jamie Parreno - marketing assistant   Jenna Savage - administrative assistant   Kevin Yuen - digital rights coordinator   Jonathan Chan - production manager
Drew Gill - art director   Tyler Shainline - print manager   Monica Garcia - production artist   Vincent Kukua - production artist   Jana Cook - production artist
www.imagecomics.com

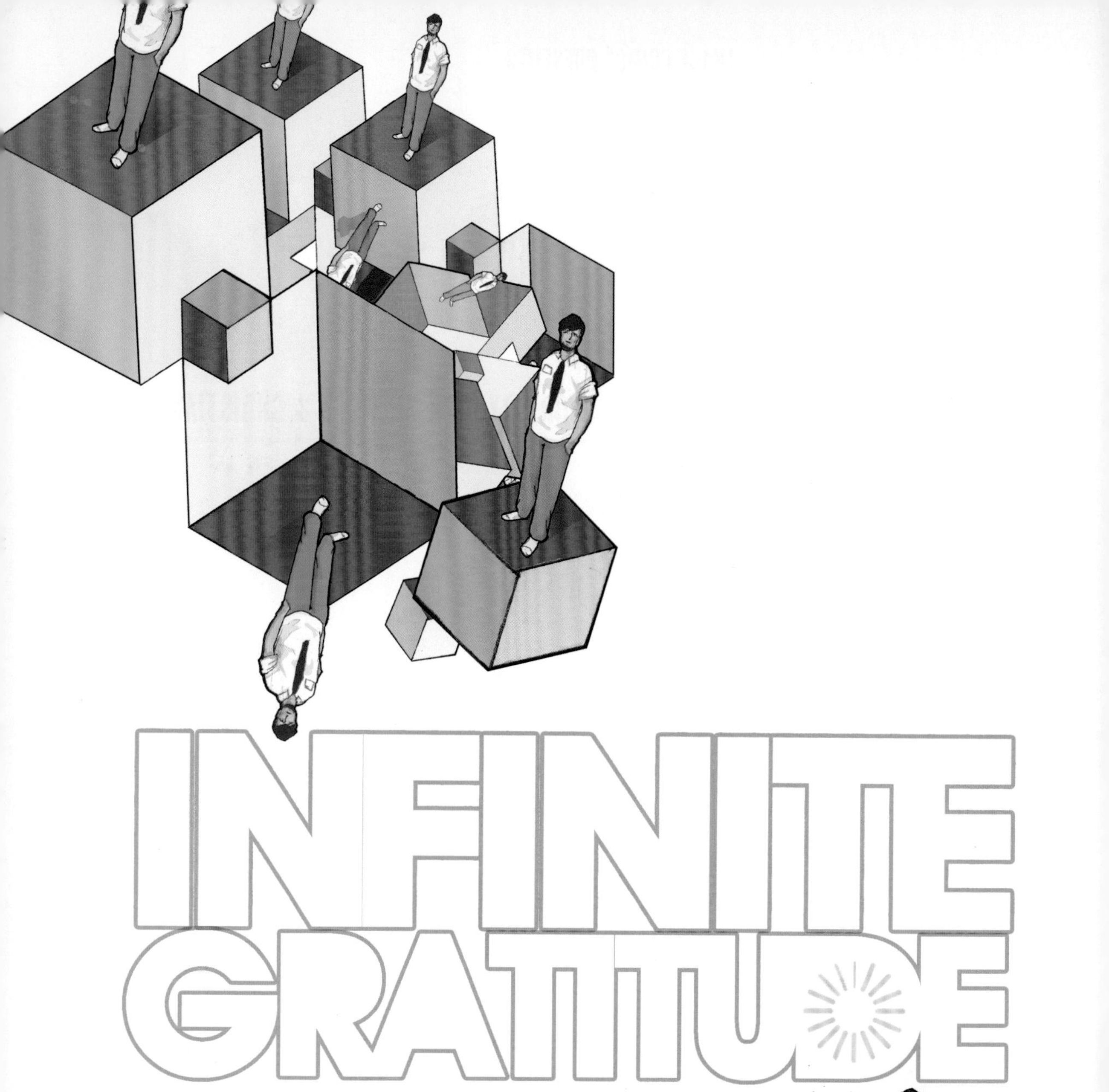

INFINITE GRATITUDE

loading.

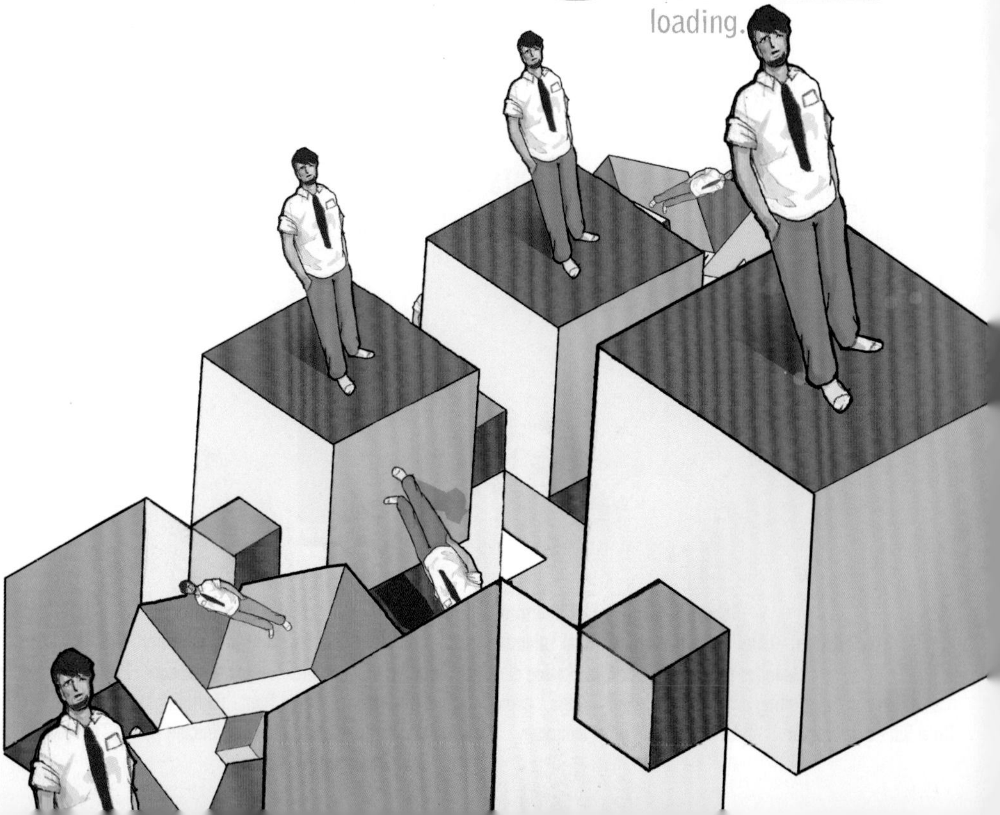

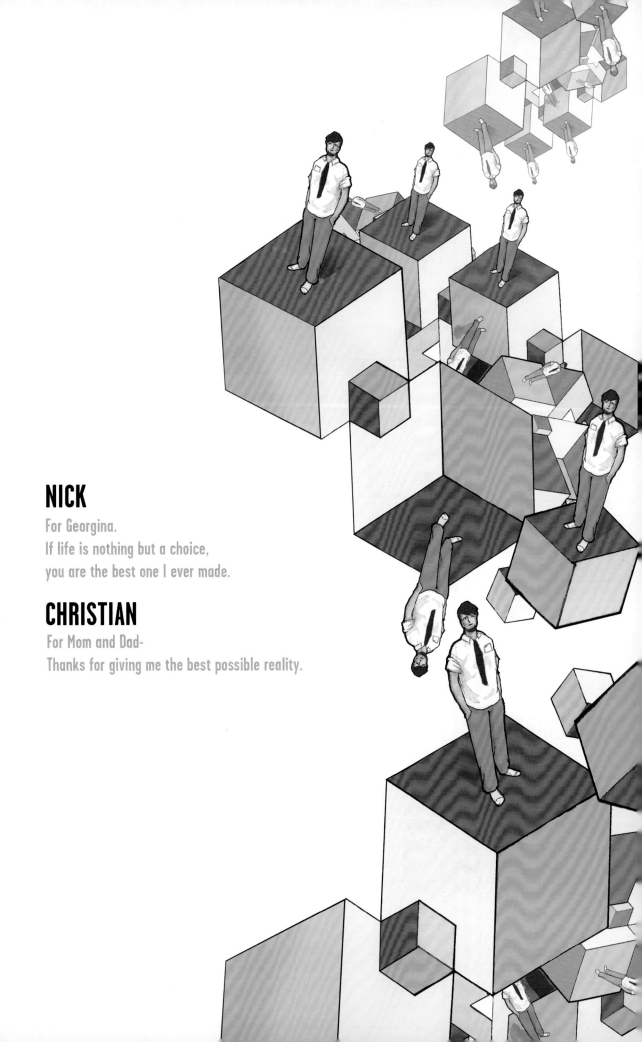

NICK

For Georgina.
If life is nothing but a choice,
you are the best one I ever made.

CHRISTIAN

For Mom and Dad-
Thanks for giving me the best possible reality.

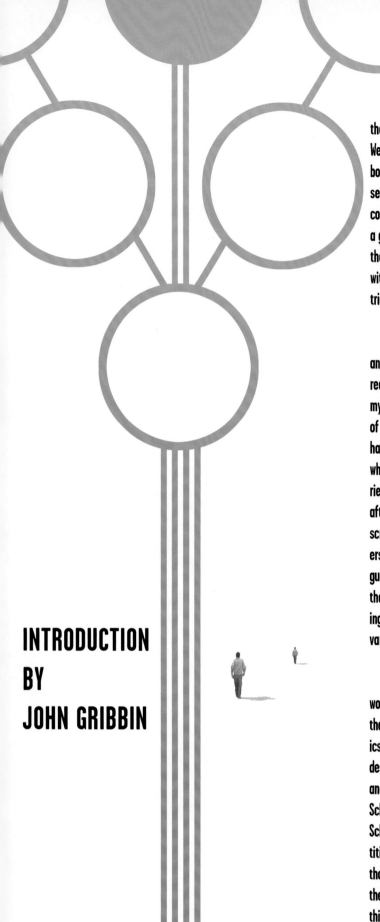

**INTRODUCTION
BY
JOHN GRIBBIN**

Parallel worlds, alternate histories, the Multiverse . . . the stuff of science fiction and comic books, right? Wrong. Well, right, but not just the stuff of science fiction and comic books. These are all serious scientific ideas that appear in serious scientific journals and are discussed at scientific conferences. So when I was asked to write an introduction to a graphic novel based on the premise "that at some point in the future you are able (for a mutually agreed price) to swap with a version of yourself in a parallel universe" I was intrigued but cautious.

Comic books are not famous for getting the science right, and as a science writer specialising in books about quantum reality, the Multiverse and the like I was wary about getting my name associated with some half-baked misrepresentation of science. Not least since Christian Ward told me that he had my book In Search of Schrödinger's Cat on his desk the whole time he was working on the book. I needn't have worried. When I read The Infinite Vacation I was impressed, page after page, with how the storyline interweaves fiction with scrupulously accurate science fact. I couldn't find any howlers - although, believe me, I tried. It seems to me - and I guess to Christian, or he wouldn't have asked me on board - that it will enhance your reading pleasure, rather than spoiling it, if I tell you a little bit about that real science in advance. So here goes.

Erwin Schrödinger was a real scientist, who was deeply worried, back in the 1930s, by the bizarre implications of the then-new theory of quantum physics (aka quantum mechanics). Quantum physics worked (and still works) beautifully to describe the behaviour of things like atoms and electrons, and light. It is based on equations (some of them derived by Schrödinger himself) which you can use (maybe not you, but Schrödinger and his succesors) to calculate how quantum entities will behave in experiments, and when you carry out those experiments the results are just the way quantum theory predicts. But it also says some deeply disturbing things. For one, it says that an entity such as an electron does not exist as a tiny hard particle (in spite of what you may have been taught in school) but as a "wave of probability" spread out across space.

If you make a measurement you always find the electron somewhere, at a definite place, as a result of what is known as the "collapse of the wave function", and the probability wave tells you the most likely places to find it. But as soon as you stop looking at it, it dissolves into a probability wave again.

Quantum theory also says that once two "particles" have interacted with one another, they are forever connected by what Albert Einstein called a spooky action at a distance, so that no matter how far apart they are if you poke one of them in a certain way the other one will jump, instantly. This "entanglement", though, does not feature in The Infinite Vacation (or does it? You decide).

You might dismiss all this as crazy theoretical ramblings of mad scientists. But quantum physics, using exactly the same equations that make these bizarre predictions, is the basis of such everyday items as the lasers in supermarket barcode readers and the chips in your smartphone. It also explains how DNA works. Nevertheless, Schrödinger was so upset by the implications of it all that he once said of the quantum theory that he had helped to invent that "I don't like it, and I'm sorry I ever had anything to do with it." And, with a little help from Einstein, he came up with his famous cat "experiment" to illustrate the absurdity of the theory.

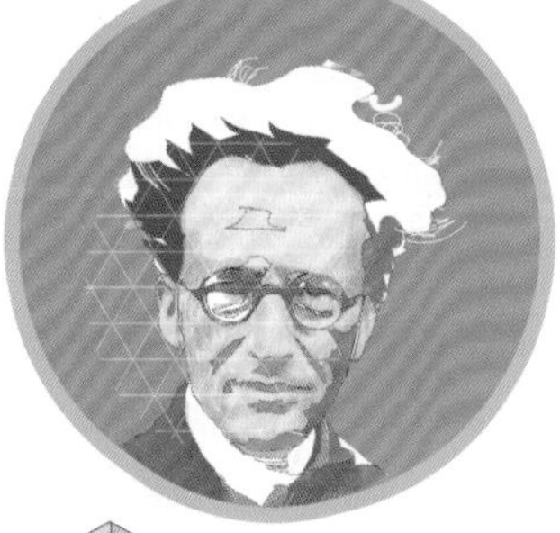

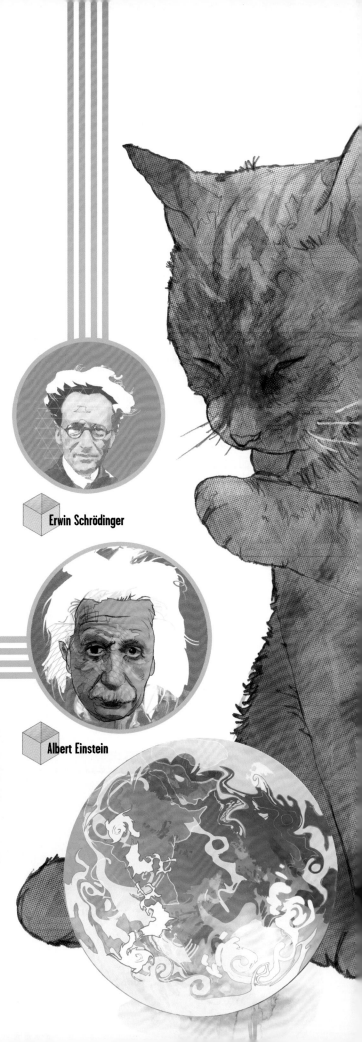

Erwin Schrödinger

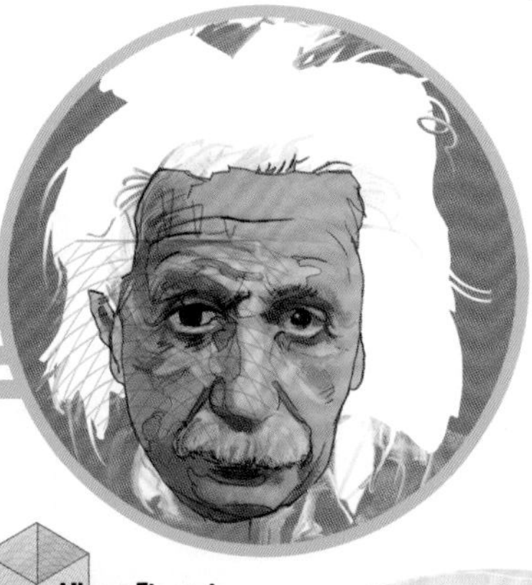

Albert Einstein

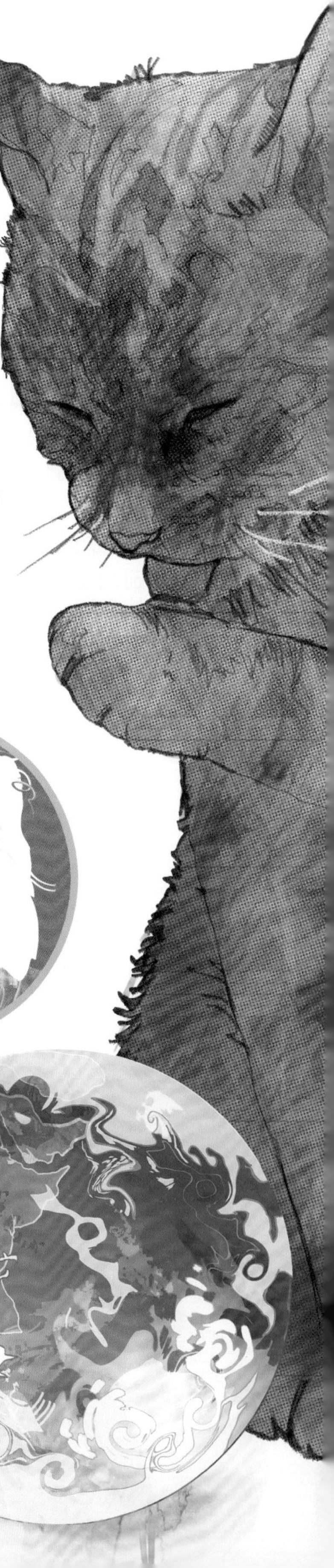

Schrödinger's cat is a mythical beast that is imagined to be involved in a quantum experiment which produces a pure mixture of two states, in one of which the cat is alive and in the other it is dead. One way of interpreting the quantum equations is to say that the Universe splits in two at the time the experiment is carried out, producing two parallel worlds, one which has a dead cat and one which has a live cat. Another interpretation says that there always were two parallel worlds, in one of which the cat dies and the other in which it lives. Either way, that makes an awful lot of worlds -- a Multiverse. Because this kind of splitting, or whatever it is, is associated with every possible choice of alternatives at a quantum level.

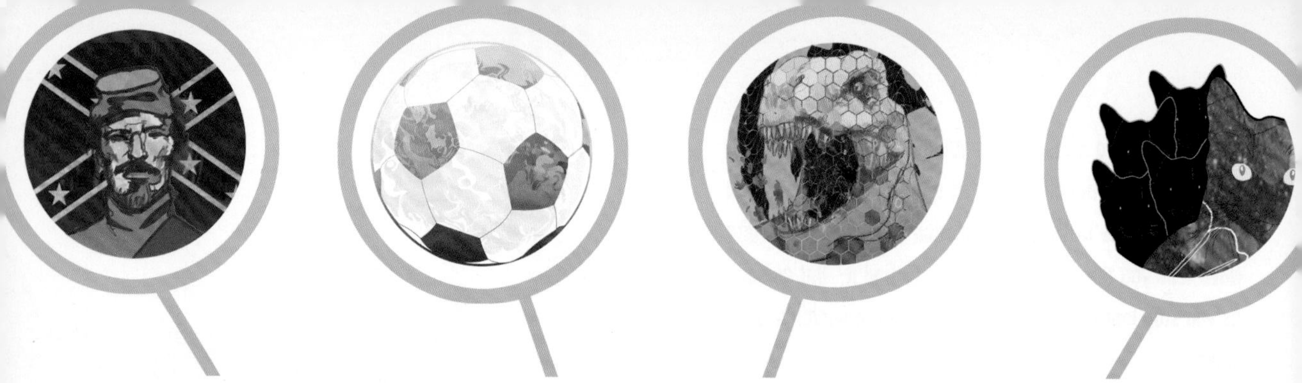

Scaling that up, it means that there are separate versions of reality in which, say you do or don't decide to get up in the morning, choose to catch the bus instead of the train, and so on. There really are worlds (an infinite number of them!) in which the South won the American Civil War, or the dinosaurs were not wiped out by a meteorite impact, or Chelsea have had the same manager for ten years. And this is real science (so real that at a very fundamental level, called the landscape in technical terminology, it provides the best explanation for why the Universe exists at all). At a more personal level, this implies the real existence of an infinite number of copies of the world including infinite copies of everybody, including you, living every possible variety of lives. This is the theme so brilliantly brought to life in The Infinite Vacation. There is a third quantum possibility (as it happens, the one I was taught at university) which says that if the cat is locked in a lab where nobody can see it, it exists in a bizarre mixture known as a "superposition of states", either both dead and alive at the same time or neither dead nor alive, until someone opens the door and checks up on it, at which point there is a "collapse of the wave function" and it becomes either dead or alive. But that is even weirder than the Multiverse.

I explore the implications of these ideas in my books In Search of Schrödinger's Cat, Schrödinger's Kittens, and In Search of the Multiverse. I also had a stab at using the same variation on the theme that you will find in The Infinite Vacation in my novel Timeswitch. But I have never seen the message got across more clearly and succinctly than in this book, which is also a cracking read even if you neither know nor care about the quantum physics. Enough of me; on with the story.

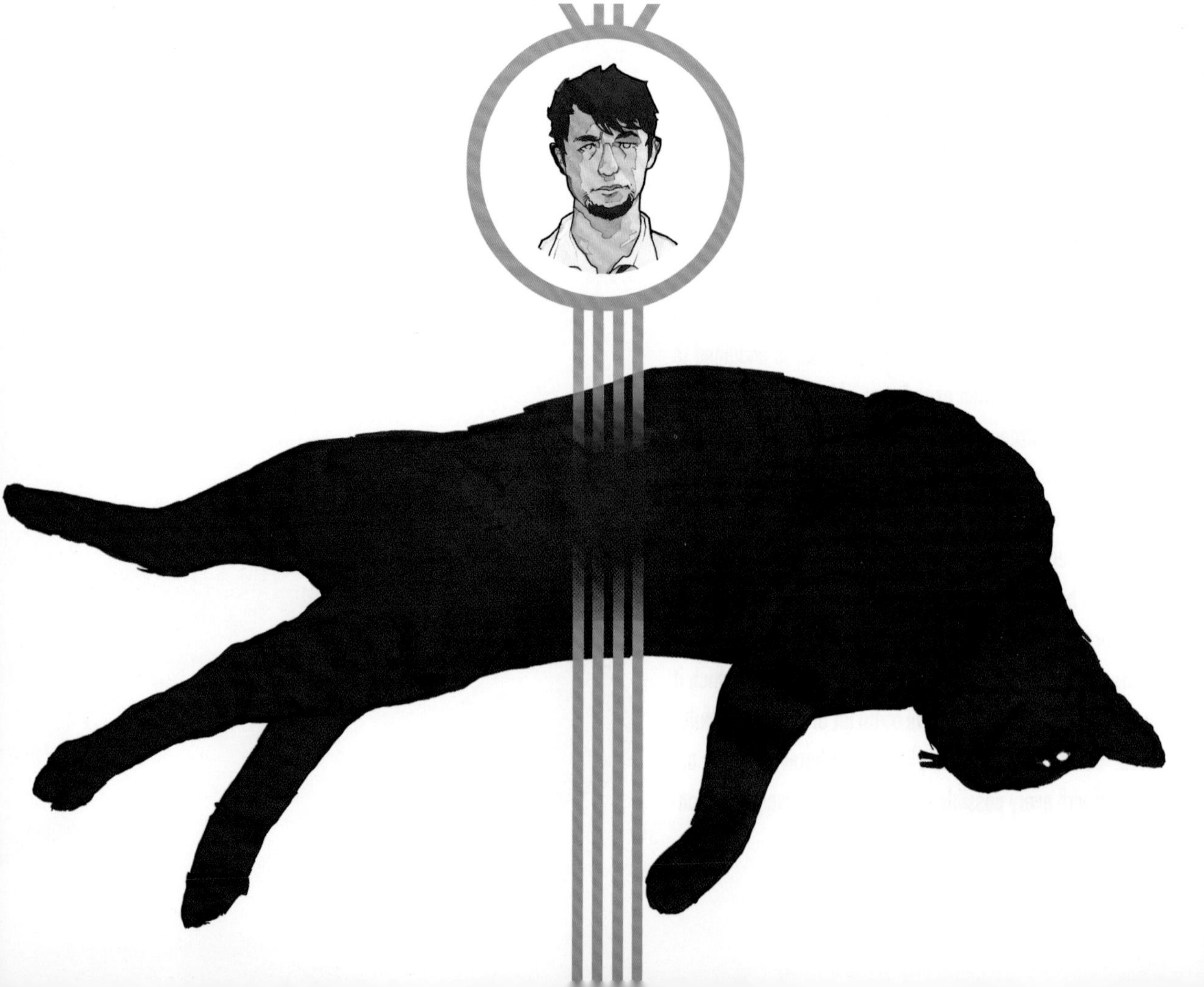

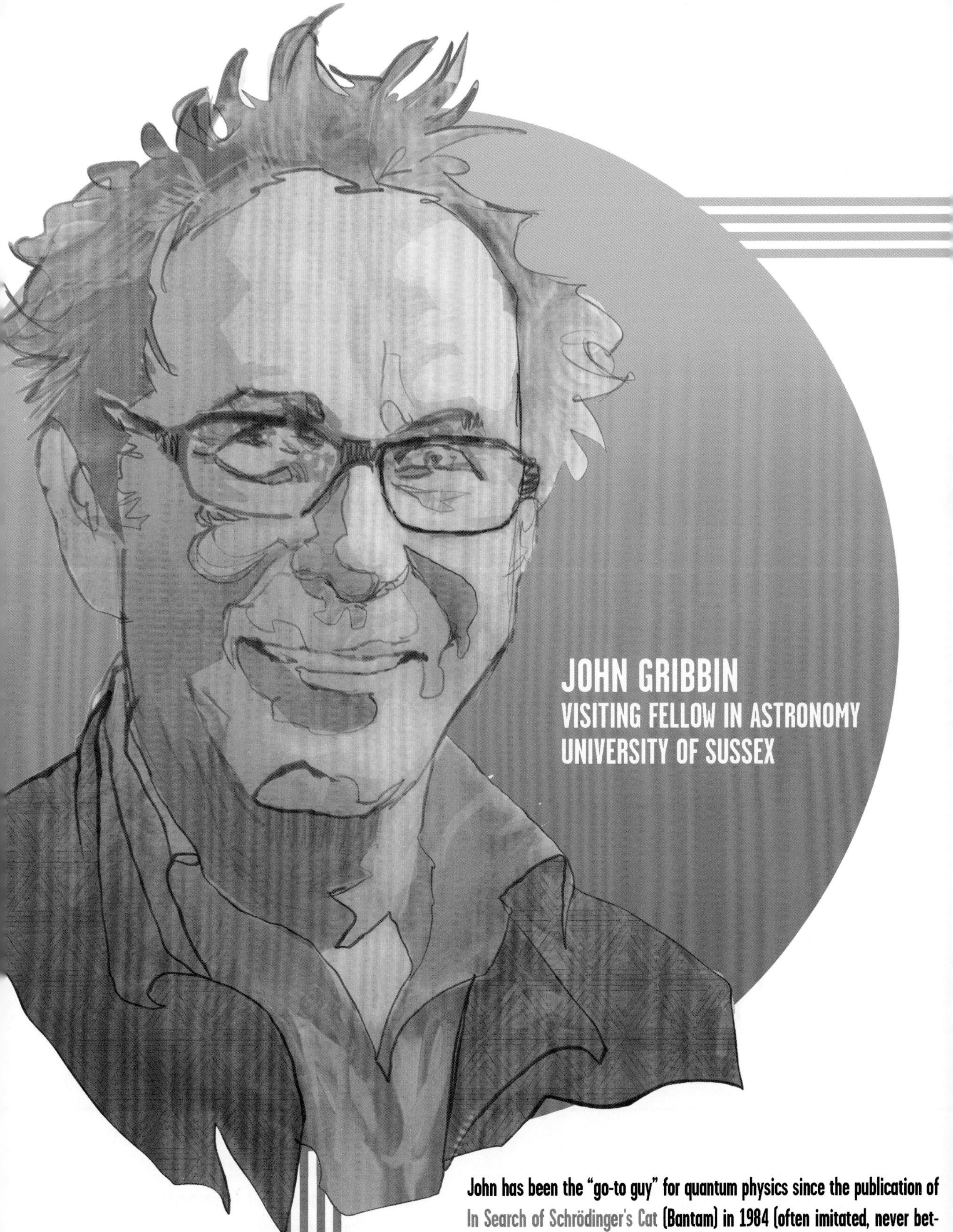
JOHN GRIBBIN
VISITING FELLOW IN ASTRONOMY
UNIVERSITY OF SUSSEX

John has been the "go-to guy" for quantum physics since the publication of In Search of Schrödinger's Cat (Bantam) in 1984 (often imitated, never bettered). Schrödinger's Kittens (Weidenfeld & Nicolson) appeared in 1995, and In Search of the Multiverse (Penguin) in 2009. Timeswitch (PS Publishing) dates from. You may also enjoy The Cartoon History of Time, illustrated by Kate Charlesworth, which has just been reprinted by Dover in the US.

He blogs as johngribbinscience.wordpress.com

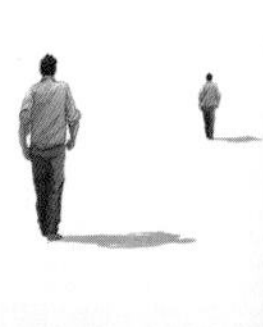

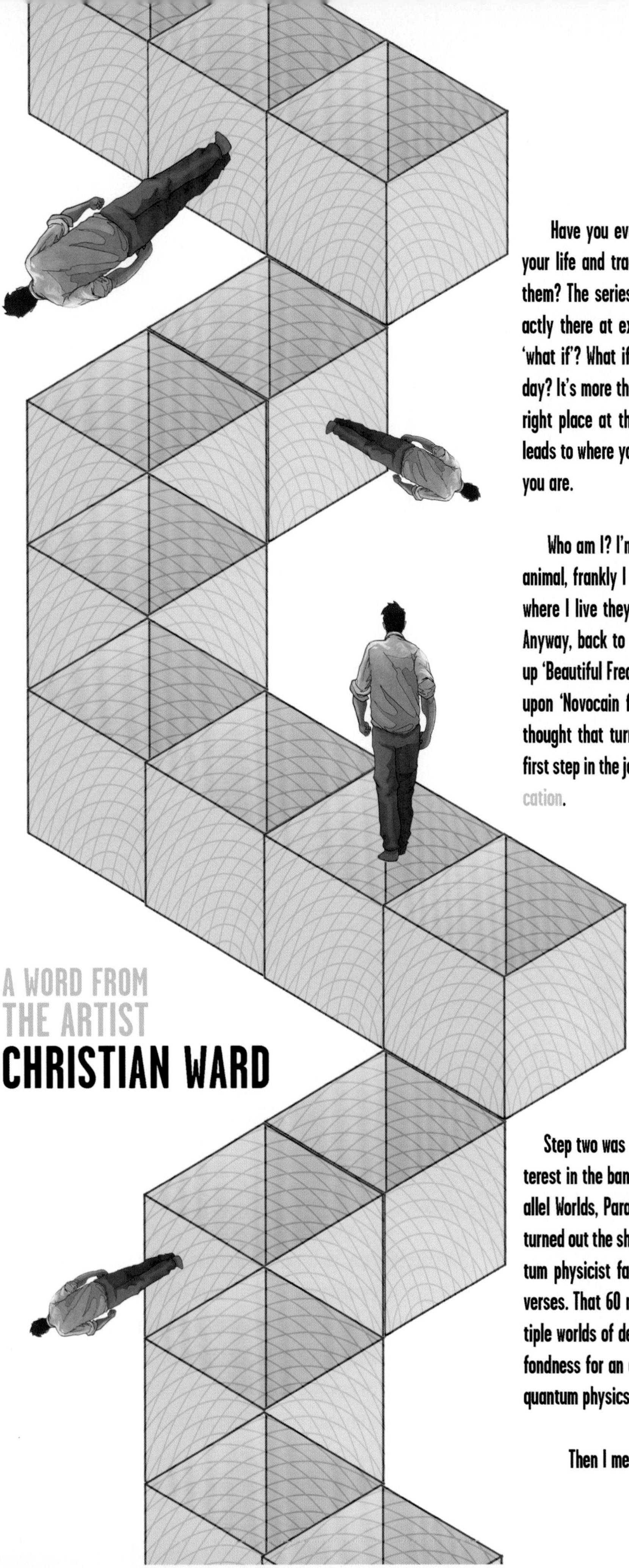

A WORD FROM THE ARTIST
CHRISTIAN WARD

WHO AM I?

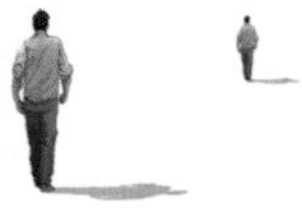

Have you ever thought about an important someone in your life and traced back the steps that lead you to meet them? The series of consequences that lead you to be exactly there at exactly that time? Have you ever wondered 'what if'? What if I hadn't gone to that coffee shop on that day? It's more than that, though. It's more than being at the right place at the right time. It's not just every step that leads to where you are but also every step that leads to who you are.

Who am I? I'm pretty fond of The EELS (the band not the animal, frankly I could live without the animal. Not far from where I live they eat jellied eels from a jar. No, thank you. Anyway, back to the musical variety...). I remember picking up 'Beautiful Freak' when I was in University after happening upon 'Novocain for the Soul' on the radio. Who would have thought that turning on the radio at that moment was the first step in the journey that would lead me to The Infinite Vacation.

Step two was in 2007 when I found myself (through my interest in the band) watching a BBC documentary called 'Parallel Worlds, Parallel Lives' presented by E from the EELS. It turned out the show was about E's relationship with his quantum physicist father and his relationship with parallel universes. That 60 minute show sent me spinning out into multiple worlds of dead cats and double slits. What started as a fondness for an alternative rock band ended up in a love of quantum physics.

Then I met Nick Spencer and Nick had an idea.

In fact, Nick had a number of ideas. He has lots of them. I think he has the ideas originally rationed out for a whole bunch of Nick's from a stream of other worlds, but our Nick got them all. I first met Nick at San Diego Comic Con back in 2009 since we were both there with our respective first releases from Image. This happenstance was step three. We knew right away we wanted to work with each other. From that point on, we chatted about different ideas and Nick would from time to time pitch a comic to me. His pitches were all great but none of them felt quite right. Then in September of that year Nick told me about an idea he was playing with which back then was just called 'Vacation'. The idea was in Nick's words a 'whole economy built around alternate realities'. There were those magic words: 'Parallel Universes'. The seed that had been planted some two years previously exploded in my head and The Infinite Vacation was born.

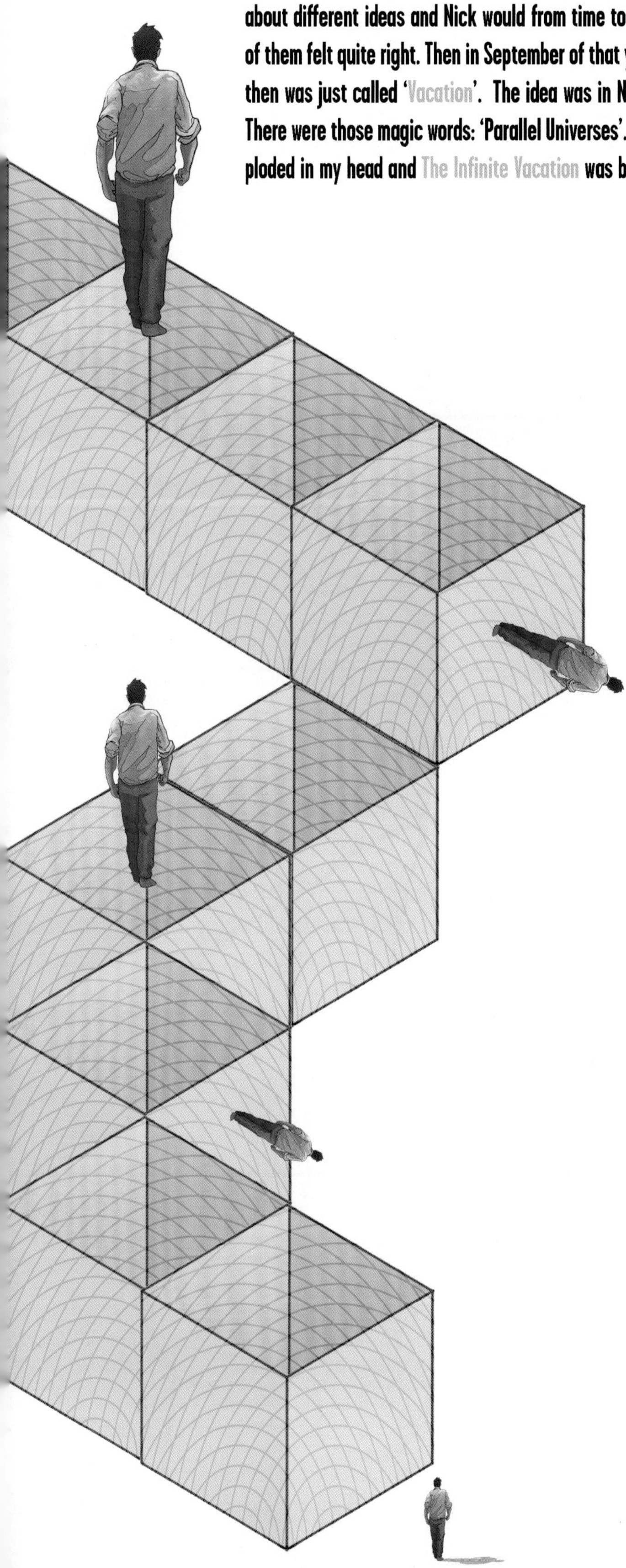

It's hard to believe in fate, but I believe in timing; in synchronicity. That synchronicity has been with us the whole time through the creation of IV. Everything happened for a reason. Like the fact that because of having a four page gatefold and having to have it land at a certain page number in this trade edition we now have to fill eight pages at the beginning of the book. This gives me the opportunity to tell you a little bit about what The Infinite Vacation means to me. I am also especially excited that we have been able to fit in an introduction written by John Gribbin, the author of 'In Search of Schroedinger's Cat' from which (after seeing E's documentary) gave me my first real taste of the dizzying quantum mechanics behind parallel universes. The book that sat on my desk as I drew The Infinite Vacation.

Those of you who have already read this book in its floppy format will know that for this story timing is everything. You see, sometimes it's not just about the right time, but about being the right you at the right time. That's something me and Mark have in common. I'm not a perfect man, I've certainly made mistakes in my life but as I get older I realize it's about being okay with who you are and embracing all the steps it took to get you to be the person you are today, because every step, even the bad ones, happen for a reason.

That's how I think about this book. It remains my favorite of all the books Nick has written and I'm immensely proud of it. I'm certainly glad that I live in the universe where we made it.

Christian Ward
London
2nd April 2013

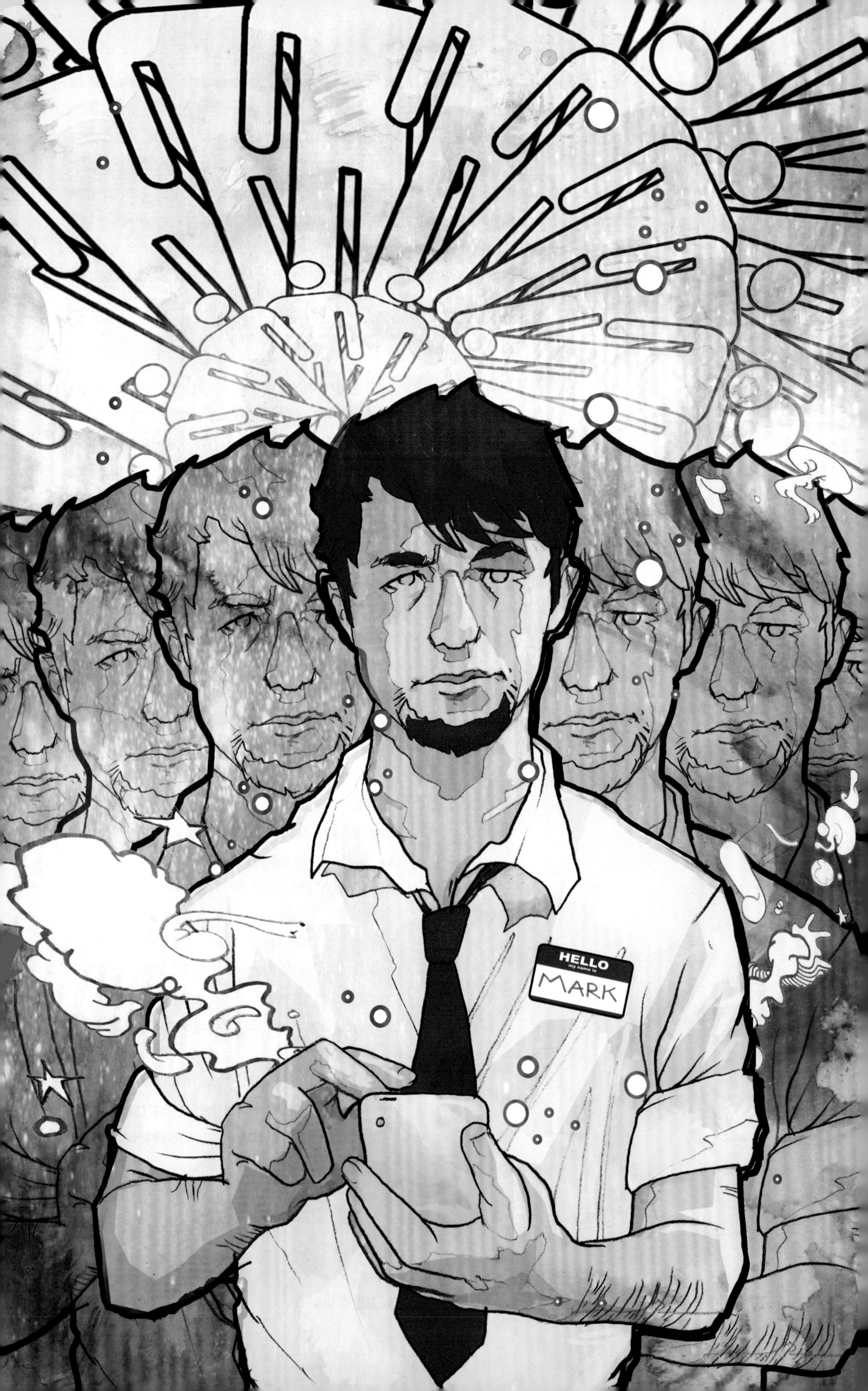
HELLO
my name is
MARK

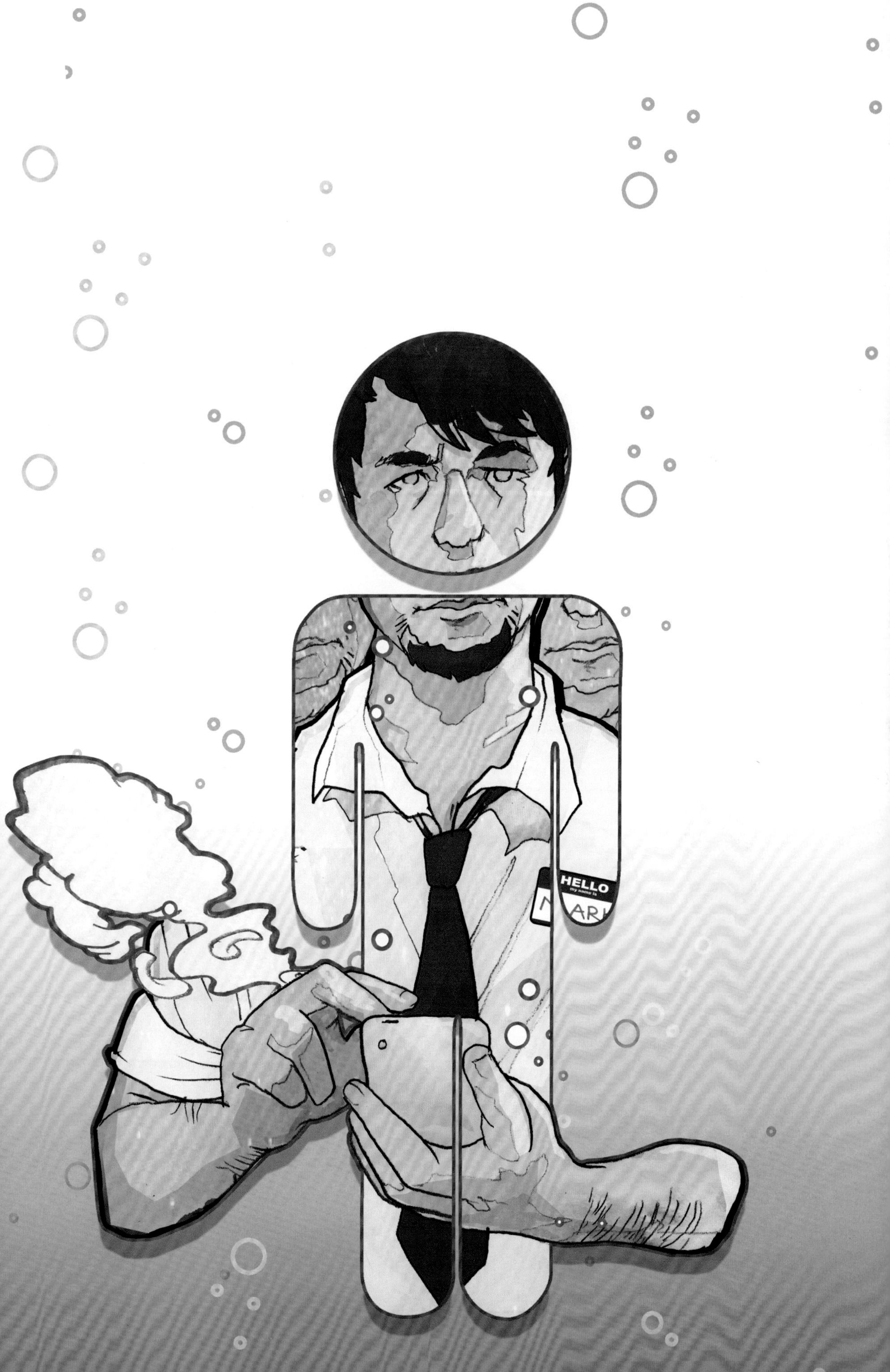
HELLO
my name is

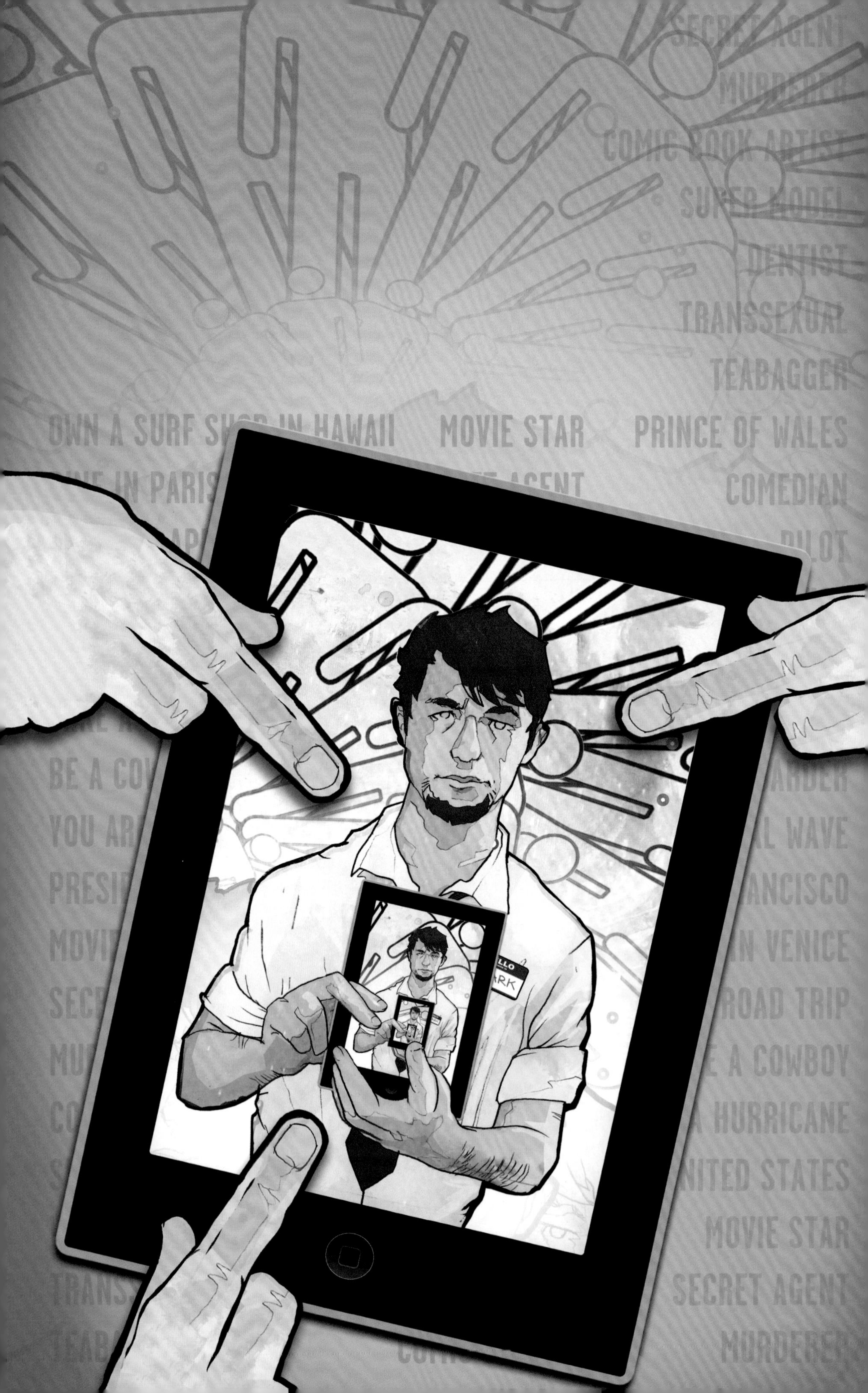
SECRET AGENT
COMIC BOOK ARTIST
DENTIST
TRANSSEXUAL
TEABAGGER
MOVIE STAR
PRINCE OF WALES
COMEDIAN
MOVIE STAR
SECRET AGENT

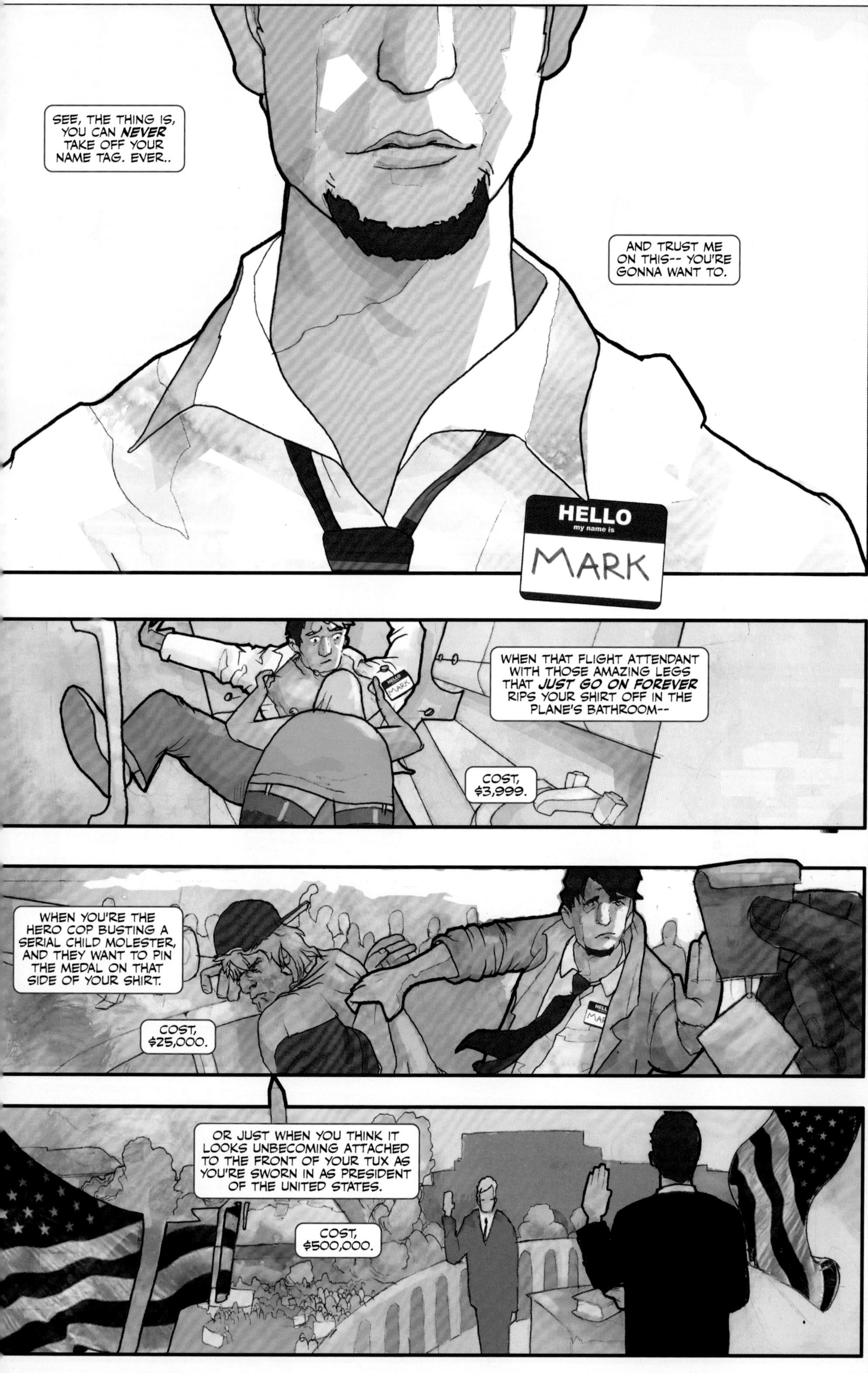
SEE, THE THING IS, YOU CAN NEVER TAKE OFF YOUR NAME TAG. EVER..
AND TRUST ME ON THIS-- YOU'RE GONNA WANT TO.
HELLO my name is MARK
WHEN THAT FLIGHT ATTENDANT WITH THOSE AMAZING LEGS THAT JUST GO ON FOREVER RIPS YOUR SHIRT OFF IN THE PLANE'S BATHROOM--
COST, $3,999.
WHEN YOU'RE THE HERO COP BUSTING A SERIAL CHILD MOLESTER, AND THEY WANT TO PIN THE MEDAL ON THAT SIDE OF YOUR SHIRT.
COST, $25,000.
OR JUST WHEN YOU THINK IT LOOKS UNBECOMING ATTACHED TO THE FRONT OF YOUR TUX AS YOU'RE SWORN IN AS PRESIDENT OF THE UNITED STATES.
COST, $500,000.

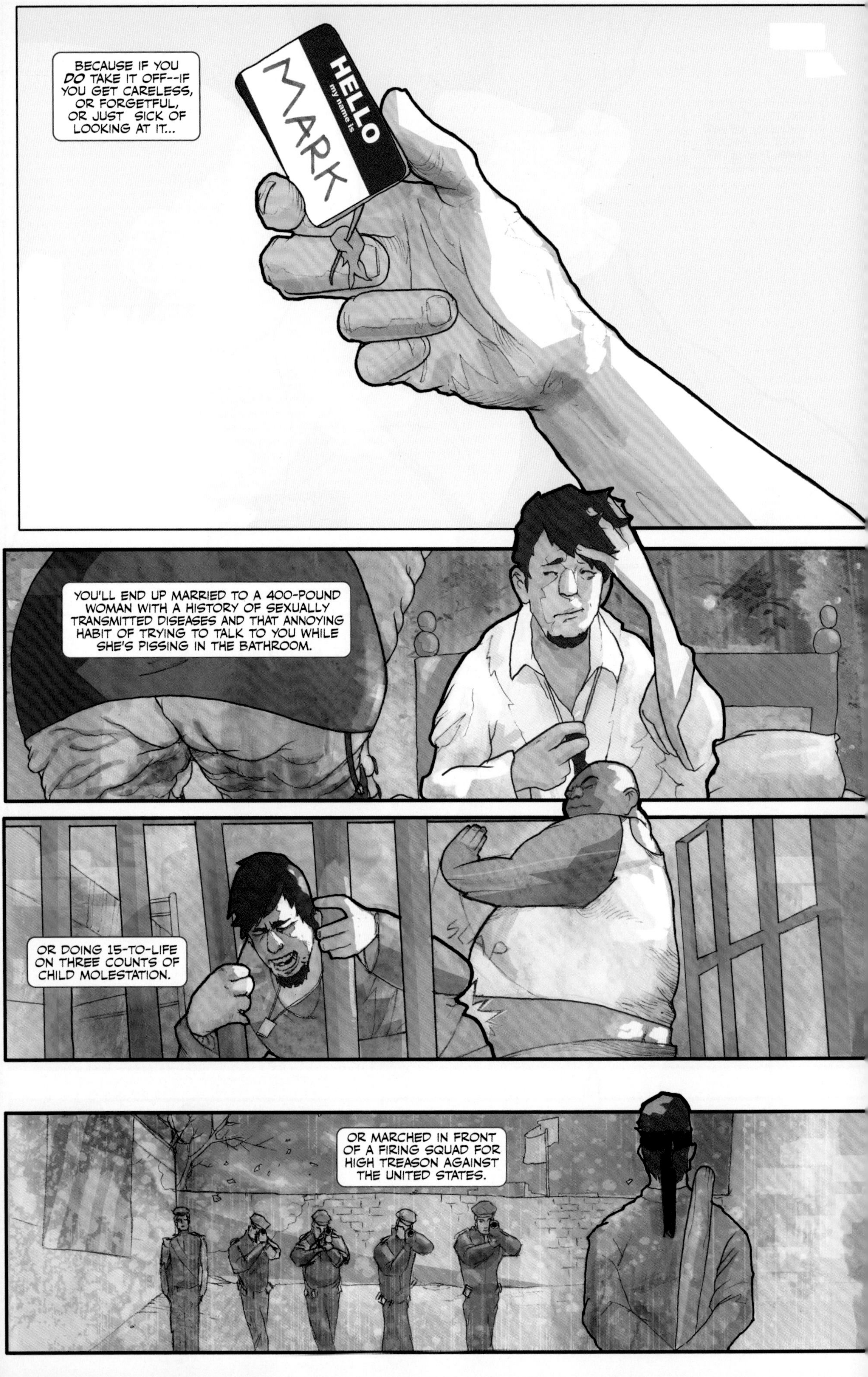

BECAUSE IF YOU DO TAKE IT OFF--IF YOU GET CARELESS, OR FORGETFUL, OR JUST SICK OF LOOKING AT IT...
HELLO my name is
MARK
YOU'LL END UP MARRIED TO A 400-POUND WOMAN WITH A HISTORY OF SEXUALLY TRANSMITTED DISEASES AND THAT ANNOYING HABIT OF TRYING TO TALK TO YOU WHILE SHE'S PISSING IN THE BATHROOM.
OR DOING 15-TO-LIFE ON THREE COUNTS OF CHILD MOLESTATION.
SLAP
OR MARCHED IN FRONT OF A FIRING SQUAD FOR HIGH TREASON AGAINST THE UNITED STATES.

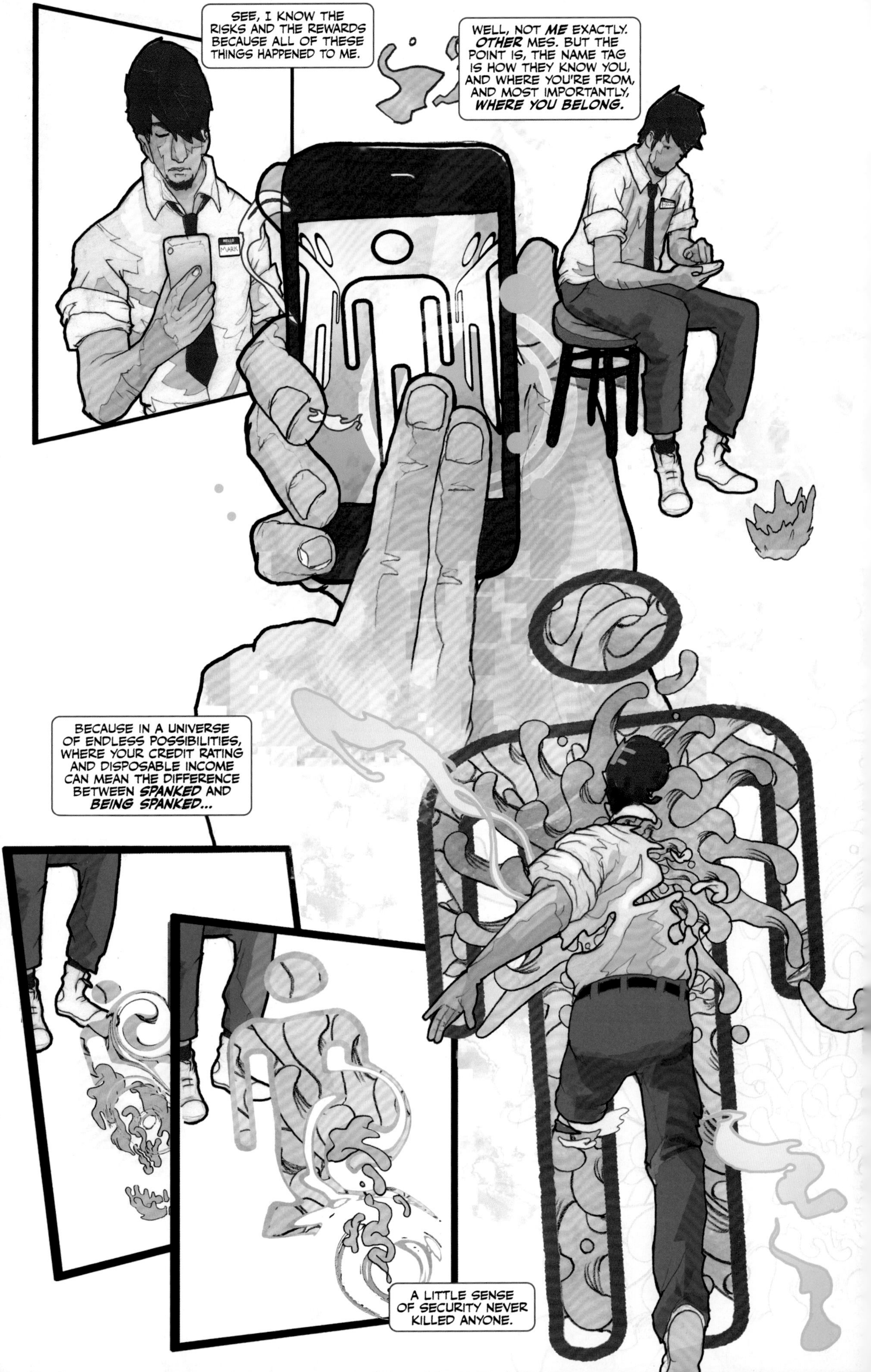
SEE, I KNOW THE RISKS AND THE REWARDS BECAUSE ALL OF THESE THINGS HAPPENED TO ME.
WELL, NOT ME EXACTLY. OTHER MES. BUT THE POINT IS, THE NAME TAG IS HOW THEY KNOW YOU, AND WHERE YOU'RE FROM, AND MOST IMPORTANTLY, WHERE YOU BELONG.
HELLO MARK
BECAUSE IN A UNIVERSE OF ENDLESS POSSIBILITIES, WHERE YOUR CREDIT RATING AND DISPOSABLE INCOME CAN MEAN THE DIFFERENCE BETWEEN SPANKED AND BEING SPANKED...
A LITTLE SENSE OF SECURITY NEVER KILLED ANYONE.

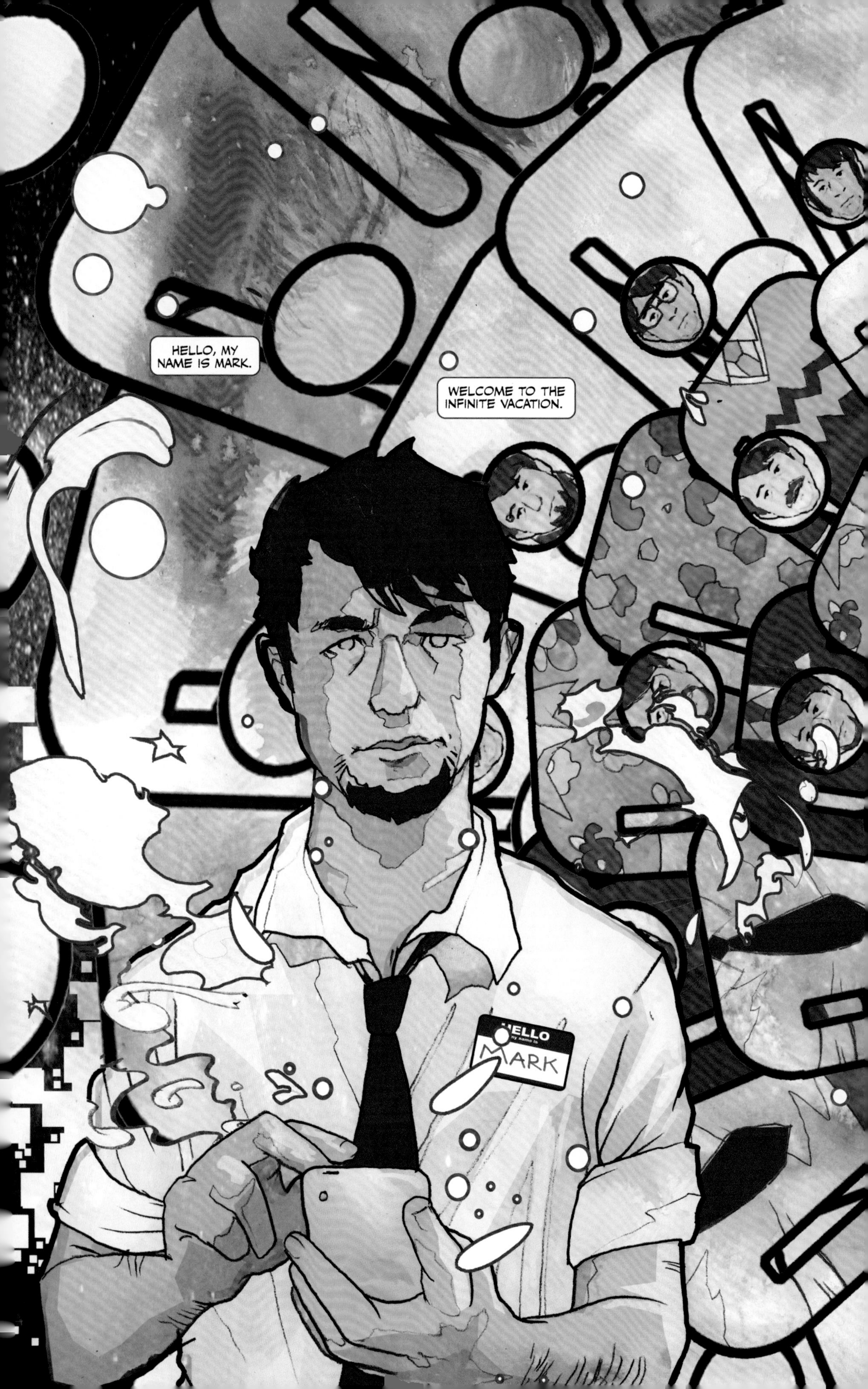
HELLO, MY NAME IS MARK.
WELCOME TO THE INFINITE VACATION.
HELLO
my name is
MARK

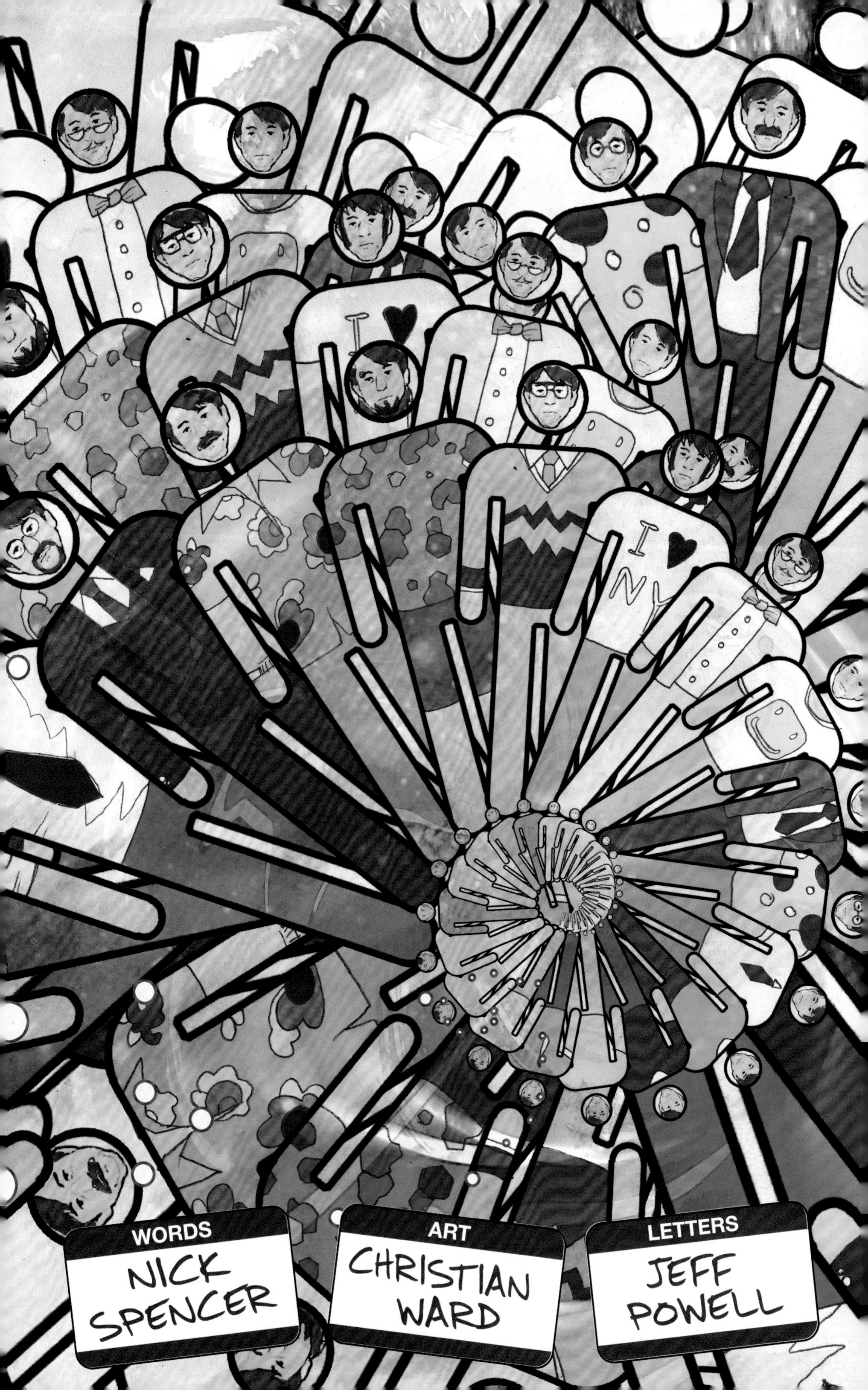

WORDS
NICK SPENCER
ART
CHRISTIAN WARD
LETTERS
JEFF POWELL

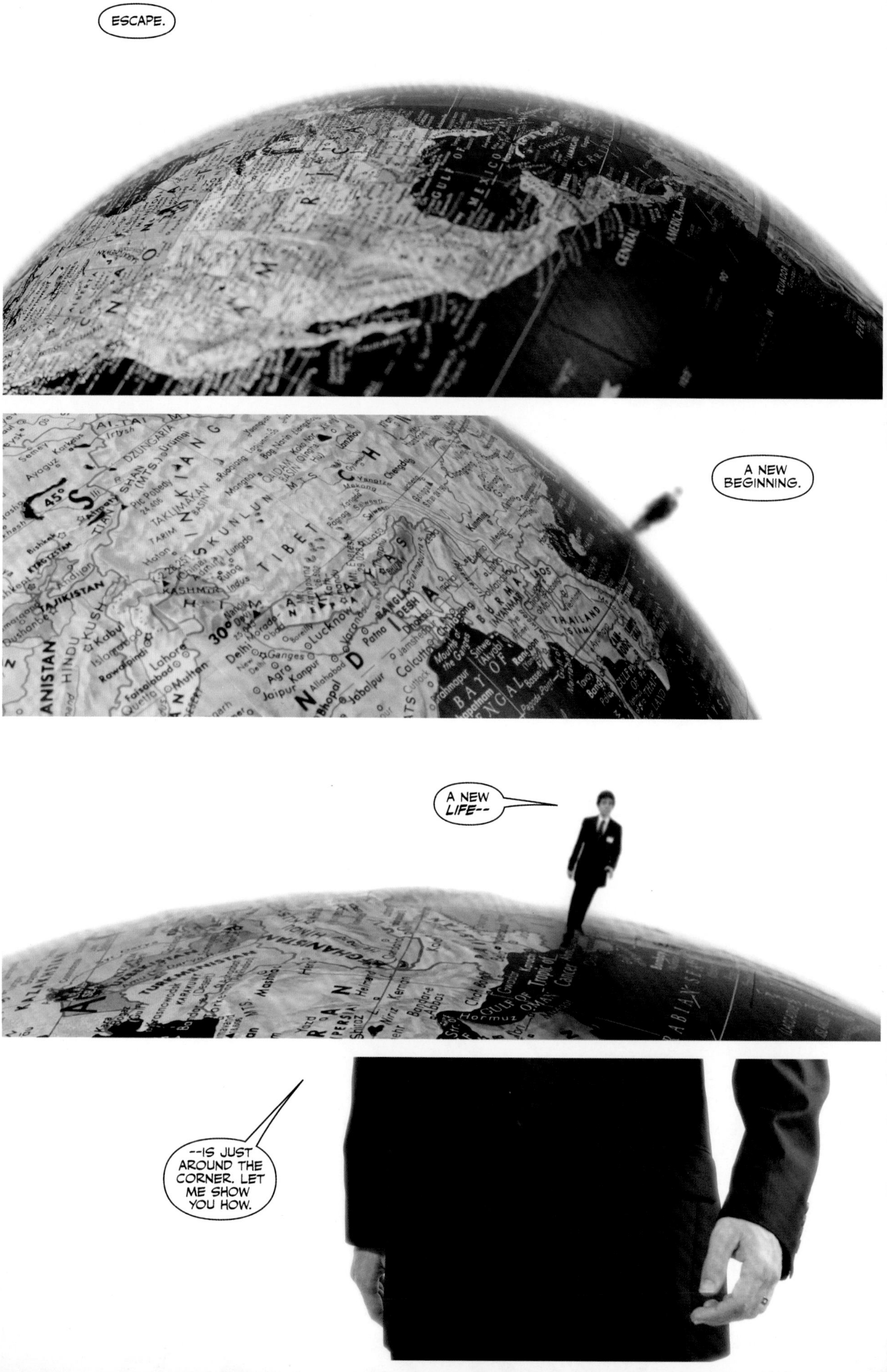
ESCAPE.
A NEW BEGINNING.
A NEW *LIFE*--
--IS JUST AROUND THE CORNER. LET ME SHOW YOU HOW.

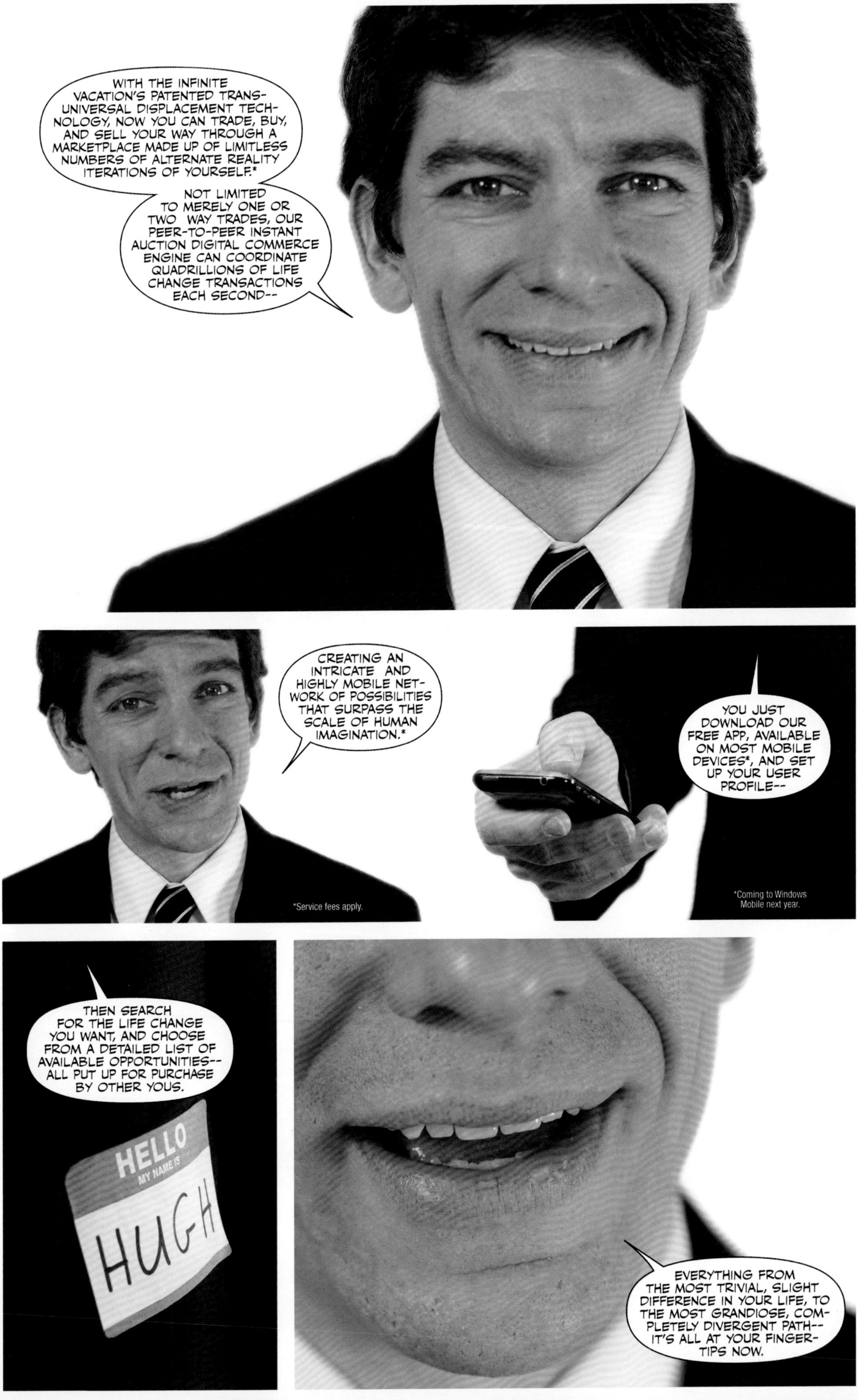
WITH THE INFINITE VACATION'S PATENTED TRANS-UNIVERSAL DISPLACEMENT TECH-NOLOGY, NOW YOU CAN TRADE, BUY, AND SELL YOUR WAY THROUGH A MARKETPLACE MADE UP OF LIMITLESS NUMBERS OF ALTERNATE REALITY ITERATIONS OF YOURSELF.*
NOT LIMITED TO MERELY ONE OR TWO WAY TRADES, OUR PEER-TO-PEER INSTANT AUCTION DIGITAL COMMERCE ENGINE CAN COORDINATE QUADRILLIONS OF LIFE CHANGE TRANSACTIONS EACH SECOND--
CREATING AN INTRICATE AND HIGHLY MOBILE NET-WORK OF POSSIBILITIES THAT SURPASS THE SCALE OF HUMAN IMAGINATION.*
*Service fees apply.
YOU JUST DOWNLOAD OUR FREE APP, AVAILABLE ON MOST MOBILE DEVICES*, AND SET UP YOUR USER PROFILE--
*Coming to Windows Mobile next year.
THEN SEARCH FOR THE LIFE CHANGE YOU WANT, AND CHOOSE FROM A DETAILED LIST OF AVAILABLE OPPORTUNITIES-- ALL PUT UP FOR PURCHASE BY OTHER YOUS.
HELLO
MY NAME IS
HUGH
EVERYTHING FROM THE MOST TRIVIAL, SLIGHT DIFFERENCE IN YOUR LIFE, TO THE MOST GRANDIOSE, COM-PLETELY DIVERGENT PATH-- IT'S ALL AT YOUR FINGER-TIPS NOW.

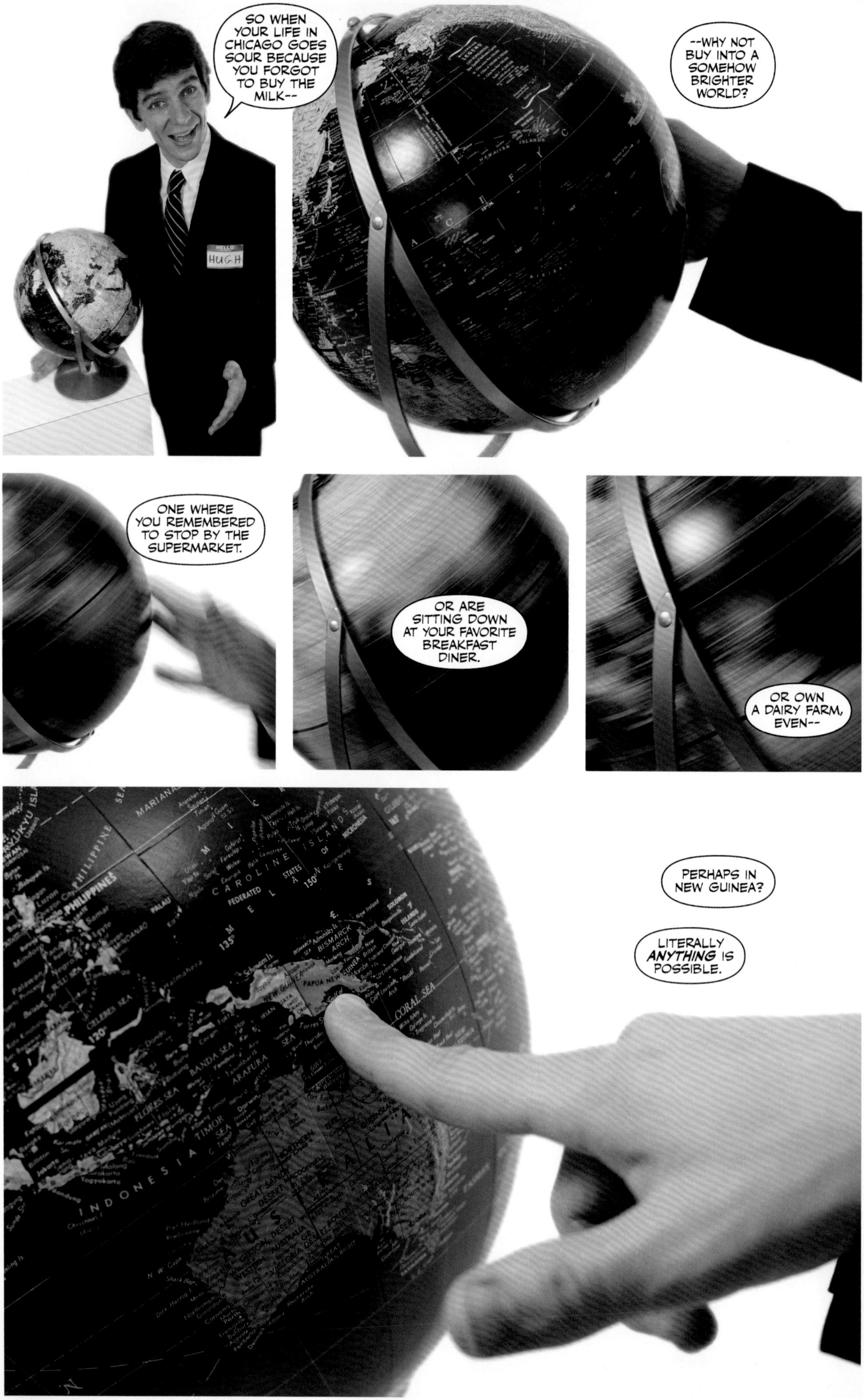
SO WHEN YOUR LIFE IN CHICAGO GOES SOUR BECAUSE YOU FORGOT TO BUY THE MILK--
HELLO
HUGH
--WHY NOT BUY INTO A SOMEHOW BRIGHTER WORLD?
ONE WHERE YOU REMEMBERED TO STOP BY THE SUPERMARKET.
OR ARE SITTING DOWN AT YOUR FAVORITE BREAKFAST DINER.
OR OWN A DAIRY FARM, EVEN--
PERHAPS IN NEW GUINEA?
LITERALLY *ANYTHING* IS POSSIBLE.

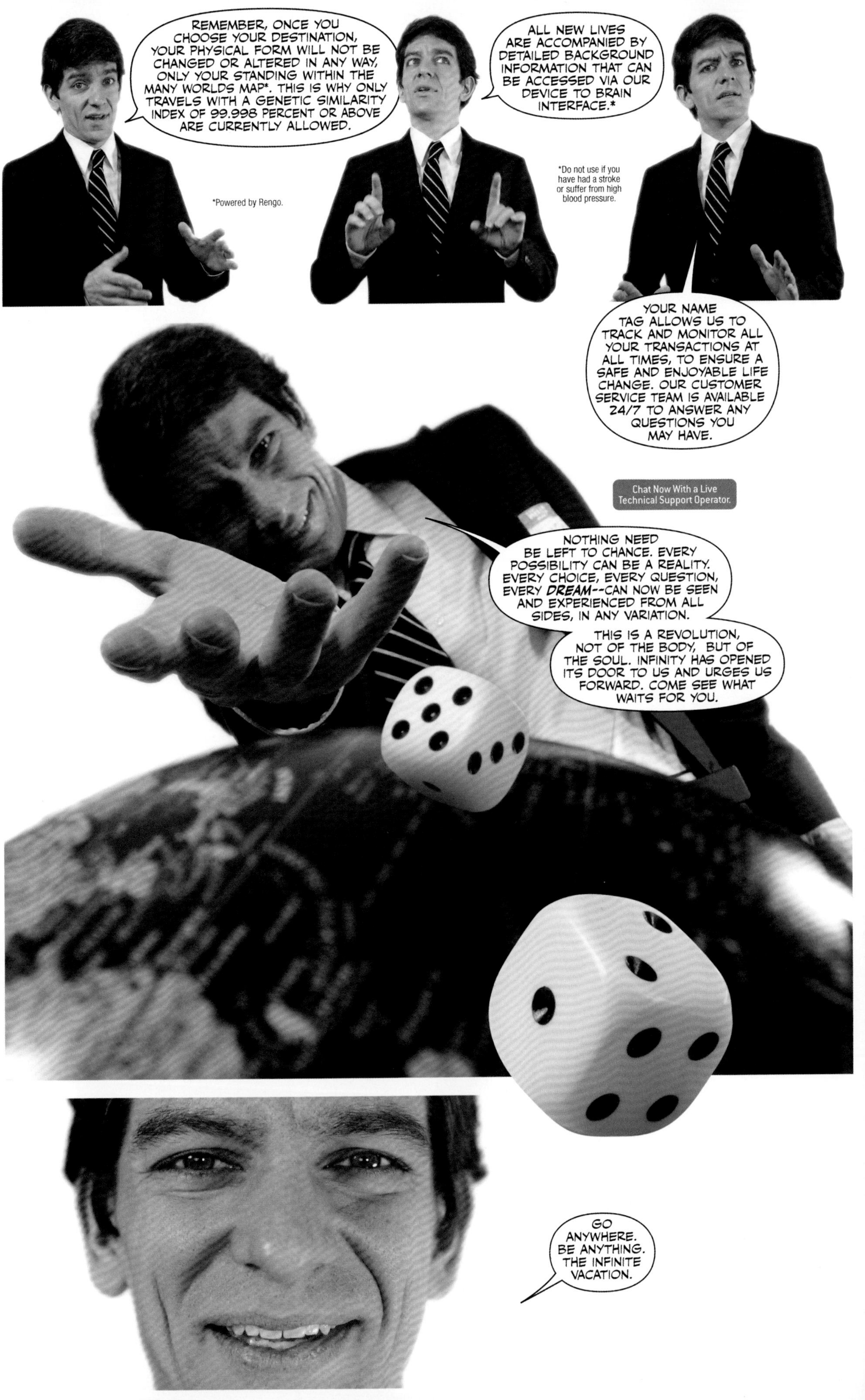
REMEMBER, ONCE YOU CHOOSE YOUR DESTINATION, YOUR PHYSICAL FORM WILL NOT BE CHANGED OR ALTERED IN ANY WAY, ONLY YOUR STANDING WITHIN THE MANY WORLDS MAP*. THIS IS WHY ONLY TRAVELS WITH A GENETIC SIMILARITY INDEX OF 99.998 PERCENT OR ABOVE ARE CURRENTLY ALLOWED.
*Powered by Rengo.
ALL NEW LIVES ARE ACCOMPANIED BY DETAILED BACKGROUND INFORMATION THAT CAN BE ACCESSED VIA OUR DEVICE TO BRAIN INTERFACE.*
*Do not use if you have had a stroke or suffer from high blood pressure.
YOUR NAME TAG ALLOWS US TO TRACK AND MONITOR ALL YOUR TRANSACTIONS AT ALL TIMES, TO ENSURE A SAFE AND ENJOYABLE LIFE CHANGE. OUR CUSTOMER SERVICE TEAM IS AVAILABLE 24/7 TO ANSWER ANY QUESTIONS YOU MAY HAVE.
Chat Now With a Live Technical Support Operator.
NOTHING NEED BE LEFT TO CHANCE. EVERY POSSIBILITY CAN BE A REALITY. EVERY CHOICE, EVERY QUESTION, EVERY DREAM--CAN NOW BE SEEN AND EXPERIENCED FROM ALL SIDES, IN ANY VARIATION.
THIS IS A REVOLUTION, NOT OF THE BODY, BUT OF THE SOUL. INFINITY HAS OPENED ITS DOOR TO US AND URGES US FORWARD. COME SEE WHAT WAITS FOR YOU.
GO ANYWHERE. BE ANYTHING. THE INFINITE VACATION.

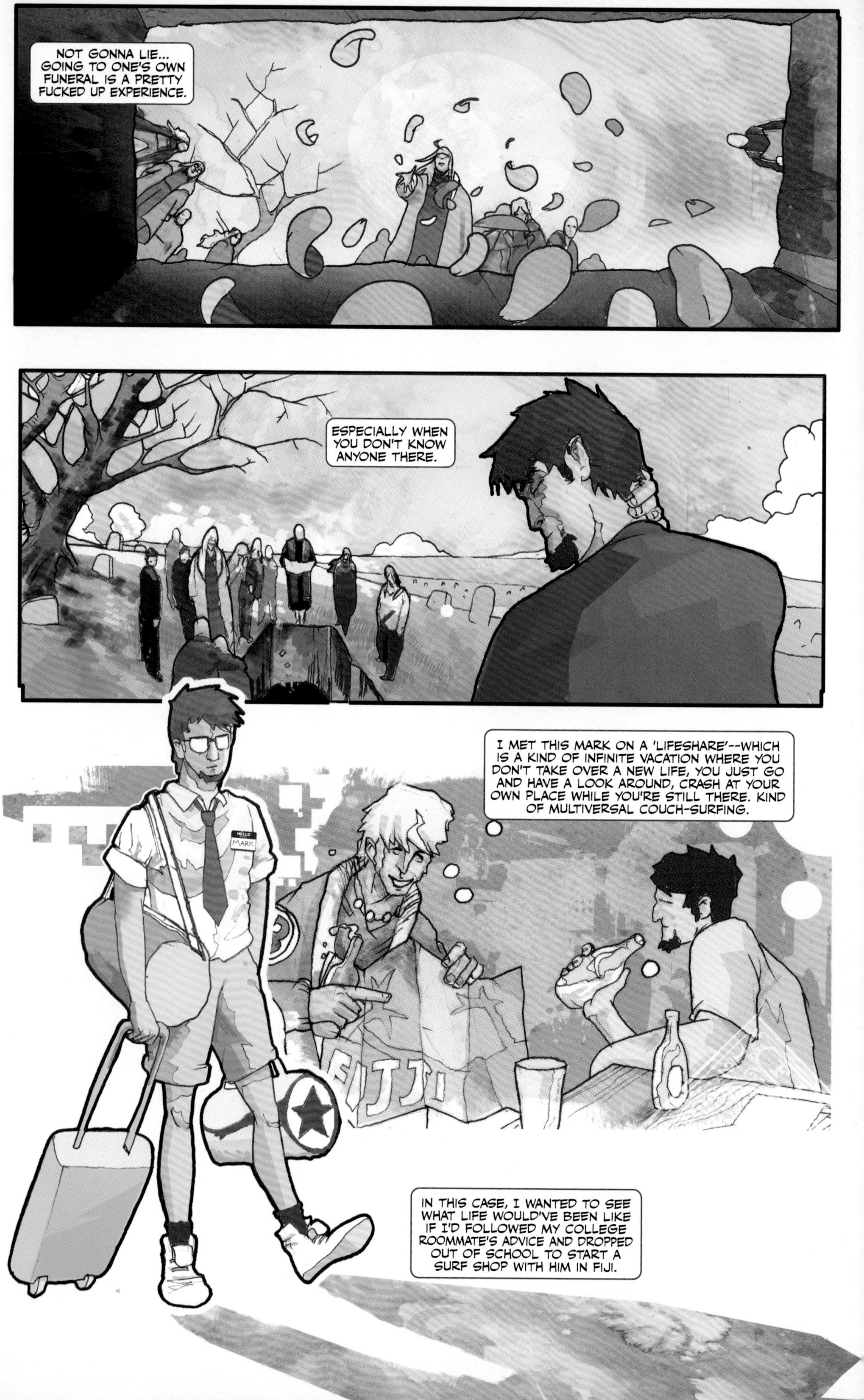
NOT GONNA LIE... GOING TO ONE'S OWN FUNERAL IS A PRETTY FUCKED UP EXPERIENCE.
ESPECIALLY WHEN YOU DON'T KNOW ANYONE THERE.
HELLO MARK
I MET THIS MARK ON A 'LIFESHARE'--WHICH IS A KIND OF INFINITE VACATION WHERE YOU DON'T TAKE OVER A NEW LIFE, YOU JUST GO AND HAVE A LOOK AROUND, CRASH AT YOUR OWN PLACE WHILE YOU'RE STILL THERE. KIND OF MULTIVERSAL COUCH-SURFING.
FIJI
IN THIS CASE, I WANTED TO SEE WHAT LIFE WOULD'VE BEEN LIKE IF I'D FOLLOWED MY COLLEGE ROOMMATE'S ADVICE AND DROPPED OUT OF SCHOOL TO START A SURF SHOP WITH HIM IN FIJI.

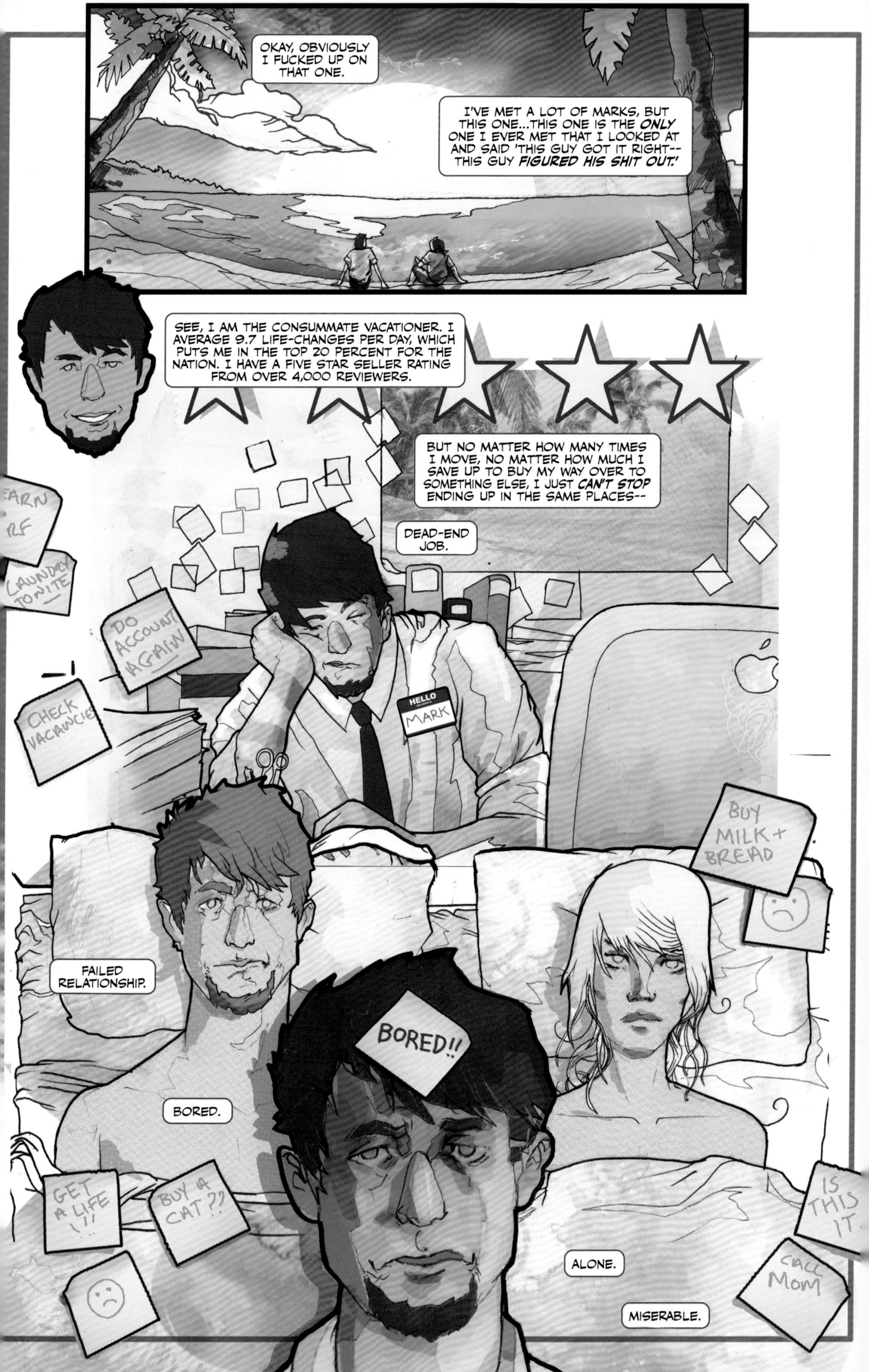
OKAY, OBVIOUSLY I FUCKED UP ON THAT ONE.
I'VE MET A LOT OF MARKS, BUT THIS ONE...THIS ONE IS THE *ONLY* ONE I EVER MET THAT I LOOKED AT AND SAID 'THIS GUY GOT IT RIGHT-- THIS GUY *FIGURED HIS SHIT OUT.*'
SEE, I AM THE CONSUMMATE VACATIONER. I AVERAGE 9.7 LIFE-CHANGES PER DAY, WHICH PUTS ME IN THE TOP 20 PERCENT FOR THE NATION. I HAVE A FIVE STAR SELLER RATING FROM OVER 4,000 REVIEWERS.
BUT NO MATTER HOW MANY TIMES I MOVE, NO MATTER HOW MUCH I SAVE UP TO BUY MY WAY OVER TO SOMETHING ELSE, I JUST *CAN'T STOP* ENDING UP IN THE SAME PLACES--
DEAD-END JOB.
LAUNDRY TONITE
DO ACCOUNT AGAIN
CHECK VACANCIES
HELLO
MARK
BUY MILK + BREAD
FAILED RELATIONSHIP.
BORED!!
BORED.
GET A LIFE !!!
BUY A CAT??
IS THIS IT.
ALONE.
CALL MOM
MISERABLE.

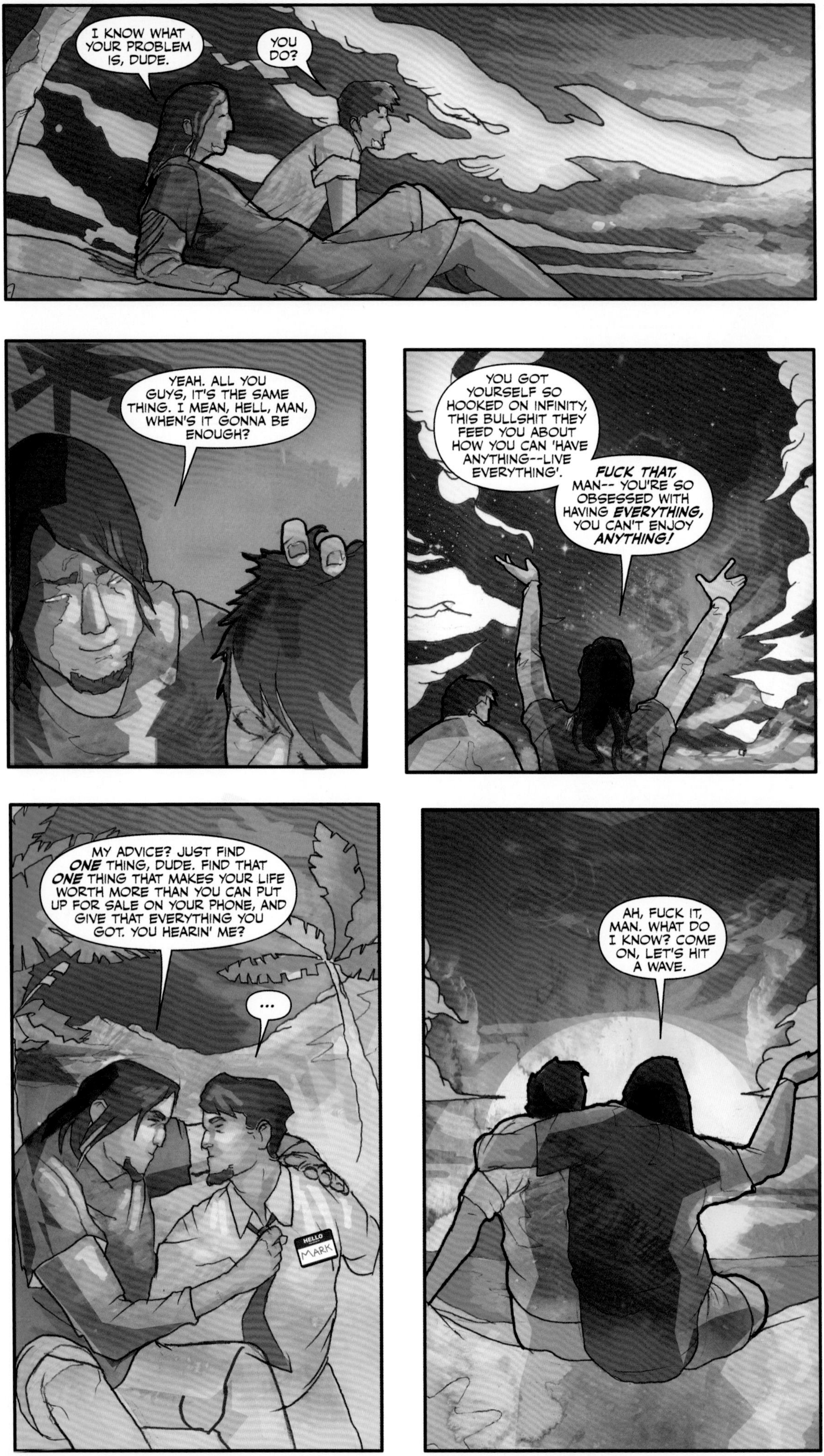
I KNOW WHAT YOUR PROBLEM IS, DUDE.
YOU DO?
YEAH. ALL YOU GUYS, IT'S THE SAME THING. I MEAN, HELL, MAN, WHEN'S IT GONNA BE ENOUGH?
YOU GOT YOURSELF SO HOOKED ON INFINITY, THIS BULLSHIT THEY FEED YOU ABOUT HOW YOU CAN 'HAVE ANYTHING--LIVE EVERYTHING'.
FUCK THAT, MAN-- YOU'RE SO OBSESSED WITH HAVING EVERYTHING, YOU CAN'T ENJOY ANYTHING!
MY ADVICE? JUST FIND ONE THING, DUDE. FIND THAT ONE THING THAT MAKES YOUR LIFE WORTH MORE THAN YOU CAN PUT UP FOR SALE ON YOUR PHONE, AND GIVE THAT EVERYTHING YOU GOT. YOU HEARIN' ME?
...
HELLO
MARK
AH, FUCK IT, MAN. WHAT DO I KNOW? COME ON, LET'S HIT A WAVE.

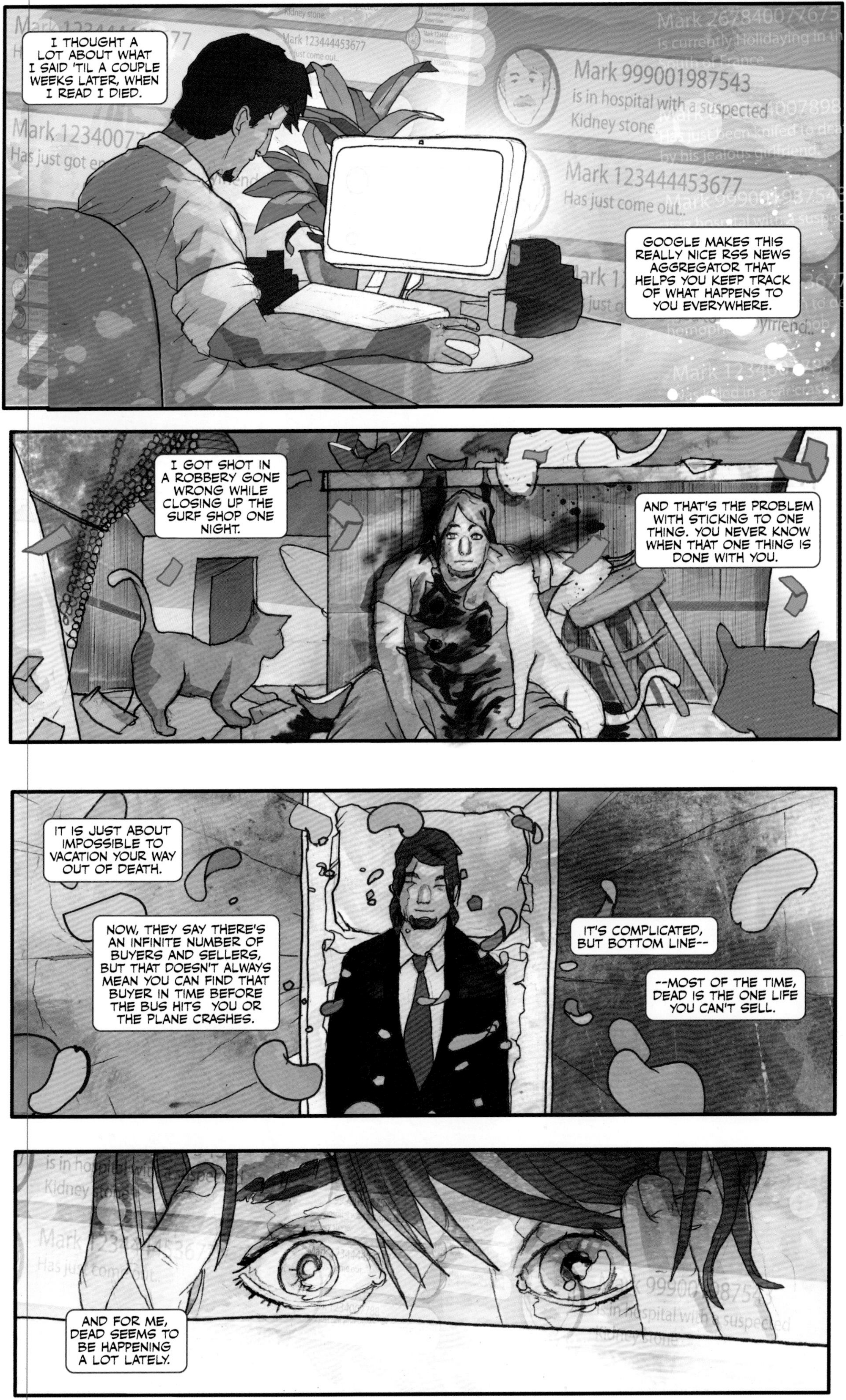
I THOUGHT A LOT ABOUT WHAT I SAID 'TIL A COUPLE WEEKS LATER, WHEN I READ I DIED.
GOOGLE MAKES THIS REALLY NICE RSS NEWS AGGREGATOR THAT HELPS YOU KEEP TRACK OF WHAT HAPPENS TO YOU EVERYWHERE.
I GOT SHOT IN A ROBBERY GONE WRONG WHILE CLOSING UP THE SURF SHOP ONE NIGHT.
AND THAT'S THE PROBLEM WITH STICKING TO ONE THING. YOU NEVER KNOW WHEN THAT ONE THING IS DONE WITH YOU.
IT IS JUST ABOUT IMPOSSIBLE TO VACATION YOUR WAY OUT OF DEATH.
NOW, THEY SAY THERE'S AN INFINITE NUMBER OF BUYERS AND SELLERS, BUT THAT DOESN'T ALWAYS MEAN YOU CAN FIND THAT BUYER IN TIME BEFORE THE BUS HITS YOU OR THE PLANE CRASHES.
IT'S COMPLICATED, BUT BOTTOM LINE--
--MOST OF THE TIME, DEAD IS THE ONE LIFE YOU CAN'T SELL.
AND FOR ME, DEAD SEEMS TO BE HAPPENING A LOT LATELY.
Mark 999001987543
is in hospital with a suspected Kidney stone.
Mark 123444453677
Has just come out..

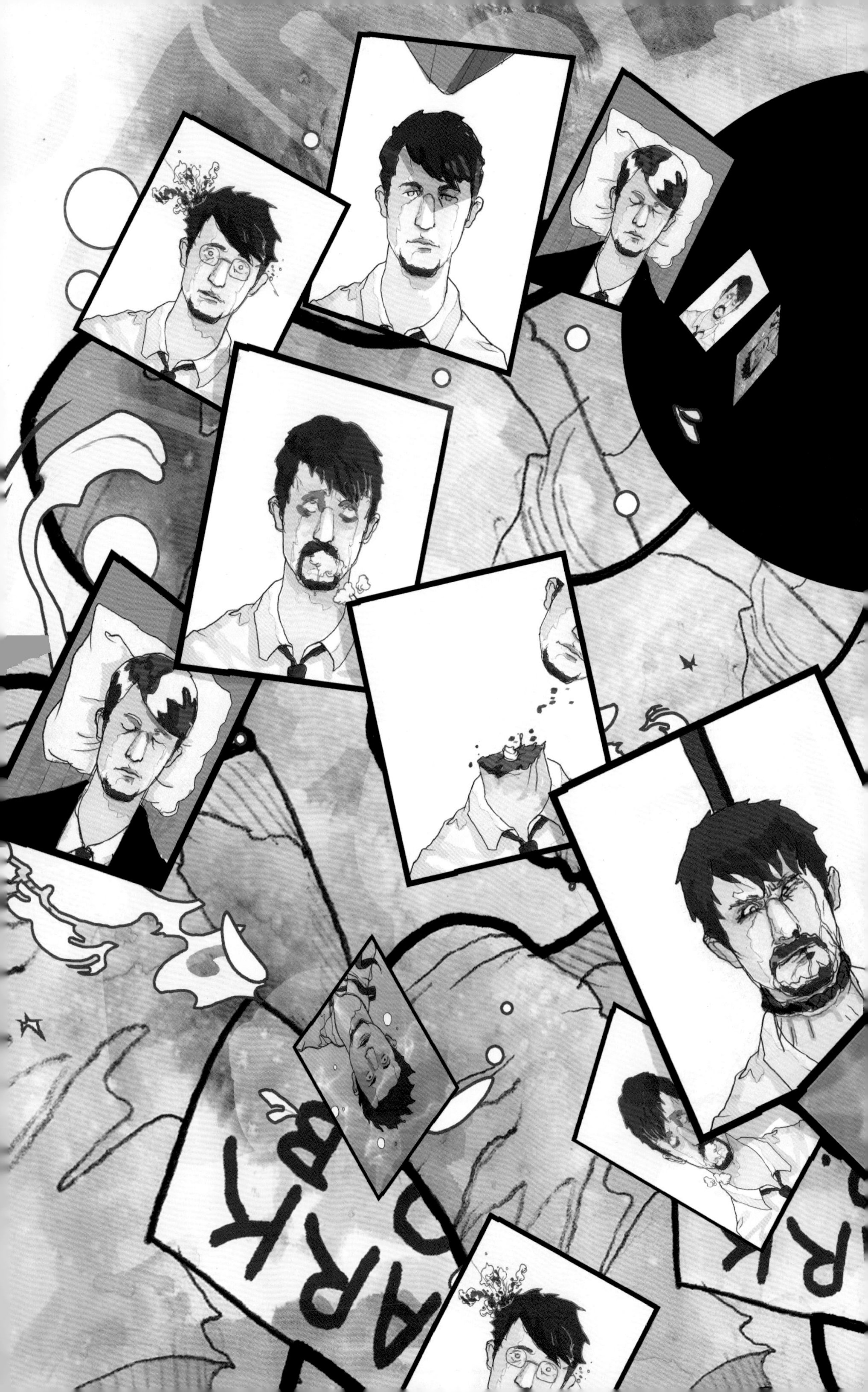

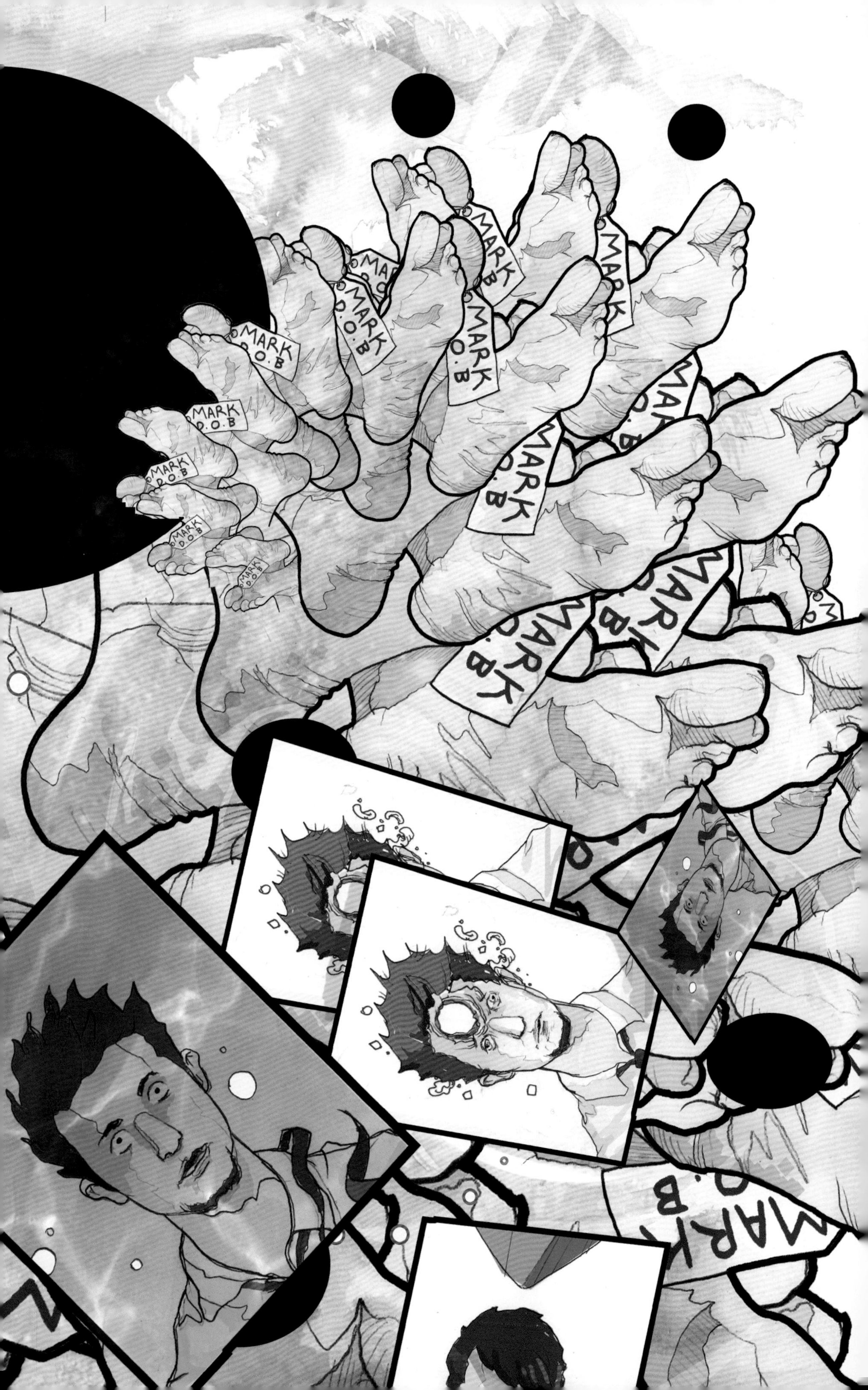

MARK
MARK D.O.B
MARK D.O.B
MARK D.O.B
MARK D.O.B
MARK D.O.B
MARK D.O.B
MARK D.O.B
MARK D.O.B
MARK D.O.B
MARK D.O.B
MARK D.O.B
MARK D.O.B

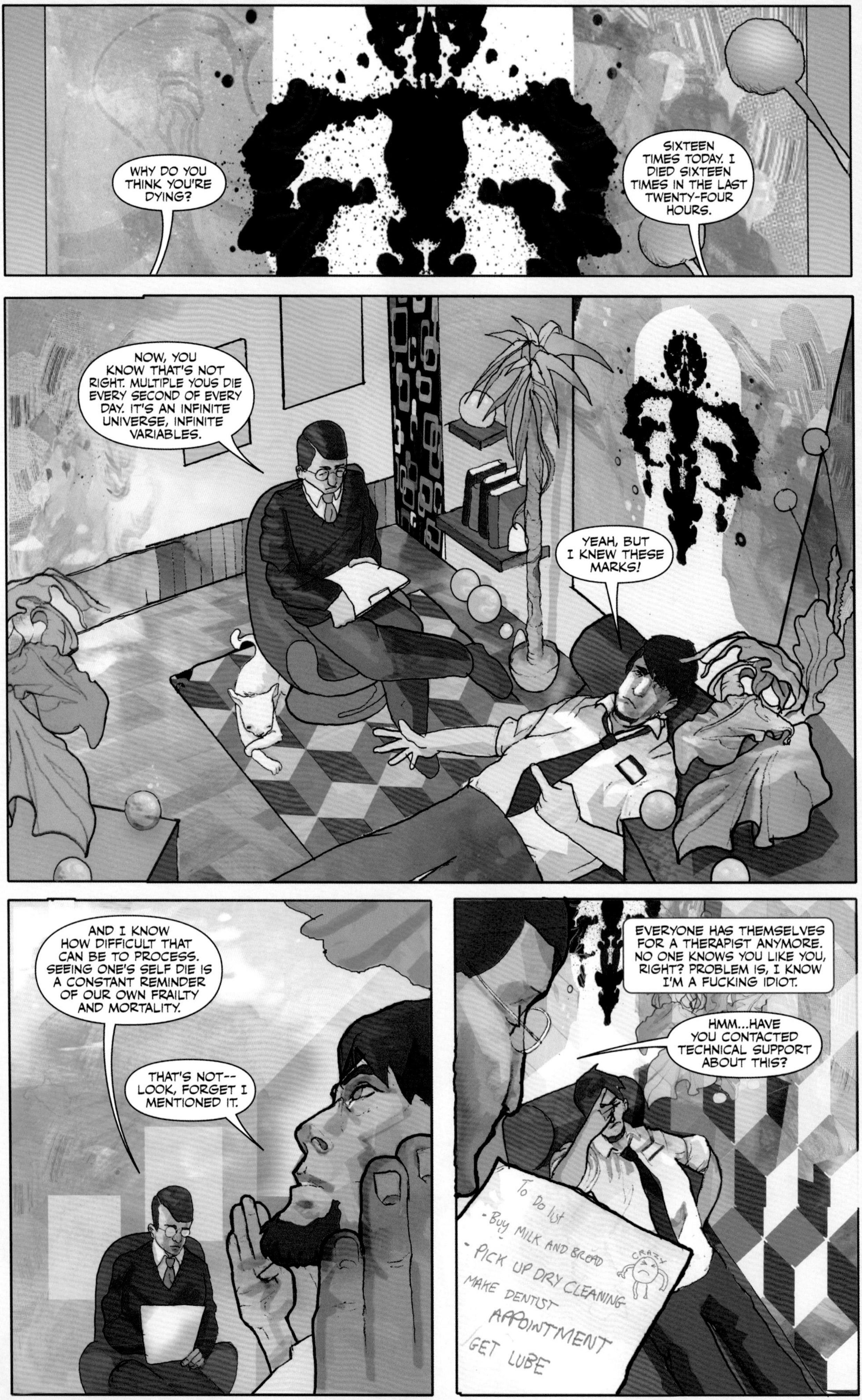
WHY DO YOU THINK YOU'RE DYING?
SIXTEEN TIMES TODAY. I DIED SIXTEEN TIMES IN THE LAST TWENTY-FOUR HOURS.
NOW, YOU KNOW THAT'S NOT RIGHT. MULTIPLE YOUS DIE EVERY SECOND OF EVERY DAY. IT'S AN INFINITE UNIVERSE, INFINITE VARIABLES.
YEAH, BUT I KNEW THESE MARKS!
AND I KNOW HOW DIFFICULT THAT CAN BE TO PROCESS. SEEING ONE'S SELF DIE IS A CONSTANT REMINDER OF OUR OWN FRAILTY AND MORTALITY.
THAT'S NOT-- LOOK, FORGET I MENTIONED IT.
EVERYONE HAS THEMSELVES FOR A THERAPIST ANYMORE. NO ONE KNOWS YOU LIKE YOU, RIGHT? PROBLEM IS, I KNOW I'M A FUCKING IDIOT.
HMM...HAVE YOU CONTACTED TECHNICAL SUPPORT ABOUT THIS?
To Do list
-Buy MILK AND BREAD
-PICK UP DRY CLEANING
MAKE DENTIST APPOINTMENT
GET LUBE
CRAZY

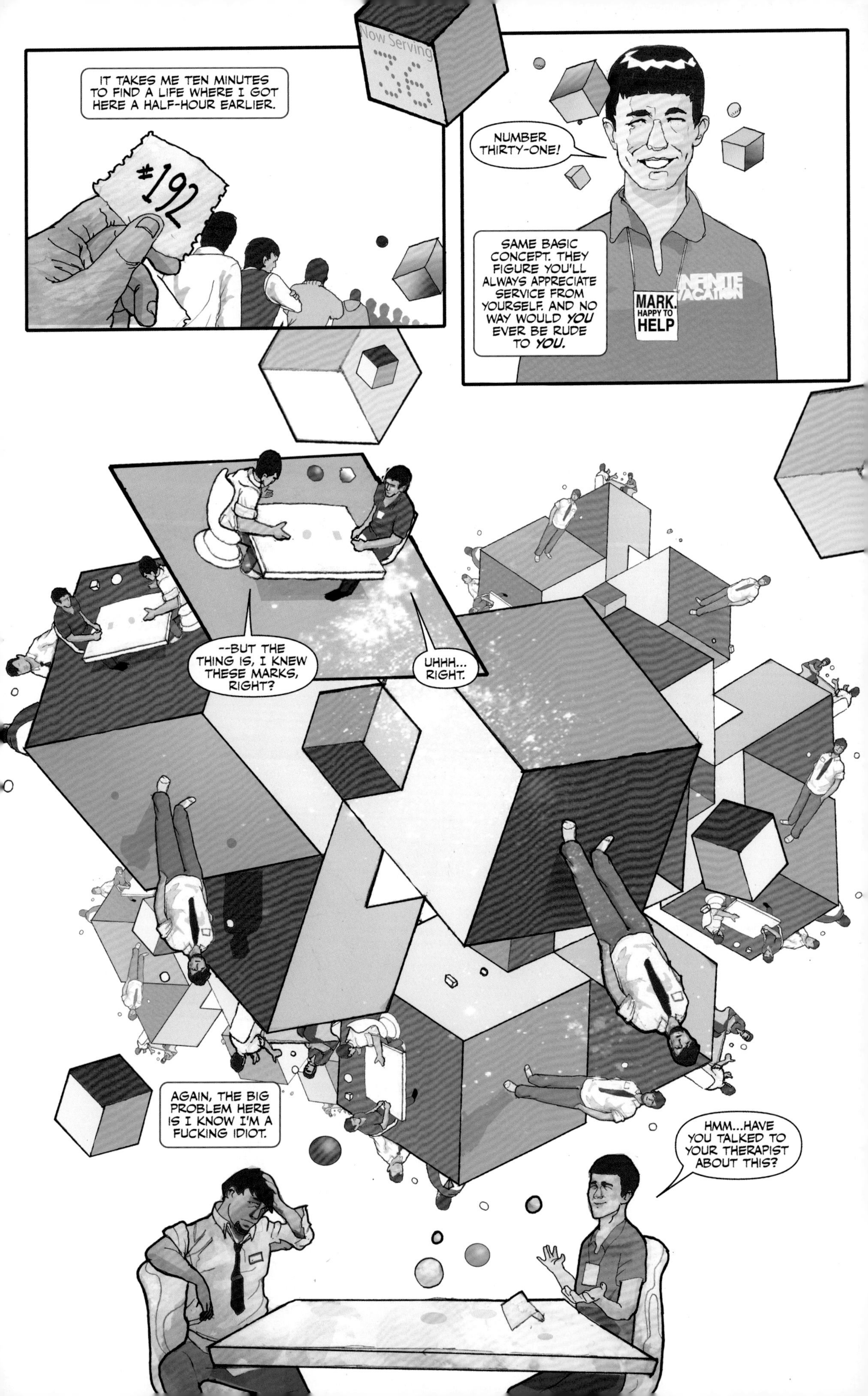
Now Serving
36
IT TAKES ME TEN MINUTES TO FIND A LIFE WHERE I GOT HERE A HALF-HOUR EARLIER.
#192
NUMBER THIRTY-ONE!
SAME BASIC CONCEPT. THEY FIGURE YOU'LL ALWAYS APPRECIATE SERVICE FROM YOURSELF. AND NO WAY WOULD YOU EVER BE RUDE TO YOU.
INFINITE VACATION
MARK. HAPPY TO HELP
--BUT THE THING IS, I KNEW THESE MARKS, RIGHT?
UHHH... RIGHT.
AGAIN, THE BIG PROBLEM HERE IS I KNOW I'M A FUCKING IDIOT.
HMM...HAVE YOU TALKED TO YOUR THERAPIST ABOUT THIS?

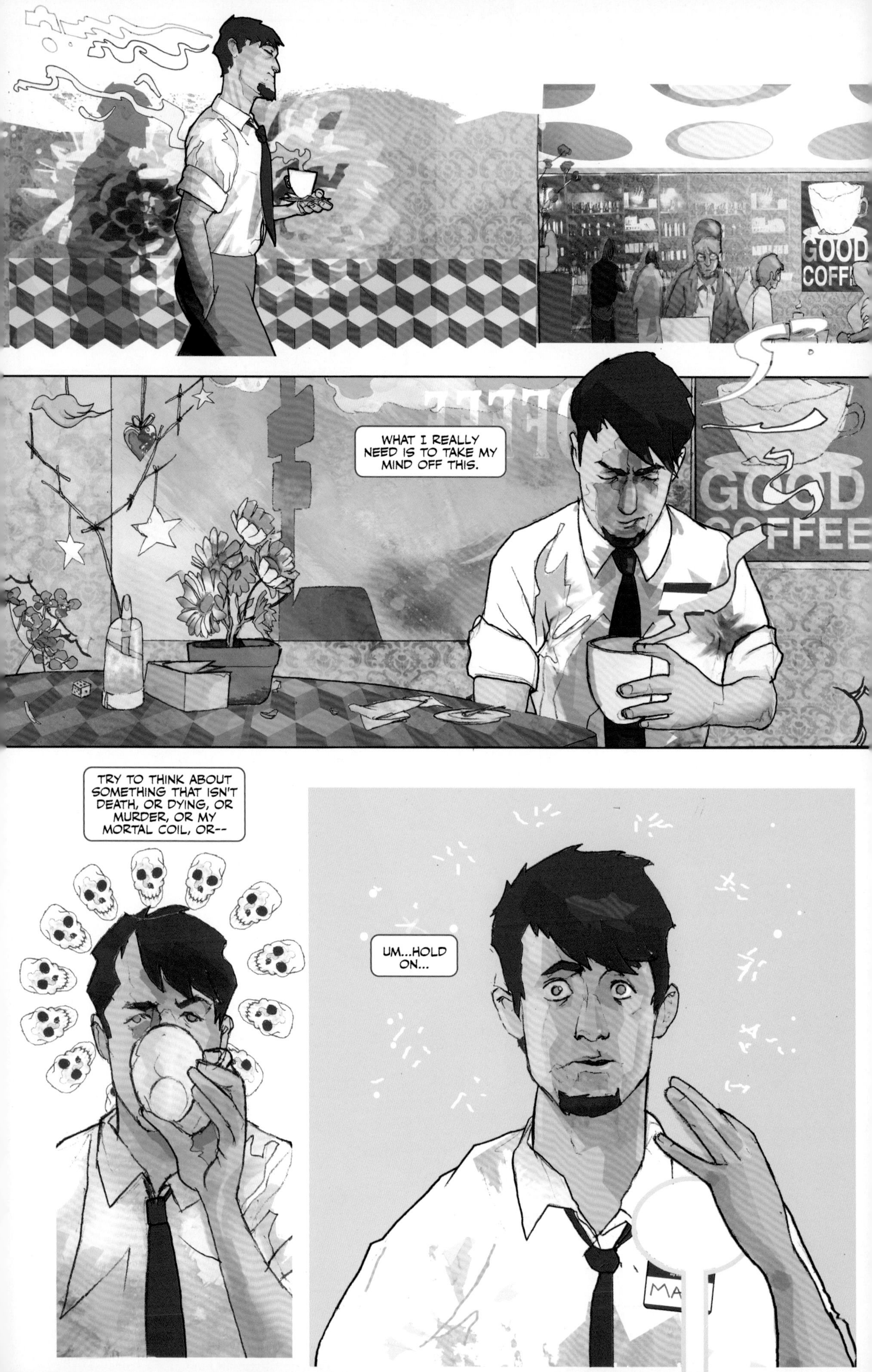
GOOD COFFE
GOOD COFFEE
WHAT I REALLY NEED IS TO TAKE MY MIND OFF THIS.
TRY TO THINK ABOUT SOMETHING THAT ISN'T DEATH, OR DYING, OR MURDER, OR MY MORTAL COIL, OR--
UM...HOLD ON...

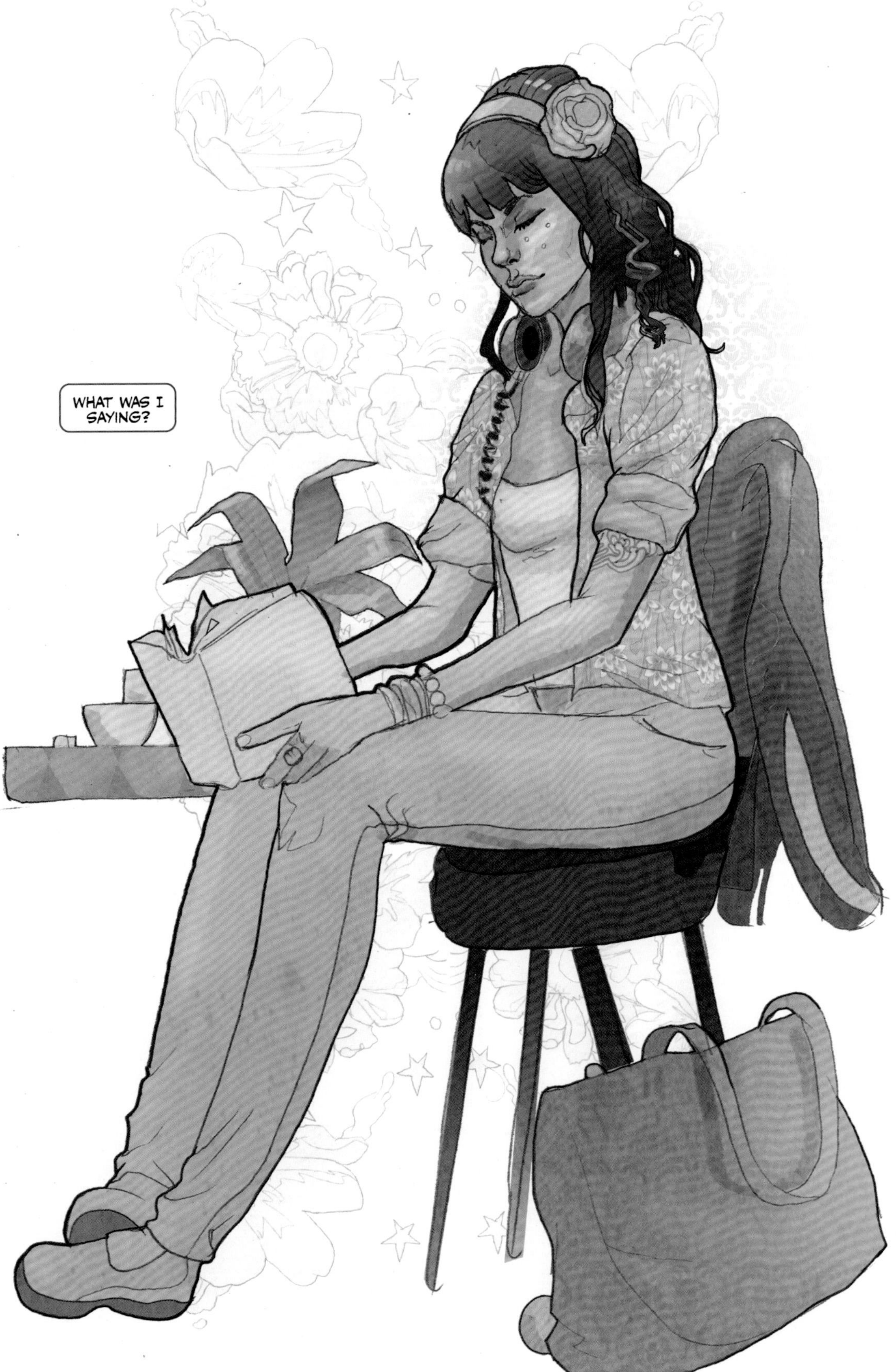
WHAT WAS I SAYING?

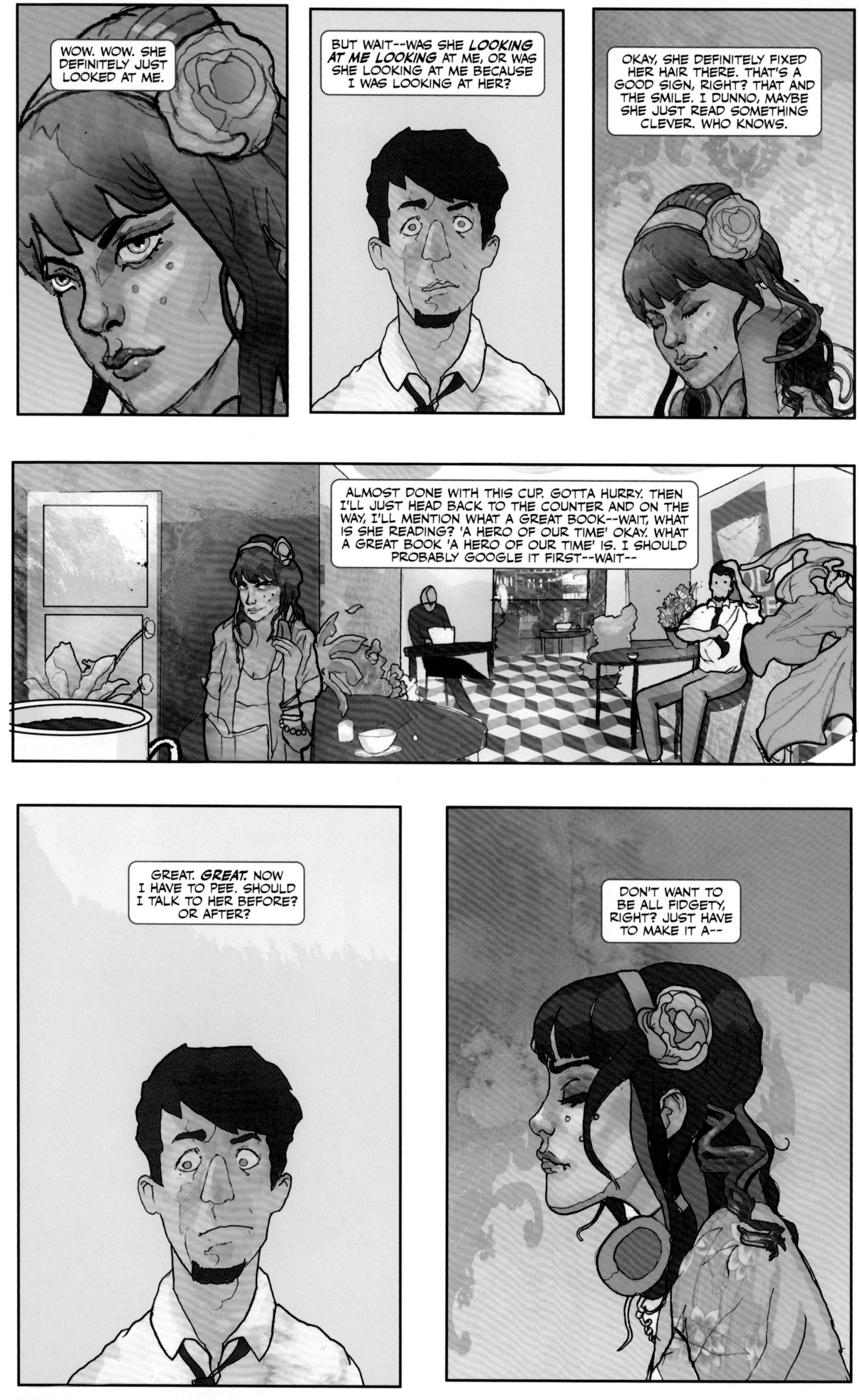
WOW. WOW. SHE DEFINITELY JUST LOOKED AT ME.
BUT WAIT--WAS SHE *LOOKING AT ME LOOKING* AT ME, OR WAS SHE LOOKING AT ME BECAUSE I WAS LOOKING AT HER?
OKAY, SHE DEFINITELY FIXED HER HAIR THERE. THAT'S A GOOD SIGN, RIGHT? THAT AND THE SMILE. I DUNNO, MAYBE SHE JUST READ SOMETHING CLEVER. WHO KNOWS.
ALMOST DONE WITH THIS CUP. GOTTA HURRY. THEN I'LL JUST HEAD BACK TO THE COUNTER AND ON THE WAY, I'LL MENTION WHAT A GREAT BOOK--WAIT, WHAT IS SHE READING? 'A HERO OF OUR TIME' OKAY. WHAT A GREAT BOOK 'A HERO OF OUR TIME' IS. I SHOULD PROBABLY GOOGLE IT FIRST--WAIT--
GREAT. ***GREAT.*** NOW I HAVE TO PEE. SHOULD I TALK TO HER BEFORE? OR AFTER?
DON'T WANT TO BE ALL FIDGETY, RIGHT? JUST HAVE TO MAKE IT A--

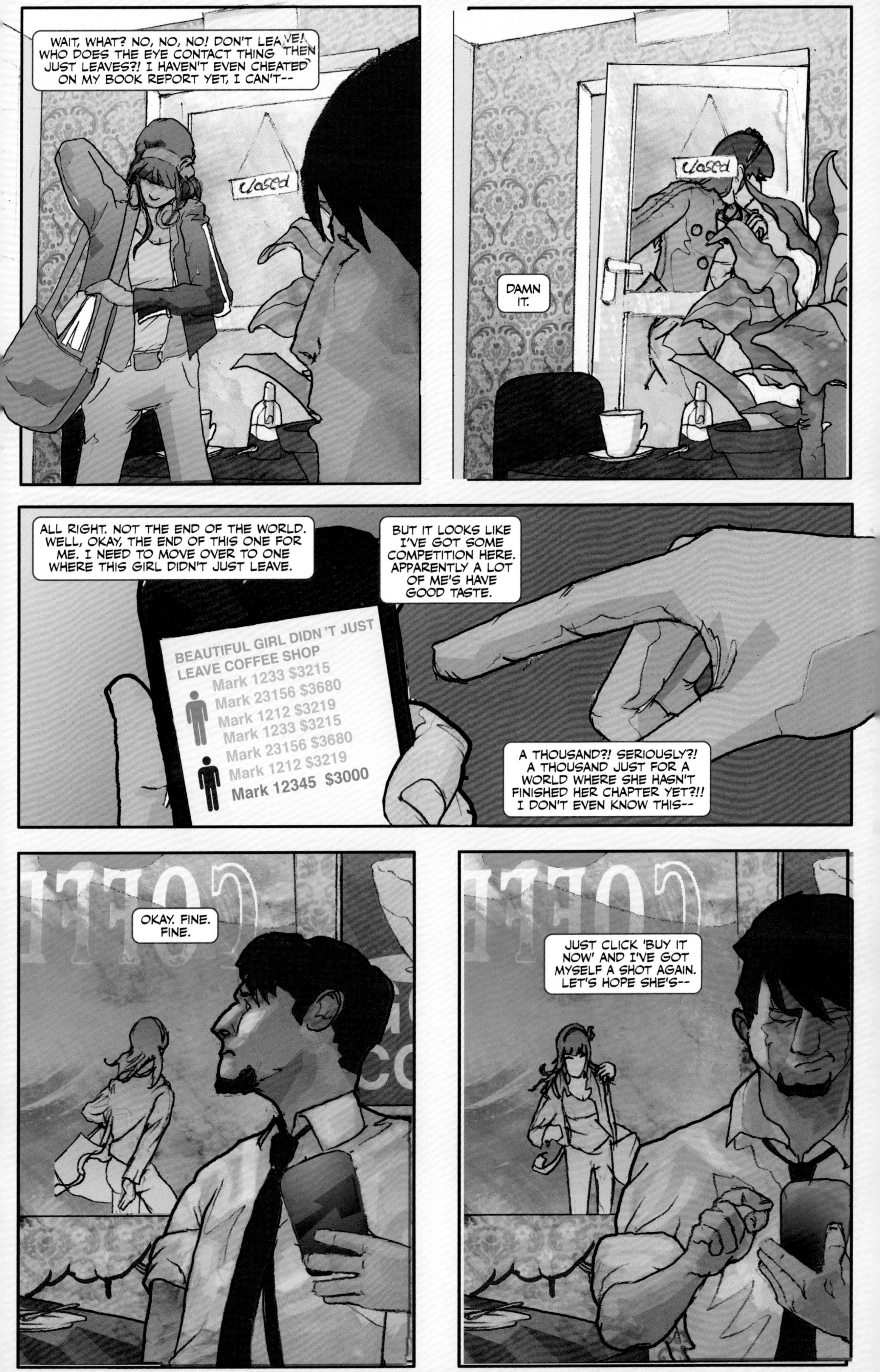
WAIT, WHAT? NO, NO, NO! DON'T LEAVE! WHO DOES THE EYE CONTACT THING THEN JUST LEAVES?! I HAVEN'T EVEN CHEATED ON MY BOOK REPORT YET, I CAN'T--
Closed
Closed
DAMN IT.
ALL RIGHT. NOT THE END OF THE WORLD. WELL, OKAY, THE END OF THIS ONE FOR ME. I NEED TO MOVE OVER TO ONE WHERE THIS GIRL DIDN'T JUST LEAVE.
BUT IT LOOKS LIKE I'VE GOT SOME COMPETITION HERE. APPARENTLY A LOT OF ME'S HAVE GOOD TASTE.
BEAUTIFUL GIRL DIDN 'T JUST LEAVE COFFEE SHOP
Mark 1233 $3215
Mark 23156 $3680
Mark 1212 $3219
Mark 1233 $3215
Mark 23156 $3680
Mark 1212 $3219
Mark 12345 $3000
A THOUSAND?! SERIOUSLY?! A THOUSAND JUST FOR A WORLD WHERE SHE HASN'T FINISHED HER CHAPTER YET?!! I DON'T EVEN KNOW THIS--
OKAY. FINE. FINE.
JUST CLICK 'BUY IT NOW' AND I'VE GOT MYSELF A SHOT AGAIN. LET'S HOPE SHE'S--

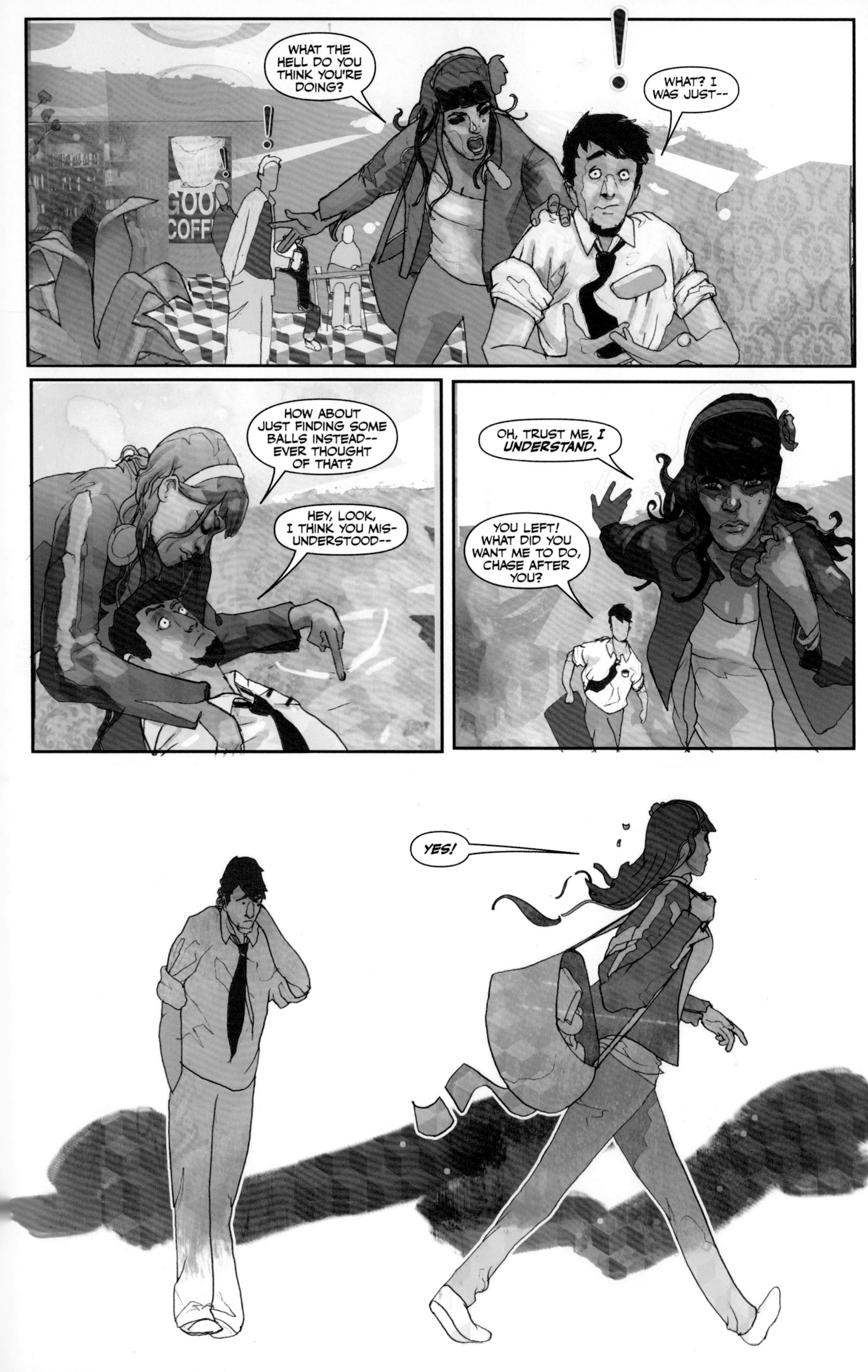
WHAT THE HELL DO YOU THINK YOU'RE DOING?
WHAT? I WAS JUST--
GOOD COFFEE
HOW ABOUT JUST FINDING SOME BALLS INSTEAD-- EVER THOUGHT OF THAT?
HEY, LOOK, I THINK YOU MIS-UNDERSTOOD--
OH, TRUST ME, I *UNDERSTAND.*
YOU LEFT! WHAT DID YOU WANT ME TO DO, CHASE AFTER YOU?
YES!

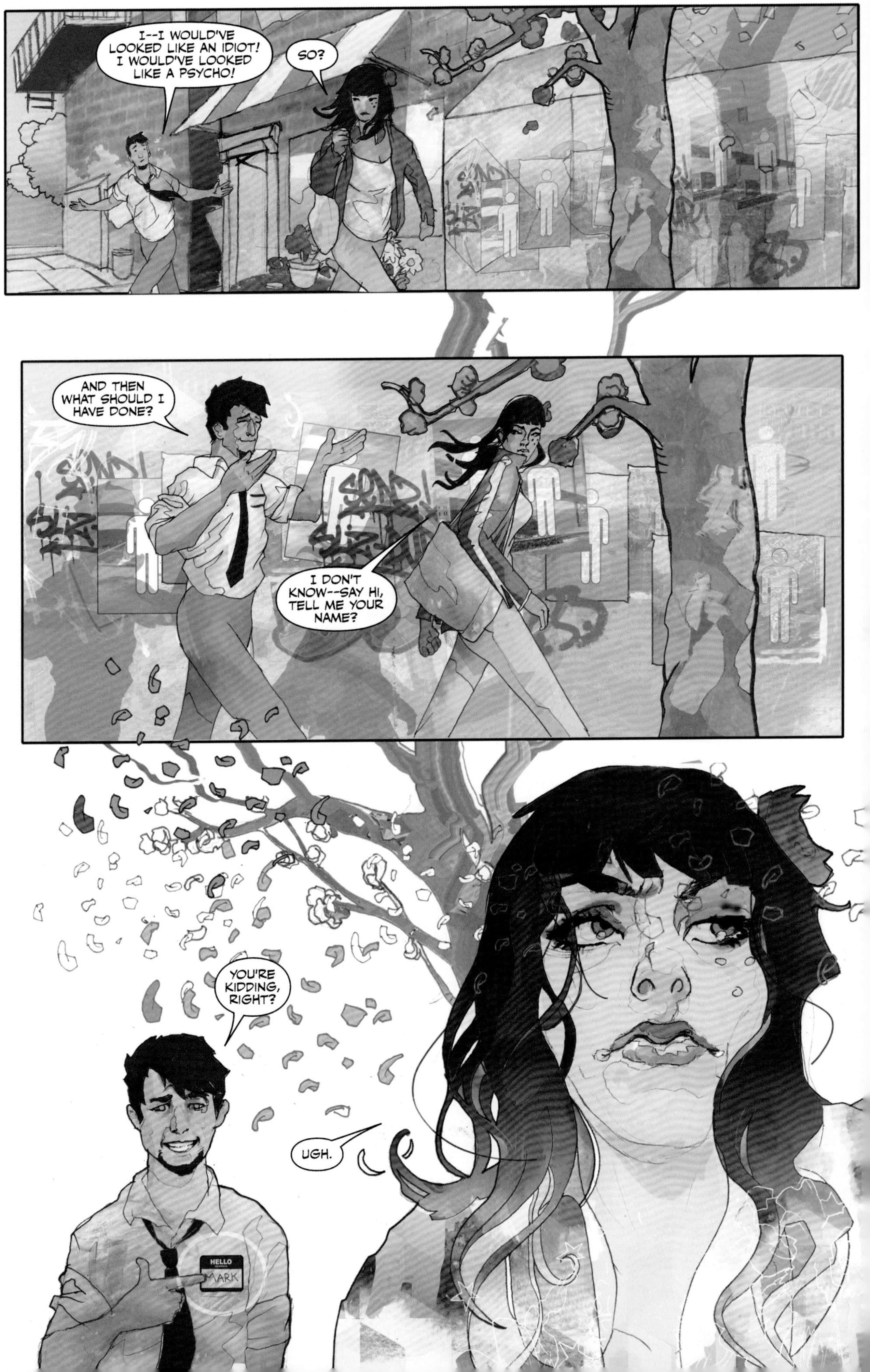
I--I WOULD'VE LOOKED LIKE AN IDIOT! I WOULD'VE LOOKED LIKE A PSYCHO!
SO?
AND THEN WHAT SHOULD I HAVE DONE?
I DON'T KNOW--SAY HI, TELL ME YOUR NAME?
YOU'RE KIDDING, RIGHT?
HELLO
MARK
UGH.

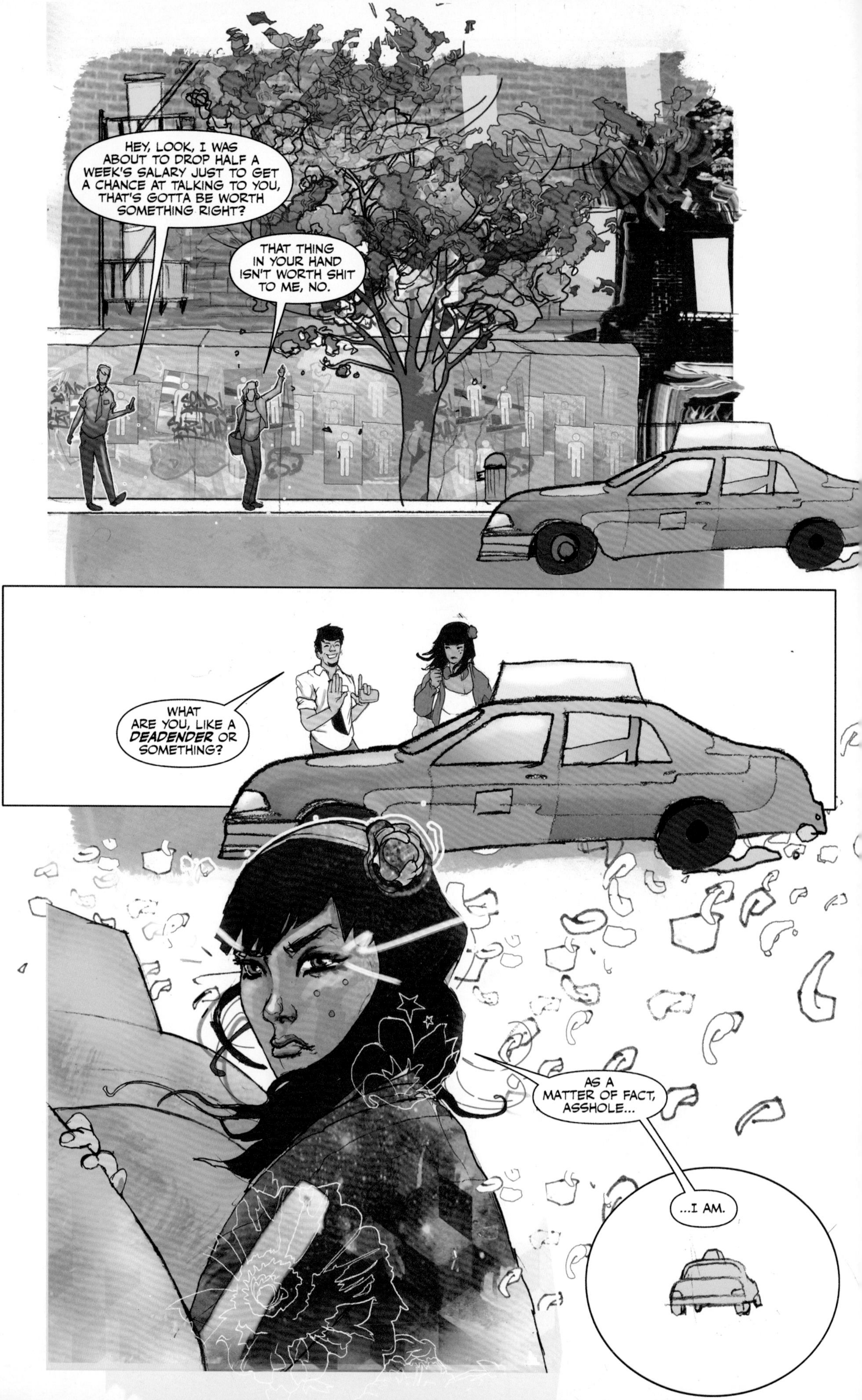
HEY, LOOK, I WAS ABOUT TO DROP HALF A WEEK'S SALARY JUST TO GET A CHANCE AT TALKING TO YOU, THAT'S GOTTA BE WORTH SOMETHING RIGHT?
THAT THING IN YOUR HAND ISN'T WORTH SHIT TO ME, NO.
WHAT ARE YOU, LIKE A DEADENDER OR SOMETHING?
AS A MATTER OF FACT, ASSHOLE...
...I AM.

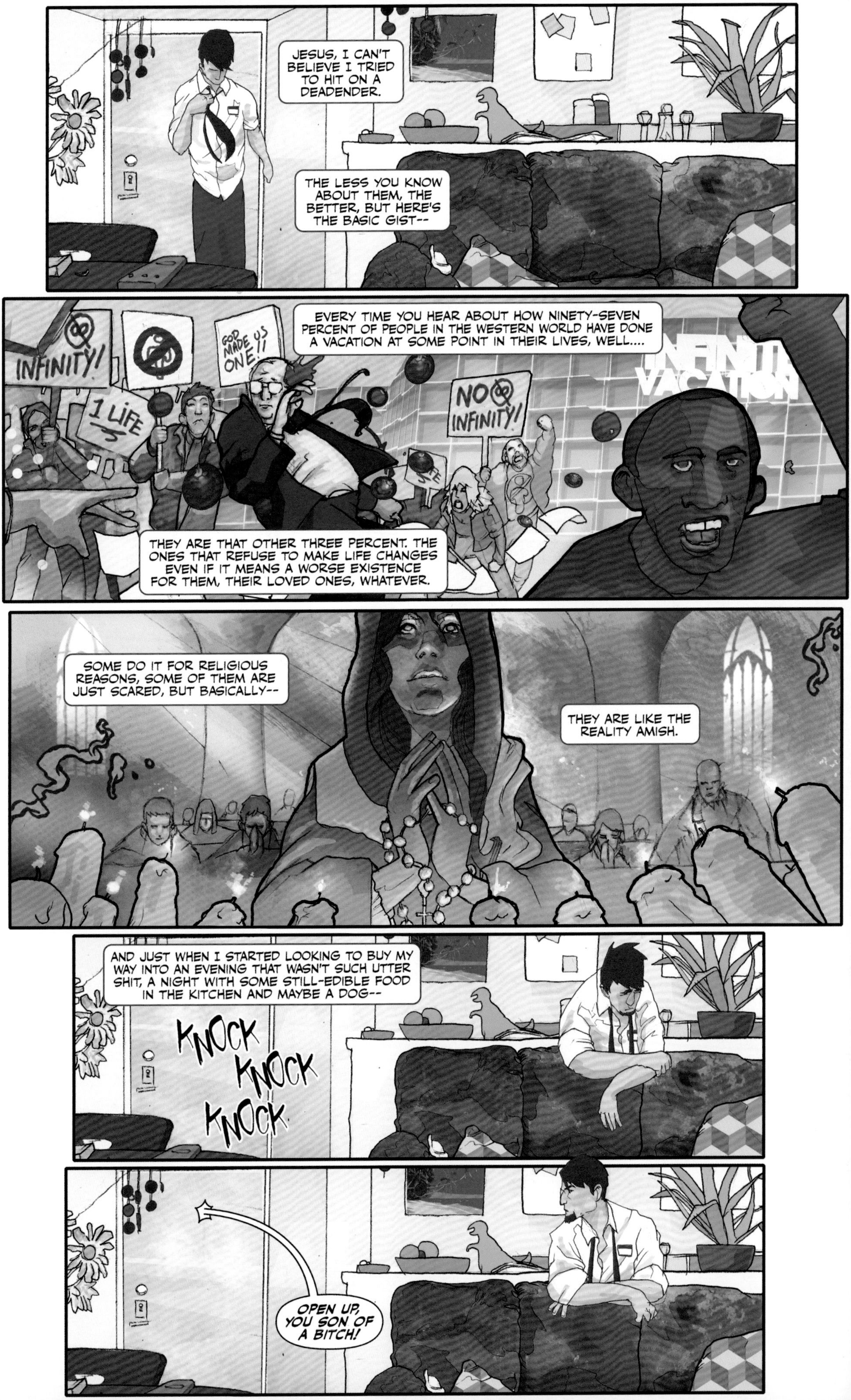

JESUS, I CAN'T BELIEVE I TRIED TO HIT ON A DEADENDER.
THE LESS YOU KNOW ABOUT THEM, THE BETTER, BUT HERE'S THE BASIC GIST--
INFINITY!
GOD MADE US ONE!!
1 LIFE
EVERY TIME YOU HEAR ABOUT HOW NINETY-SEVEN PERCENT OF PEOPLE IN THE WESTERN WORLD HAVE DONE A VACATION AT SOME POINT IN THEIR LIVES, WELL....
VACATION
NO INFINITY!
THEY ARE THAT OTHER THREE PERCENT. THE ONES THAT REFUSE TO MAKE LIFE CHANGES EVEN IF IT MEANS A WORSE EXISTENCE FOR THEM, THEIR LOVED ONES, WHATEVER.
SOME DO IT FOR RELIGIOUS REASONS, SOME OF THEM ARE JUST SCARED, BUT BASICALLY--
THEY ARE LIKE THE REALITY AMISH.
AND JUST WHEN I STARTED LOOKING TO BUY MY WAY INTO AN EVENING THAT WASN'T SUCH UTTER SHIT, A NIGHT WITH SOME STILL-EDIBLE FOOD IN THE KITCHEN AND MAYBE A DOG--
KNOCK KNOCK KNOCK
OPEN UP, YOU SON OF A BITCH!

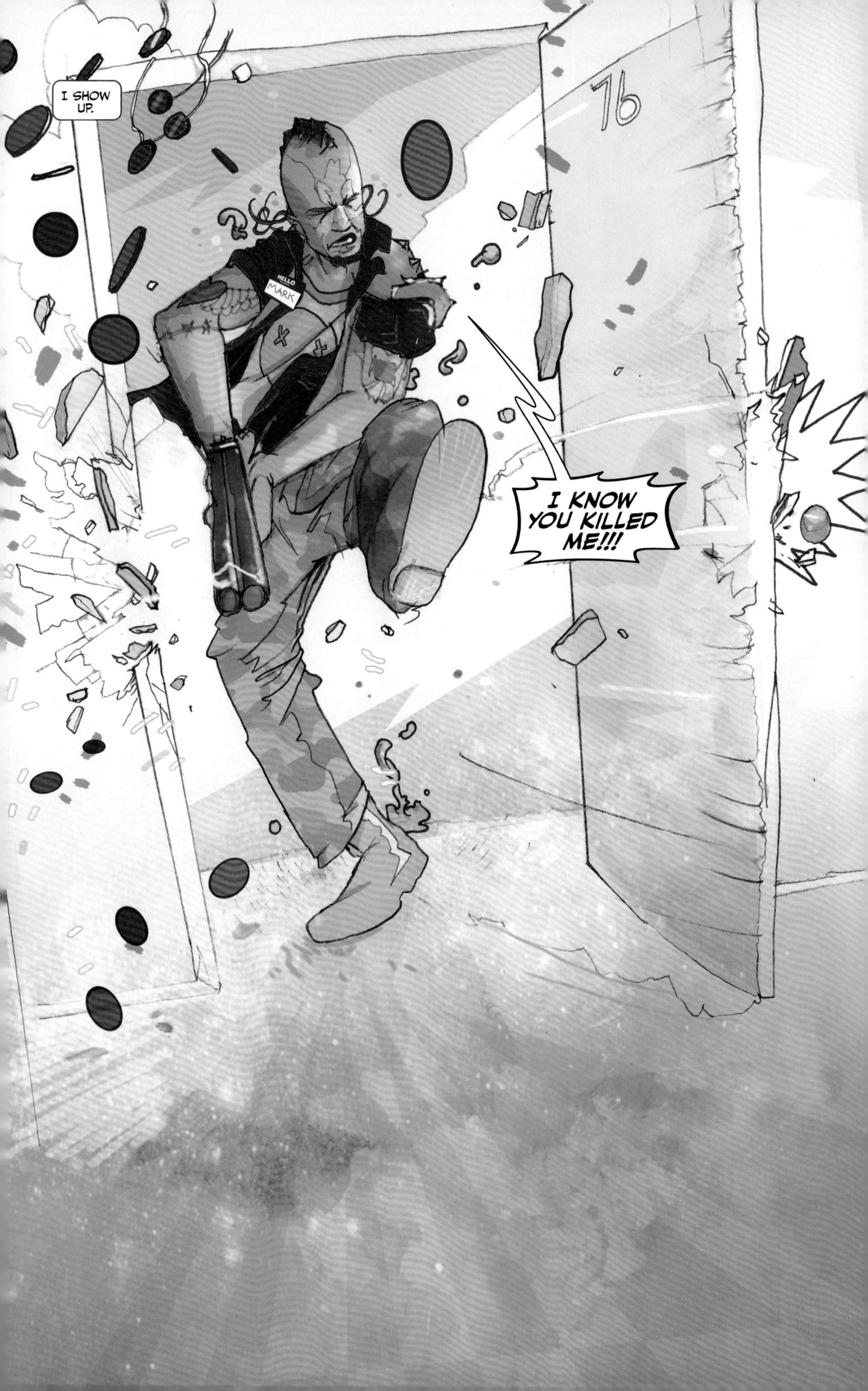
I SHOW UP.
HELLO
MARK
76
I KNOW YOU KILLED ME!!!

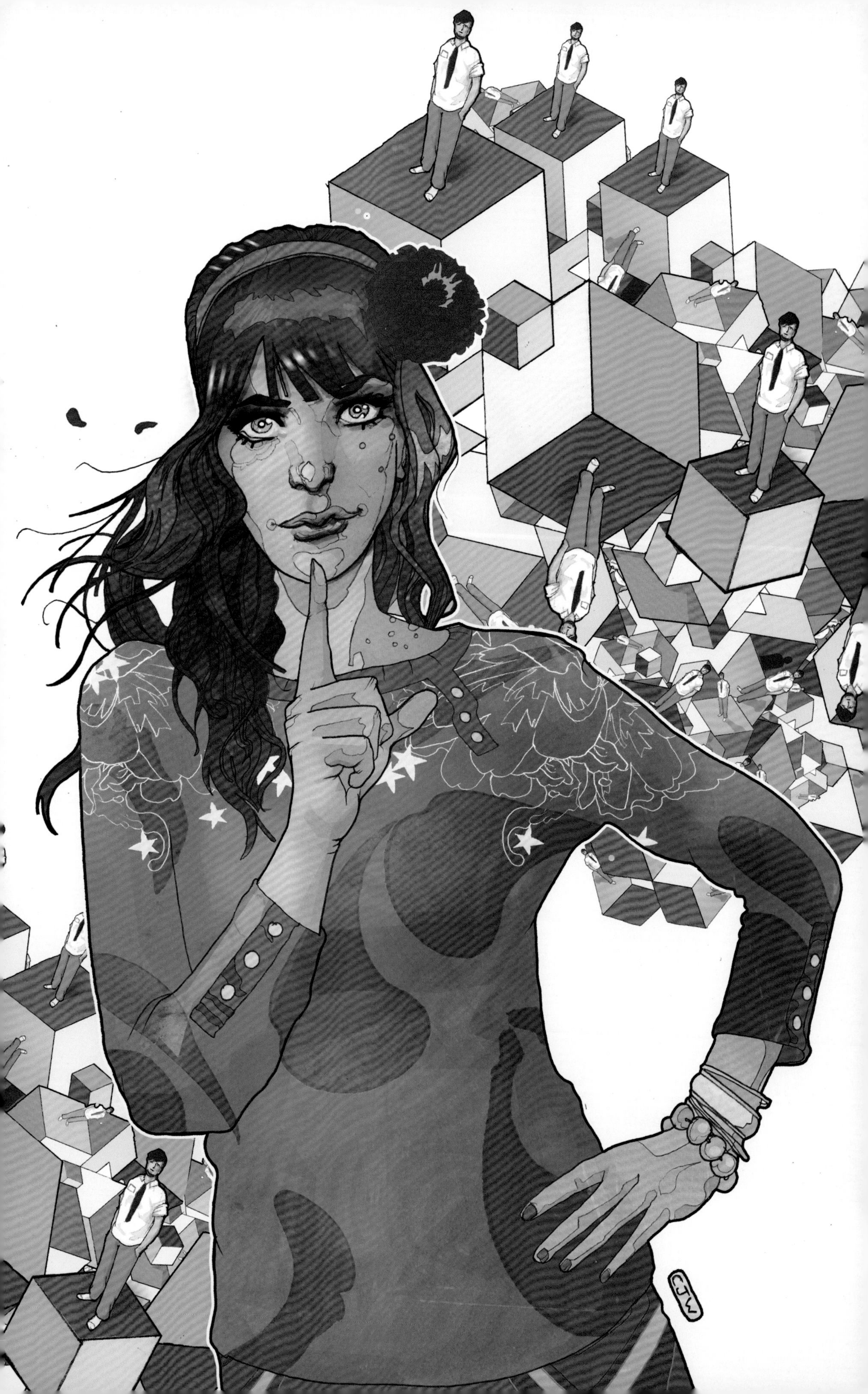
CJW

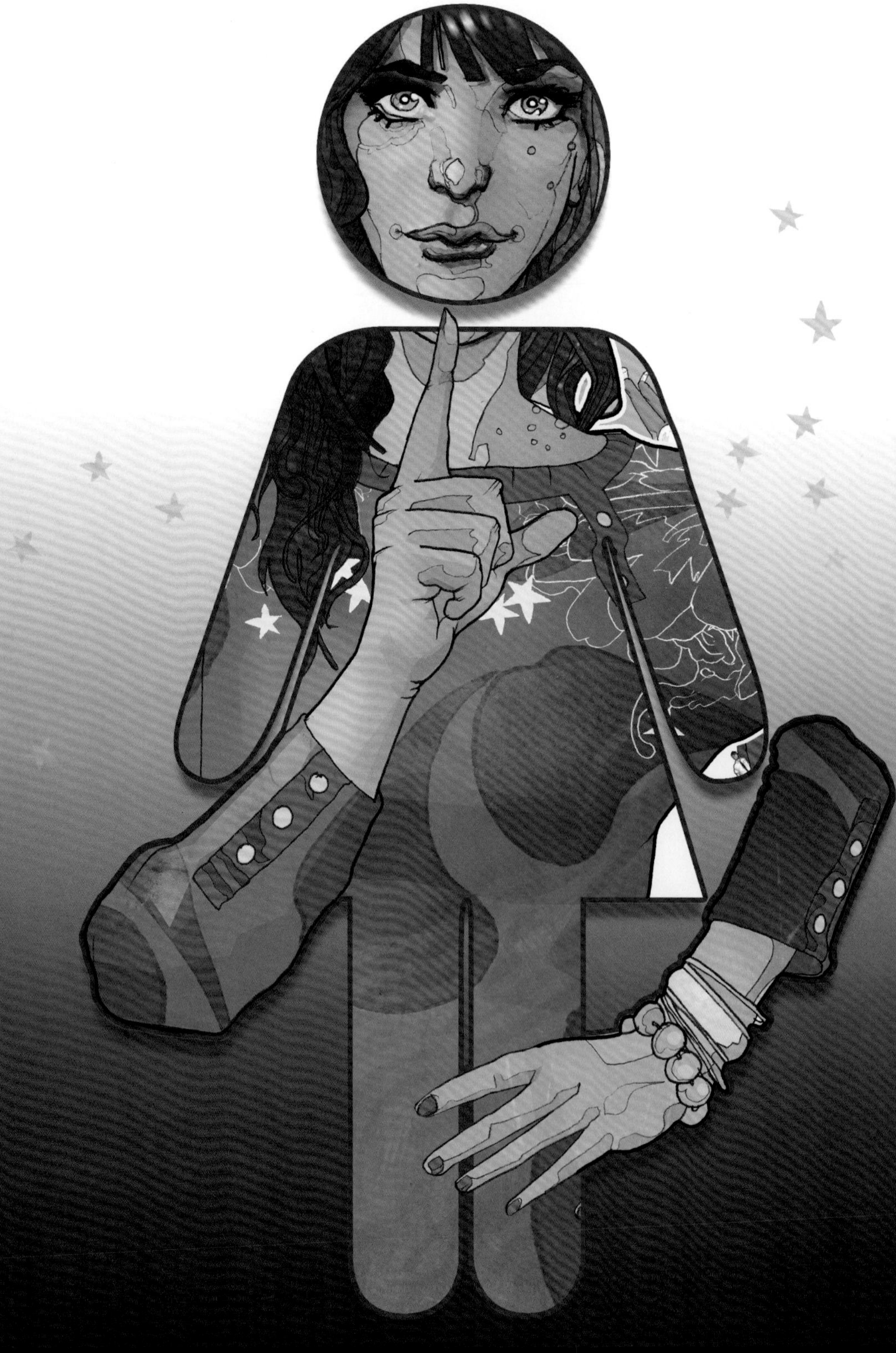

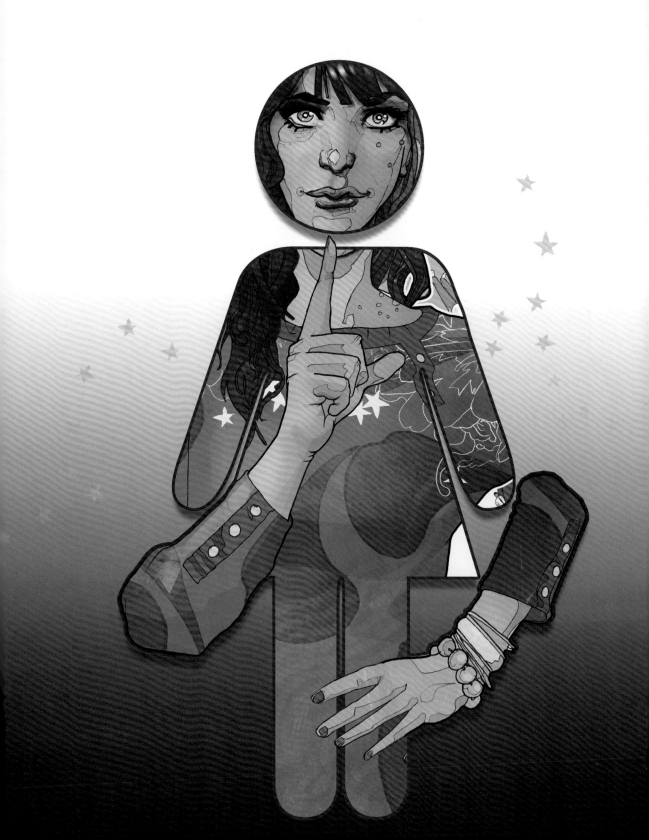

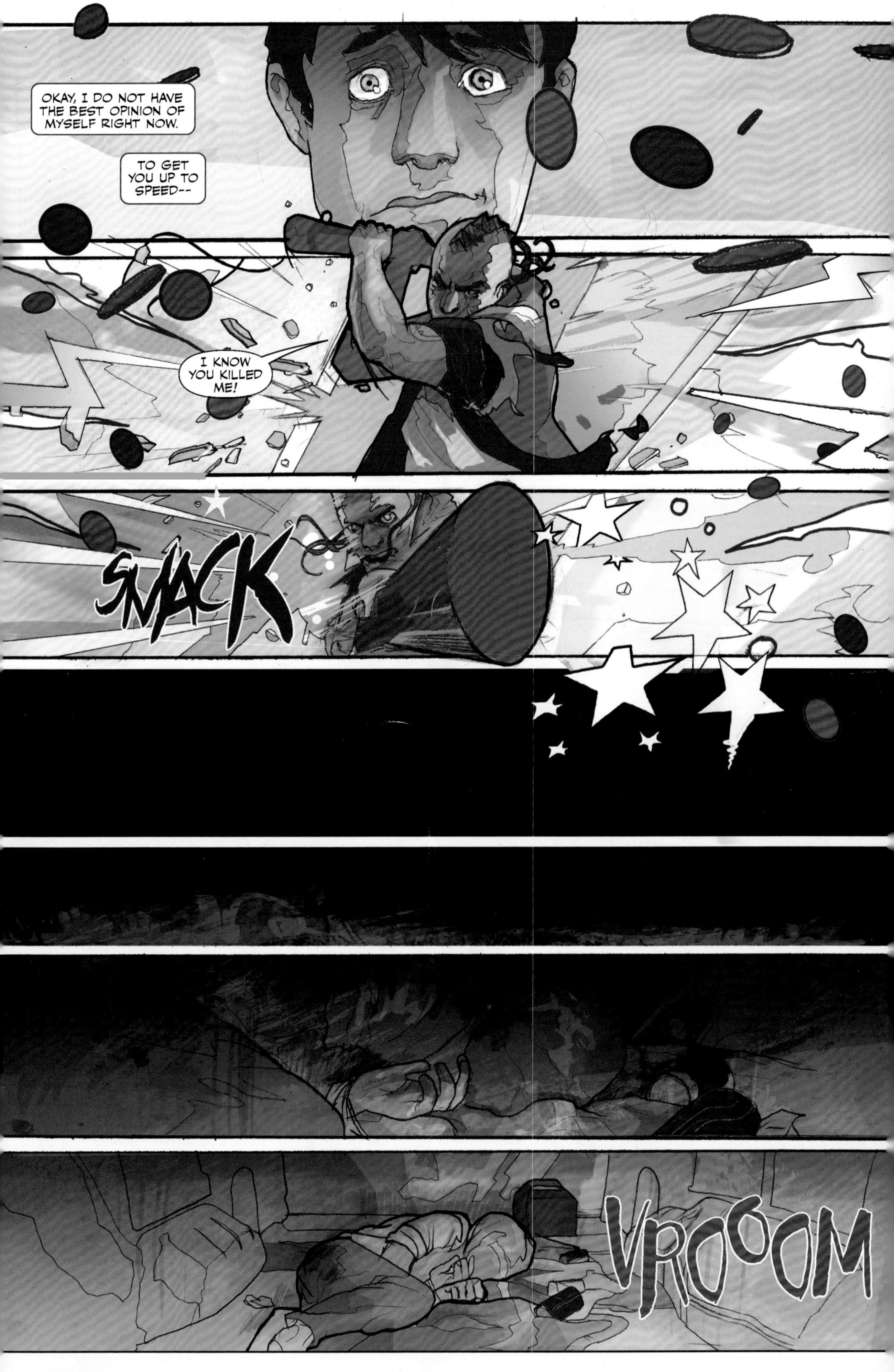
OKAY, I DO NOT HAVE THE BEST OPINION OF MYSELF RIGHT NOW.
TO GET YOU UP TO SPEED--
I KNOW YOU KILLED ME!
SMACK
VROOOOM

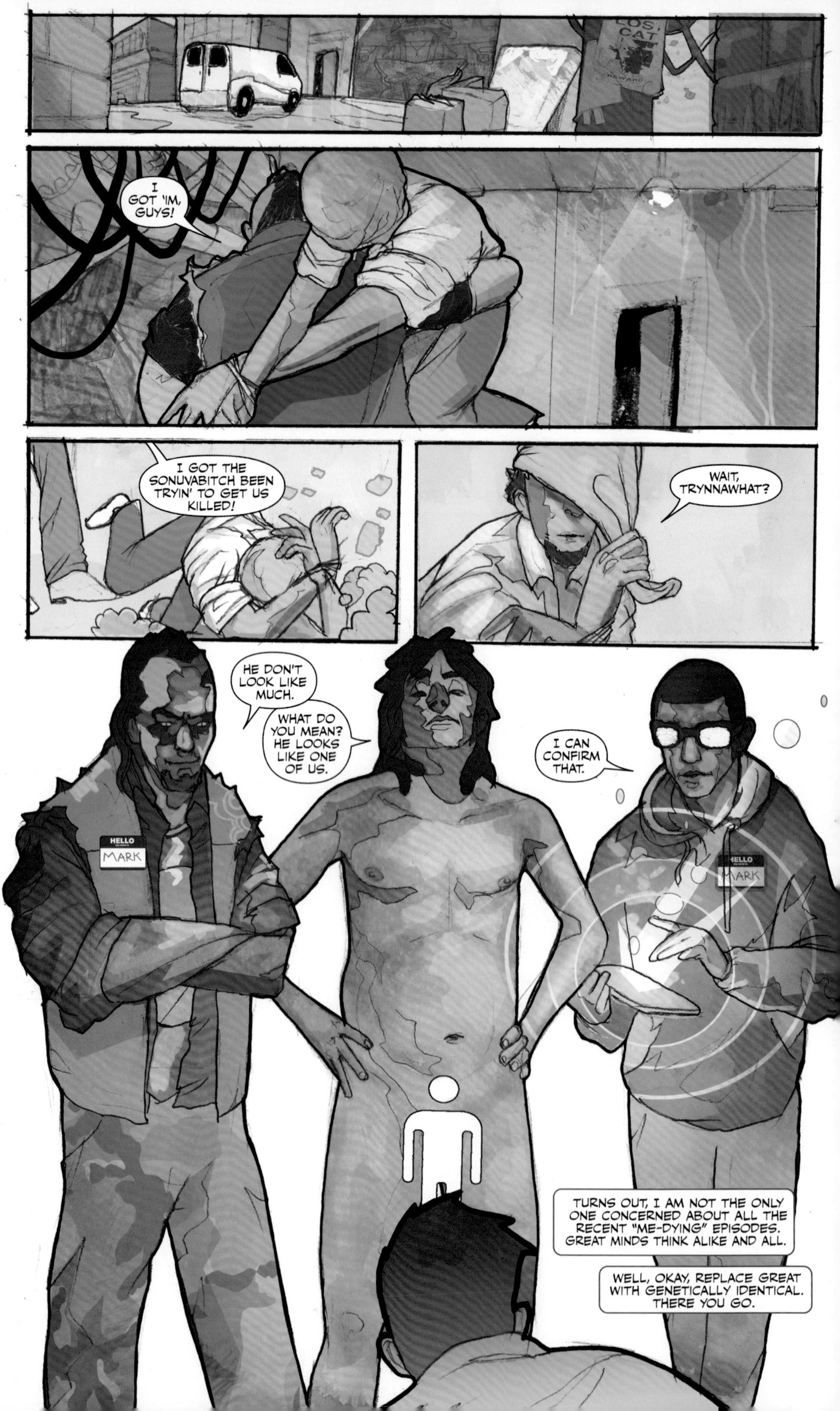
LOS. CAT
REWARD
I GOT 'IM, GUYS!
I GOT THE SONUVABITCH BEEN TRYIN' TO GET US KILLED!
WAIT, TRYNNAWHAT?
HE DON'T LOOK LIKE MUCH.
WHAT DO YOU MEAN? HE LOOKS LIKE ONE OF US.
I CAN CONFIRM THAT.
HELLO
MARK
HELLO
MARK
TURNS OUT, I AM NOT THE ONLY ONE CONCERNED ABOUT ALL THE RECENT "ME-DYING" EPISODES. GREAT MINDS THINK ALIKE AND ALL.
WELL, OKAY, REPLACE GREAT WITH GENETICALLY IDENTICAL. THERE YOU GO.

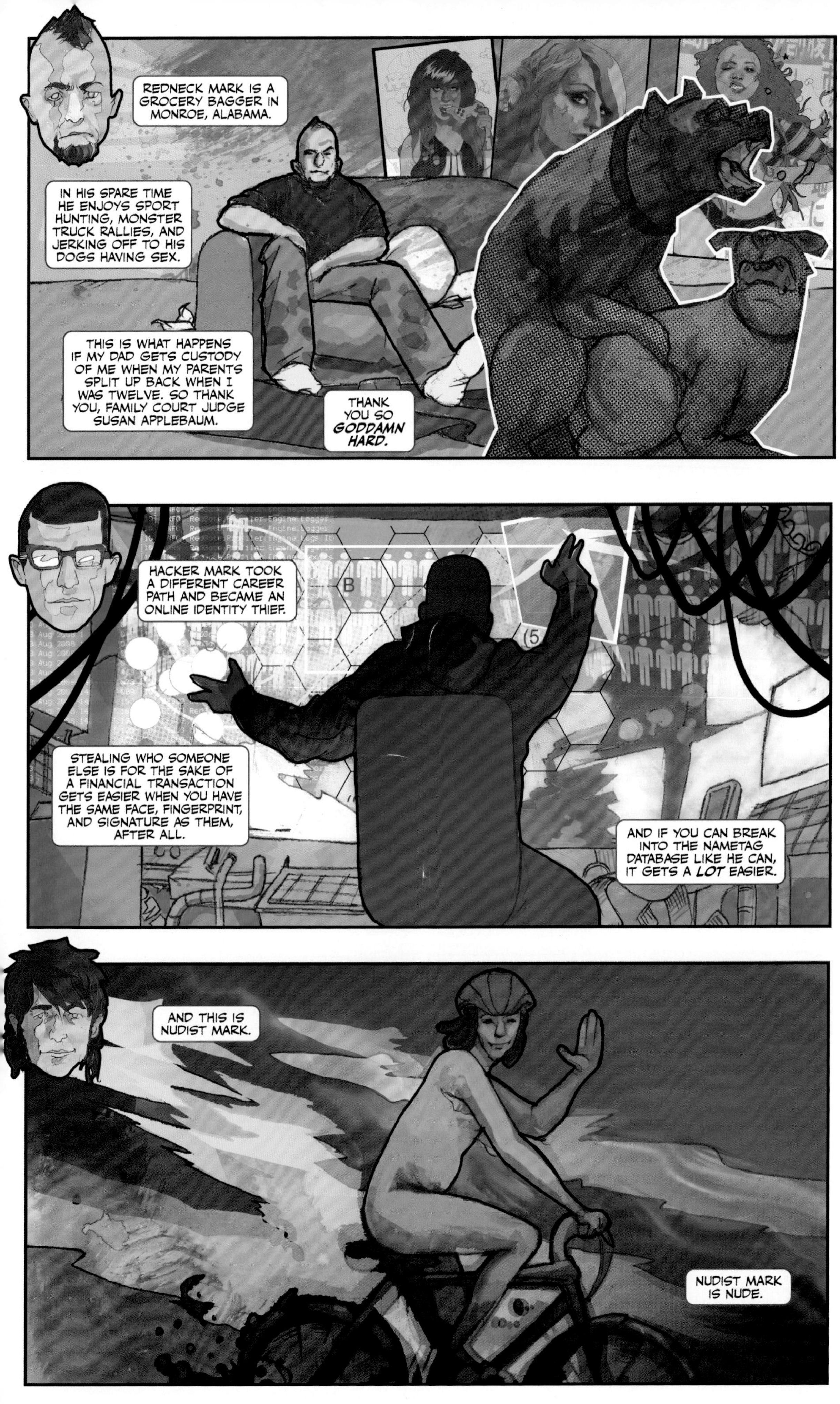

REDNECK MARK IS A GROCERY BAGGER IN MONROE, ALABAMA.
IN HIS SPARE TIME HE ENJOYS SPORT HUNTING, MONSTER TRUCK RALLIES, AND JERKING OFF TO HIS DOGS HAVING SEX.
THIS IS WHAT HAPPENS IF MY DAD GETS CUSTODY OF ME WHEN MY PARENTS SPLIT UP BACK WHEN I WAS TWELVE. SO THANK YOU, FAMILY COURT JUDGE SUSAN APPLEBAUM.
THANK YOU SO *GODDAMN HARD.*
HACKER MARK TOOK A DIFFERENT CAREER PATH AND BECAME AN ONLINE IDENTITY THIEF.
STEALING WHO SOMEONE ELSE IS FOR THE SAKE OF A FINANCIAL TRANSACTION GETS EASIER WHEN YOU HAVE THE SAME FACE, FINGERPRINT, AND SIGNATURE AS THEM, AFTER ALL.
AND IF YOU CAN BREAK INTO THE NAMETAG DATABASE LIKE HE CAN, IT GETS A *LOT* EASIER.
AND THIS IS NUDIST MARK.
NUDIST MARK IS NUDE.

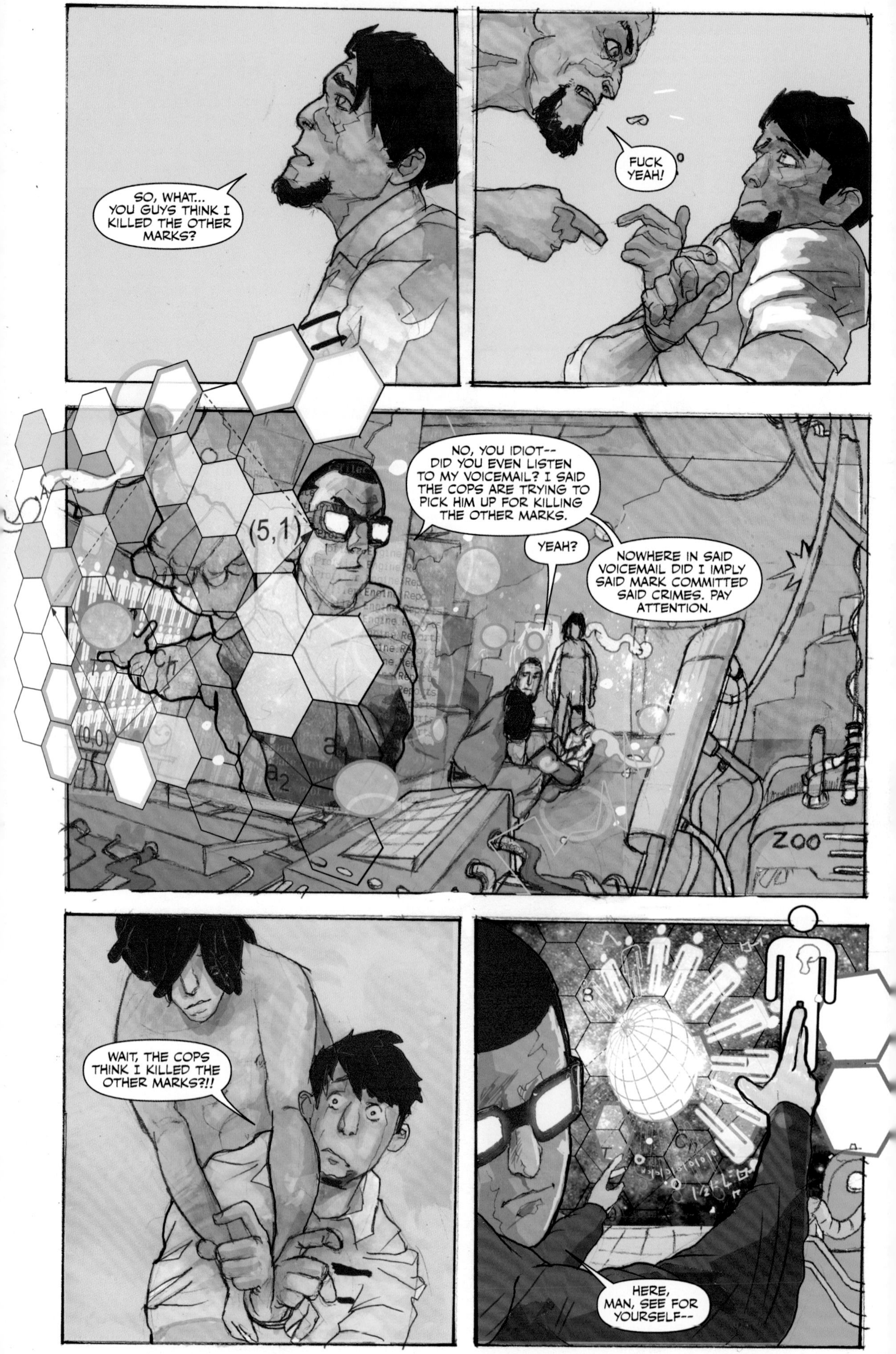
SO, WHAT... YOU GUYS THINK I KILLED THE OTHER MARKS?
FUCK YEAH!
NO, YOU IDIOT-- DID YOU EVEN LISTEN TO MY VOICEMAIL? I SAID THE COPS ARE TRYING TO PICK HIM UP FOR KILLING THE OTHER MARKS.
YEAH?
NOWHERE IN SAID VOICEMAIL DID I IMPLY SAID MARK COMMITTED SAID CRIMES. PAY ATTENTION.
(5,1)
(0,0)
ZOO
WAIT, THE COPS THINK I KILLED THE OTHER MARKS?!!
HERE, MAN, SEE FOR YOURSELF--

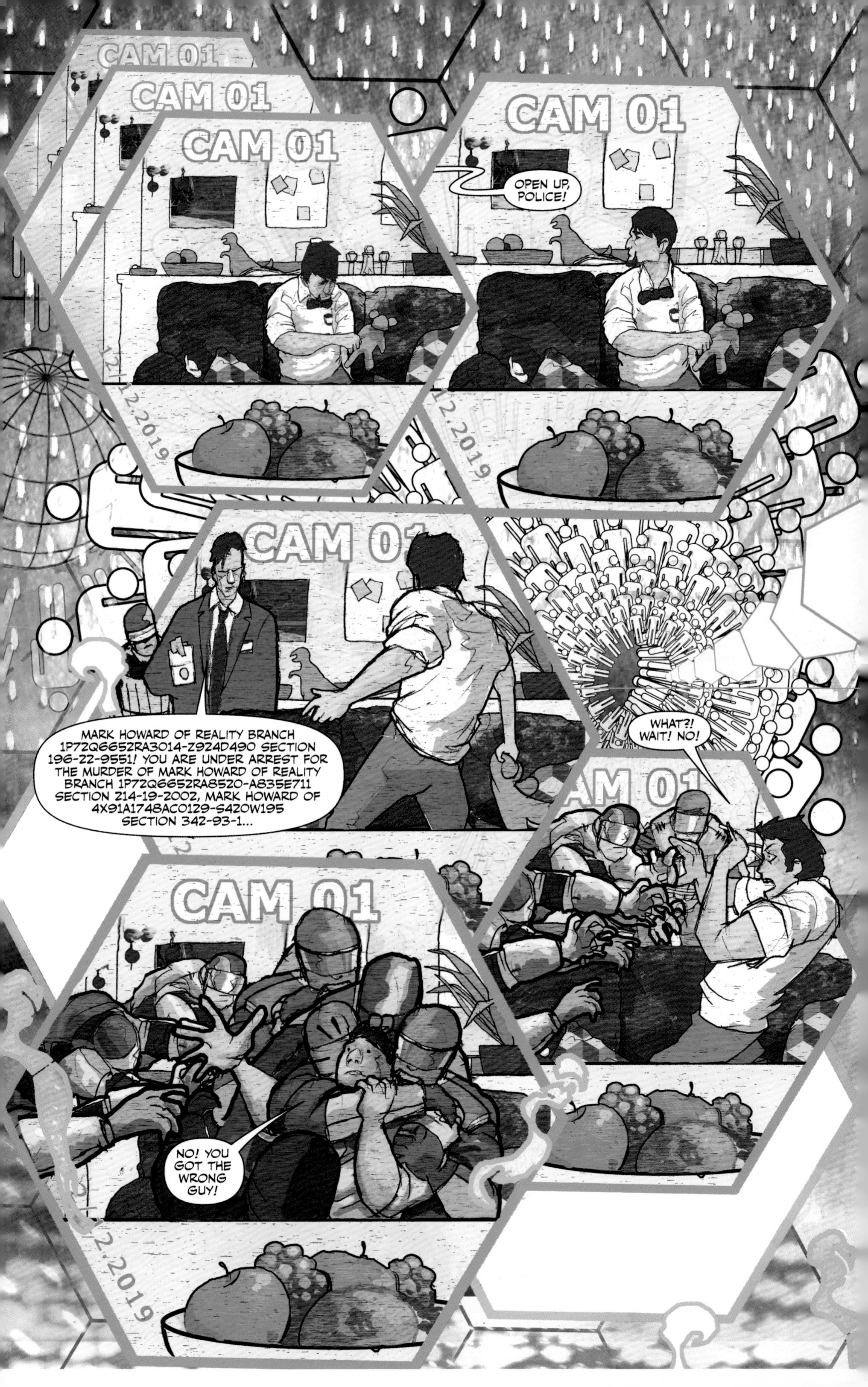
CAM 01
CAM 01
CAM 01
12.12.2019
CAM 01
OPEN UP, POLICE!
12.12.2019
CAM 01
MARK HOWARD OF REALITY BRANCH 1P72Q6652RA3014-Z924D490 SECTION 196-22-9551! YOU ARE UNDER ARREST FOR THE MURDER OF MARK HOWARD OF REALITY BRANCH 1P72Q6652RA8520-A835E711 SECTION 214-19-2002, MARK HOWARD OF 4X91A1748AC0129-S420W195 SECTION 342-93-1...
WHAT?! WAIT! NO!
CAM 01
NO! YOU GOT THE WRONG GUY!
12.12.2019

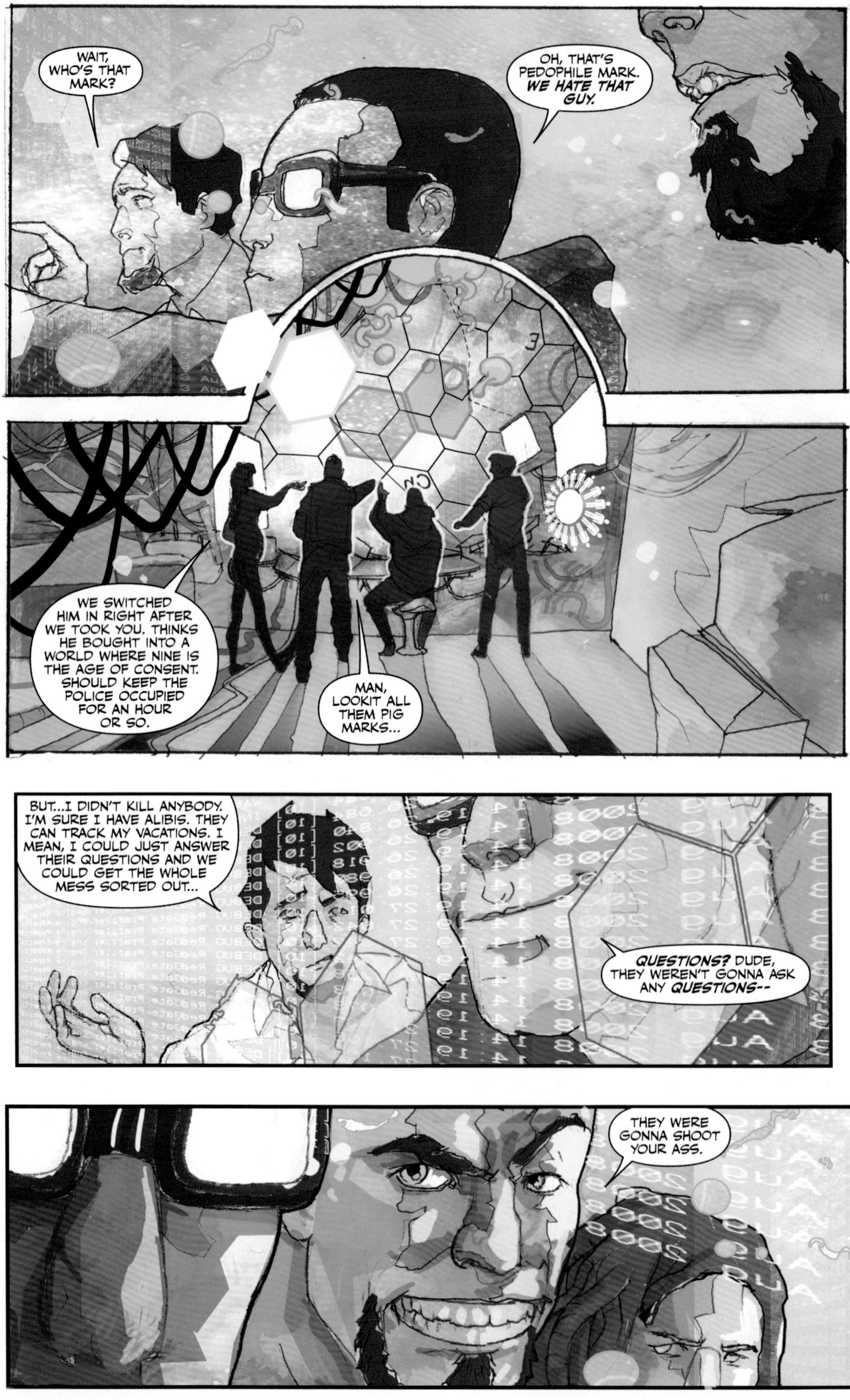
WAIT, WHO'S THAT MARK?
OH, THAT'S PEDOPHILE MARK. *WE HATE THAT GUY.*
WE SWITCHED HIM IN RIGHT AFTER WE TOOK YOU. THINKS HE BOUGHT INTO A WORLD WHERE NINE IS THE AGE OF CONSENT. SHOULD KEEP THE POLICE OCCUPIED FOR AN HOUR OR SO.
MAN, LOOKIT ALL THEM PIG MARKS...
BUT...I DIDN'T KILL ANYBODY. I'M SURE I HAVE ALIBIS. THEY CAN TRACK MY VACATIONS. I MEAN, I COULD JUST ANSWER THEIR QUESTIONS AND WE COULD GET THE WHOLE MESS SORTED OUT...
QUESTIONS? DUDE, THEY WEREN'T GONNA ASK ANY *QUESTIONS--*
THEY WERE GONNA SHOOT YOUR ASS.

TURNS OUT THESE THREE MARKS HAD ALL SURVIVED ATTEMPTS ON THEIR OWN LIVES IN THE LAST WEEK.

SOMEONE CAME AFTER THEM, AND TRIED TO OFF US IN A WAY THAT LOOKED LIKE AN ACCIDENT OR RANDOM FOUL PLAY.

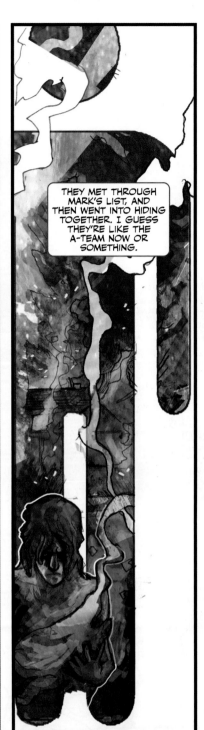

THEY MET THROUGH MARK'S LIST, AND THEN WENT INTO HIDING TOGETHER. I GUESS THEY'RE LIKE THE A-TEAM NOW OR SOMETHING.

SO...HOW MANY MARKS HAVE YOU GUYS MANAGED TO SAVE, THEN?

INCLUDING YOU?

SURE.

YOU, THEN.

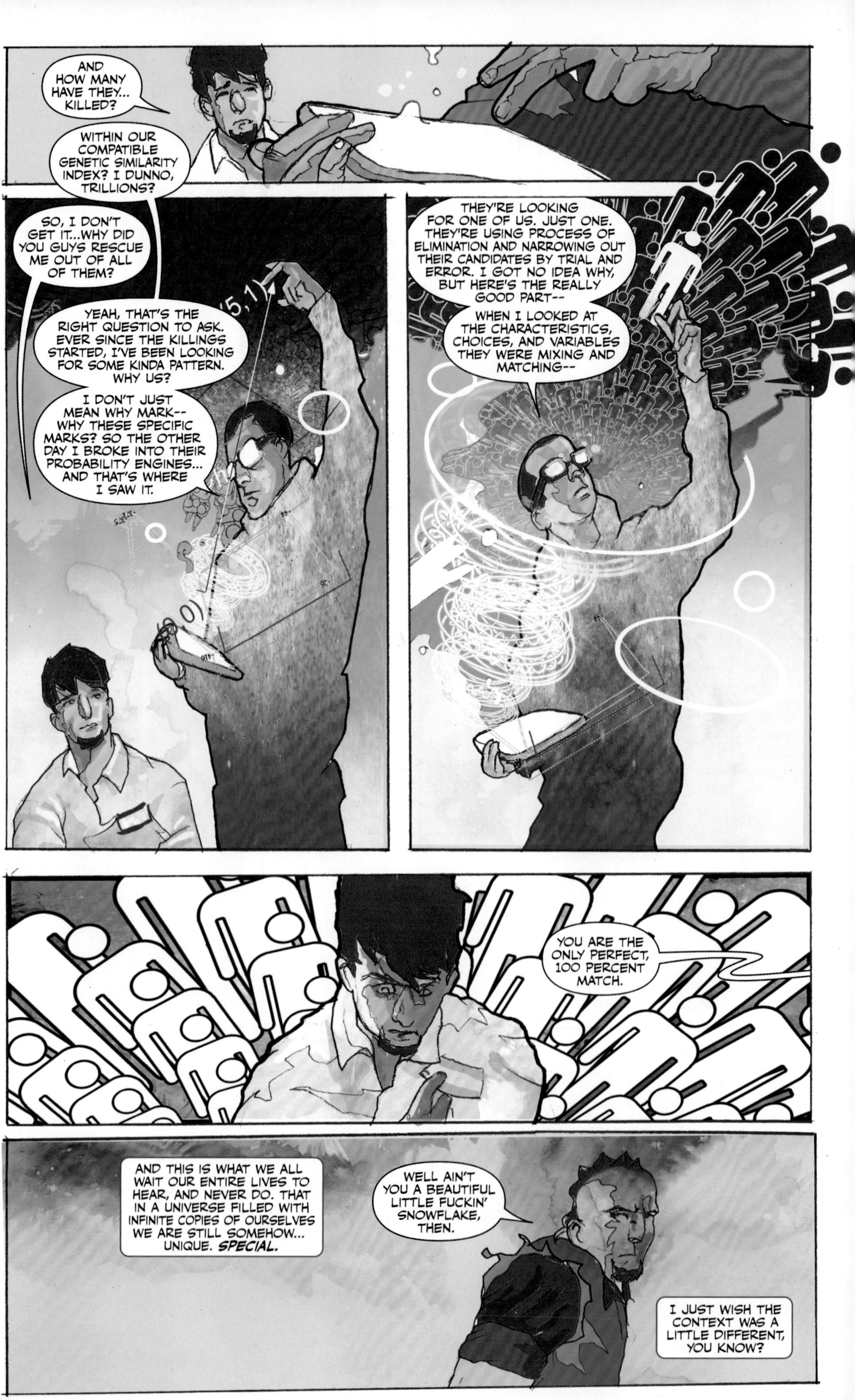
AND HOW MANY HAVE THEY... KILLED?
WITHIN OUR COMPATIBLE GENETIC SIMILARITY INDEX? I DUNNO, TRILLIONS?
SO, I DON'T GET IT...WHY DID YOU GUYS RESCUE ME OUT OF ALL OF THEM?
YEAH, THAT'S THE RIGHT QUESTION TO ASK. EVER SINCE THE KILLINGS STARTED, I'VE BEEN LOOKING FOR SOME KINDA PATTERN. WHY US?
I DON'T JUST MEAN WHY MARK-- WHY THESE SPECIFIC MARKS? SO THE OTHER DAY I BROKE INTO THEIR PROBABILITY ENGINES... AND THAT'S WHERE I SAW IT.
THEY'RE LOOKING FOR ONE OF US. JUST ONE. THEY'RE USING PROCESS OF ELIMINATION AND NARROWING OUT THEIR CANDIDATES BY TRIAL AND ERROR. I GOT NO IDEA WHY, BUT HERE'S THE REALLY GOOD PART--
WHEN I LOOKED AT THE CHARACTERISTICS, CHOICES, AND VARIABLES THEY WERE MIXING AND MATCHING--
YOU ARE THE ONLY PERFECT, 100 PERCENT MATCH.
AND THIS IS WHAT WE ALL WAIT OUR ENTIRE LIVES TO HEAR, AND NEVER DO. THAT IN A UNIVERSE FILLED WITH INFINITE COPIES OF OURSELVES WE ARE STILL SOMEHOW... UNIQUE. *SPECIAL.*
WELL AIN'T YOU A BEAUTIFUL LITTLE FUCKIN' SNOWFLAKE, THEN.
I JUST WISH THE CONTEXT WAS A LITTLE DIFFERENT, YOU KNOW?

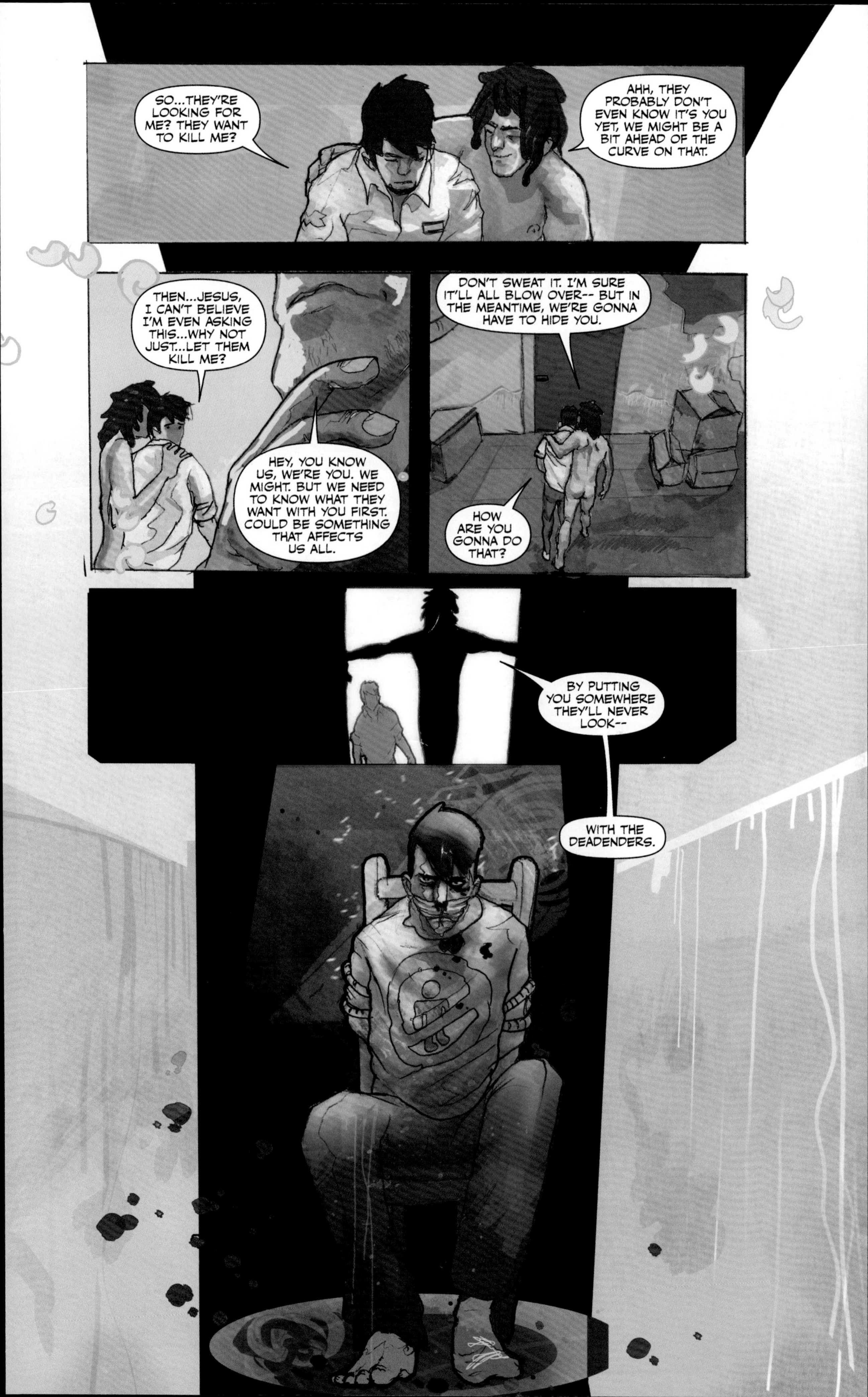
SO...THEY'RE LOOKING FOR ME? THEY WANT TO KILL ME?
AHH, THEY PROBABLY DON'T EVEN KNOW IT'S YOU YET, WE MIGHT BE A BIT AHEAD OF THE CURVE ON THAT.
THEN...JESUS, I CAN'T BELIEVE I'M EVEN ASKING THIS...WHY NOT JUST...LET THEM KILL ME?
HEY, YOU KNOW US, WE'RE YOU. WE MIGHT. BUT WE NEED TO KNOW WHAT THEY WANT WITH YOU FIRST. COULD BE SOMETHING THAT AFFECTS US ALL.
DON'T SWEAT IT. I'M SURE IT'LL ALL BLOW OVER-- BUT IN THE MEANTIME, WE'RE GONNA HAVE TO HIDE YOU.
HOW ARE YOU GONNA DO THAT?
BY PUTTING YOU SOMEWHERE THEY'LL NEVER LOOK--
WITH THE DEADENDERS.

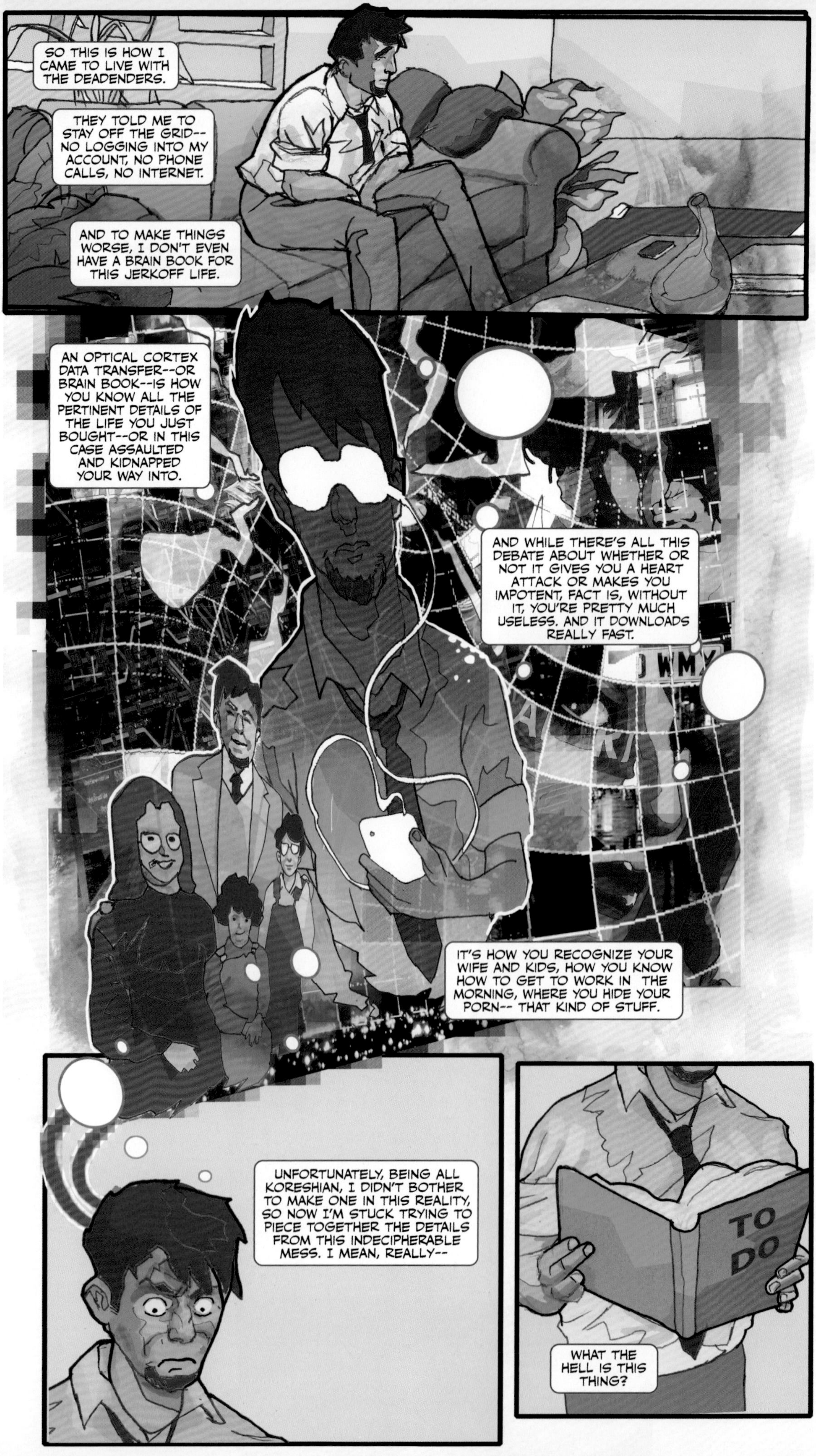
SO THIS IS HOW I CAME TO LIVE WITH THE DEADENDERS.
THEY TOLD ME TO STAY OFF THE GRID-- NO LOGGING INTO MY ACCOUNT, NO PHONE CALLS, NO INTERNET.
AND TO MAKE THINGS WORSE, I DON'T EVEN HAVE A BRAIN BOOK FOR THIS JERKOFF LIFE.
AN OPTICAL CORTEX DATA TRANSFER--OR BRAIN BOOK--IS HOW YOU KNOW ALL THE PERTINENT DETAILS OF THE LIFE YOU JUST BOUGHT--OR IN THIS CASE ASSAULTED AND KIDNAPPED YOUR WAY INTO.
AND WHILE THERE'S ALL THIS DEBATE ABOUT WHETHER OR NOT IT GIVES YOU A HEART ATTACK OR MAKES YOU IMPOTENT, FACT IS, WITHOUT IT, YOU'RE PRETTY MUCH USELESS. AND IT DOWNLOADS REALLY FAST.
IT'S HOW YOU RECOGNIZE YOUR WIFE AND KIDS, HOW YOU KNOW HOW TO GET TO WORK IN THE MORNING, WHERE YOU HIDE YOUR PORN-- THAT KIND OF STUFF.
UNFORTUNATELY, BEING ALL KORESHIAN, I DIDN'T BOTHER TO MAKE ONE IN THIS REALITY, SO NOW I'M STUCK TRYING TO PIECE TOGETHER THE DETAILS FROM THIS INDECIPHERABLE MESS. I MEAN, REALLY--
TO DO
WHAT THE HELL IS THIS THING?

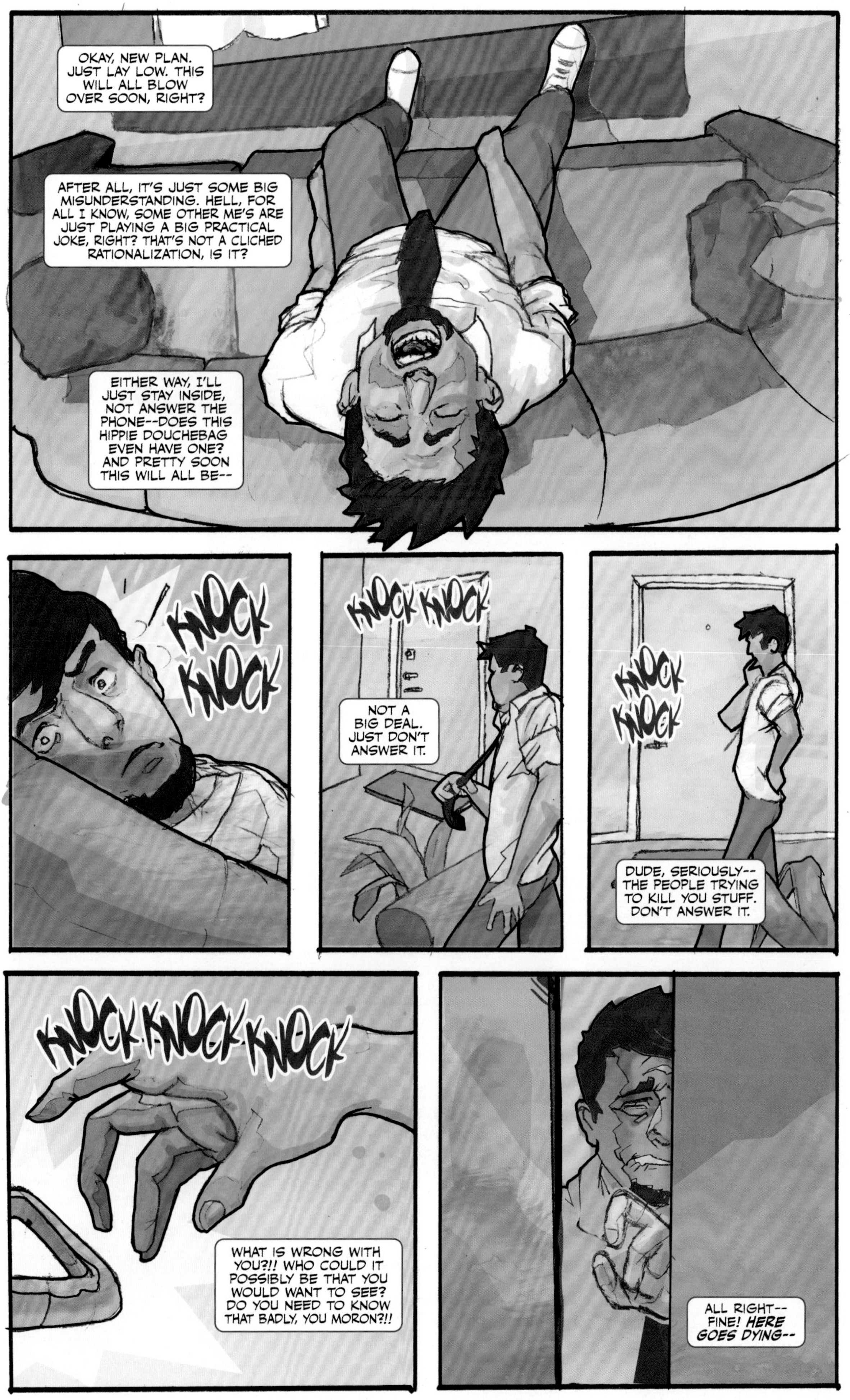
OKAY, NEW PLAN. JUST LAY LOW. THIS WILL ALL BLOW OVER SOON, RIGHT?
AFTER ALL, IT'S JUST SOME BIG MISUNDERSTANDING. HELL, FOR ALL I KNOW, SOME OTHER ME'S ARE JUST PLAYING A BIG PRACTICAL JOKE, RIGHT? THAT'S NOT A CLICHED RATIONALIZATION, IS IT?
EITHER WAY, I'LL JUST STAY INSIDE, NOT ANSWER THE PHONE--DOES THIS HIPPIE DOUCHEBAG EVEN HAVE ONE? AND PRETTY SOON THIS WILL ALL BE--
KNOCK KNOCK
KNOCK KNOCK
NOT A BIG DEAL. JUST DON'T ANSWER IT.
KNOCK KNOCK
DUDE, SERIOUSLY-- THE PEOPLE TRYING TO KILL YOU STUFF. DON'T ANSWER IT.
KNOCK KNOCK KNOCK
WHAT IS WRONG WITH YOU?!! WHO COULD IT POSSIBLY BE THAT YOU WOULD WANT TO SEE? DO YOU NEED TO KNOW THAT BADLY, YOU MORON?!!
ALL RIGHT-- FINE! *HERE GOES DYING--*

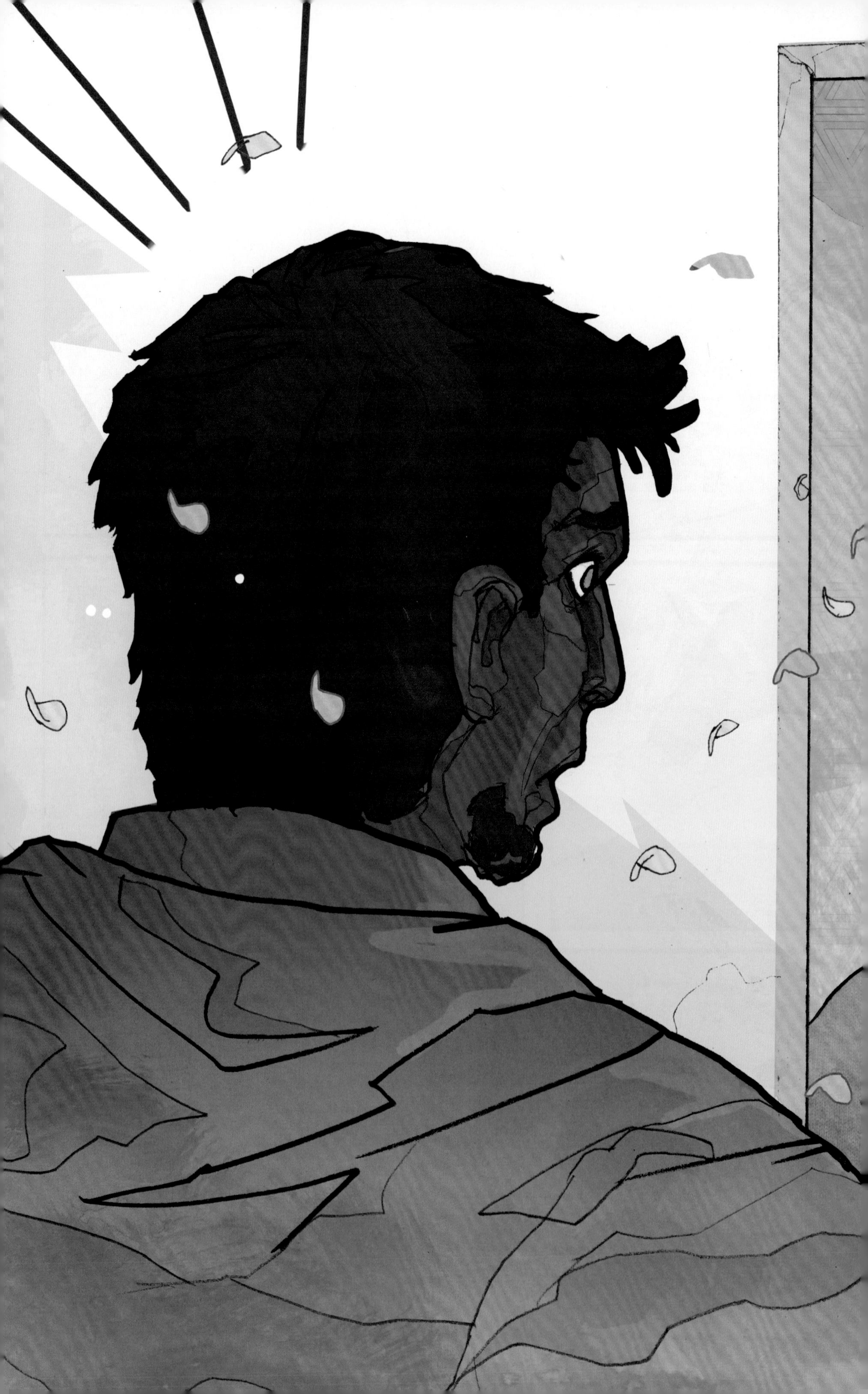

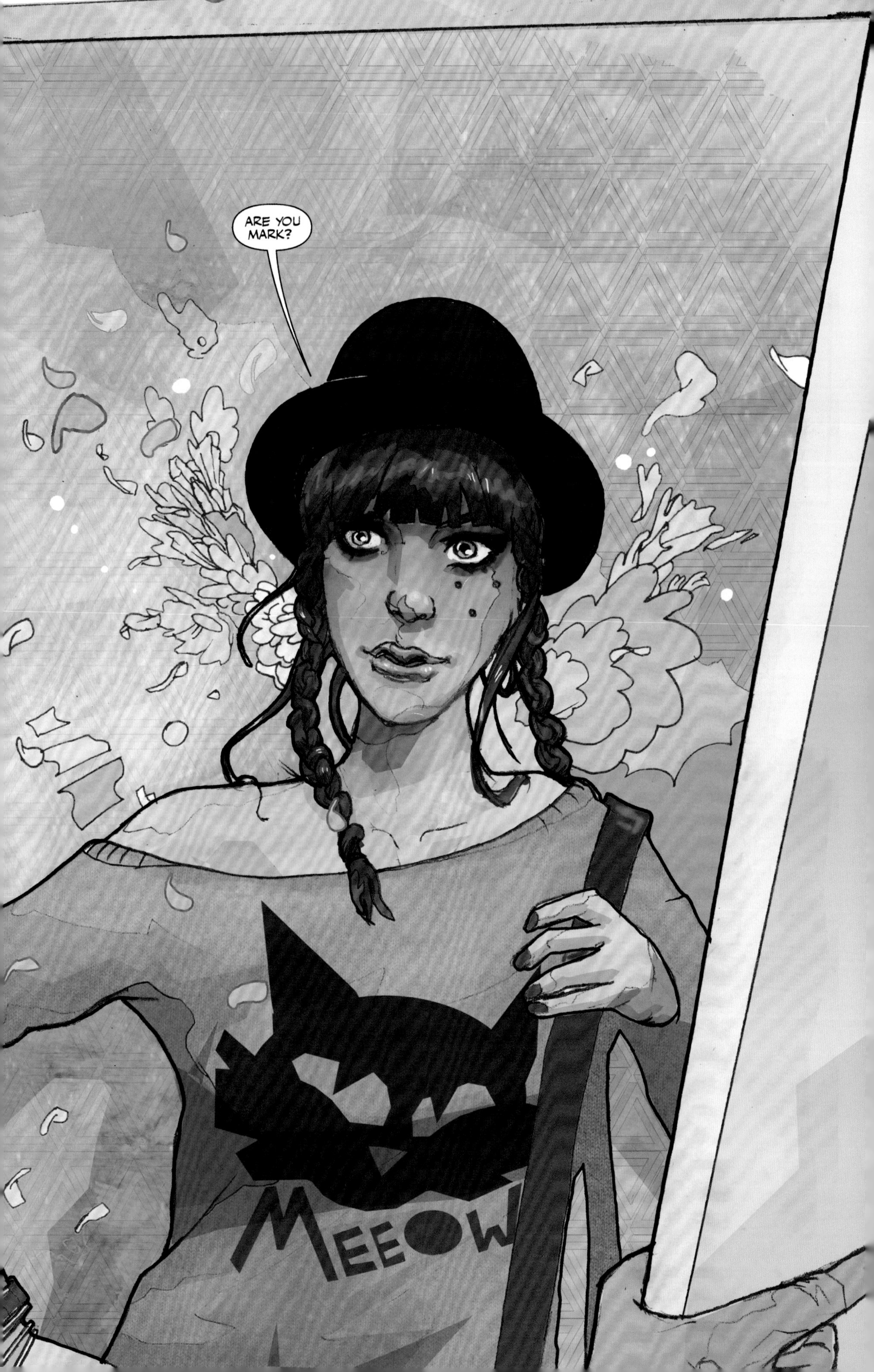
ARE YOU MARK?
MEEOW

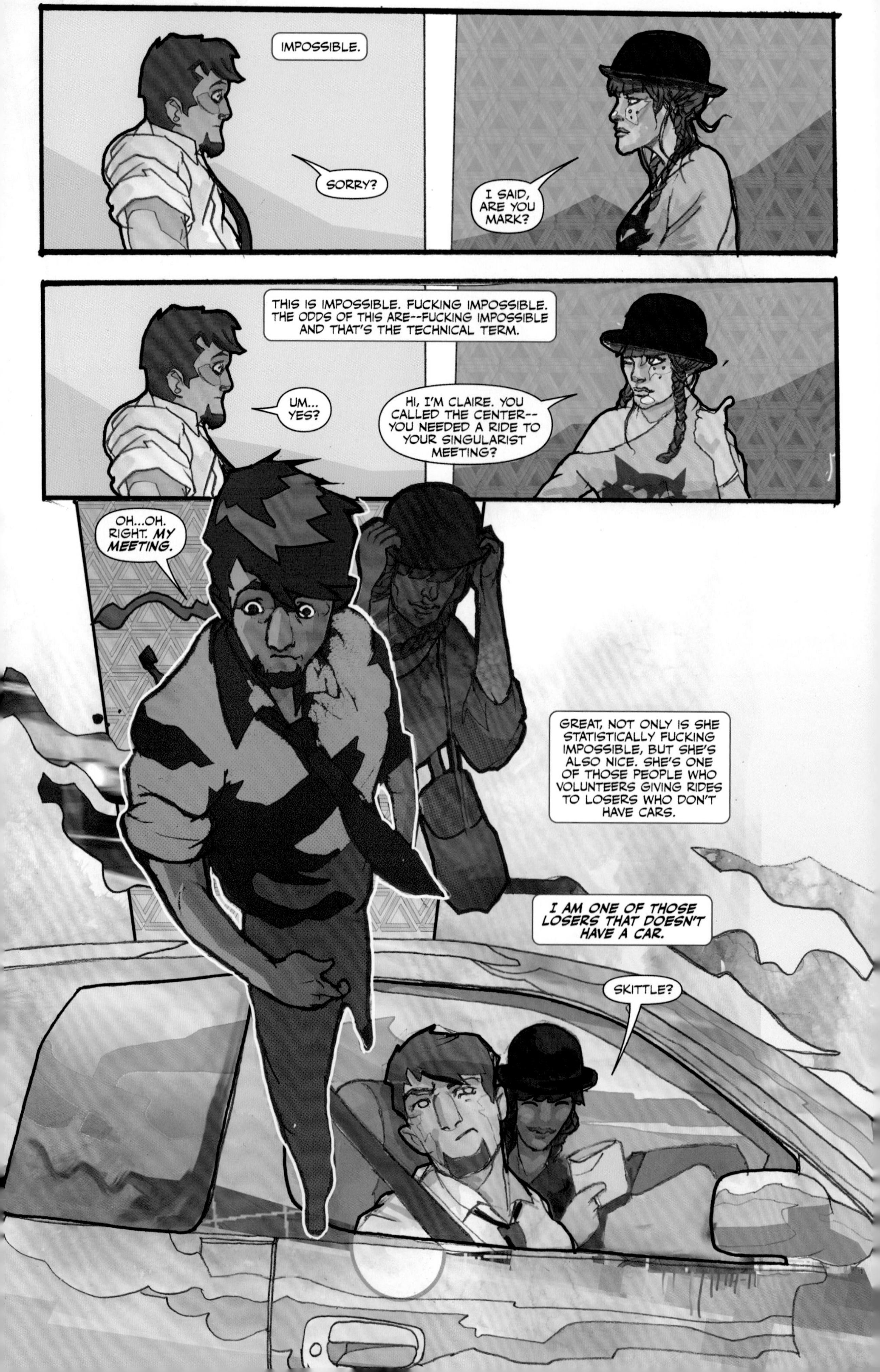
IMPOSSIBLE.
SORRY?
I SAID, ARE YOU MARK?
THIS IS IMPOSSIBLE. FUCKING IMPOSSIBLE. THE ODDS OF THIS ARE--FUCKING IMPOSSIBLE AND THAT'S THE TECHNICAL TERM.
UM... YES?
HI, I'M CLAIRE. YOU CALLED THE CENTER--YOU NEEDED A RIDE TO YOUR SINGULARIST MEETING?
OH...OH. RIGHT. *MY MEETING.*
GREAT, NOT ONLY IS SHE STATISTICALLY FUCKING IMPOSSIBLE, BUT SHE'S ALSO NICE. SHE'S ONE OF THOSE PEOPLE WHO VOLUNTEERS GIVING RIDES TO LOSERS WHO DON'T HAVE CARS.
I AM ONE OF THOSE LOSERS THAT DOESN'T HAVE A CAR.
SKITTLE?

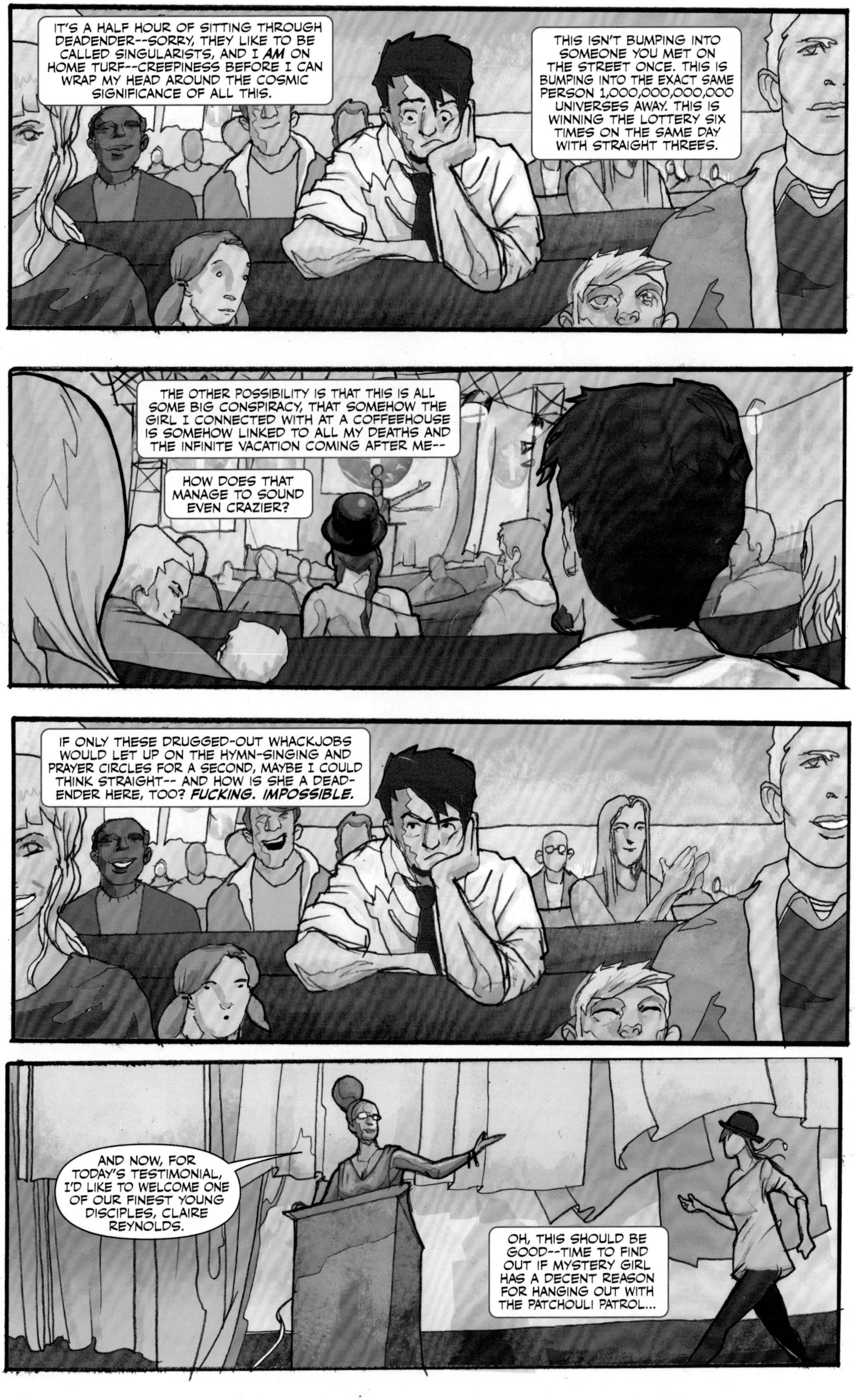
IT'S A HALF HOUR OF SITTING THROUGH DEADENDER--SORRY, THEY LIKE TO BE CALLED SINGULARISTS, AND I *AM* ON HOME TURF--CREEPINESS BEFORE I CAN WRAP MY HEAD AROUND THE COSMIC SIGNIFICANCE OF ALL THIS.
THIS ISN'T BUMPING INTO SOMEONE YOU MET ON THE STREET ONCE. THIS IS BUMPING INTO THE EXACT SAME PERSON 1,000,000,000,000 UNIVERSES AWAY. THIS IS WINNING THE LOTTERY SIX TIMES ON THE SAME DAY WITH STRAIGHT THREES.
THE OTHER POSSIBILITY IS THAT THIS IS ALL SOME BIG CONSPIRACY, THAT SOMEHOW THE GIRL I CONNECTED WITH AT A COFFEEHOUSE IS SOMEHOW LINKED TO ALL MY DEATHS AND THE INFINITE VACATION COMING AFTER ME--
HOW DOES THAT MANAGE TO SOUND EVEN CRAZIER?
IF ONLY THESE DRUGGED-OUT WHACKJOBS WOULD LET UP ON THE HYMN-SINGING AND PRAYER CIRCLES FOR A SECOND, MAYBE I COULD THINK STRAIGHT-- AND HOW IS SHE A DEAD-ENDER HERE, TOO? ***FUCKING. IMPOSSIBLE.***
AND NOW, FOR TODAY'S TESTIMONIAL, I'D LIKE TO WELCOME ONE OF OUR FINEST YOUNG DISCIPLES, CLAIRE REYNOLDS.
OH, THIS SHOULD BE GOOD--TIME TO FIND OUT IF MYSTERY GIRL HAS A DECENT REASON FOR HANGING OUT WITH THE PATCHOULI PATROL...

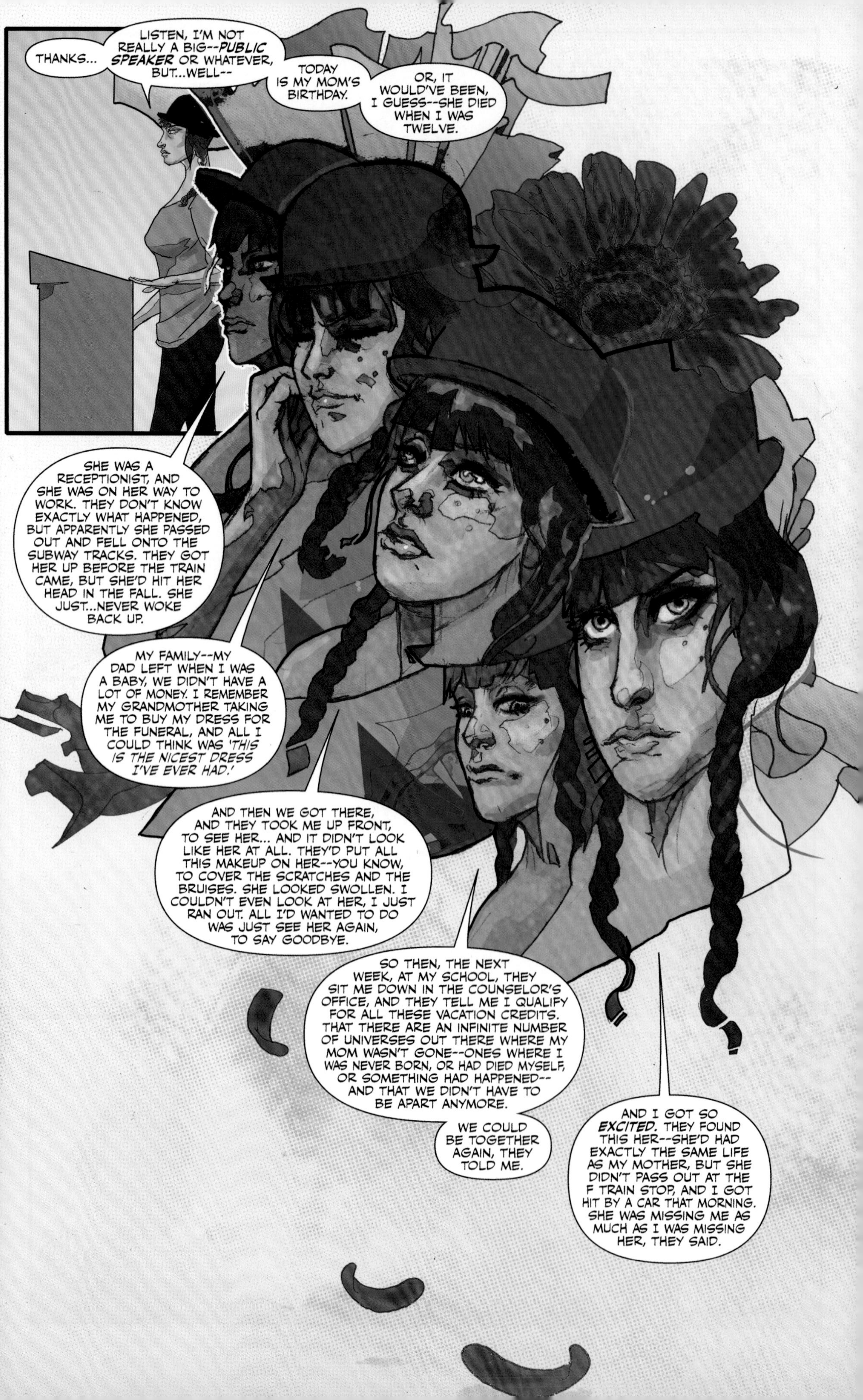
THANKS...
LISTEN, I'M NOT REALLY A BIG--*PUBLIC SPEAKER* OR WHATEVER, BUT...WELL--
TODAY IS MY MOM'S BIRTHDAY.
OR, IT WOULD'VE BEEN, I GUESS--SHE DIED WHEN I WAS TWELVE.
SHE WAS A RECEPTIONIST, AND SHE WAS ON HER WAY TO WORK. THEY DON'T KNOW EXACTLY WHAT HAPPENED, BUT APPARENTLY SHE PASSED OUT AND FELL ONTO THE SUBWAY TRACKS. THEY GOT HER UP BEFORE THE TRAIN CAME, BUT SHE'D HIT HER HEAD IN THE FALL. SHE JUST...NEVER WOKE BACK UP.
MY FAMILY--MY DAD LEFT WHEN I WAS A BABY, WE DIDN'T HAVE A LOT OF MONEY. I REMEMBER MY GRANDMOTHER TAKING ME TO BUY MY DRESS FOR THE FUNERAL, AND ALL I COULD THINK WAS *'THIS IS THE NICEST DRESS I'VE EVER HAD.'*
AND THEN WE GOT THERE, AND THEY TOOK ME UP FRONT, TO SEE HER... AND IT DIDN'T LOOK LIKE HER AT ALL. THEY'D PUT ALL THIS MAKEUP ON HER--YOU KNOW, TO COVER THE SCRATCHES AND THE BRUISES. SHE LOOKED SWOLLEN. I COULDN'T EVEN LOOK AT HER, I JUST RAN OUT. ALL I'D WANTED TO DO WAS JUST SEE HER AGAIN, TO SAY GOODBYE.
SO THEN, THE NEXT WEEK, AT MY SCHOOL, THEY SIT ME DOWN IN THE COUNSELOR'S OFFICE, AND THEY TELL ME I QUALIFY FOR ALL THESE VACATION CREDITS. THAT THERE ARE AN INFINITE NUMBER OF UNIVERSES OUT THERE WHERE MY MOM WASN'T GONE--ONES WHERE I WAS NEVER BORN, OR HAD DIED MYSELF, OR SOMETHING HAD HAPPENED--AND THAT WE DIDN'T HAVE TO BE APART ANYMORE.
WE COULD BE TOGETHER AGAIN, THEY TOLD ME.
AND I GOT SO *EXCITED.* THEY FOUND THIS HER--SHE'D HAD EXACTLY THE SAME LIFE AS MY MOTHER, BUT SHE DIDN'T PASS OUT AT THE F TRAIN STOP, AND I GOT HIT BY A CAR THAT MORNING. SHE WAS MISSING ME AS MUCH AS I WAS MISSING HER, THEY SAID.

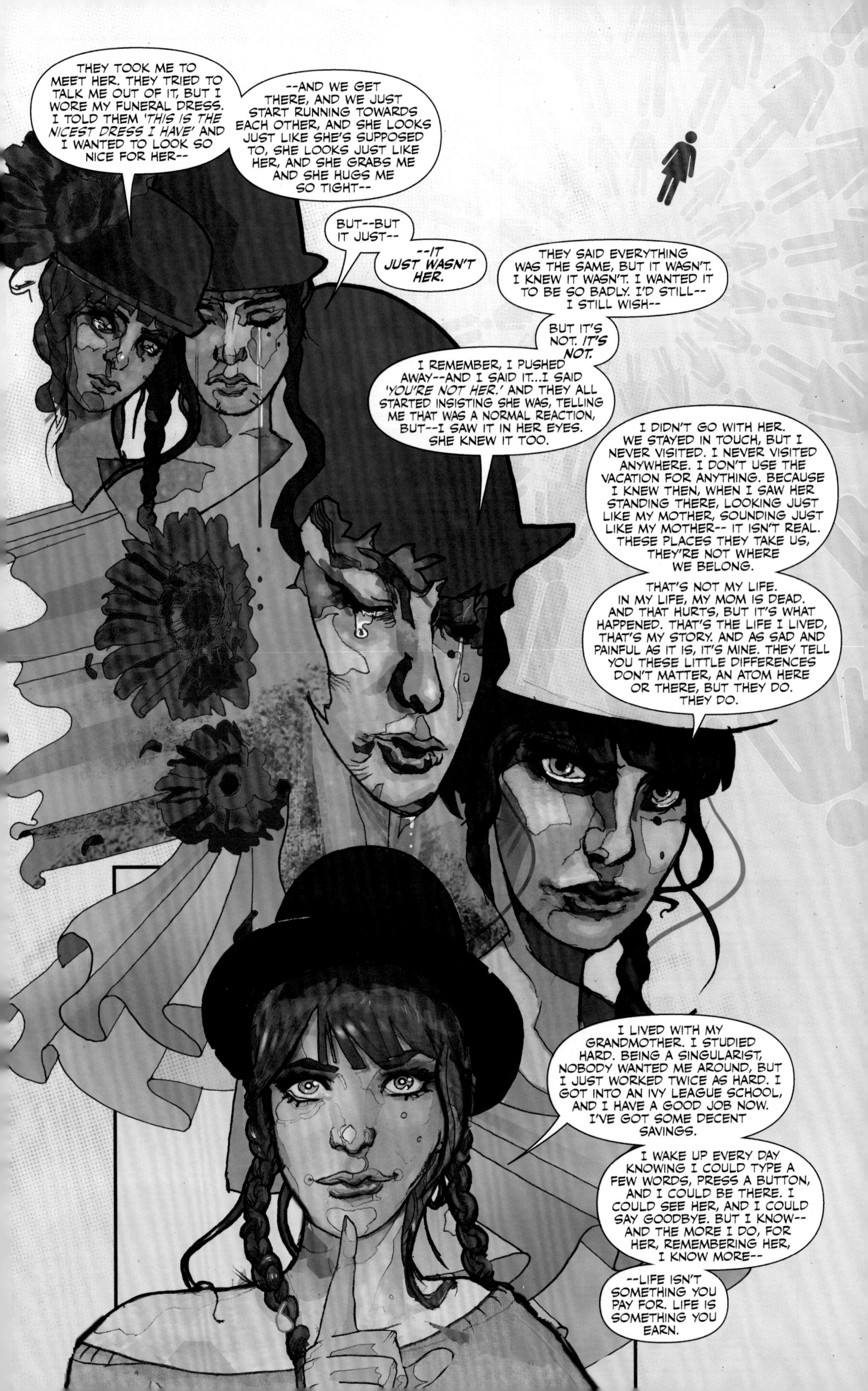
THEY TOOK ME TO MEET HER. THEY TRIED TO TALK ME OUT OF IT, BUT I WORE MY FUNERAL DRESS. I TOLD THEM *'THIS IS THE NICEST DRESS I HAVE'* AND I WANTED TO LOOK SO NICE FOR HER--
--AND WE GET THERE, AND WE JUST START RUNNING TOWARDS EACH OTHER, AND SHE LOOKS JUST LIKE SHE'S SUPPOSED TO, SHE LOOKS JUST LIKE HER, AND SHE GRABS ME AND SHE HUGS ME SO TIGHT--
BUT--BUT IT JUST--
--IT JUST WASN'T HER.
THEY SAID EVERYTHING WAS THE SAME, BUT IT WASN'T. I KNEW IT WASN'T. I WANTED IT TO BE SO BADLY. I'D STILL-- I STILL WISH--
BUT IT'S NOT. ***IT'S NOT.***
I REMEMBER, I PUSHED AWAY--AND I SAID IT...I SAID *'YOU'RE NOT HER.'* AND THEY ALL STARTED INSISTING SHE WAS, TELLING ME THAT WAS A NORMAL REACTION, BUT--I SAW IT IN HER EYES. SHE KNEW IT TOO.
I DIDN'T GO WITH HER. WE STAYED IN TOUCH, BUT I NEVER VISITED. I NEVER VISITED ANYWHERE. I DON'T USE THE VACATION FOR ANYTHING. BECAUSE I KNEW THEN, WHEN I SAW HER STANDING THERE, LOOKING JUST LIKE MY MOTHER, SOUNDING JUST LIKE MY MOTHER-- IT ISN'T REAL. THESE PLACES THEY TAKE US, THEY'RE NOT WHERE WE BELONG.
THAT'S NOT MY LIFE. IN MY LIFE, MY MOM IS DEAD. AND THAT HURTS, BUT IT'S WHAT HAPPENED. THAT'S THE LIFE I LIVED, THAT'S MY STORY. AND AS SAD AND PAINFUL AS IT IS, IT'S MINE. THEY TELL YOU THESE LITTLE DIFFERENCES DON'T MATTER, AN ATOM HERE OR THERE, BUT THEY DO. THEY DO.
I LIVED WITH MY GRANDMOTHER. I STUDIED HARD. BEING A SINGULARIST, NOBODY WANTED ME AROUND, BUT I JUST WORKED TWICE AS HARD. I GOT INTO AN IVY LEAGUE SCHOOL, AND I HAVE A GOOD JOB NOW. I'VE GOT SOME DECENT SAVINGS.
I WAKE UP EVERY DAY KNOWING I COULD TYPE A FEW WORDS, PRESS A BUTTON, AND I COULD BE THERE. I COULD SEE HER, AND I COULD SAY GOODBYE. BUT I KNOW-- AND THE MORE I DO, FOR HER, REMEMBERING HER, I KNOW MORE--
--LIFE ISN'T SOMETHING YOU PAY FOR. LIFE IS SOMETHING YOU EARN.

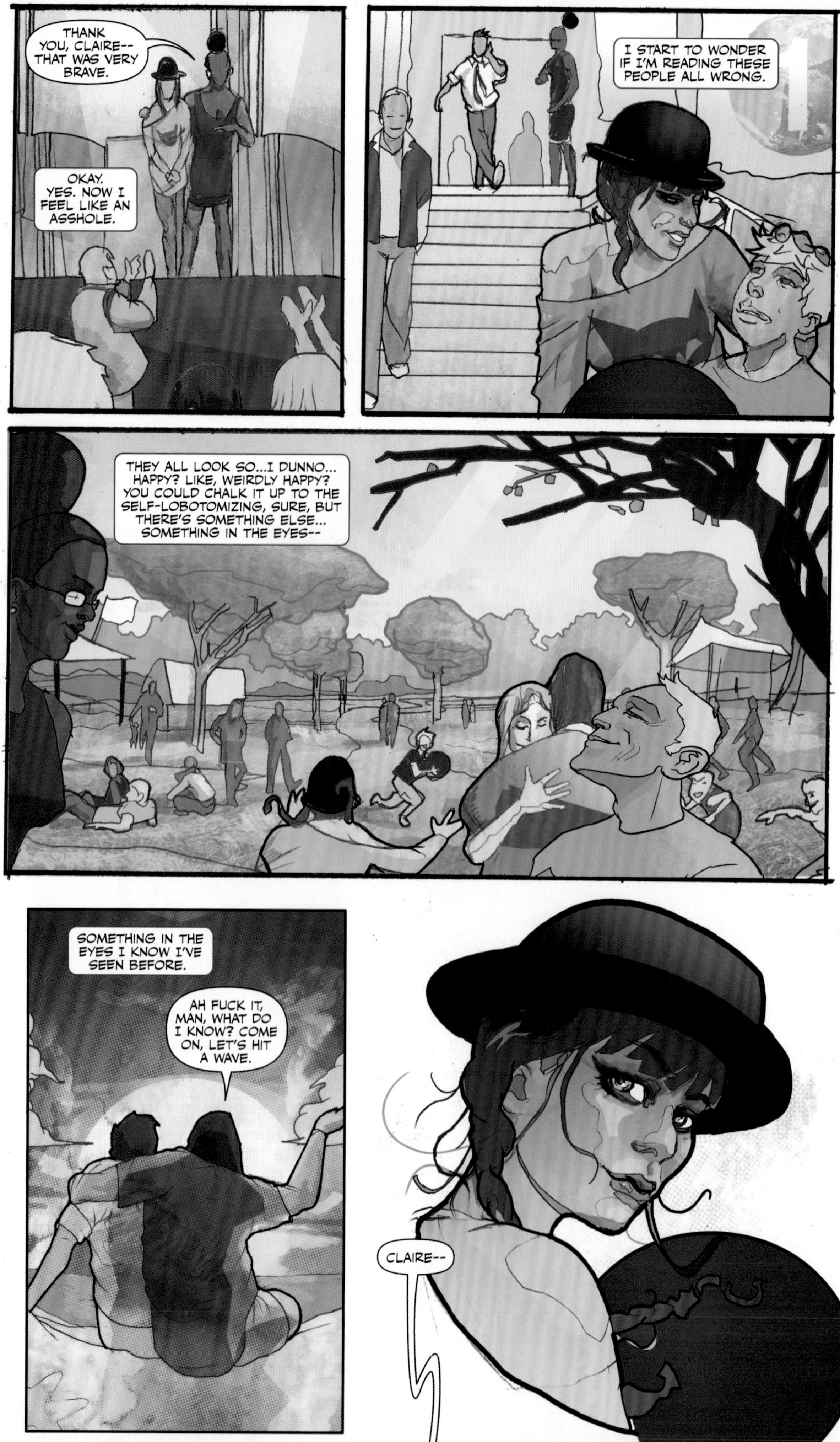
THANK YOU, CLAIRE--THAT WAS VERY BRAVE.
OKAY. YES. NOW I FEEL LIKE AN ASSHOLE.
I START TO WONDER IF I'M READING THESE PEOPLE ALL WRONG.
THEY ALL LOOK SO...I DUNNO... HAPPY? LIKE, WEIRDLY HAPPY? YOU COULD CHALK IT UP TO THE SELF-LOBOTOMIZING, SURE, BUT THERE'S SOMETHING ELSE... SOMETHING IN THE EYES--
SOMETHING IN THE EYES I KNOW I'VE SEEN BEFORE.
AH FUCK IT, MAN, WHAT DO I KNOW? COME ON, LET'S HIT A WAVE.
CLAIRE--

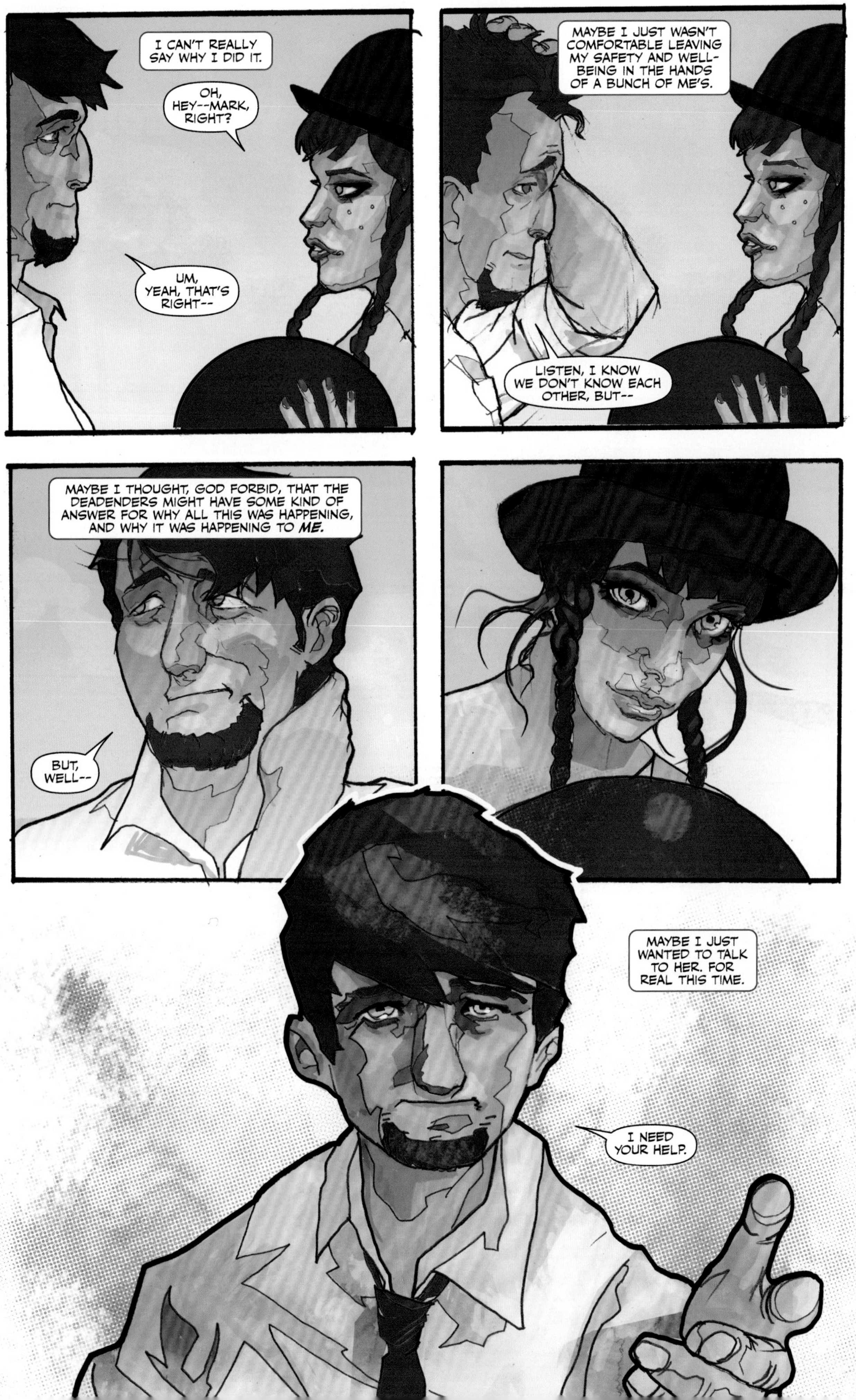
I CAN'T REALLY SAY WHY I DID IT.
OH, HEY--MARK, RIGHT?
UM, YEAH, THAT'S RIGHT--
MAYBE I JUST WASN'T COMFORTABLE LEAVING MY SAFETY AND WELL-BEING IN THE HANDS OF A BUNCH OF ME'S.
LISTEN, I KNOW WE DON'T KNOW EACH OTHER, BUT--
MAYBE I THOUGHT, GOD FORBID, THAT THE DEADENDERS MIGHT HAVE SOME KIND OF ANSWER FOR WHY ALL THIS WAS HAPPENING, AND WHY IT WAS HAPPENING TO *ME.*
BUT, WELL--
MAYBE I JUST WANTED TO TALK TO HER. FOR REAL THIS TIME.
I NEED YOUR HELP.

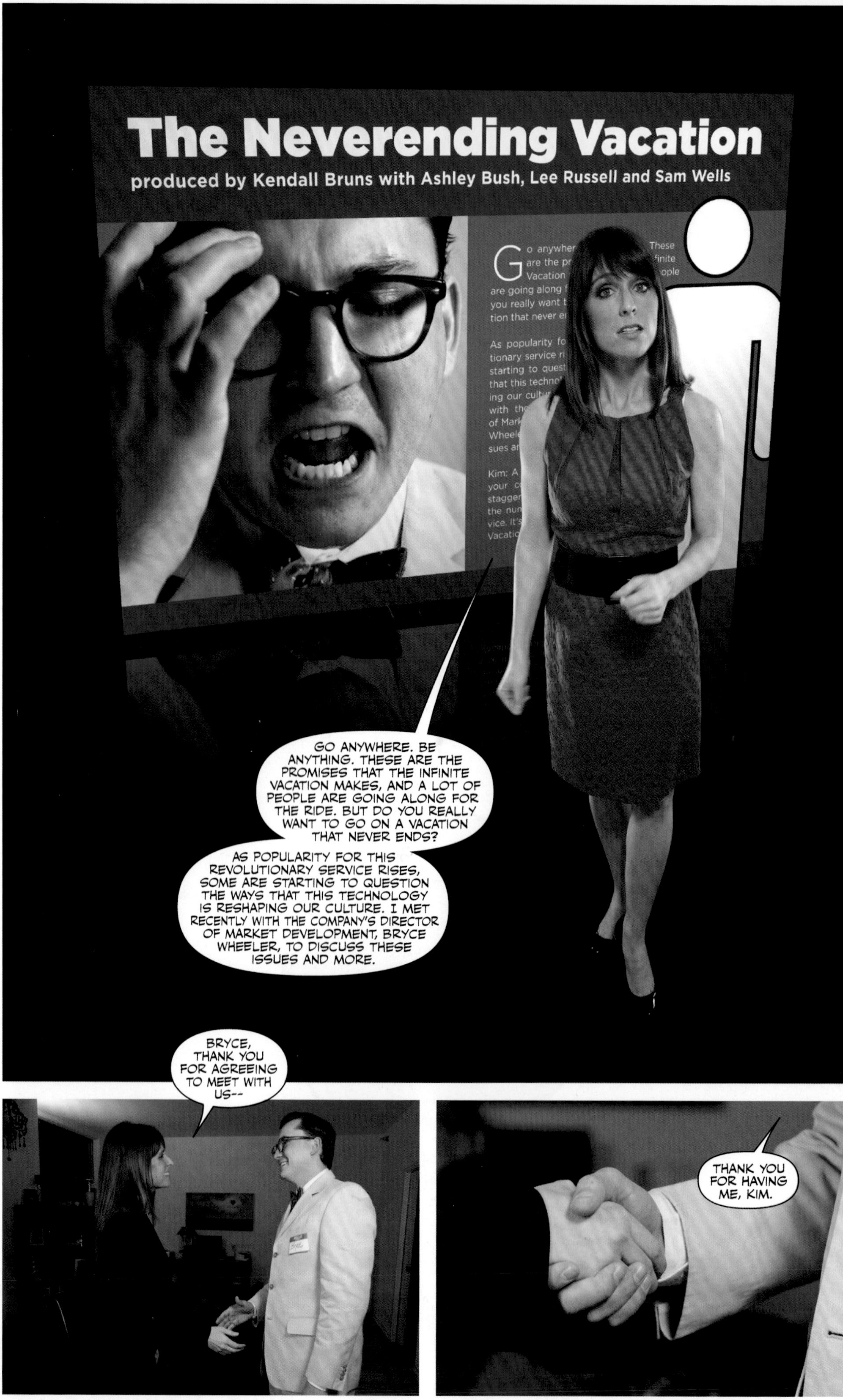
The Neverending Vacation
produced by Kendall Bruns with Ashley Bush, Lee Russell and Sam Wells
GO ANYWHERE. BE ANYTHING. THESE ARE THE PROMISES THAT THE INFINITE VACATION MAKES, AND A LOT OF PEOPLE ARE GOING ALONG FOR THE RIDE. BUT DO YOU REALLY WANT TO GO ON A VACATION THAT NEVER ENDS?
AS POPULARITY FOR THIS REVOLUTIONARY SERVICE RISES, SOME ARE STARTING TO QUESTION THE WAYS THAT THIS TECHNOLOGY IS RESHAPING OUR CULTURE. I MET RECENTLY WITH THE COMPANY'S DIRECTOR OF MARKET DEVELOPMENT, BRYCE WHEELER, TO DISCUSS THESE ISSUES AND MORE.
BRYCE, THANK YOU FOR AGREEING TO MEET WITH US--
THANK YOU FOR HAVING ME, KIM.

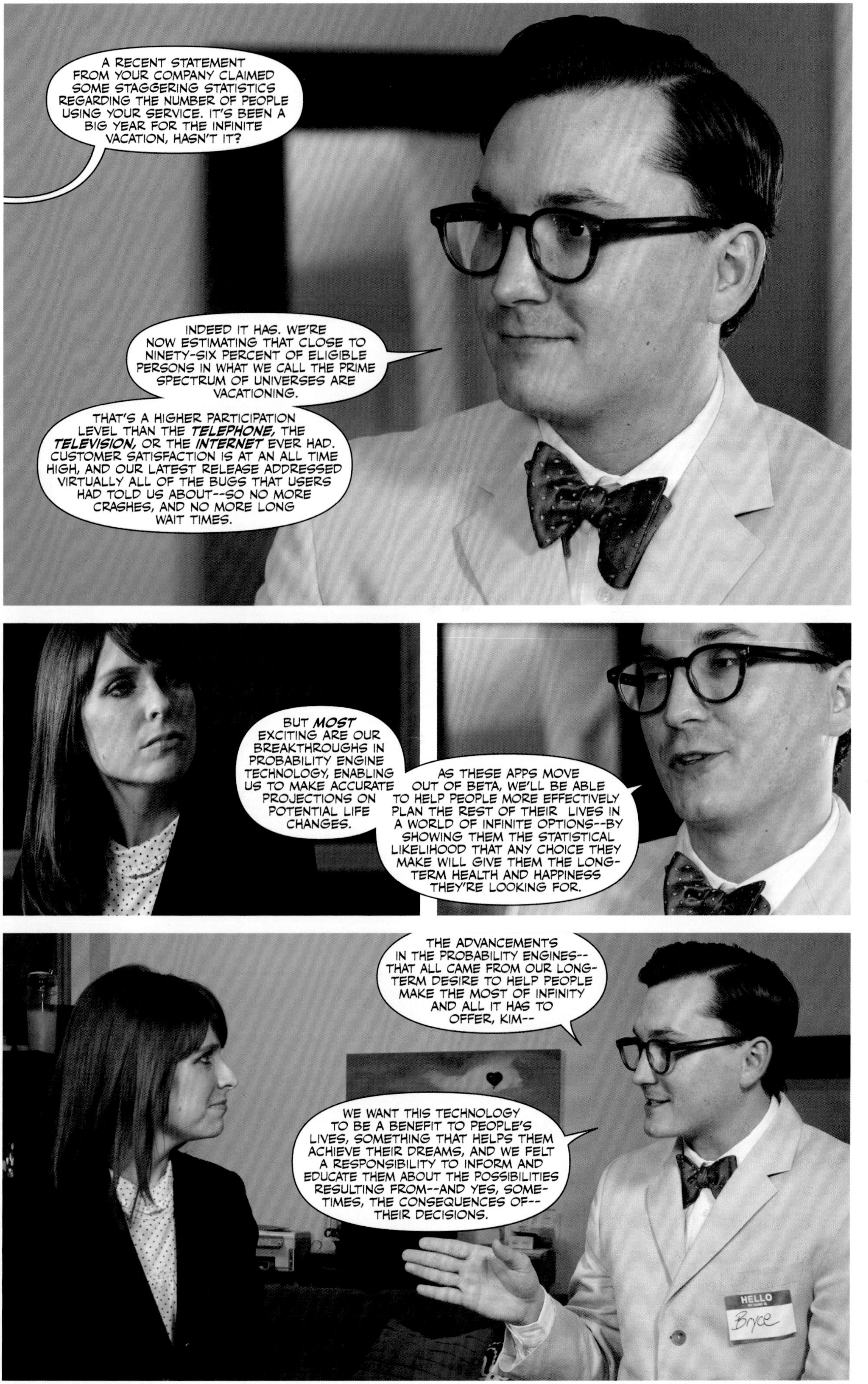
A RECENT STATEMENT FROM YOUR COMPANY CLAIMED SOME STAGGERING STATISTICS REGARDING THE NUMBER OF PEOPLE USING YOUR SERVICE. IT'S BEEN A BIG YEAR FOR THE INFINITE VACATION, HASN'T IT?
INDEED IT HAS. WE'RE NOW ESTIMATING THAT CLOSE TO NINETY-SIX PERCENT OF ELIGIBLE PERSONS IN WHAT WE CALL THE PRIME SPECTRUM OF UNIVERSES ARE VACATIONING.
THAT'S A HIGHER PARTICIPATION LEVEL THAN THE ***TELEPHONE,*** THE ***TELEVISION,*** OR THE ***INTERNET*** EVER HAD. CUSTOMER SATISFACTION IS AT AN ALL TIME HIGH, AND OUR LATEST RELEASE ADDRESSED VIRTUALLY ALL OF THE BUGS THAT USERS HAD TOLD US ABOUT--SO NO MORE CRASHES, AND NO MORE LONG WAIT TIMES.
BUT ***MOST*** EXCITING ARE OUR BREAKTHROUGHS IN PROBABILITY ENGINE TECHNOLOGY, ENABLING US TO MAKE ACCURATE PROJECTIONS ON POTENTIAL LIFE CHANGES.
AS THESE APPS MOVE OUT OF BETA, WE'LL BE ABLE TO HELP PEOPLE MORE EFFECTIVELY PLAN THE REST OF THEIR LIVES IN A WORLD OF INFINITE OPTIONS--BY SHOWING THEM THE STATISTICAL LIKELIHOOD THAT ANY CHOICE THEY MAKE WILL GIVE THEM THE LONG-TERM HEALTH AND HAPPINESS THEY'RE LOOKING FOR.
THE ADVANCEMENTS IN THE PROBABILITY ENGINES--THAT ALL CAME FROM OUR LONG-TERM DESIRE TO HELP PEOPLE MAKE THE MOST OF INFINITY AND ALL IT HAS TO OFFER, KIM--
WE WANT THIS TECHNOLOGY TO BE A BENEFIT TO PEOPLE'S LIVES, SOMETHING THAT HELPS THEM ACHIEVE THEIR DREAMS, AND WE FELT A RESPONSIBILITY TO INFORM AND EDUCATE THEM ABOUT THE POSSIBILITIES RESULTING FROM--AND YES, SOME-TIMES, THE CONSEQUENCES OF--THEIR DECISIONS.
HELLO
Bryce

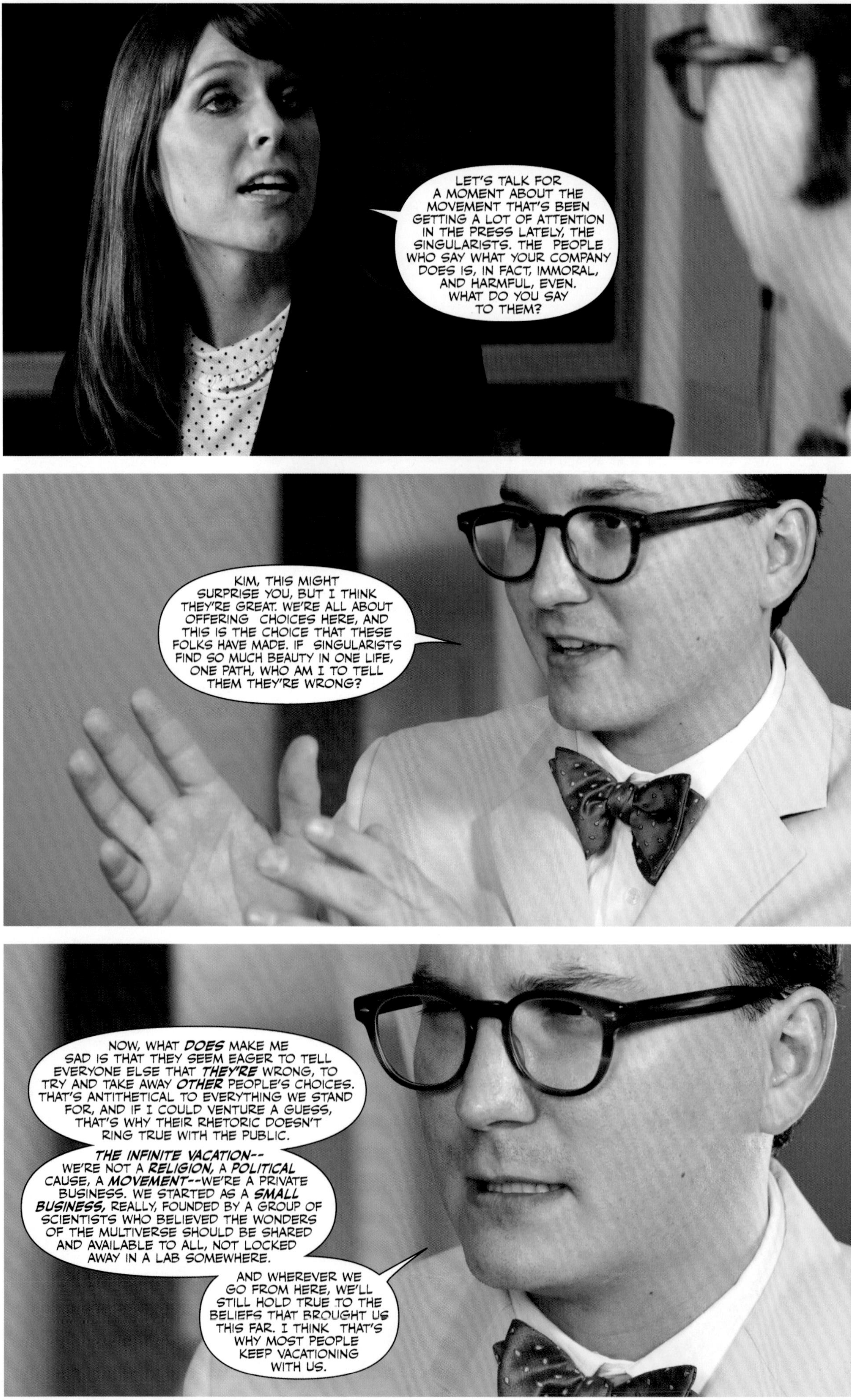
LET'S TALK FOR A MOMENT ABOUT THE MOVEMENT THAT'S BEEN GETTING A LOT OF ATTENTION IN THE PRESS LATELY, THE SINGULARISTS. THE PEOPLE WHO SAY WHAT YOUR COMPANY DOES IS, IN FACT, IMMORAL, AND HARMFUL, EVEN. WHAT DO YOU SAY TO THEM?
KIM, THIS MIGHT SURPRISE YOU, BUT I THINK THEY'RE GREAT. WE'RE ALL ABOUT OFFERING CHOICES HERE, AND THIS IS THE CHOICE THAT THESE FOLKS HAVE MADE. IF SINGULARISTS FIND SO MUCH BEAUTY IN ONE LIFE, ONE PATH, WHO AM I TO TELL THEM THEY'RE WRONG?
NOW, WHAT DOES MAKE ME SAD IS THAT THEY SEEM EAGER TO TELL EVERYONE ELSE THAT THEY'RE WRONG, TO TRY AND TAKE AWAY OTHER PEOPLE'S CHOICES. THAT'S ANTITHETICAL TO EVERYTHING WE STAND FOR, AND IF I COULD VENTURE A GUESS, THAT'S WHY THEIR RHETORIC DOESN'T RING TRUE WITH THE PUBLIC.
THE INFINITE VACATION-- WE'RE NOT A RELIGION, A POLITICAL CAUSE, A MOVEMENT--WE'RE A PRIVATE BUSINESS. WE STARTED AS A SMALL BUSINESS, REALLY, FOUNDED BY A GROUP OF SCIENTISTS WHO BELIEVED THE WONDERS OF THE MULTIVERSE SHOULD BE SHARED AND AVAILABLE TO ALL, NOT LOCKED AWAY IN A LAB SOMEWHERE.
AND WHEREVER WE GO FROM HERE, WE'LL STILL HOLD TRUE TO THE BELIEFS THAT BROUGHT US THIS FAR. I THINK THAT'S WHY MOST PEOPLE KEEP VACATIONING WITH US.

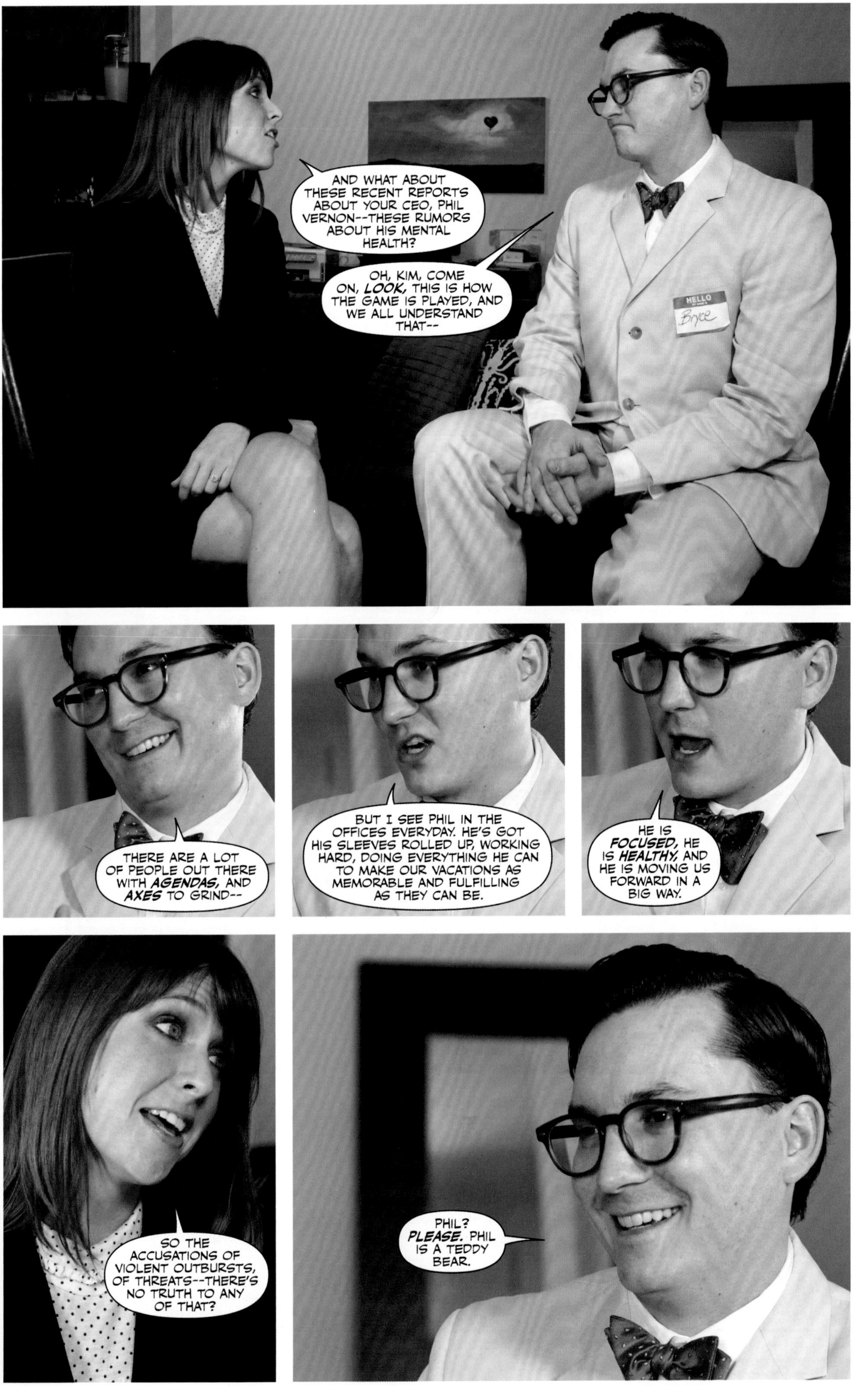
AND WHAT ABOUT THESE RECENT REPORTS ABOUT YOUR CEO, PHIL VERNON--THESE RUMORS ABOUT HIS MENTAL HEALTH?
OH, KIM, COME ON, ***LOOK,*** THIS IS HOW THE GAME IS PLAYED, AND WE ALL UNDERSTAND THAT--
HELLO
Bryce
THERE ARE A LOT OF PEOPLE OUT THERE WITH ***AGENDAS,*** AND ***AXES*** TO GRIND--
BUT I SEE PHIL IN THE OFFICES EVERYDAY. HE'S GOT HIS SLEEVES ROLLED UP, WORKING HARD, DOING EVERYTHING HE CAN TO MAKE OUR VACATIONS AS MEMORABLE AND FULFILLING AS THEY CAN BE.
HE IS ***FOCUSED,*** HE IS ***HEALTHY,*** AND HE IS MOVING US FORWARD IN A BIG WAY.
SO THE ACCUSATIONS OF VIOLENT OUTBURSTS, OF THREATS--THERE'S NO TRUTH TO ANY OF THAT?
PHIL? ***PLEASE.*** PHIL IS A TEDDY BEAR.

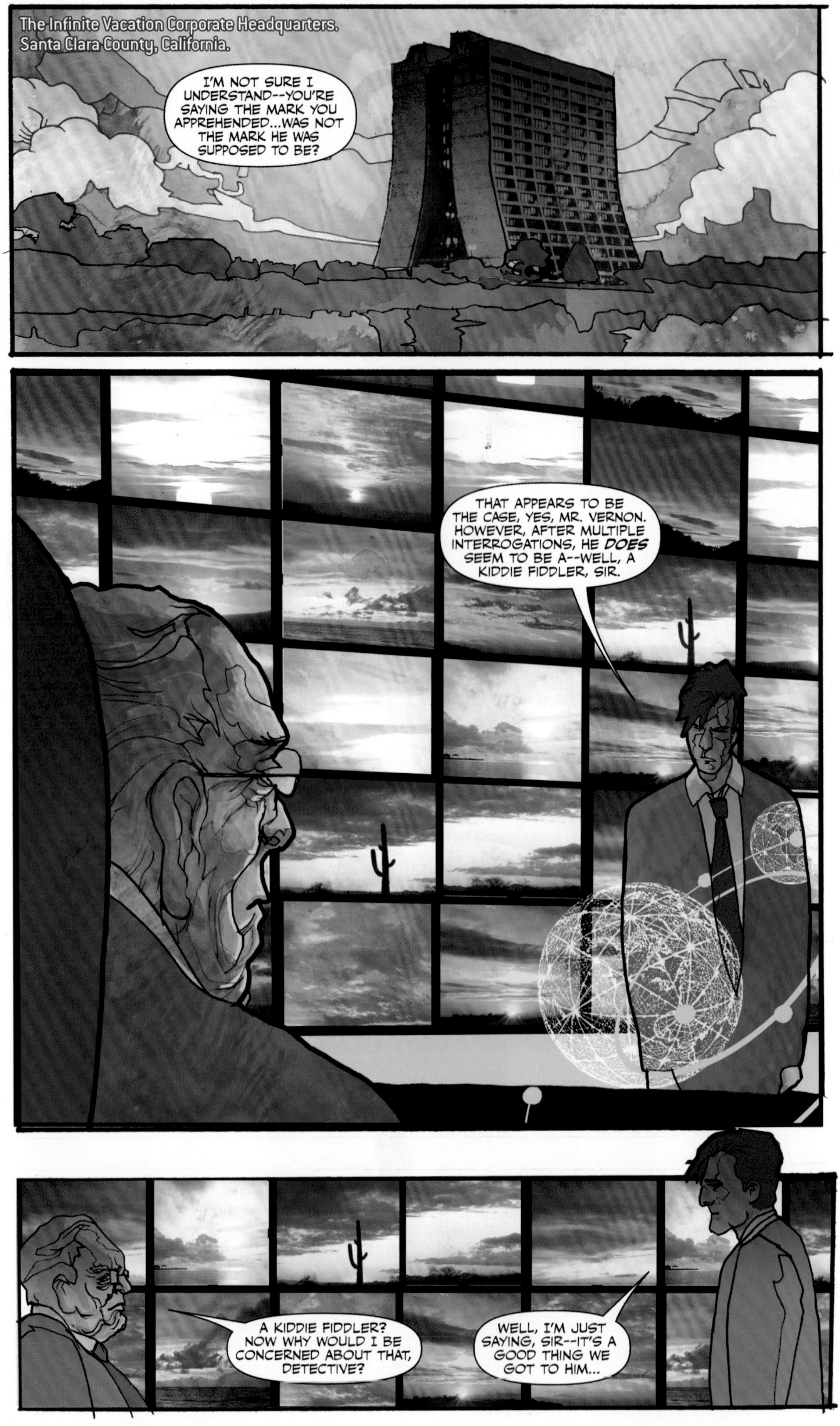
The Infinite Vacation Corporate Headquarters.
Santa Clara County, California.
I'M NOT SURE I UNDERSTAND--YOU'RE SAYING THE MARK YOU APPREHENDED...WAS NOT THE MARK HE WAS SUPPOSED TO BE?
THAT APPEARS TO BE THE CASE, YES, MR. VERNON. HOWEVER, AFTER MULTIPLE INTERROGATIONS, HE DOES SEEM TO BE A--WELL, A KIDDIE FIDDLER, SIR.
A KIDDIE FIDDLER? NOW WHY WOULD I BE CONCERNED ABOUT THAT, DETECTIVE?
WELL, I'M JUST SAYING, SIR--IT'S A GOOD THING WE GOT TO HIM...

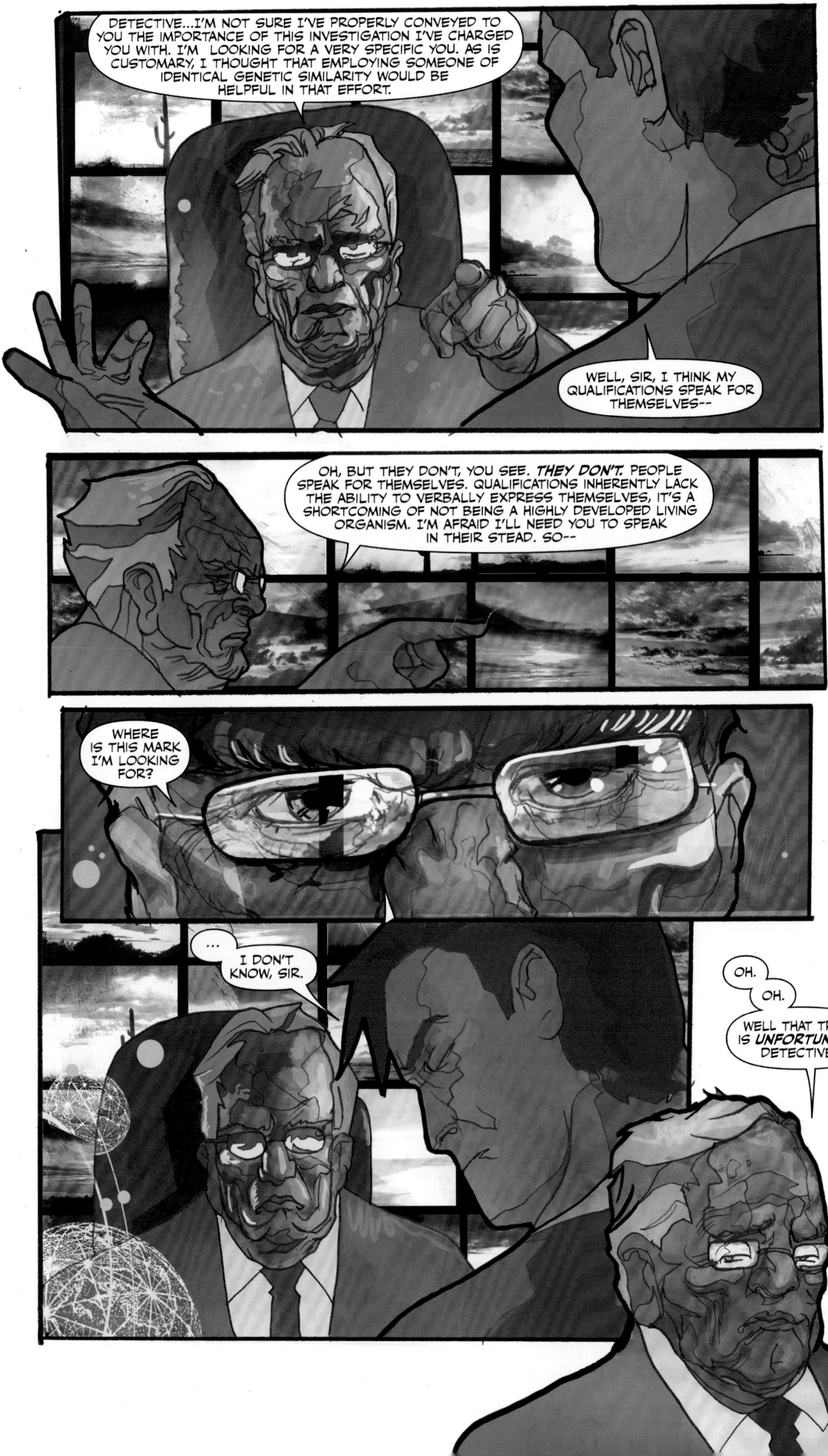
DETECTIVE...I'M NOT SURE I'VE PROPERLY CONVEYED TO YOU THE IMPORTANCE OF THIS INVESTIGATION I'VE CHARGED YOU WITH. I'M LOOKING FOR A VERY SPECIFIC YOU. AS IS CUSTOMARY, I THOUGHT THAT EMPLOYING SOMEONE OF IDENTICAL GENETIC SIMILARITY WOULD BE HELPFUL IN THAT EFFORT.
WELL, SIR, I THINK MY QUALIFICATIONS SPEAK FOR THEMSELVES--
OH, BUT THEY DON'T, YOU SEE. *THEY DON'T.* PEOPLE SPEAK FOR THEMSELVES. QUALIFICATIONS INHERENTLY LACK THE ABILITY TO VERBALLY EXPRESS THEMSELVES, IT'S A SHORTCOMING OF NOT BEING A HIGHLY DEVELOPED LIVING ORGANISM. I'M AFRAID I'LL NEED YOU TO SPEAK IN THEIR STEAD. SO--
WHERE IS THIS MARK I'M LOOKING FOR?
...
I DON'T KNOW, SIR.
OH.
OH.
WELL THAT TRULY IS ***UNFORTUNATE,*** DETECTIVE.

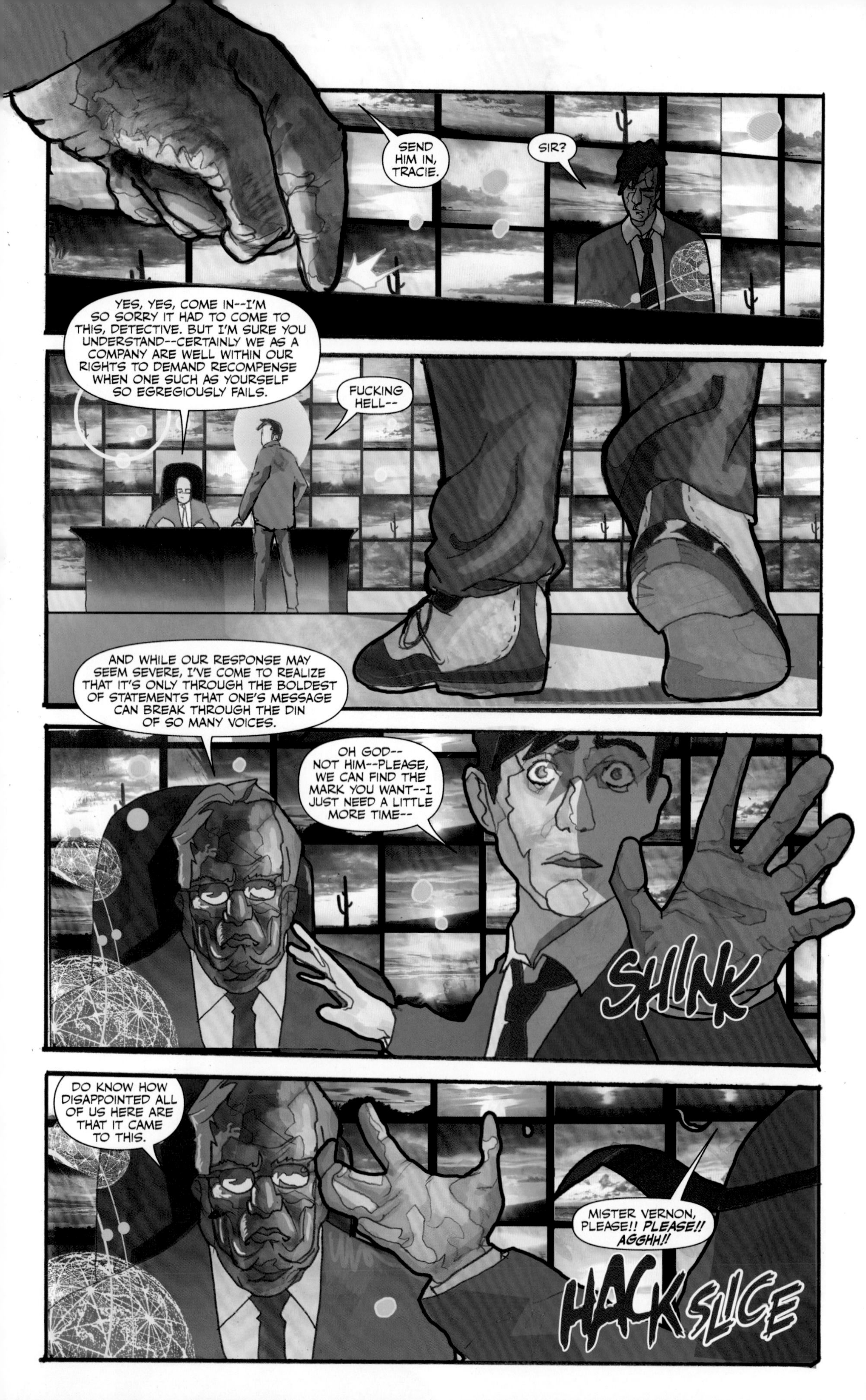
SEND HIM IN, TRACIE.
SIR?
YES, YES, COME IN--I'M SO SORRY IT HAD TO COME TO THIS, DETECTIVE. BUT I'M SURE YOU UNDERSTAND--CERTAINLY WE AS A COMPANY ARE WELL WITHIN OUR RIGHTS TO DEMAND RECOMPENSE WHEN ONE SUCH AS YOURSELF SO EGREGIOUSLY FAILS.
FUCKING HELL--
AND WHILE OUR RESPONSE MAY SEEM SEVERE, I'VE COME TO REALIZE THAT IT'S ONLY THROUGH THE BOLDEST OF STATEMENTS THAT ONE'S MESSAGE CAN BREAK THROUGH THE DIN OF SO MANY VOICES.
OH GOD-- NOT HIM--PLEASE, WE CAN FIND THE MARK YOU WANT--I JUST NEED A LITTLE MORE TIME--
SHINK
DO KNOW HOW DISAPPOINTED ALL OF US HERE ARE THAT IT CAME TO THIS.
MISTER VERNON, PLEASE!! *PLEASE!!* AGGHH!!
HACK SLICE

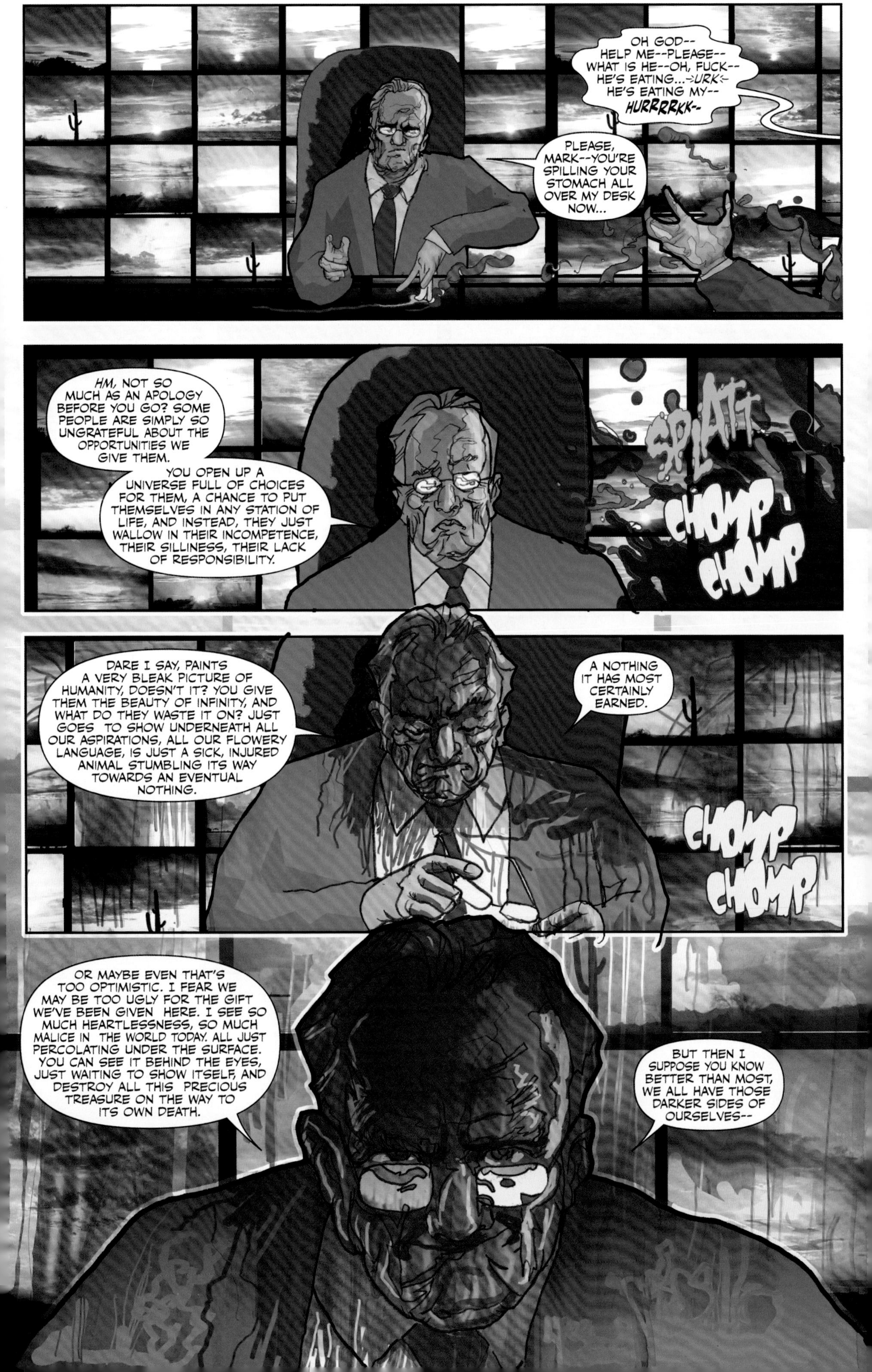
OH GOD-- HELP ME--PLEASE-- WHAT IS HE--OH, FUCK-- HE'S EATING...>URK< HE'S EATING MY-- HURRRRKK--
PLEASE, MARK--YOU'RE SPILLING YOUR STOMACH ALL OVER MY DESK NOW...
HM, NOT SO MUCH AS AN APOLOGY BEFORE YOU GO? SOME PEOPLE ARE SIMPLY SO UNGRATEFUL ABOUT THE OPPORTUNITIES WE GIVE THEM.
YOU OPEN UP A UNIVERSE FULL OF CHOICES FOR THEM, A CHANCE TO PUT THEMSELVES IN ANY STATION OF LIFE, AND INSTEAD, THEY JUST WALLOW IN THEIR INCOMPETENCE, THEIR SILLINESS, THEIR LACK OF RESPONSIBILITY.
SPLATT
CHOMP CHOMP
DARE I SAY, PAINTS A VERY BLEAK PICTURE OF HUMANITY, DOESN'T IT? YOU GIVE THEM THE BEAUTY OF INFINITY, AND WHAT DO THEY WASTE IT ON? JUST GOES TO SHOW UNDERNEATH ALL OUR ASPIRATIONS, ALL OUR FLOWERY LANGUAGE, IS JUST A SICK, INJURED ANIMAL STUMBLING ITS WAY TOWARDS AN EVENTUAL NOTHING.
A NOTHING IT HAS MOST CERTAINLY EARNED.
CHOMP CHOMP
OR MAYBE EVEN THAT'S TOO OPTIMISTIC. I FEAR WE MAY BE TOO UGLY FOR THE GIFT WE'VE BEEN GIVEN HERE. I SEE SO MUCH HEARTLESSNESS, SO MUCH MALICE IN THE WORLD TODAY. ALL JUST PERCOLATING UNDER THE SURFACE. YOU CAN SEE IT BEHIND THE EYES, JUST WAITING TO SHOW ITSELF, AND DESTROY ALL THIS PRECIOUS TREASURE ON THE WAY TO ITS OWN DEATH.
BUT THEN I SUPPOSE YOU KNOW BETTER THAN MOST, WE ALL HAVE THOSE DARKER SIDES OF OURSELVES--

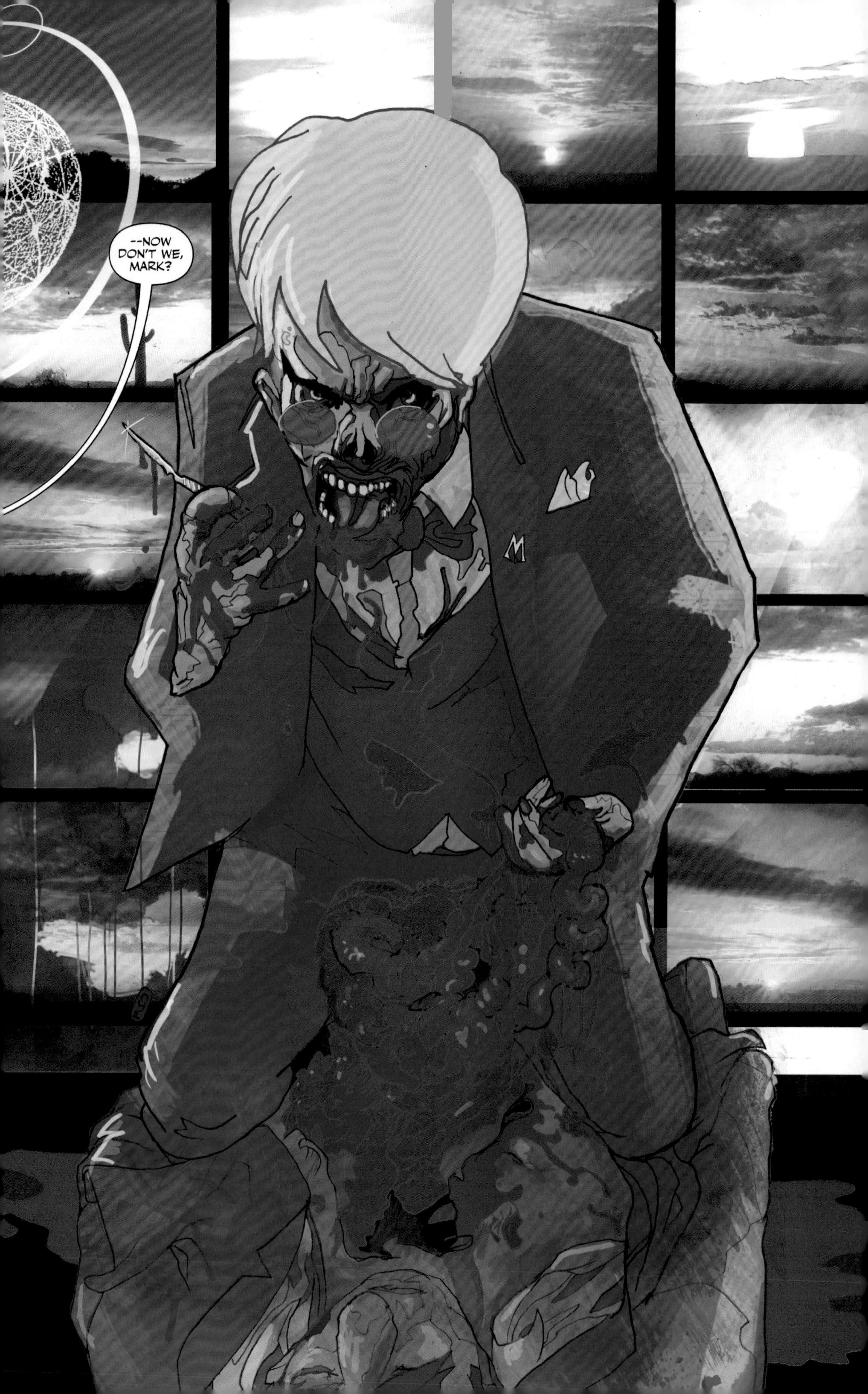
--NOW DON'T WE, MARK?

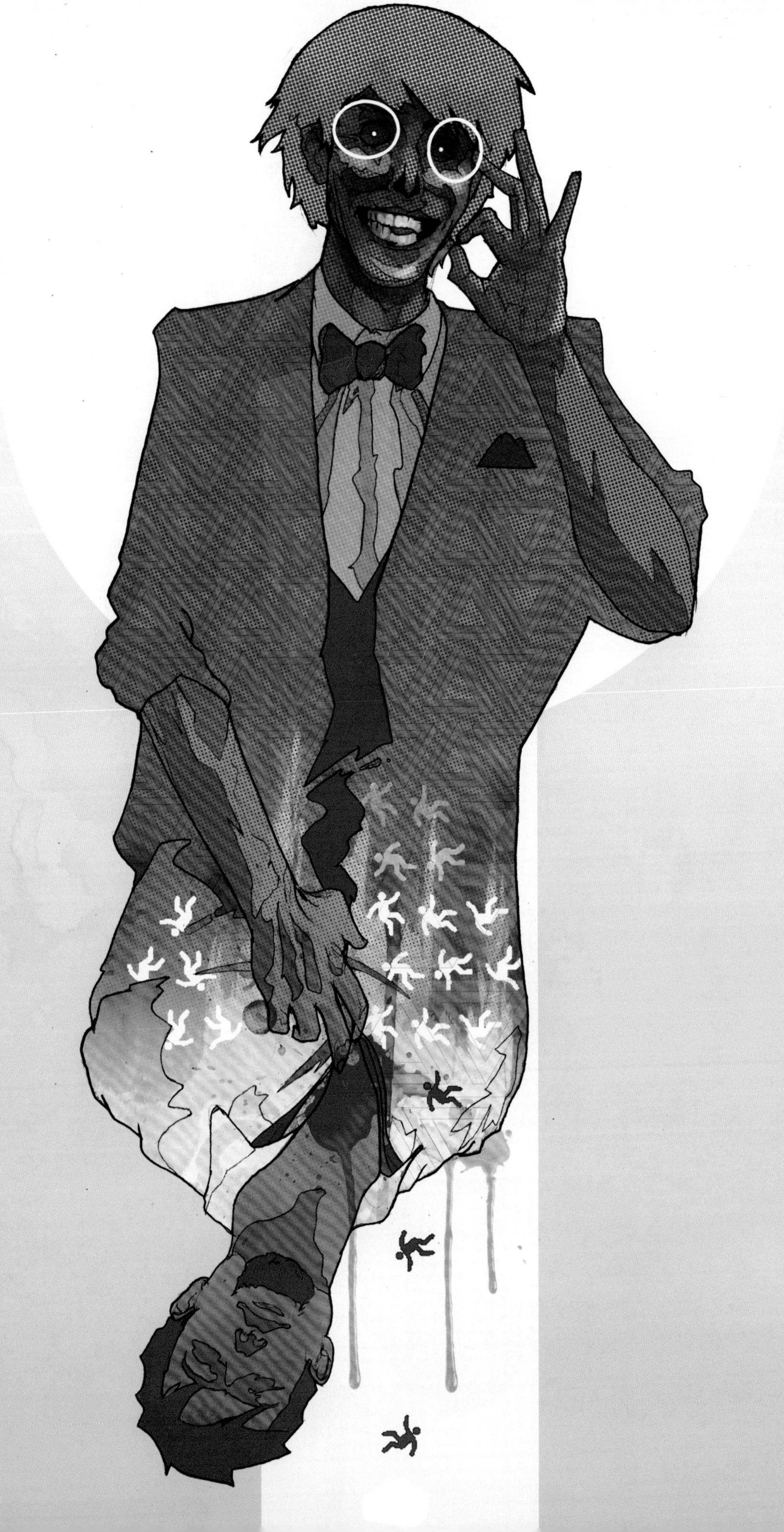

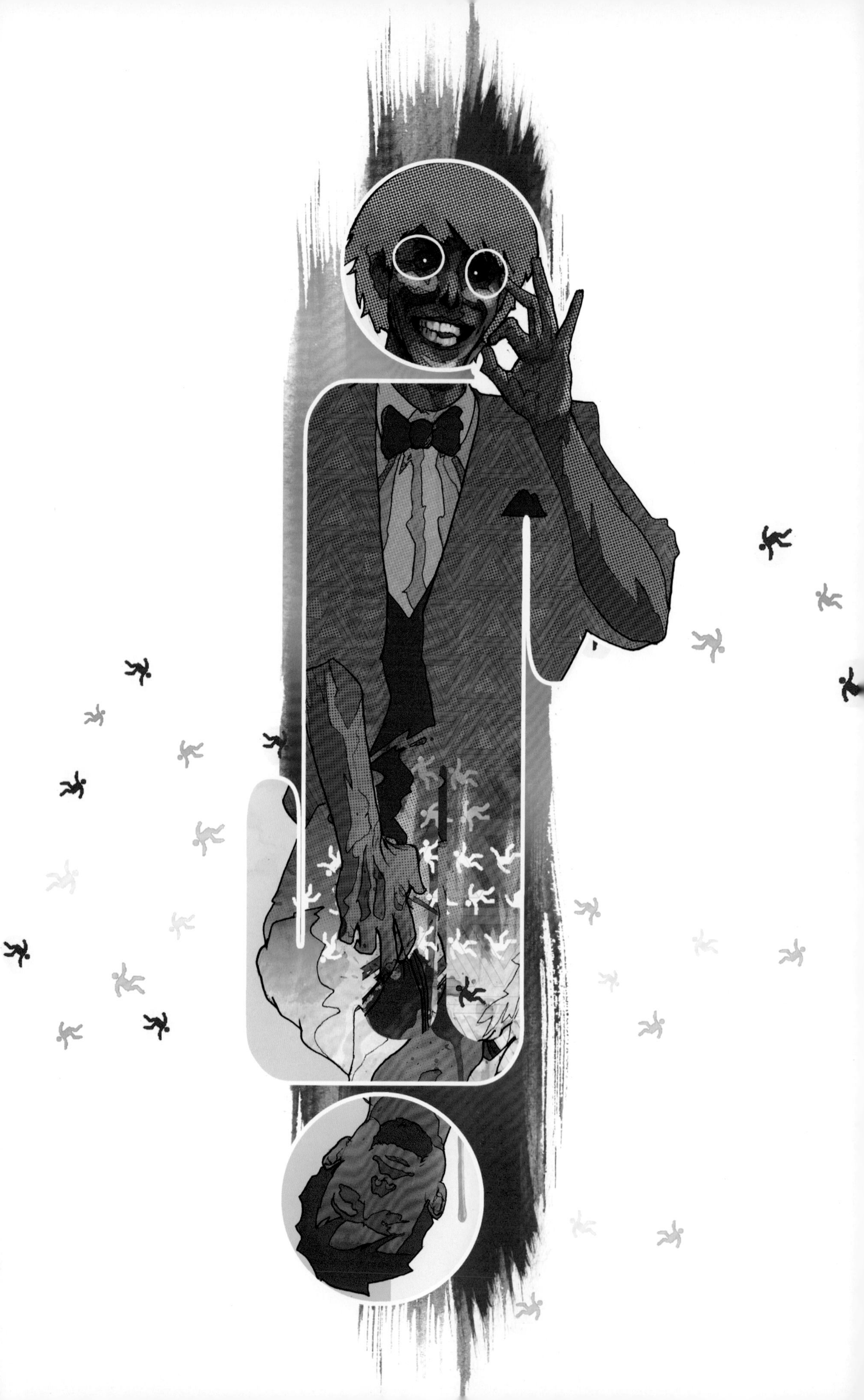

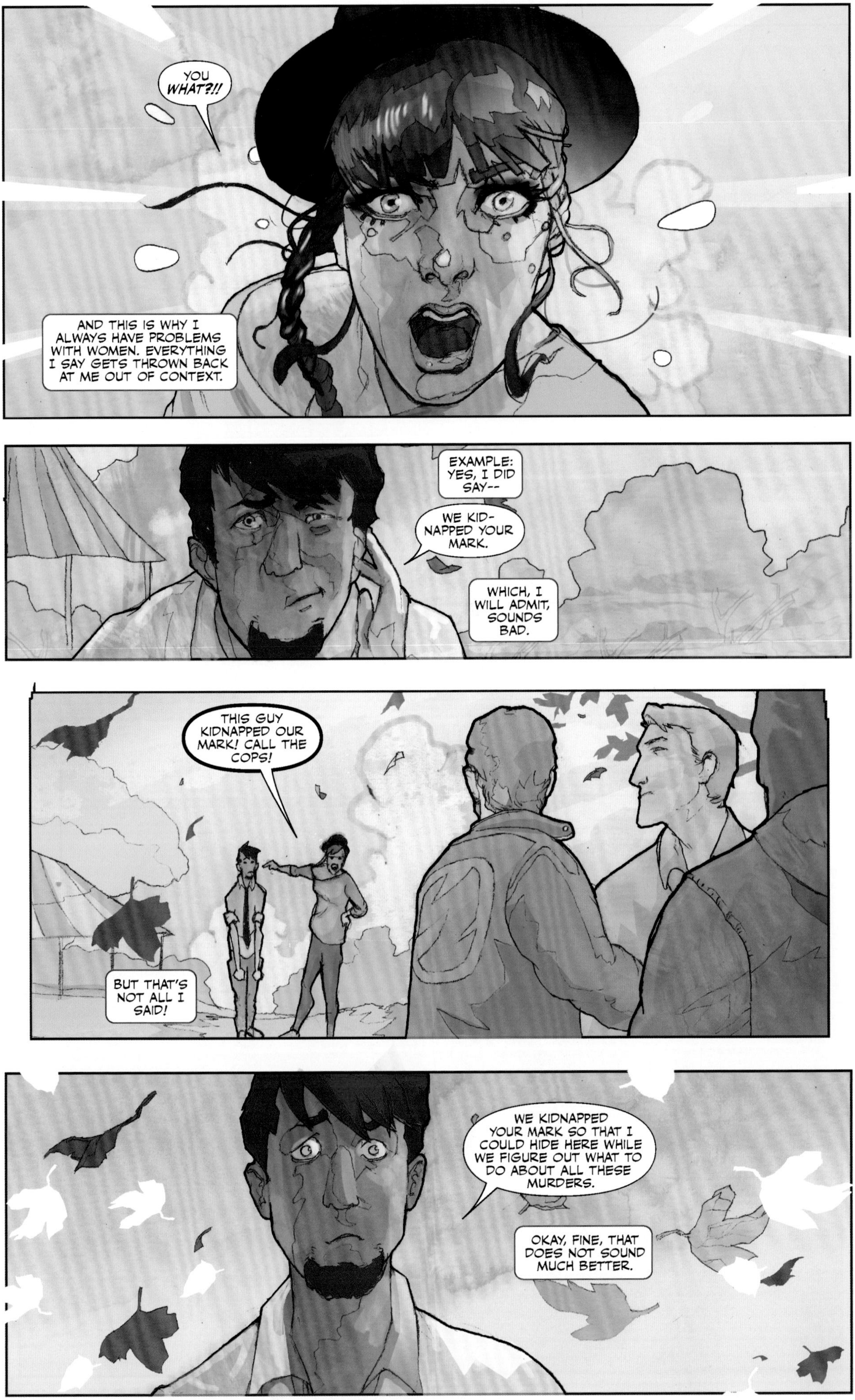
YOU WHAT?!!
AND THIS IS WHY I ALWAYS HAVE PROBLEMS WITH WOMEN. EVERYTHING I SAY GETS THROWN BACK AT ME OUT OF CONTEXT.
EXAMPLE: YES, I DID SAY--
WE KID-NAPPED YOUR MARK.
WHICH, I WILL ADMIT, SOUNDS BAD.
THIS GUY KIDNAPPED OUR MARK! CALL THE COPS!
BUT THAT'S NOT ALL I SAID!
WE KIDNAPPED YOUR MARK SO THAT I COULD HIDE HERE WHILE WE FIGURE OUT WHAT TO DO ABOUT ALL THESE MURDERS.
OKAY, FINE, THAT DOES NOT SOUND MUCH BETTER.

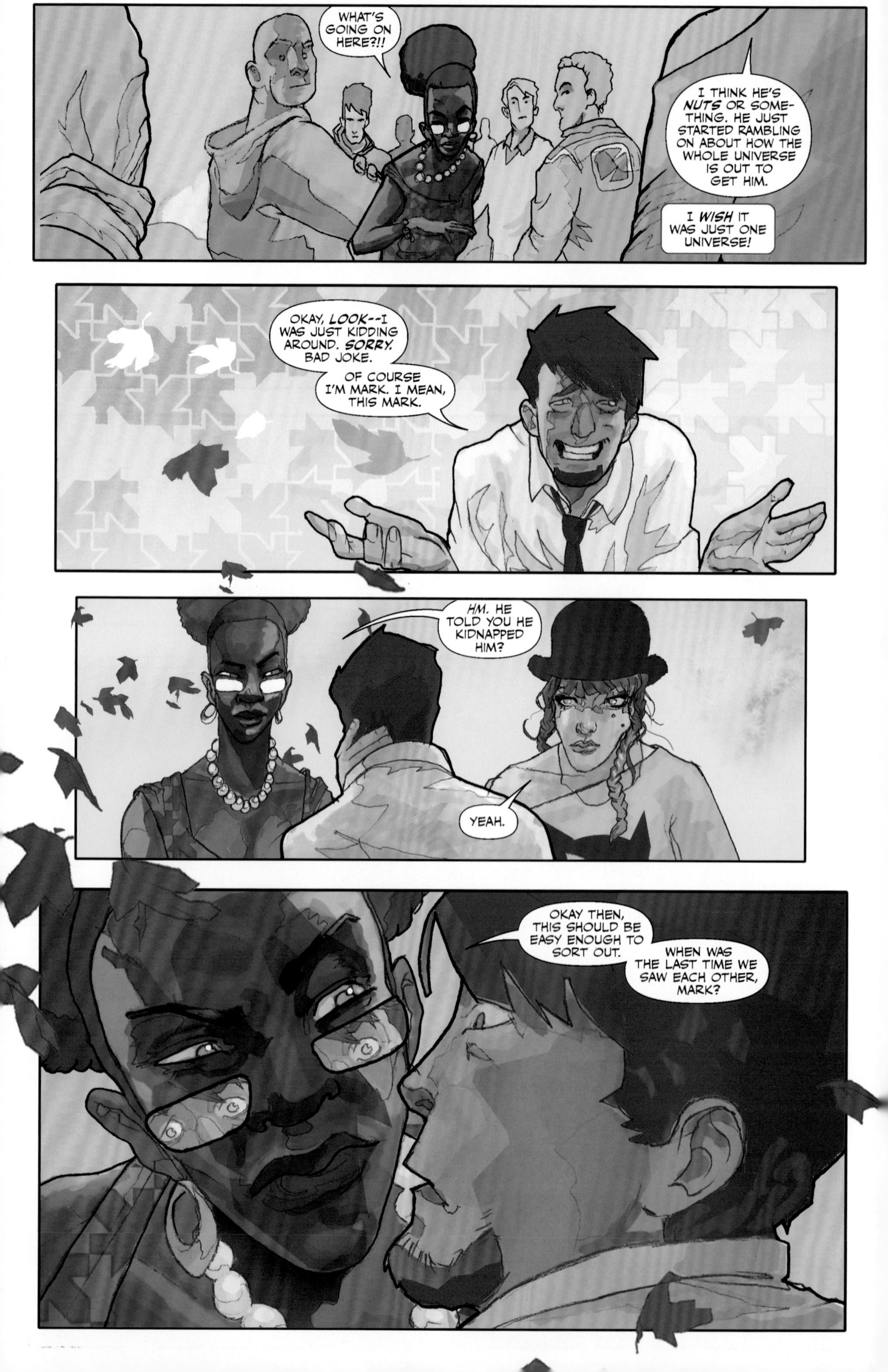
WHAT'S GOING ON HERE?!!
I THINK HE'S *NUTS* OR SOMETHING. HE JUST STARTED RAMBLING ON ABOUT HOW THE WHOLE UNIVERSE IS OUT TO GET HIM.
I *WISH* IT WAS JUST ONE UNIVERSE!
OKAY, *LOOK*--I WAS JUST KIDDING AROUND. *SORRY.* BAD JOKE.
OF COURSE I'M MARK. I MEAN, THIS MARK.
HM. HE TOLD YOU HE KIDNAPPED HIM?
YEAH.
OKAY THEN, THIS SHOULD BE EASY ENOUGH TO SORT OUT.
WHEN WAS THE LAST TIME WE SAW EACH OTHER, MARK?

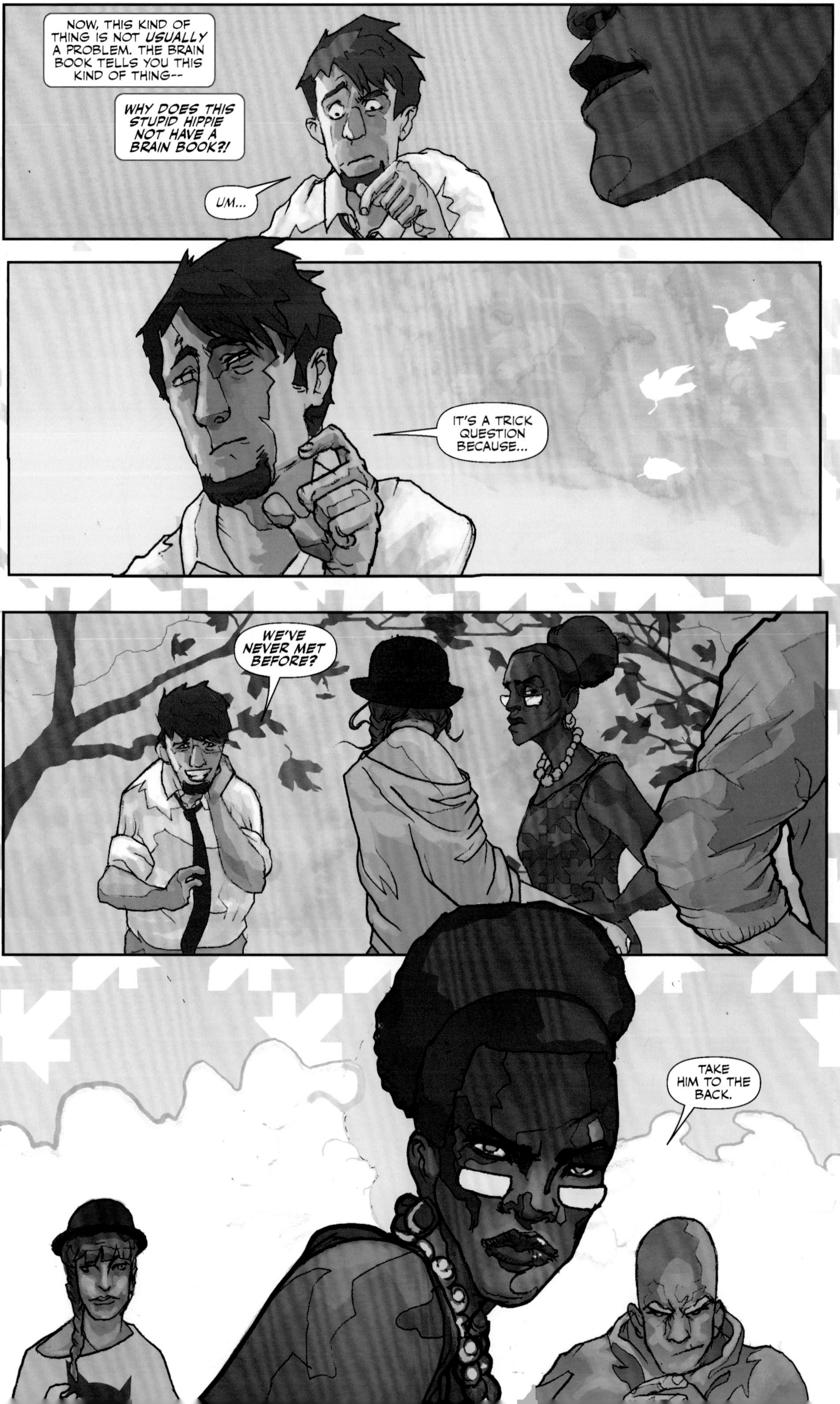
NOW, THIS KIND OF THING IS NOT USUALLY A PROBLEM. THE BRAIN BOOK TELLS YOU THIS KIND OF THING--
WHY DOES THIS STUPID HIPPIE NOT HAVE A BRAIN BOOK?!
UM...
IT'S A TRICK QUESTION BECAUSE...
WE'VE NEVER MET BEFORE?
TAKE HIM TO THE BACK.

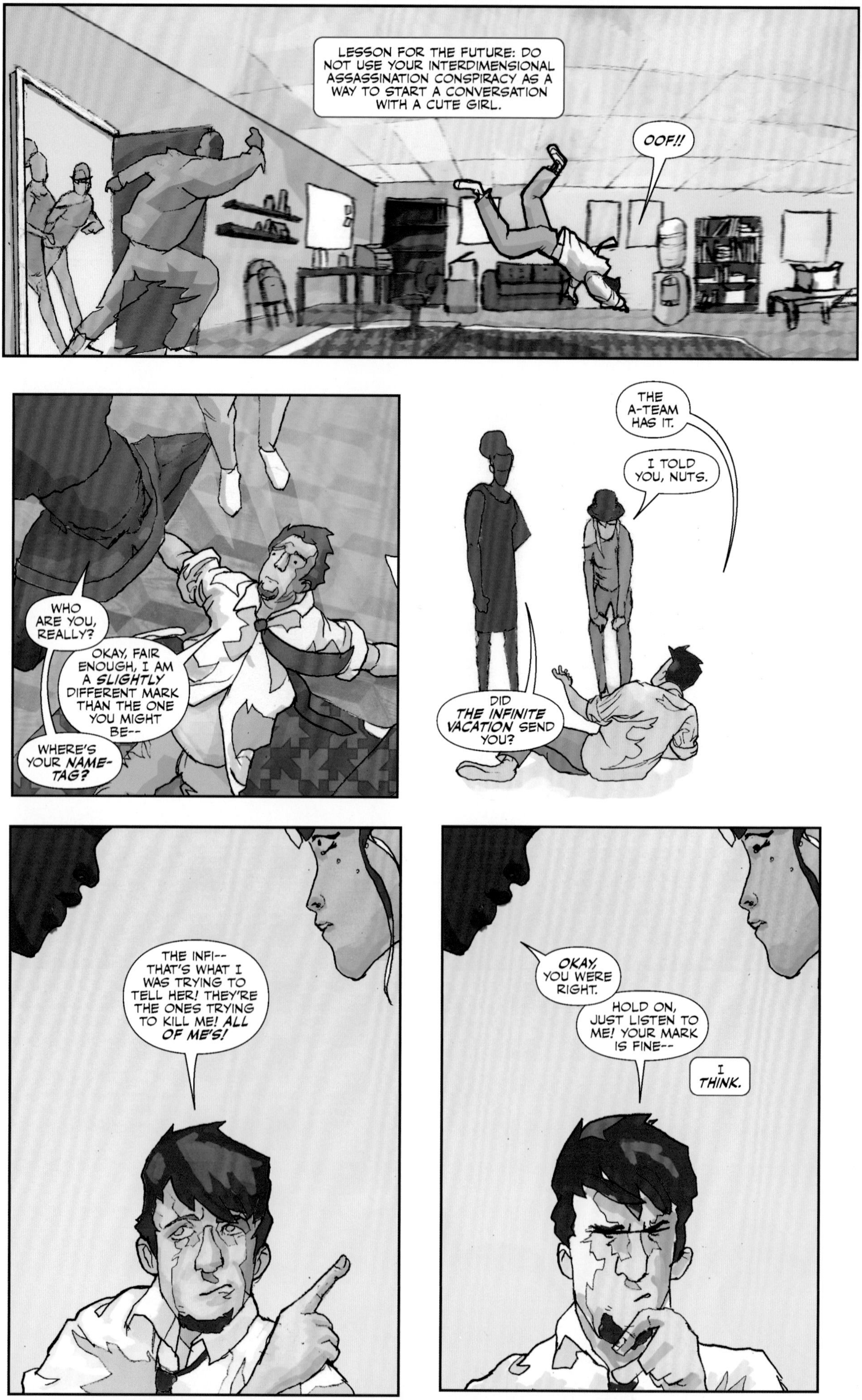

LESSON FOR THE FUTURE: DO NOT USE YOUR INTERDIMENSIONAL ASSASSINATION CONSPIRACY AS A WAY TO START A CONVERSATION WITH A CUTE GIRL.
OOF!!
WHO ARE YOU, REALLY?
OKAY, FAIR ENOUGH, I AM A *SLIGHTLY* DIFFERENT MARK THAN THE ONE YOU MIGHT BE--
WHERE'S YOUR *NAME-TAG?*
THE A-TEAM HAS IT.
I TOLD YOU, NUTS.
DID *THE INFINITE VACATION* SEND YOU?
THE INFI-- THAT'S WHAT I WAS TRYING TO TELL HER! THEY'RE THE ONES TRYING TO KILL ME! *ALL OF ME'S!*
OKAY, YOU WERE RIGHT.
HOLD ON, JUST LISTEN TO ME! YOUR MARK IS FINE--
I *THINK.*

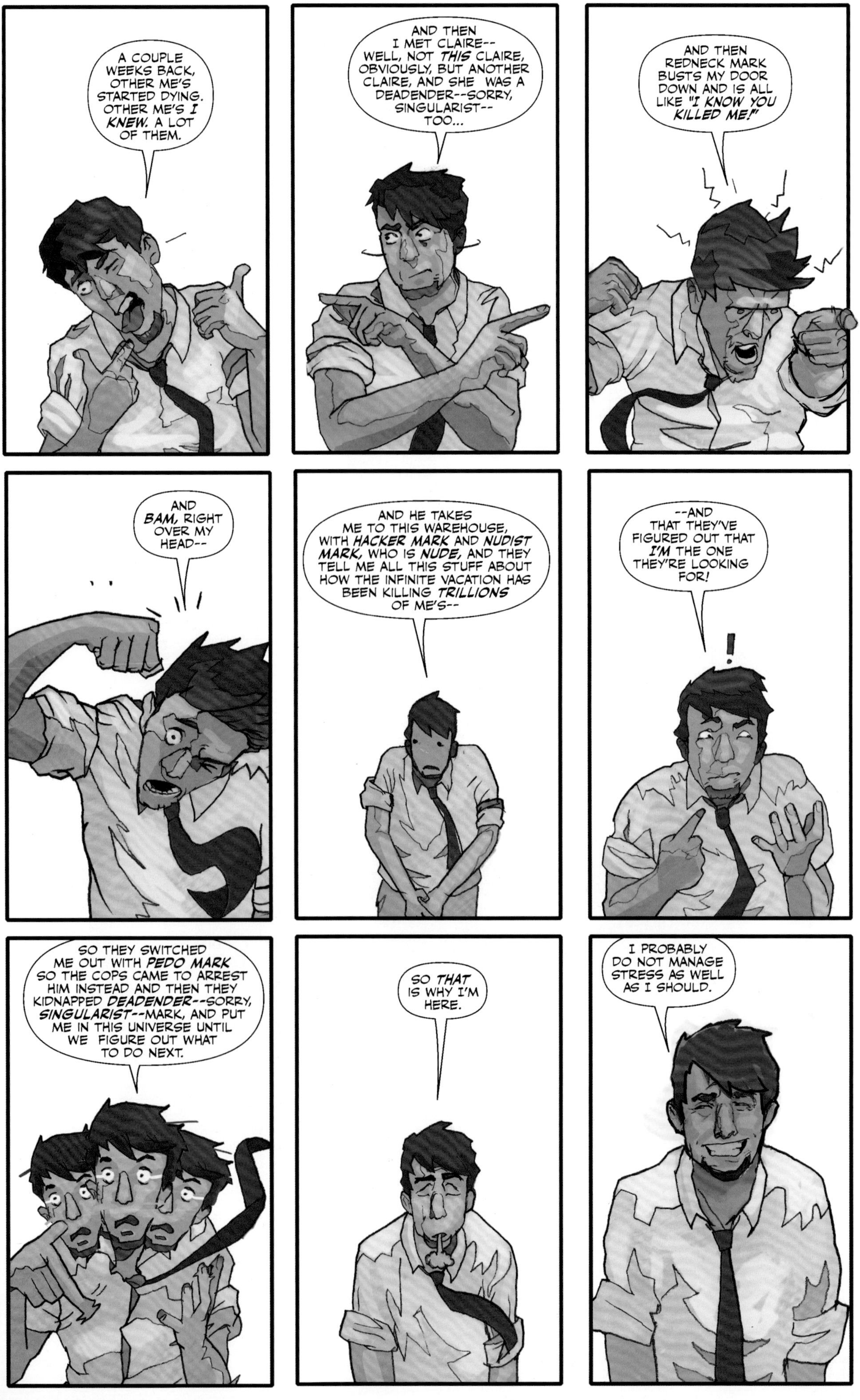
A COUPLE WEEKS BACK, OTHER ME'S STARTED DYING. OTHER ME'S *I KNEW.* A LOT OF THEM.
AND THEN I MET CLAIRE-- WELL, NOT *THIS* CLAIRE, OBVIOUSLY, BUT ANOTHER CLAIRE, AND SHE WAS A DEADENDER--SORRY, SINGULARIST-- TOO...
AND THEN REDNECK MARK BUSTS MY DOOR DOWN AND IS ALL LIKE *"I KNOW YOU KILLED ME!"*
AND *BAM,* RIGHT OVER MY HEAD--
AND HE TAKES ME TO THIS WAREHOUSE, WITH *HACKER MARK* AND *NUDIST MARK,* WHO IS *NUDE,* AND THEY TELL ME ALL THIS STUFF ABOUT HOW THE INFINITE VACATION HAS BEEN KILLING *TRILLIONS* OF ME'S--
--AND THAT THEY'VE FIGURED OUT THAT *I'M* THE ONE THEY'RE LOOKING FOR!
!
SO THEY SWITCHED ME OUT WITH *PEDO MARK* SO THE COPS CAME TO ARREST HIM INSTEAD AND THEN THEY KIDNAPPED *DEADENDER--SORRY, SINGULARIST--*MARK, AND PUT ME IN THIS UNIVERSE UNTIL WE FIGURE OUT WHAT TO DO NEXT.
SO *THAT* IS WHY I'M HERE.
I PROBABLY DO NOT MANAGE STRESS AS WELL AS I SHOULD.

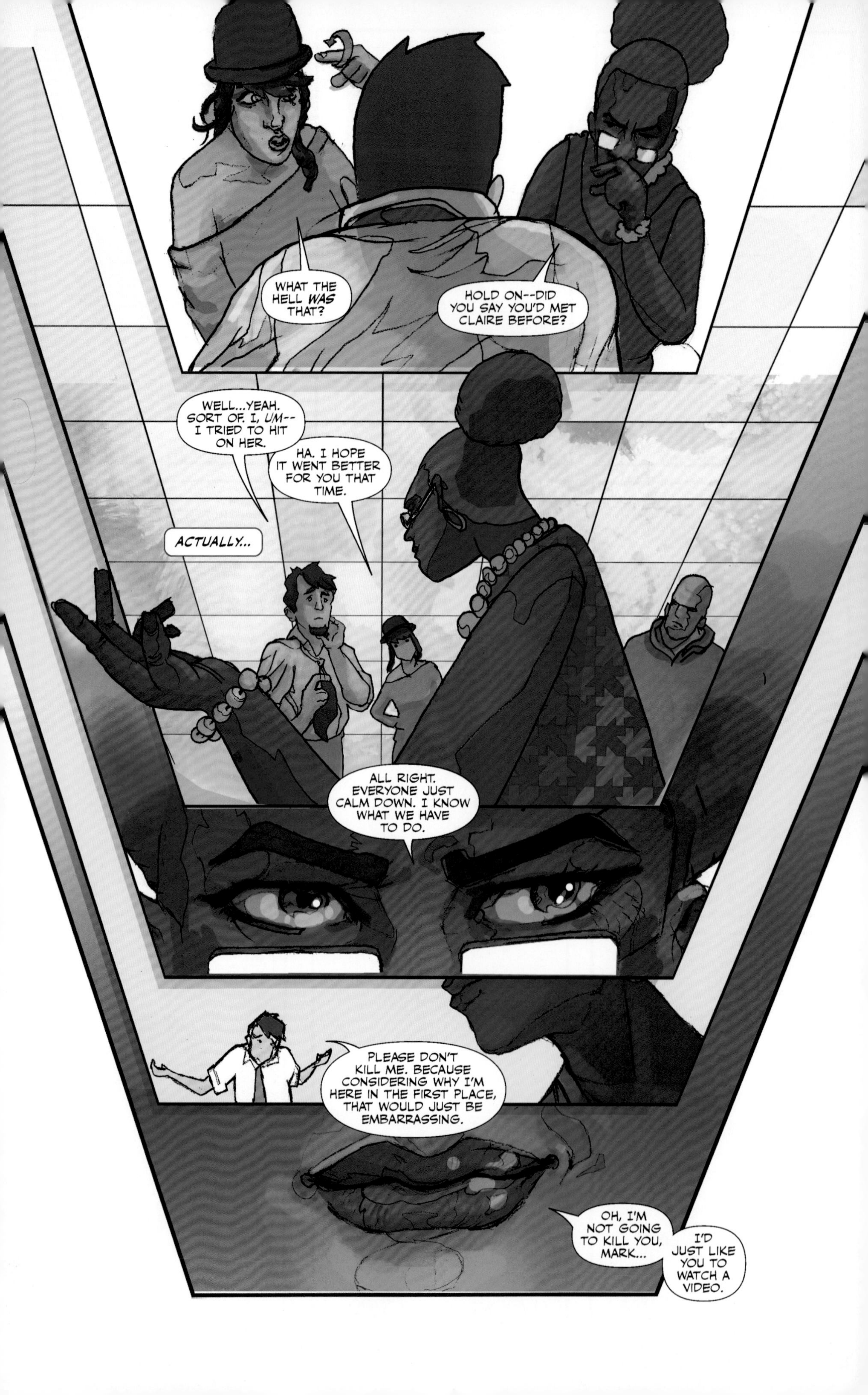
WHAT THE HELL WAS THAT?
HOLD ON--DID YOU SAY YOU'D MET CLAIRE BEFORE?
WELL...YEAH. SORT OF. I, UM-- I TRIED TO HIT ON HER.
HA. I HOPE IT WENT BETTER FOR YOU THAT TIME.
ACTUALLY...
ALL RIGHT. EVERYONE JUST CALM DOWN. I KNOW WHAT WE HAVE TO DO.
PLEASE DON'T KILL ME. BECAUSE CONSIDERING WHY I'M HERE IN THE FIRST PLACE, THAT WOULD JUST BE EMBARRASSING.
OH, I'M NOT GOING TO KILL YOU, MARK...
I'D JUST LIKE YOU TO WATCH A VIDEO.

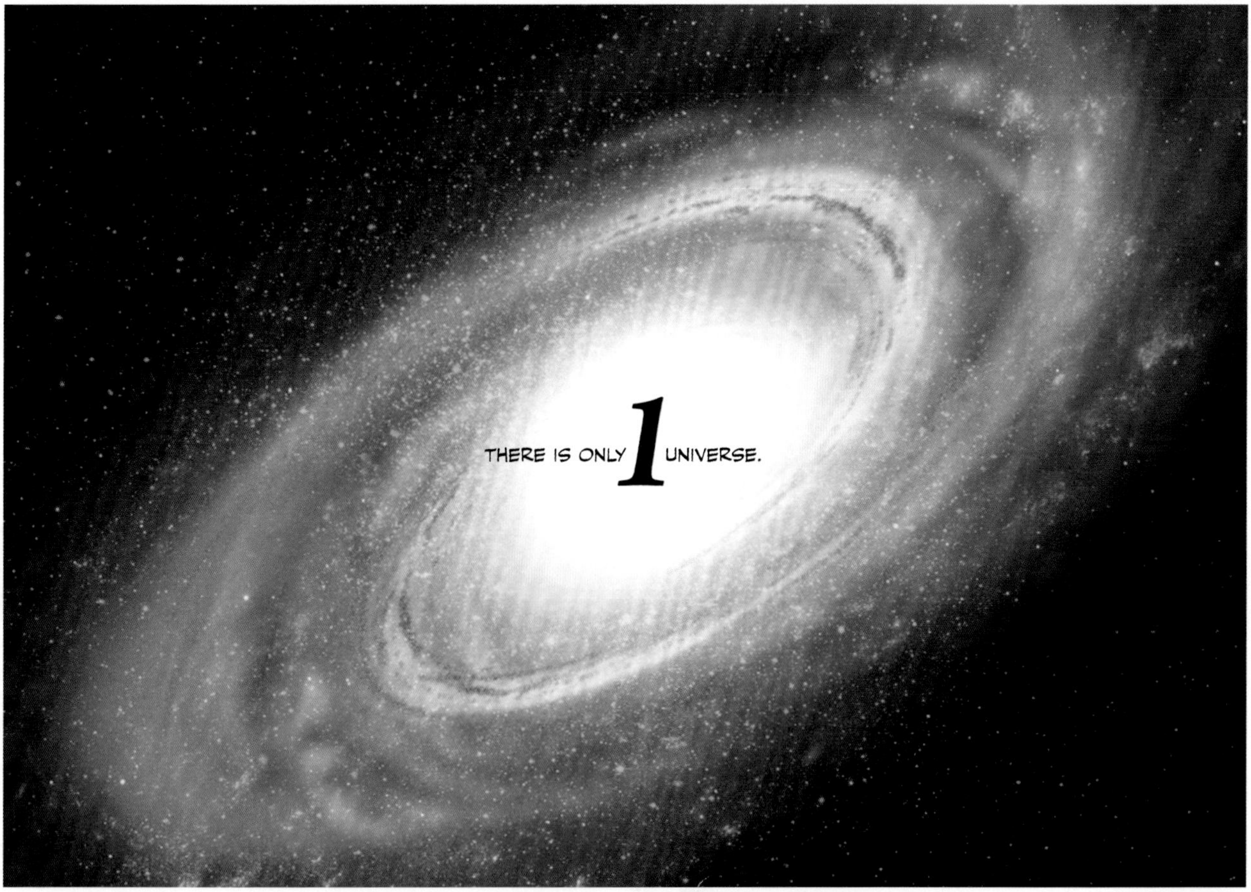
THERE IS ONLY 1 UNIVERSE.

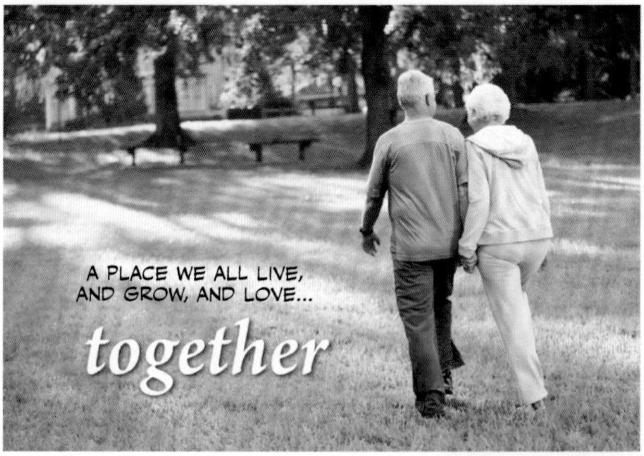
A PLACE WE ALL LIVE,
AND GROW, AND LOVE...
together

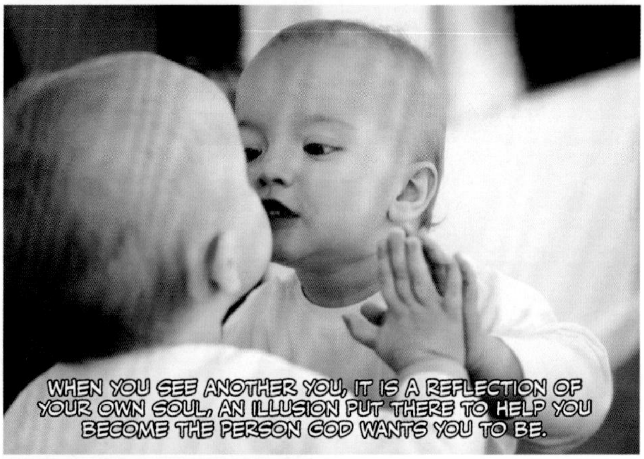
WHEN YOU SEE ANOTHER YOU, IT IS A REFLECTION OF YOUR OWN SOUL, AN ILLUSION PUT THERE TO HELP YOU BECOME THE PERSON GOD WANTS YOU TO BE.

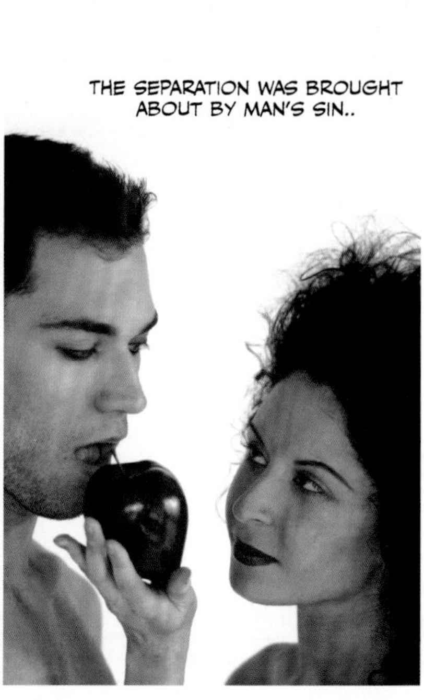
THE SEPARATION WAS BROUGHT
ABOUT BY MAN'S SIN..

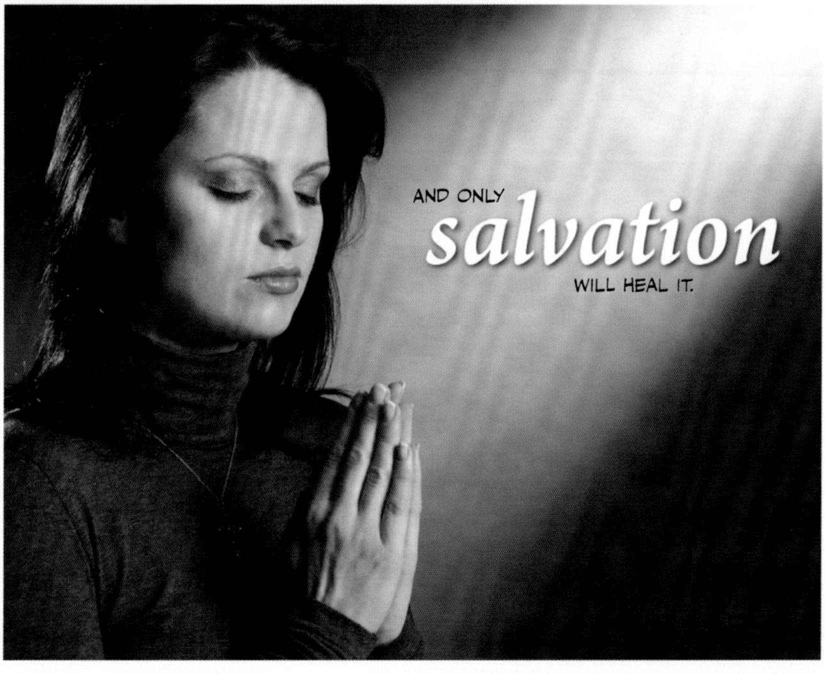
AND ONLY
salvation
WILL HEAL IT.

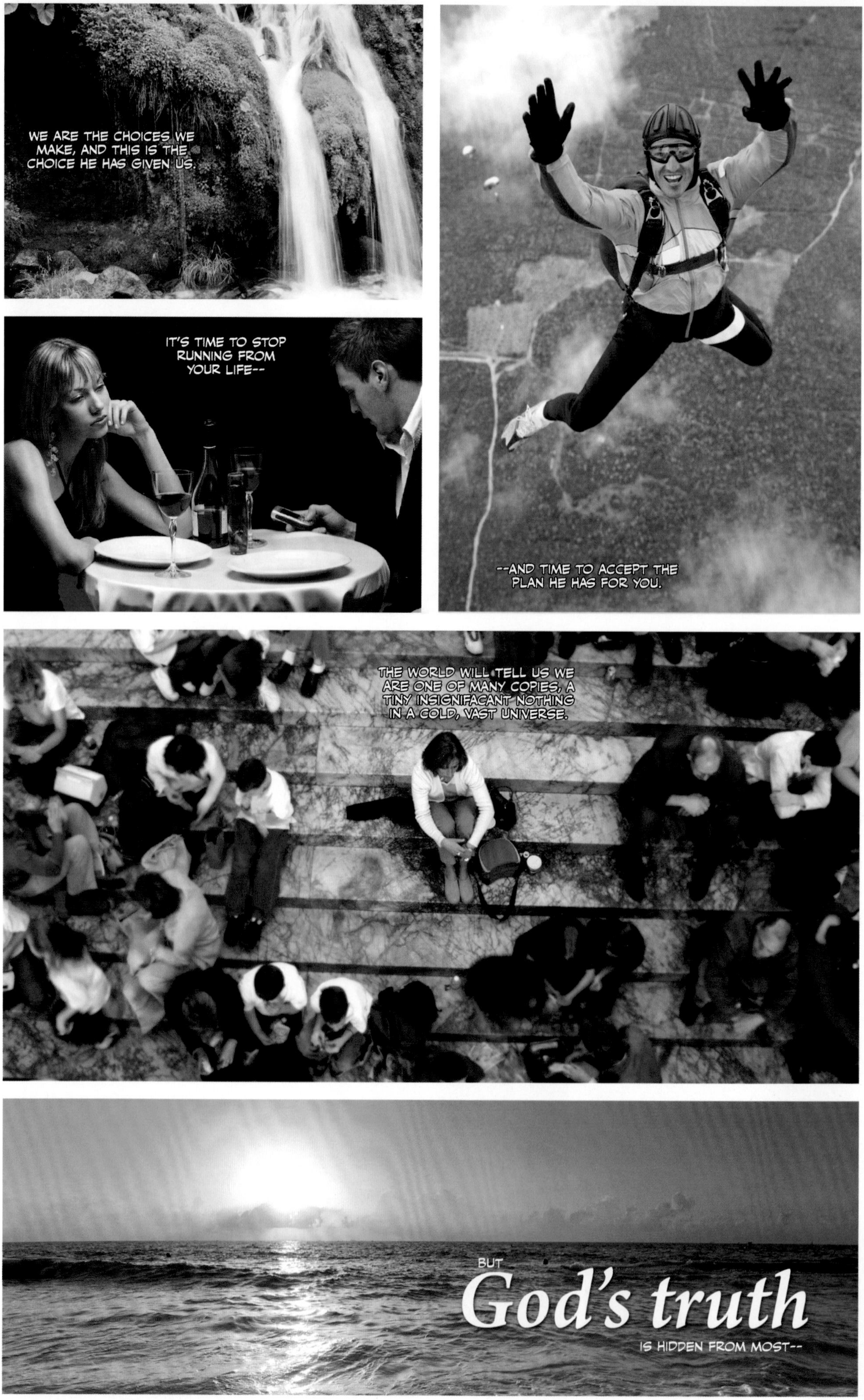
WE ARE THE CHOICES WE MAKE, AND THIS IS THE CHOICE HE HAS GIVEN US.
IT'S TIME TO STOP RUNNING FROM YOUR LIFE--
--AND TIME TO ACCEPT THE PLAN HE HAS FOR YOU.
THE WORLD WILL TELL US WE ARE ONE OF MANY COPIES, A TINY INSIGNIFACANT NOTHING IN A COLD, VAST UNIVERSE.
BUT
God's truth
IS HIDDEN FROM MOST--

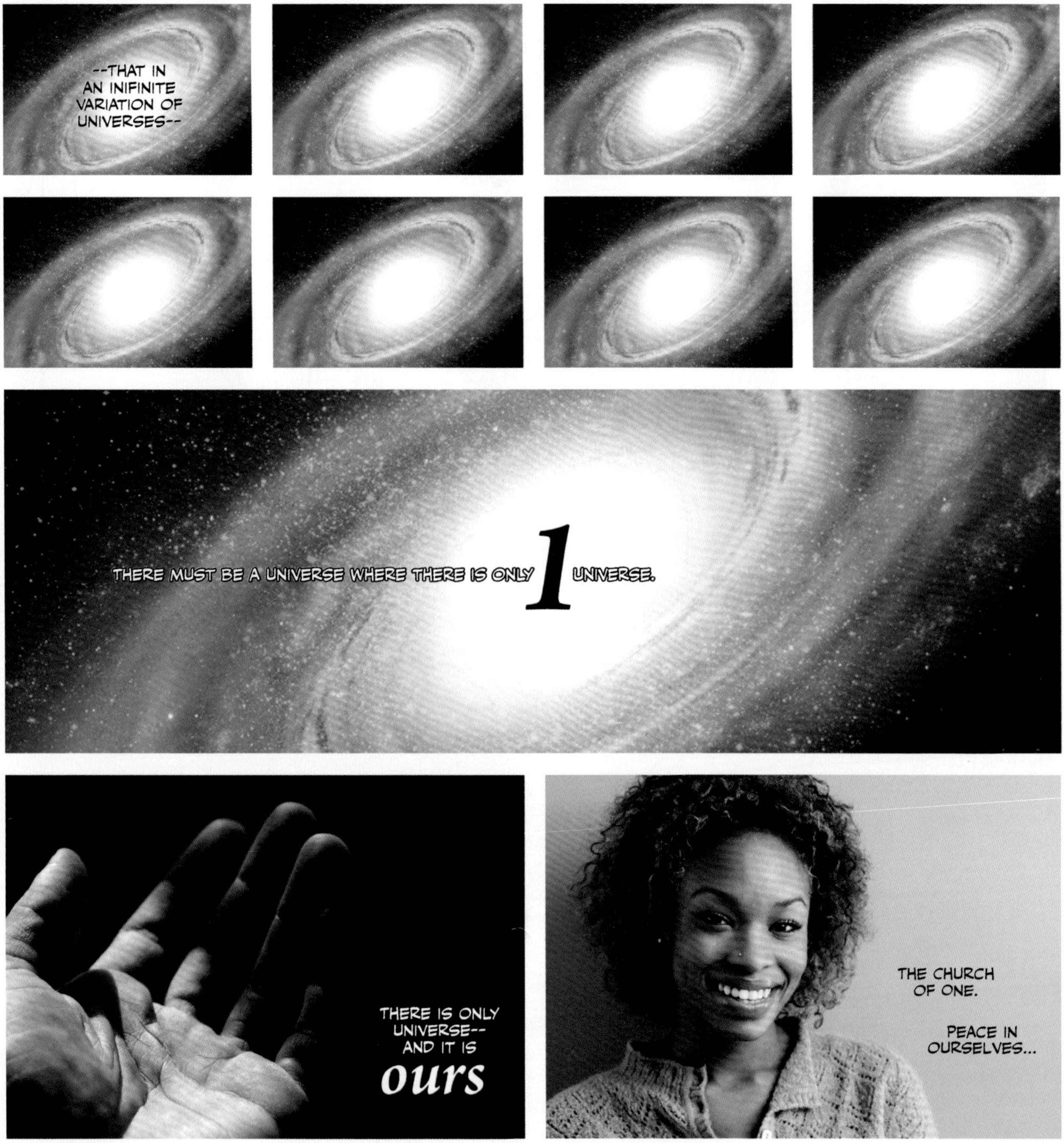
--THAT IN AN INIFINITE VARIATION OF UNIVERSES--
THERE MUST BE A UNIVERSE WHERE THERE IS ONLY 1 UNIVERSE.
THERE IS ONLY UNIVERSE-- AND IT IS
ours
THE CHURCH OF ONE.
PEACE IN OURSELVES...

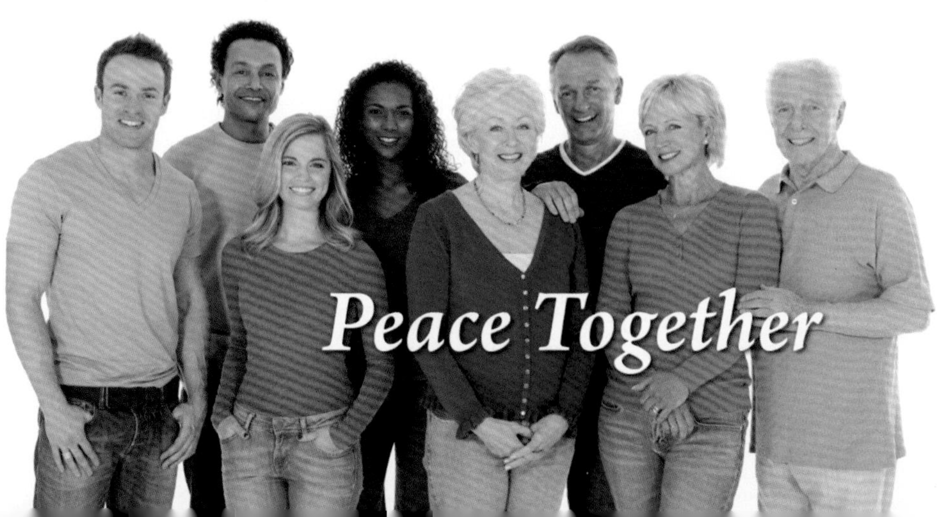
Peace Together

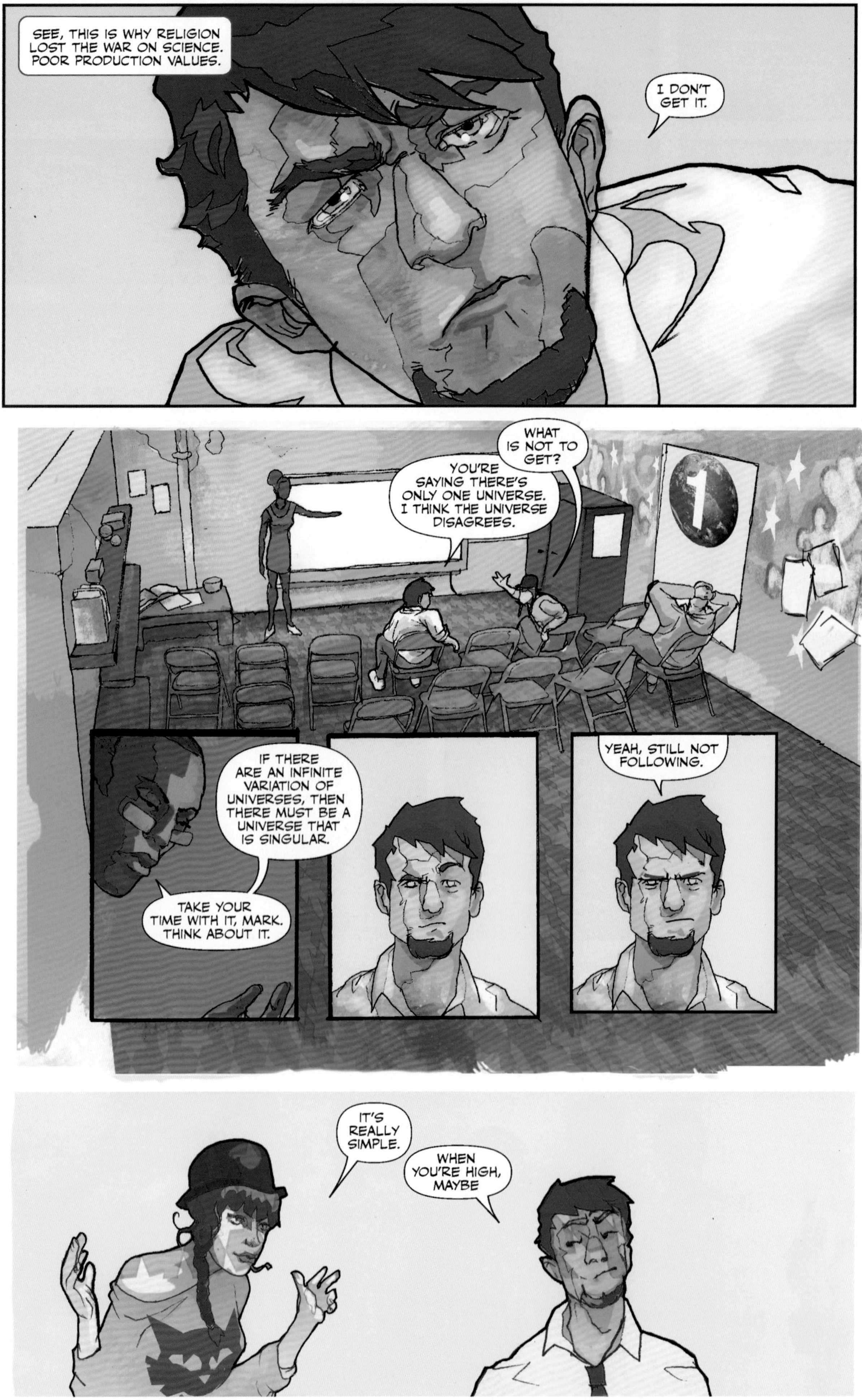
SEE, THIS IS WHY RELIGION LOST THE WAR ON SCIENCE. POOR PRODUCTION VALUES.
I DON'T GET IT.
WHAT IS NOT TO GET?
YOU'RE SAYING THERE'S ONLY ONE UNIVERSE. I THINK THE UNIVERSE DISAGREES.
IF THERE ARE AN INFINITE VARIATION OF UNIVERSES, THEN THERE MUST BE A UNIVERSE THAT IS SINGULAR.
TAKE YOUR TIME WITH IT, MARK. THINK ABOUT IT.
YEAH, STILL NOT FOLLOWING.
IT'S REALLY SIMPLE.
WHEN YOU'RE HIGH, MAYBE

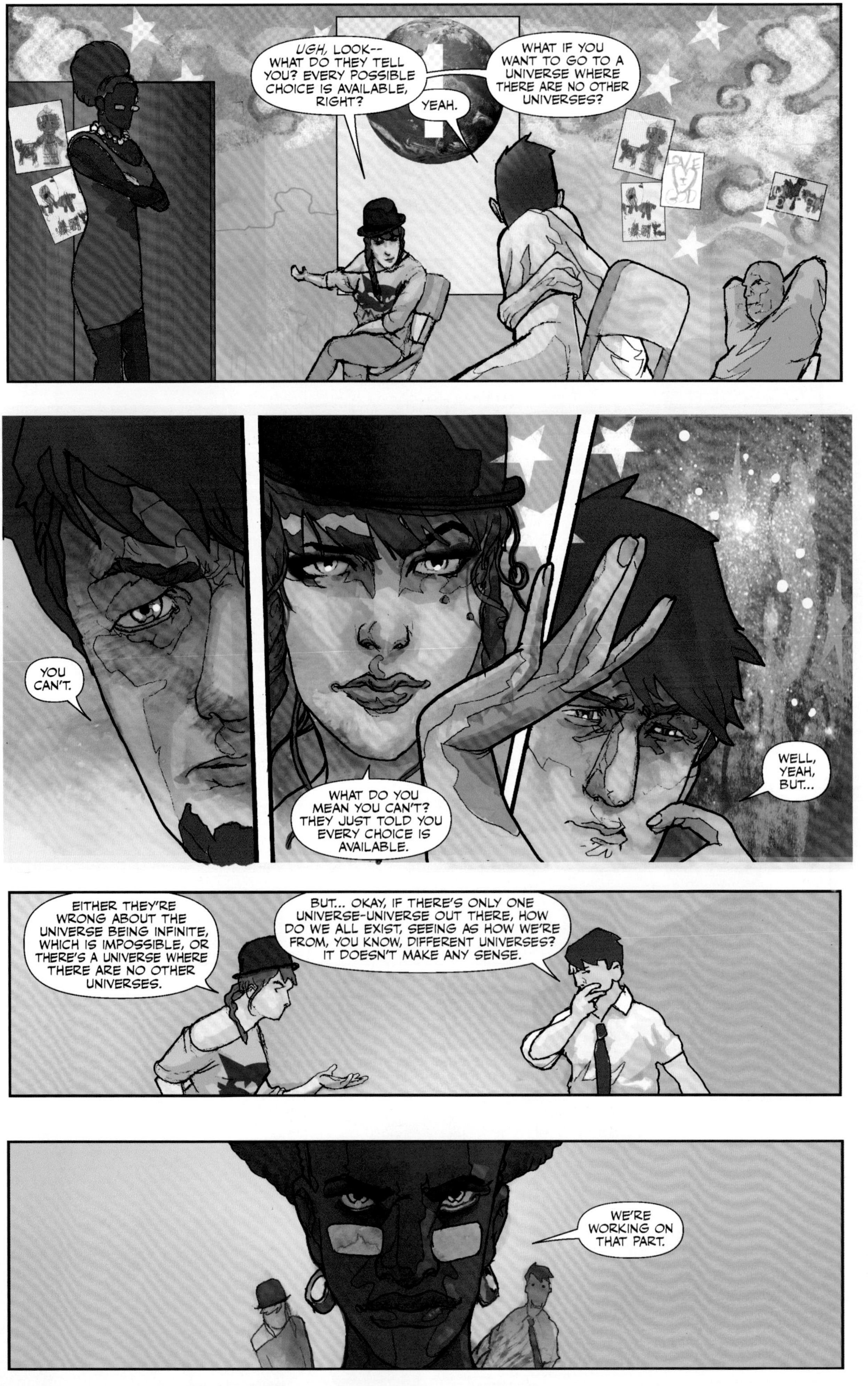
UGH, LOOK-- WHAT DO THEY TELL YOU? EVERY POSSIBLE CHOICE IS AVAILABLE, RIGHT?
YEAH.
WHAT IF YOU WANT TO GO TO A UNIVERSE WHERE THERE ARE NO OTHER UNIVERSES?
YOU CAN'T.
WHAT DO YOU MEAN YOU CAN'T? THEY JUST TOLD YOU EVERY CHOICE IS AVAILABLE.
WELL, YEAH, BUT...
EITHER THEY'RE WRONG ABOUT THE UNIVERSE BEING INFINITE, WHICH IS IMPOSSIBLE, OR THERE'S A UNIVERSE WHERE THERE ARE NO OTHER UNIVERSES.
BUT... OKAY, IF THERE'S ONLY ONE UNIVERSE-UNIVERSE OUT THERE, HOW DO WE ALL EXIST, SEEING AS HOW WE'RE FROM, YOU KNOW, DIFFERENT UNIVERSES? IT DOESN'T MAKE ANY SENSE.
WE'RE WORKING ON THAT PART.

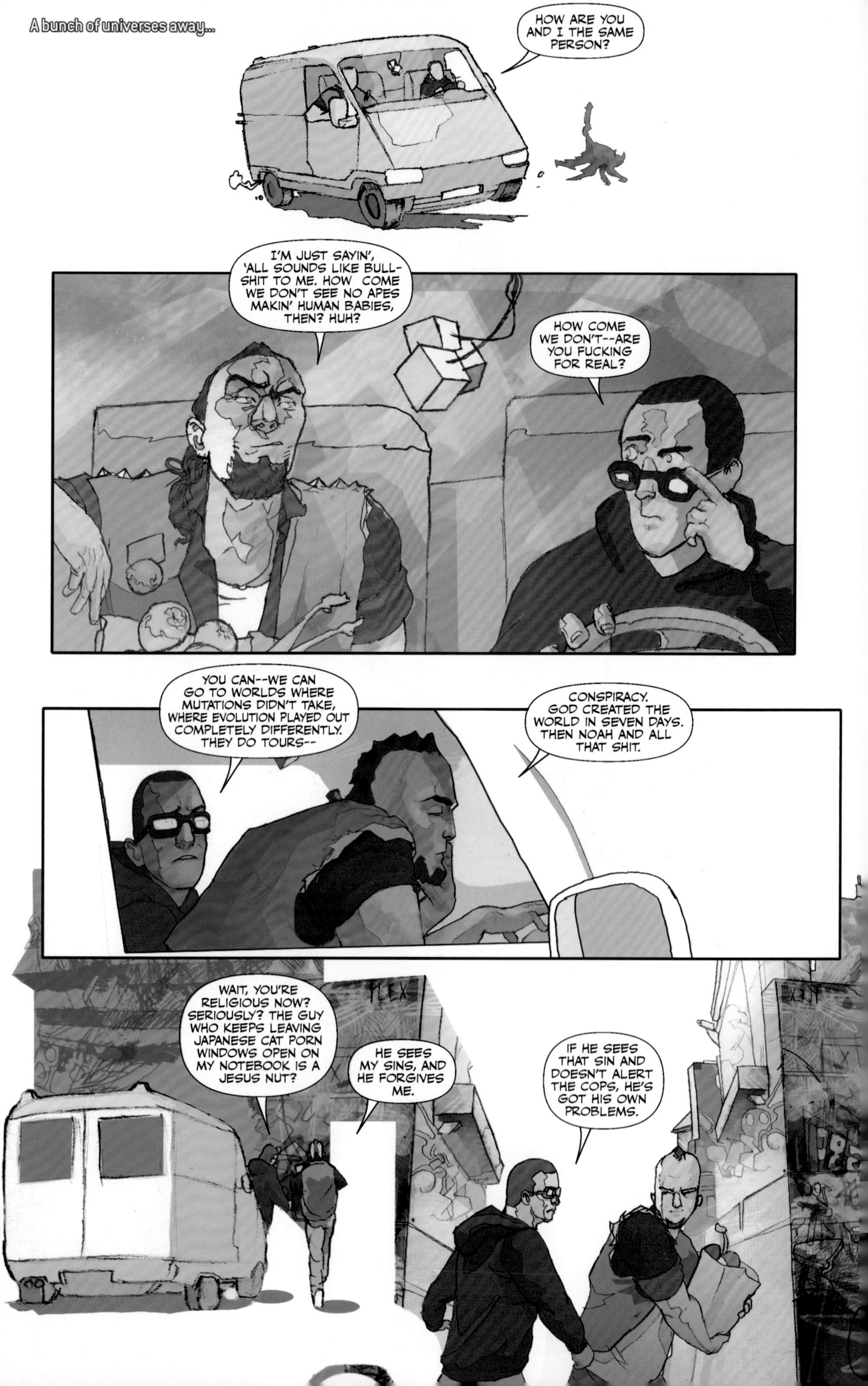
A bunch of universes away...
HOW ARE YOU AND I THE SAME PERSON?
I'M JUST SAYIN', 'ALL SOUNDS LIKE BULL-SHIT TO ME. HOW COME WE DON'T SEE NO APES MAKIN' HUMAN BABIES, THEN? HUH?
HOW COME WE DON'T--ARE YOU FUCKING FOR REAL?
YOU CAN--WE CAN GO TO WORLDS WHERE MUTATIONS DIDN'T TAKE, WHERE EVOLUTION PLAYED OUT COMPLETELY DIFFERENTLY. THEY DO TOURS--
CONSPIRACY. GOD CREATED THE WORLD IN SEVEN DAYS. THEN NOAH AND ALL THAT SHIT.
WAIT, YOU'RE RELIGIOUS NOW? SERIOUSLY? THE GUY WHO KEEPS LEAVING JAPANESE CAT PORN WINDOWS OPEN ON MY NOTEBOOK IS A JESUS NUT?
HE SEES MY SINS, AND HE FORGIVES ME.
IF HE SEES THAT SIN AND DOESN'T ALERT THE COPS, HE'S GOT HIS OWN PROBLEMS.

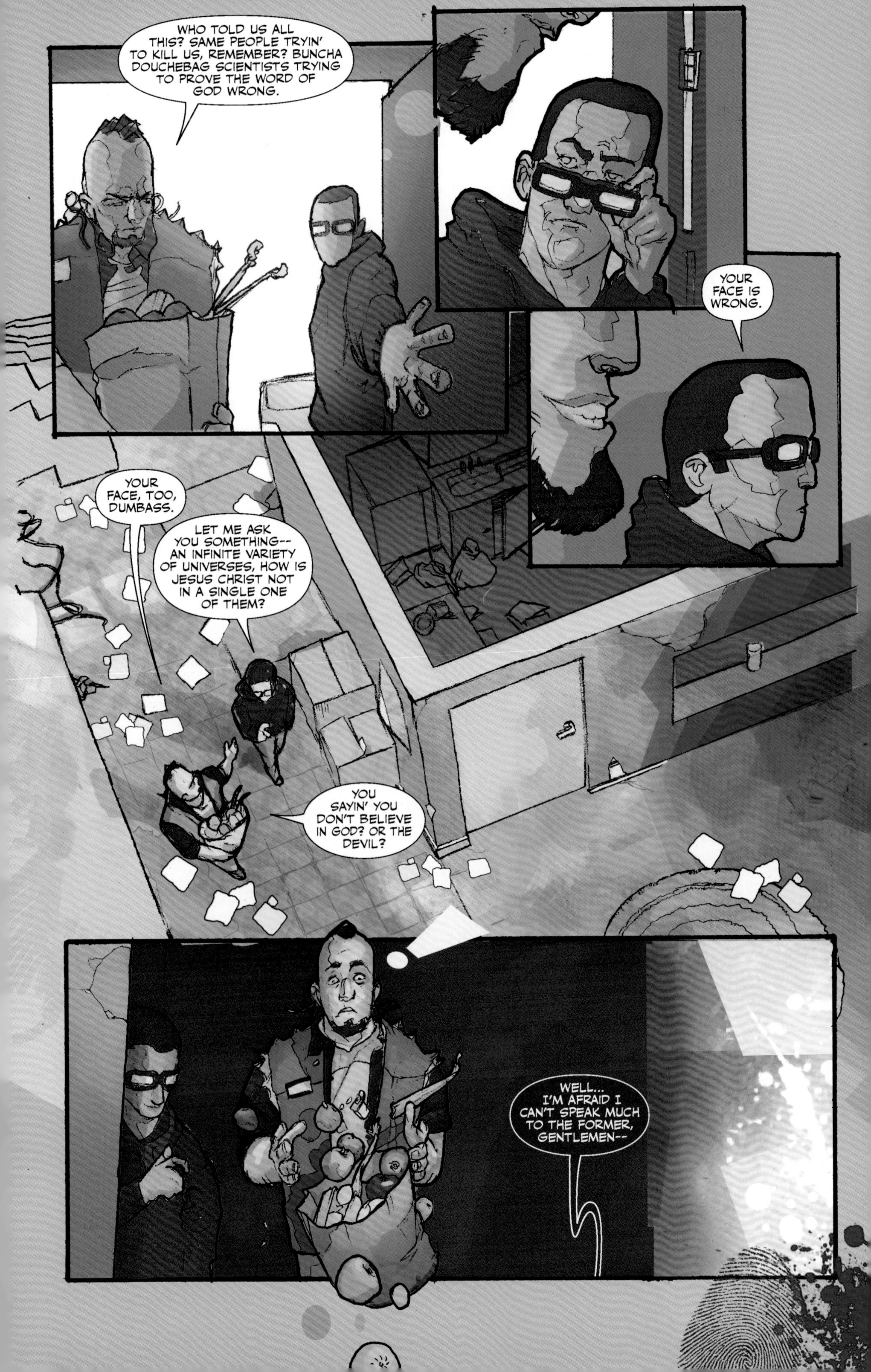
WHO TOLD US ALL THIS? SAME PEOPLE TRYIN' TO KILL US, REMEMBER? BUNCHA DOUCHEBAG SCIENTISTS TRYING TO PROVE THE WORD OF GOD WRONG.
YOUR FACE IS WRONG.
YOUR FACE, TOO, DUMBASS.
LET ME ASK YOU SOMETHING-- AN INFINITE VARIETY OF UNIVERSES, HOW IS JESUS CHRIST NOT IN A SINGLE ONE OF THEM?
YOU SAYIN' YOU DON'T BELIEVE IN GOD? OR THE DEVIL?
WELL... I'M AFRAID I CAN'T SPEAK MUCH TO THE FORMER, GENTLEMEN--

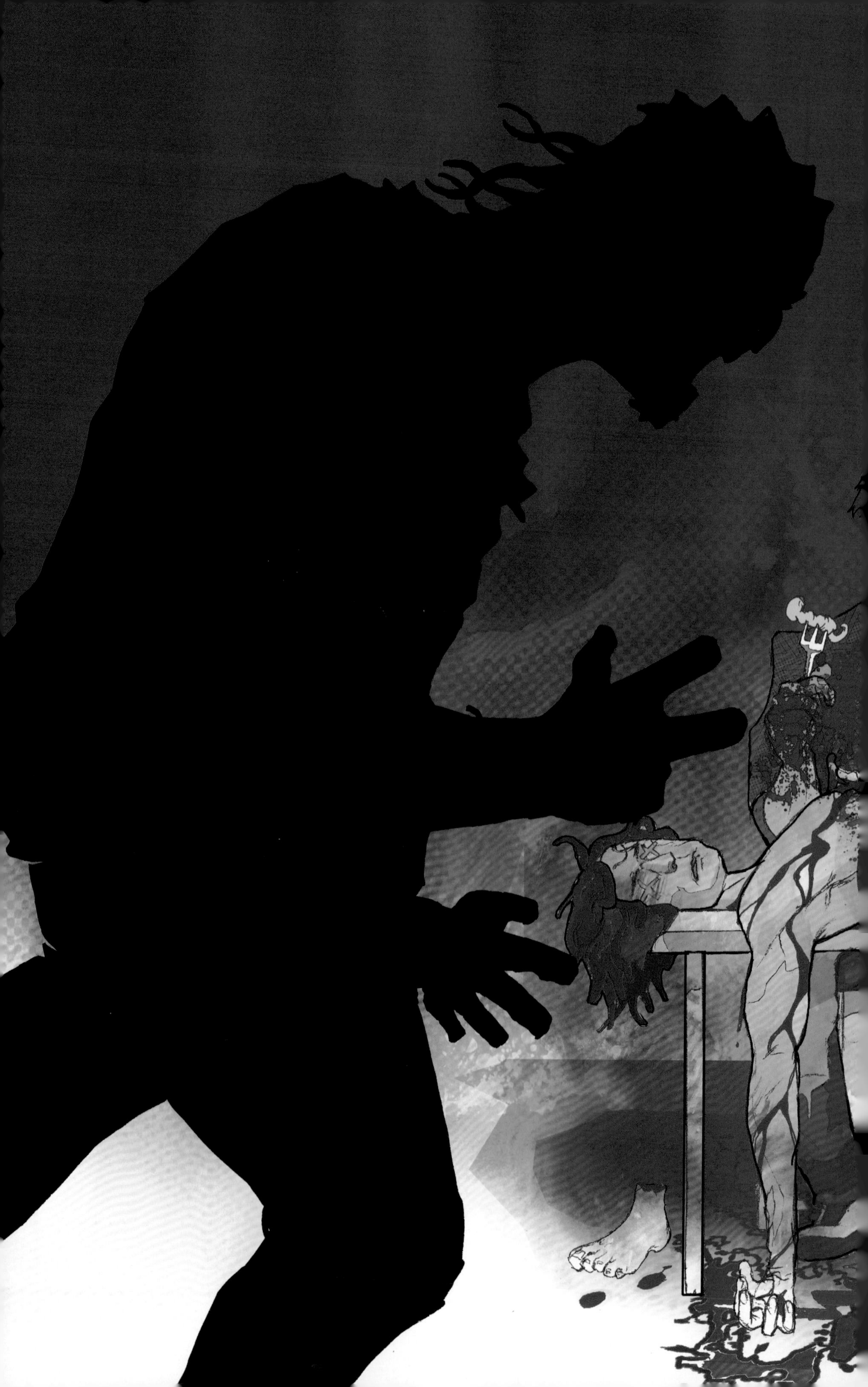

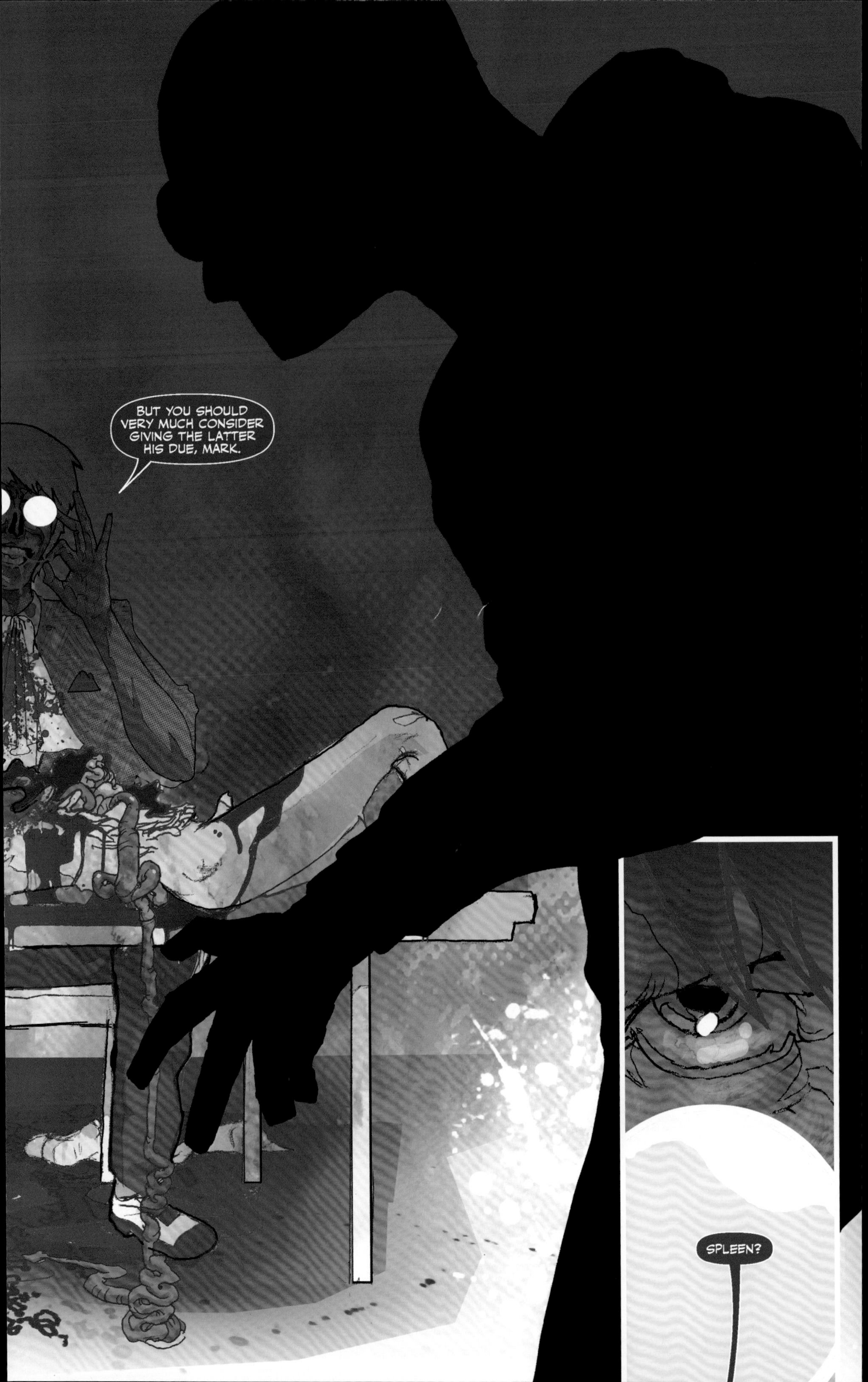
BUT YOU SHOULD VERY MUCH CONSIDER GIVING THE LATTER HIS DUE, MARK.
SPLEEN?

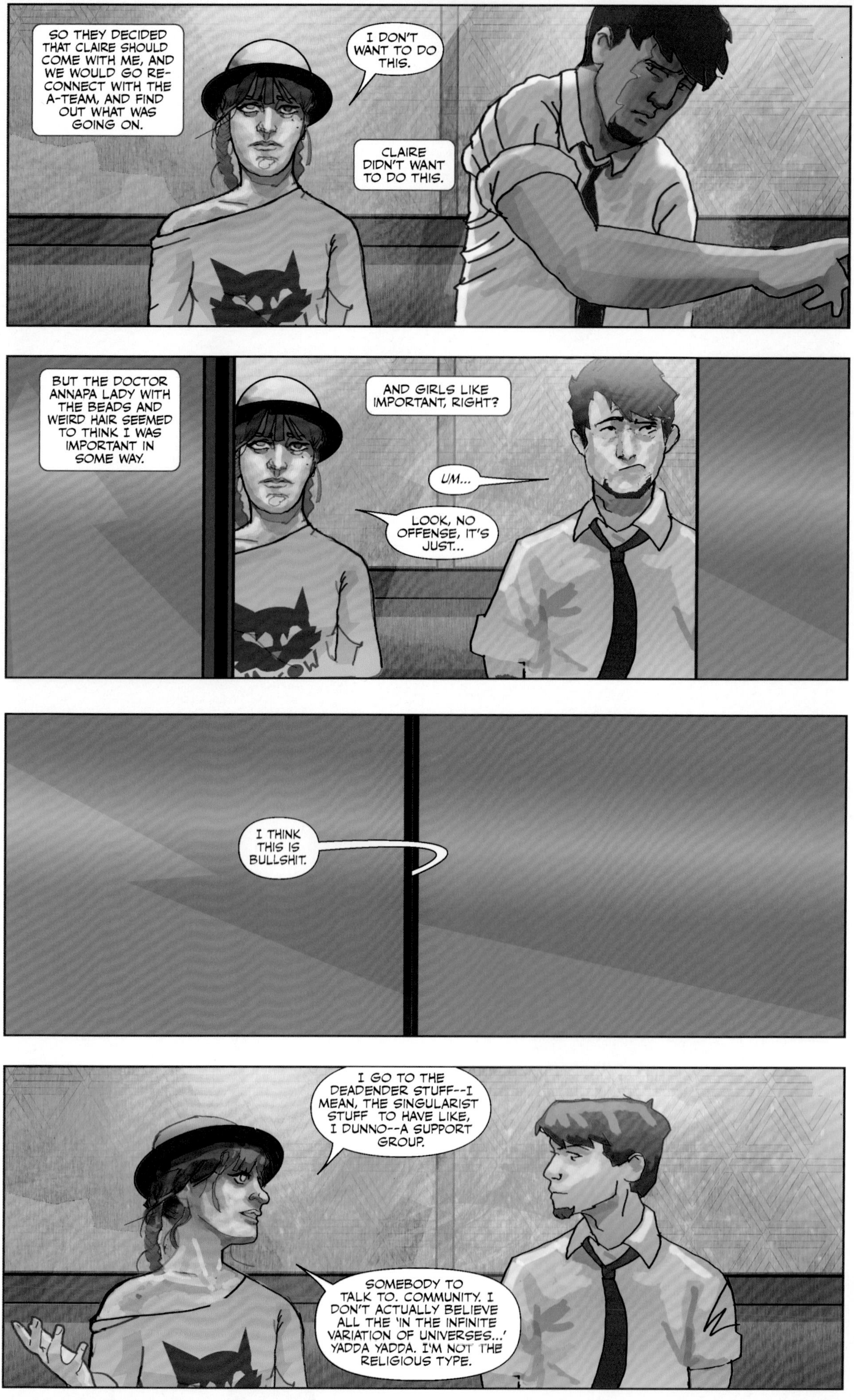
SO THEY DECIDED THAT CLAIRE SHOULD COME WITH ME, AND WE WOULD GO RE-CONNECT WITH THE A-TEAM, AND FIND OUT WHAT WAS GOING ON.
I DON'T WANT TO DO THIS.
CLAIRE DIDN'T WANT TO DO THIS.
BUT THE DOCTOR ANNAPA LADY WITH THE BEADS AND WEIRD HAIR SEEMED TO THINK I WAS IMPORTANT IN SOME WAY.
AND GIRLS LIKE IMPORTANT, RIGHT?
UM...
LOOK, NO OFFENSE, IT'S JUST...
I THINK THIS IS BULLSHIT.
I GO TO THE DEADENDER STUFF--I MEAN, THE SINGULARIST STUFF TO HAVE LIKE, I DUNNO--A SUPPORT GROUP.
SOMEBODY TO TALK TO. COMMUNITY. I DON'T ACTUALLY BELIEVE ALL THE 'IN THE INFINITE VARIATION OF UNIVERSES...' YADDA YADDA. I'M NOT THE RELIGIOUS TYPE.

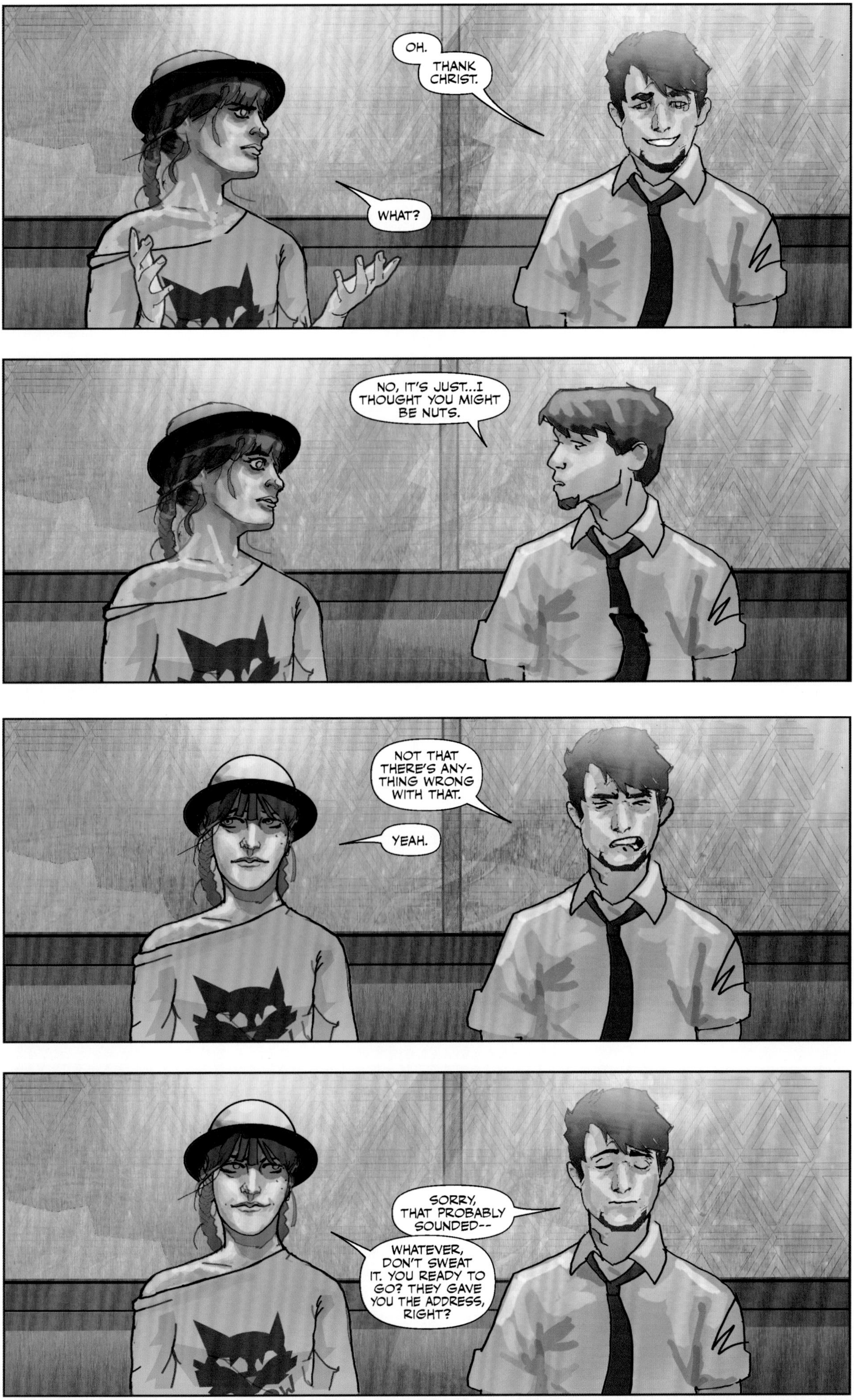
OH.
THANK CHRIST.
WHAT?
NO, IT'S JUST...I THOUGHT YOU MIGHT BE NUTS.
NOT THAT THERE'S ANY-THING WRONG WITH THAT.
YEAH.
SORRY, THAT PROBABLY SOUNDED--
WHATEVER, DON'T SWEAT IT. YOU READY TO GO? THEY GAVE YOU THE ADDRESS, RIGHT?

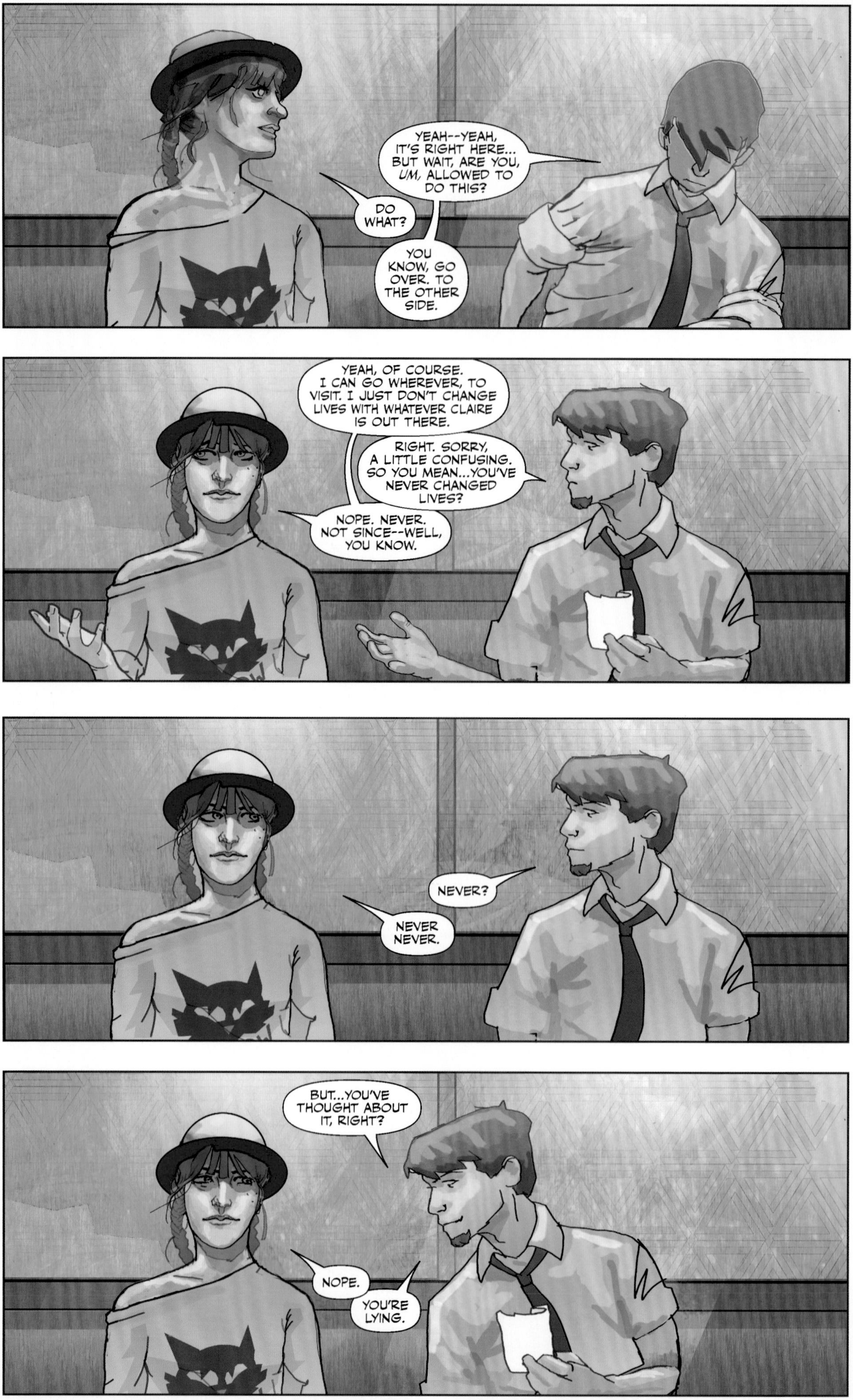
YEAH--YEAH, IT'S RIGHT HERE... BUT WAIT, ARE YOU, UM, ALLOWED TO DO THIS?
DO WHAT?
YOU KNOW, GO OVER. TO THE OTHER SIDE.
YEAH, OF COURSE. I CAN GO WHEREVER, TO VISIT. I JUST DON'T CHANGE LIVES WITH WHATEVER CLAIRE IS OUT THERE.
RIGHT. SORRY, A LITTLE CONFUSING. SO YOU MEAN...YOU'VE NEVER CHANGED LIVES?
NOPE. NEVER. NOT SINCE--WELL, YOU KNOW.
NEVER?
NEVER NEVER.
BUT...YOU'VE THOUGHT ABOUT IT, RIGHT?
NOPE.
YOU'RE LYING.

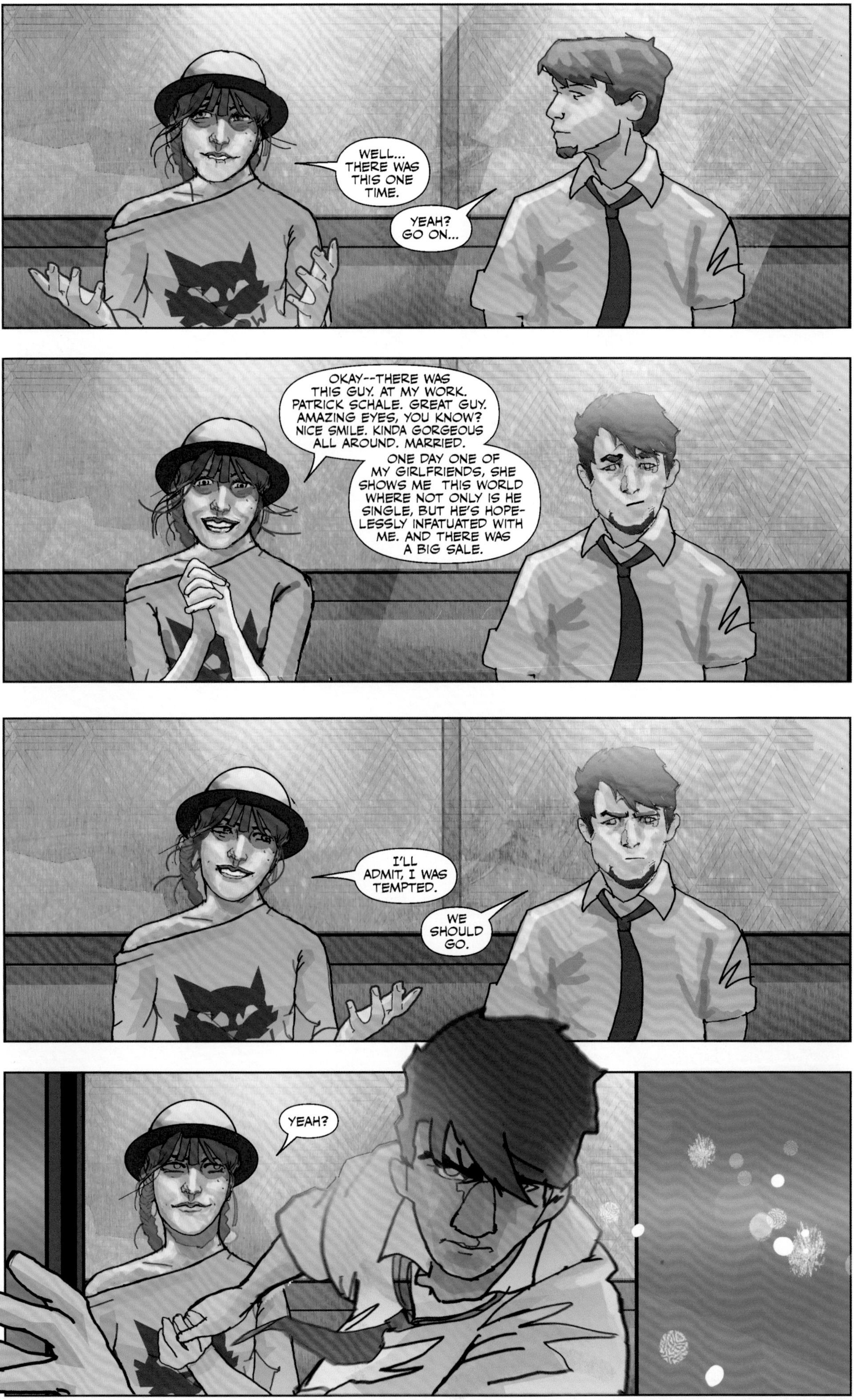
WELL... THERE WAS THIS ONE TIME.
YEAH? GO ON...
OKAY--THERE WAS THIS GUY. AT MY WORK. PATRICK SCHALE. GREAT GUY. AMAZING EYES, YOU KNOW? NICE SMILE. KINDA GORGEOUS ALL AROUND. MARRIED.
ONE DAY ONE OF MY GIRLFRIENDS, SHE SHOWS ME THIS WORLD WHERE NOT ONLY IS HE SINGLE, BUT HE'S HOPE-LESSLY INFATUATED WITH ME. AND THERE WAS A BIG SALE.
I'LL ADMIT, I WAS TEMPTED.
WE SHOULD GO.
YEAH?

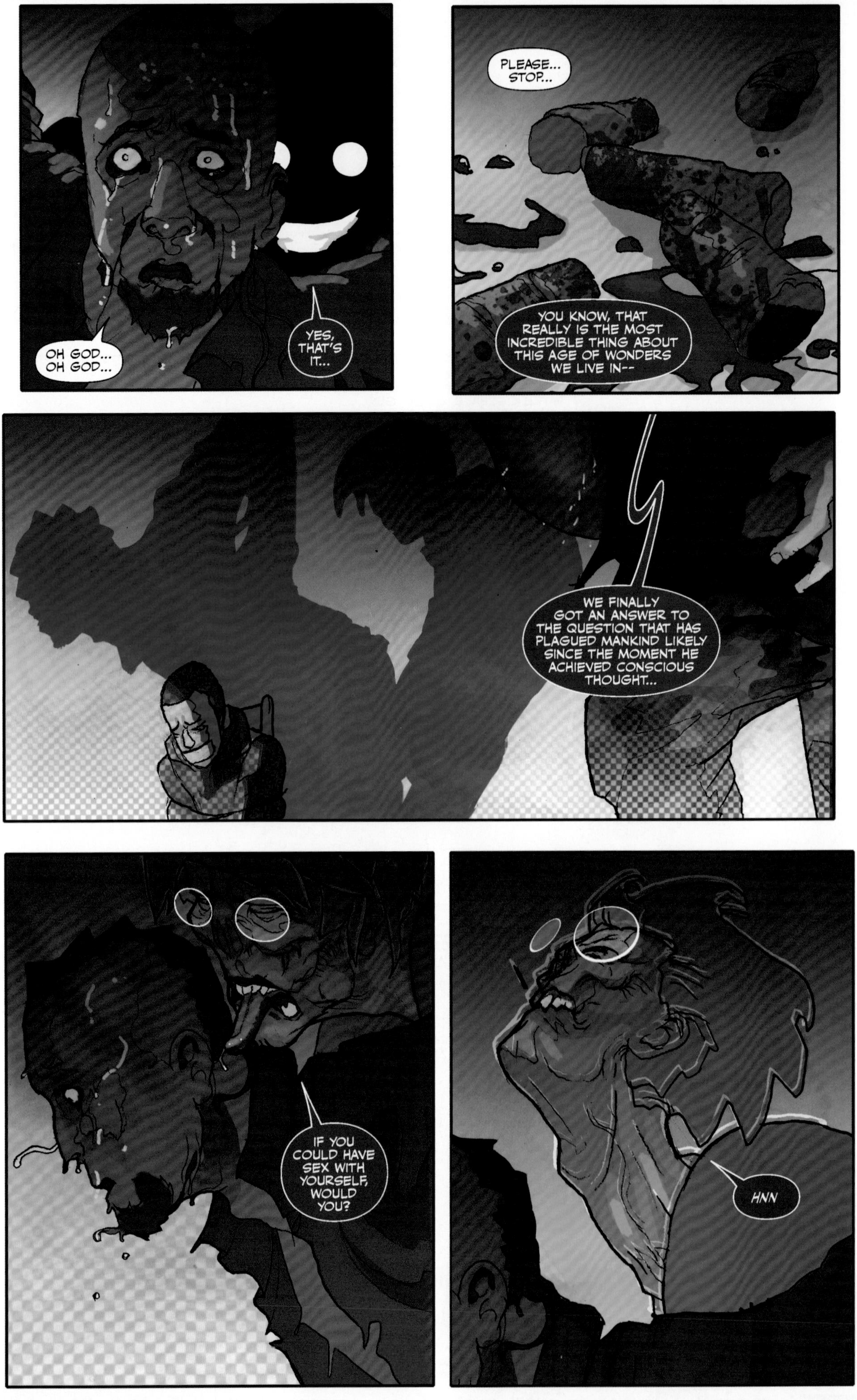
OH GOD... OH GOD...
YES, THAT'S IT...
PLEASE... STOP...
YOU KNOW, THAT REALLY IS THE MOST INCREDIBLE THING ABOUT THIS AGE OF WONDERS WE LIVE IN--
WE FINALLY GOT AN ANSWER TO THE QUESTION THAT HAS PLAGUED MANKIND LIKELY SINCE THE MOMENT HE ACHIEVED CONSCIOUS THOUGHT...
IF YOU COULD HAVE SEX WITH YOURSELF, WOULD YOU?
HNN

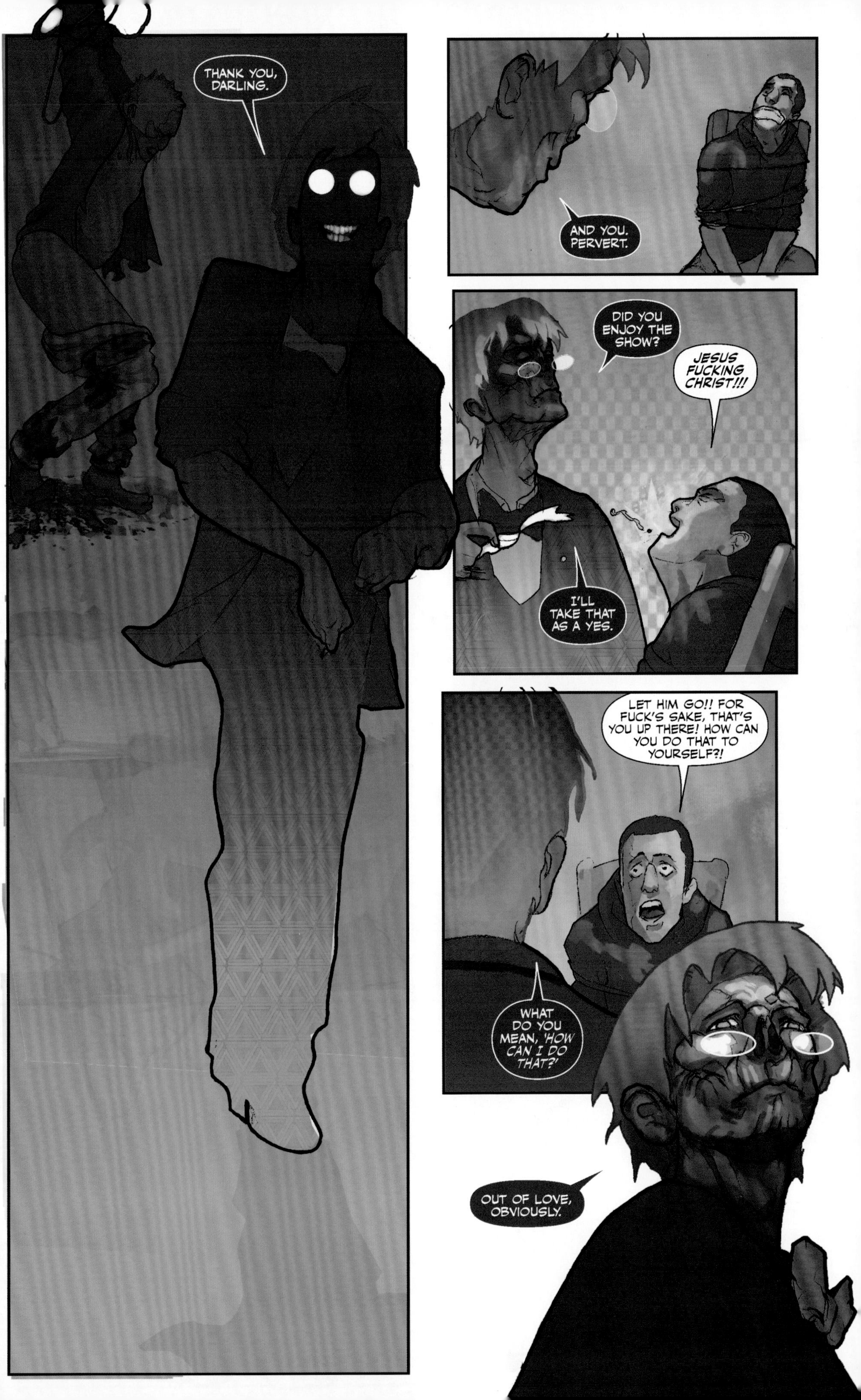
THANK YOU, DARLING.
AND YOU. PERVERT.
DID YOU ENJOY THE SHOW?
JESUS FUCKING CHRIST!!!
I'LL TAKE THAT AS A YES.
LET HIM GO!! FOR FUCK'S SAKE, THAT'S YOU UP THERE! HOW CAN YOU DO THAT TO YOURSELF?!
WHAT DO YOU MEAN, 'HOW CAN I DO THAT?'
OUT OF LOVE, OBVIOUSLY.

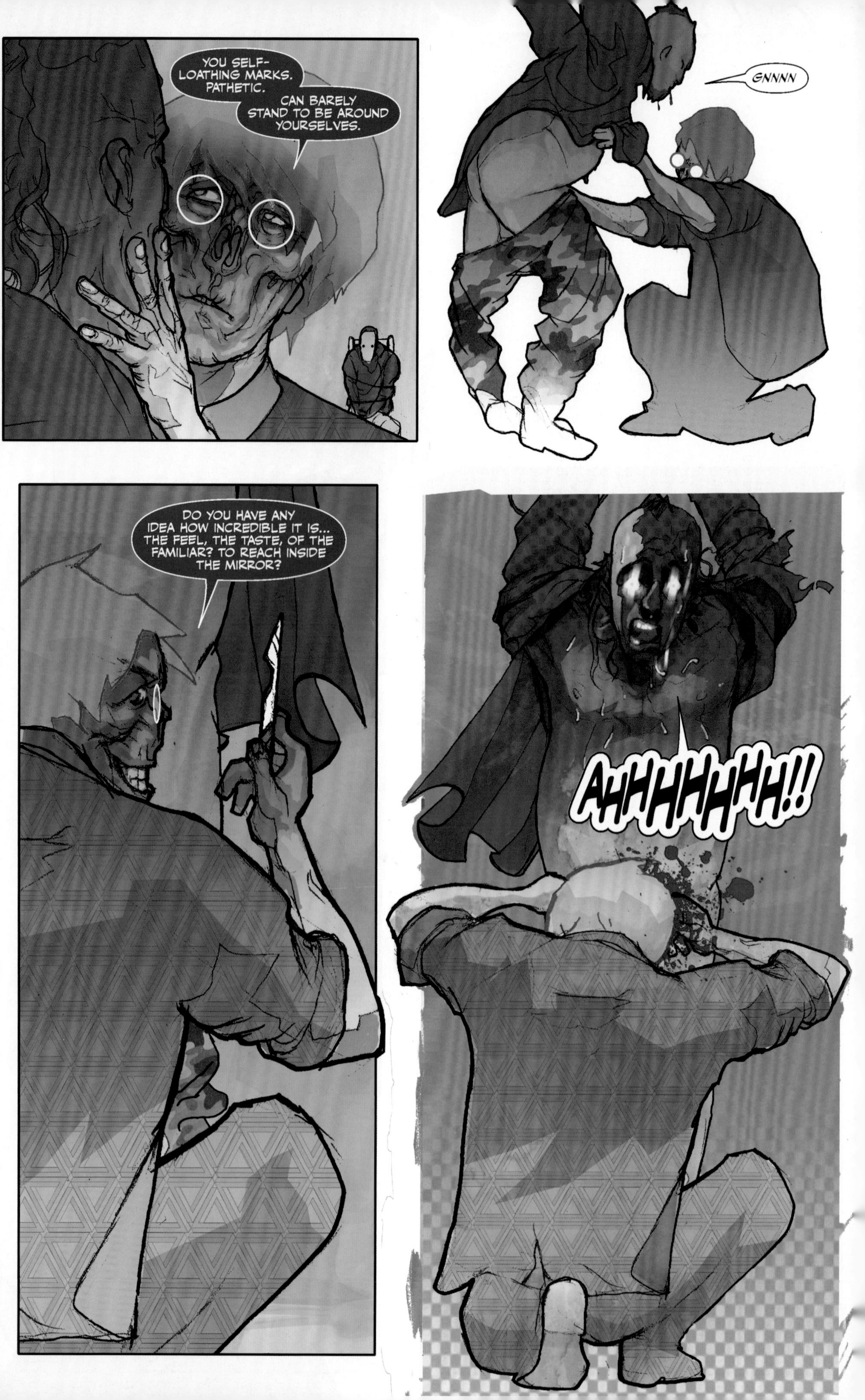
YOU SELF-LOATHING MARKS. PATHETIC.
CAN BARELY STAND TO BE AROUND YOURSELVES.
GNNNN
DO YOU HAVE ANY IDEA HOW INCREDIBLE IT IS... THE FEEL, THE TASTE, OF THE FAMILIAR? TO REACH INSIDE THE MIRROR?
AHHHHHHH!!

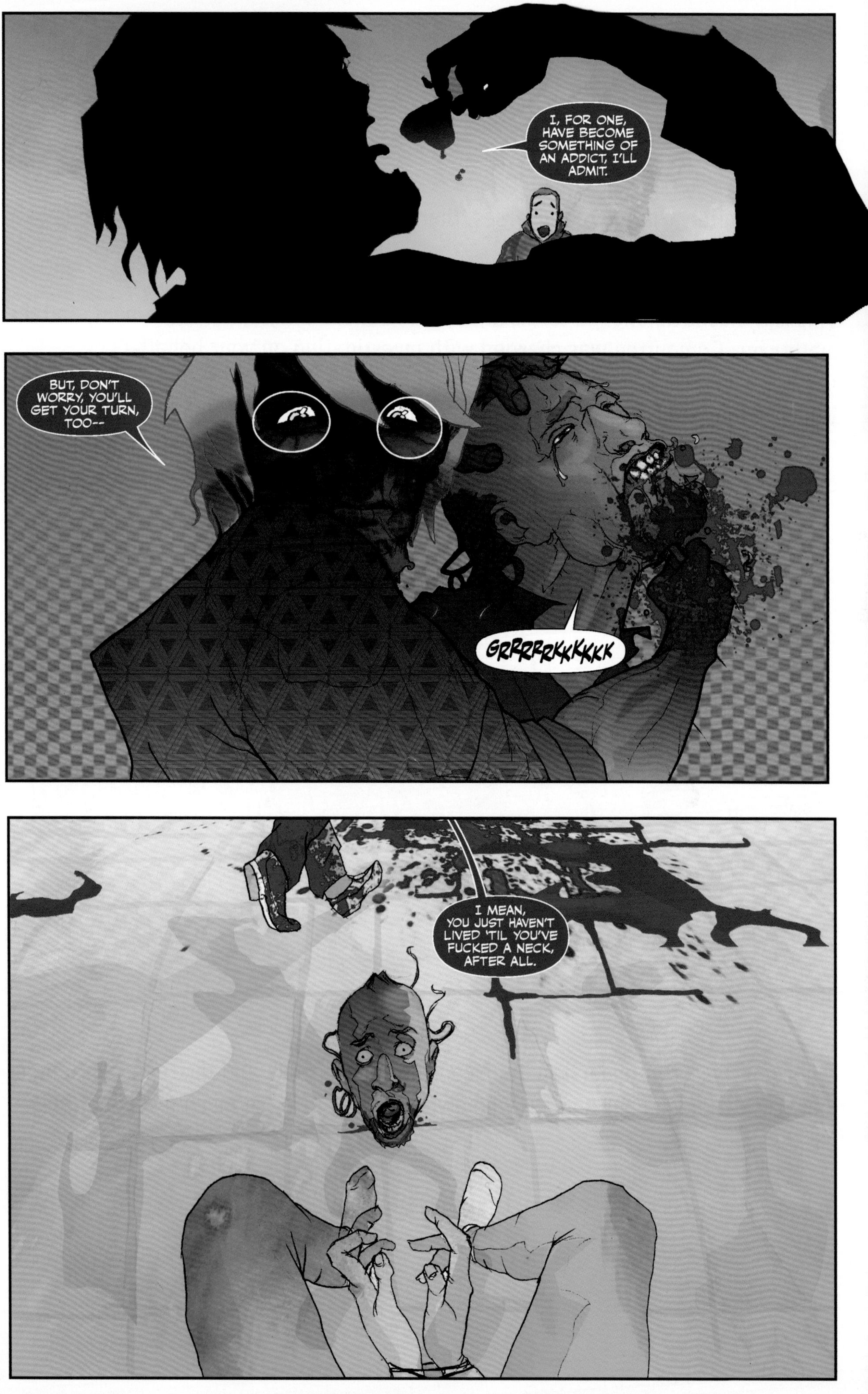
I, FOR ONE, HAVE BECOME SOMETHING OF AN ADDICT, I'LL ADMIT.
BUT, DON'T WORRY, YOU'LL GET YOUR TURN, TOO--
GRRRRRKKKKKK
I MEAN, YOU JUST HAVEN'T LIVED 'TIL YOU'VE FUCKED A NECK, AFTER ALL.

THERE IS ONLY 'ONE'

"In an infinite variation of universes, there must be a universe where there is only one universe."

This is the contradiction in terms at the heart of the Singularist movement, and the matter our Committee was charged with investigating on your behalf--

Which, I must add, we undertook gladly, and with every intention of disproving and discrediting such a nonsensical and primitive ideal. We are, after all, good students of science.

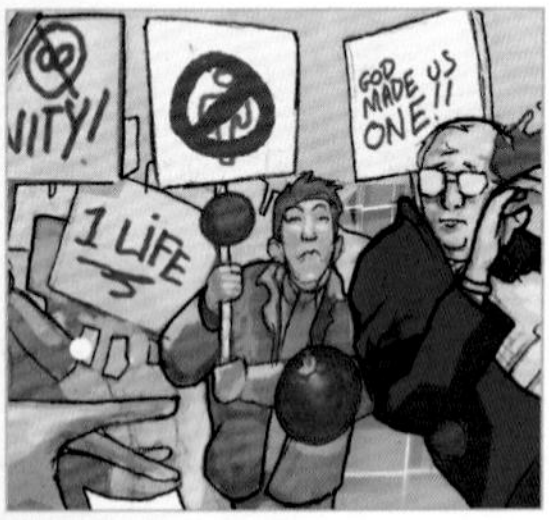
GOD MADE US ONE!!
1 LIFE

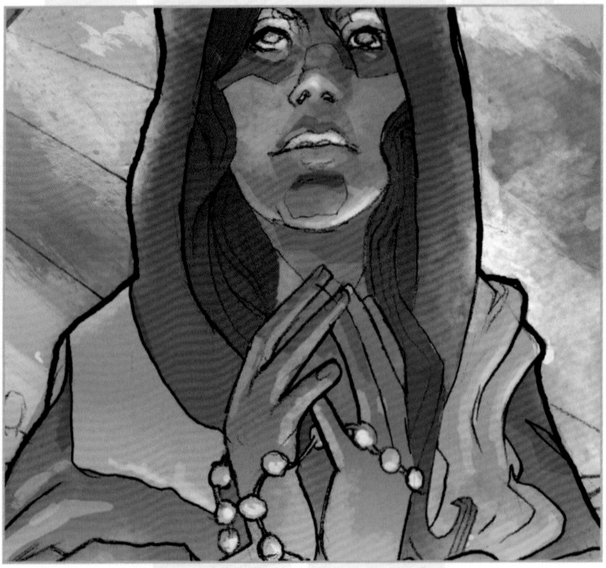

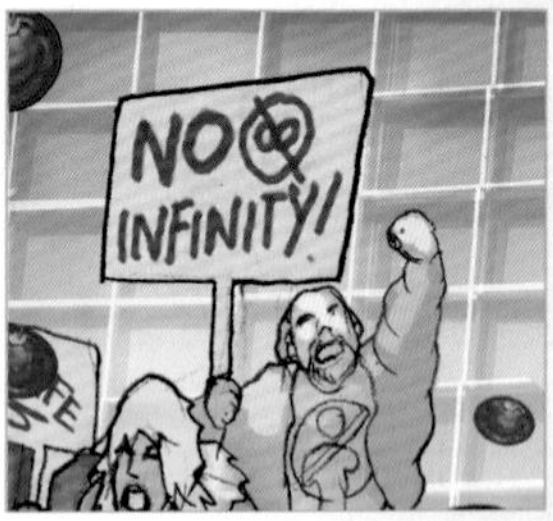
NO INFINITY!

‹ ›

Therefore you can understand our considerable dismay and distress, gentlemen-- our frustration and our anger-- when we realized, after so much investigation--

That they are right.

INFINITE ARRAY OF 'OTHERS'

Now, we understand full well that you honored gentlemen, are laypersons, so we will endeavor to make our findings as simple and plainly known as possible.

Remember that The Infinite Vacation is based on distance - the understanding that when one travels many powers beyond the speed of light, it is possible to venture well past our own hubble volume, and into an infinite array of others. Every possible configuration of particles, from those that could not be more different than our own, to those that are virtually indistinguishable.

And once such travel had been perfected, our community, perhaps a bit... shortsightedly, settled upon one understanding of what the universe really is.

After all, we had uncovered infinity - all that ever was, and all that ever could be. By definition, there was nowhere left to look.

But distance in infinity has not always been the only possiblity for so-called 'alternate universes.'

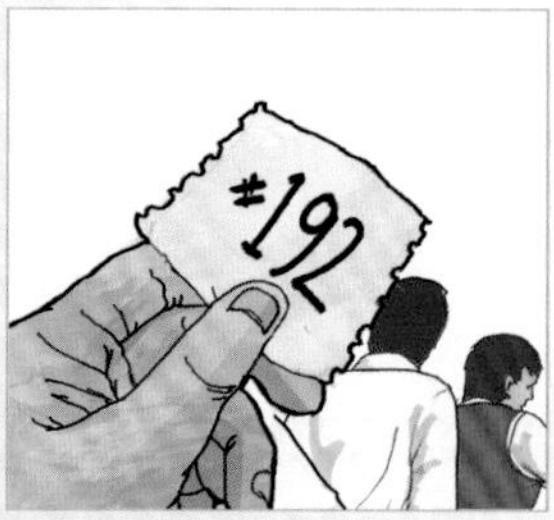
#192

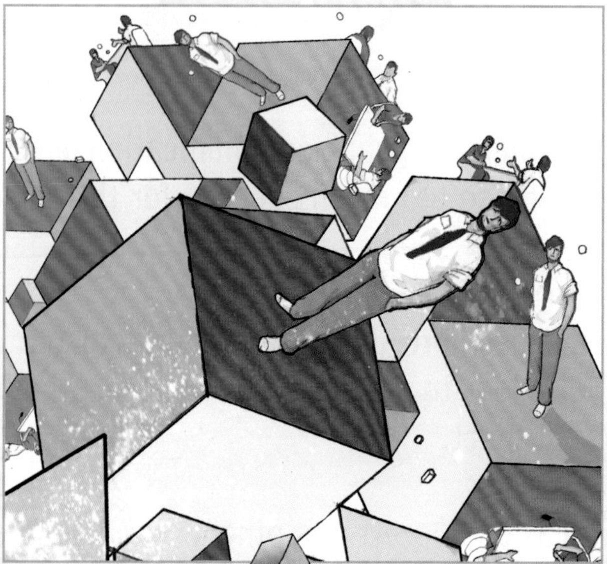

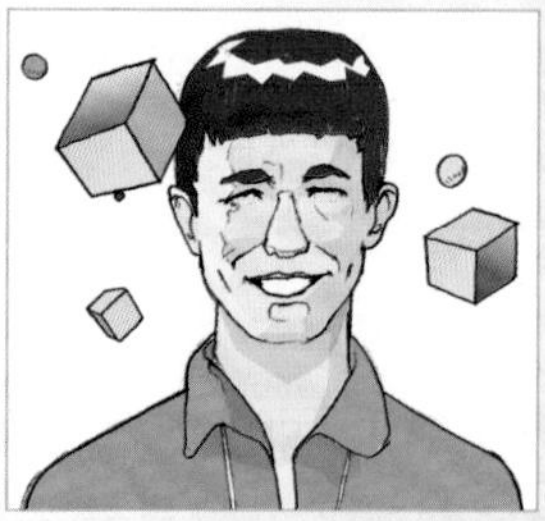

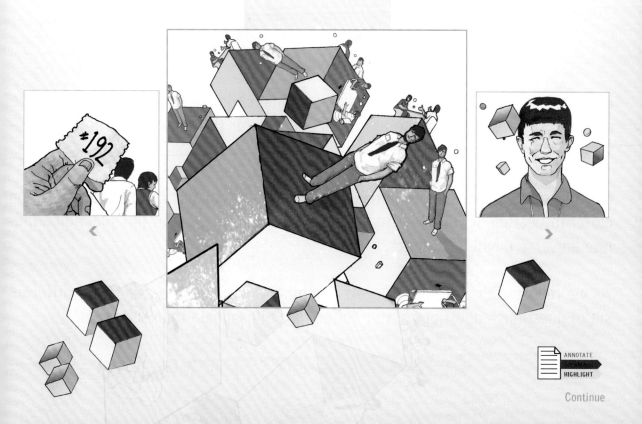

THE CAT IN QUESTION

In quantum physics, the many worlds interpretation posited the idea of infinite realities as a solution for wavefunction collapse.

We all know the thought experiment of Schrödinger's cat, for example - Many Worlds dictated that the cat in question was both alive and dead in a box, and that decoherence separates them out for our observation, but both states exist all the same.

Even still, that same decoherence made communication or interaction between the differing states impossible, so too much concern for the subject was never necessary.

But the subject arose once more during the course of our investigation, and on closer inspection, it was clear to us that our very perception of this functional infinite universe might be suspect.

As we revisited the ideas of Everett and others, we began to ask a very different set of questions - questions better suited for philosophers than scientists.

ANNOTATE
BOOKMARK
HIGHLIGHT
Continue

A PURPOSE MADE CLEAR

Questions such as, 'is there a purpose to infinity?' 'why is all of this here?' 'what role do we play, as conscious observers and participants within it?'

And finally we settled upon the possibility - the terrifying possibility, I'll readily admit - that the most likely reason choices exist is so a decision can be made.

We - this infinite universe - are the uncertain state that exists before observation. We are the box that holds the cat.

Many Worlds does not just mean that every choice made splits off and creates a new universe - it means we are the moment before the choice, the undefined awaiting observation.

We are a limitless number of paths, but we exist that just one may be walked.

And when it is - when the observation occurs, when the determination is made, all of this will collapse in on itself.

But when is a tricky prospect, one I shall expound upon shortly.

A TICKET TO THE FUNHOUSE

Think of a hallway of mirrors, reflecting upon each other endlessly, a repeating pattern. Each reflecting the quantum superposition as well.

In our vastness, we are made small. We are just one layer of the reflection. Everything that ever was and ever can be is contained within, but is just one of an infinite number of infinite, all tracing back to one singular state.

We are the all-encompassing, and yet we are just the tiniest, uncertain state.

MANY WORLD & SPOOKY ACTIONS

The Many Worlds interpretation didn't solve the problems of quantum states, or 'spooky actions' - it multiplied them by infinity. So with this in mind, with infinity collapsed atop of infinity, and the dominoes falling, we set out to ask just what a collapse would look like.

First, we dismissed notions of time and distance, as none would apply. The inifinity that lies above our infinity makes limits and quantifiables impossible; it would exist within its own set of rules.

So instead, we determined, it would be an always-occuring event, infinite itera-tions, from all sources - down to the smallest of particles, from dark matter on up, all are engaged in, and thereby the cause of, the collapse.

To test this, we used the Probability Engines to select one person - a test subject, to isolate the collapse and study it, in the hopes of delaying it's impact on the illu-sory universe it exists in. His photo is below.

If our findings are correct, using the stimuli we have applied, this person will effect the collapse of his own sphere of existence, just as all do. And while this will mean the end of the universe, one shouldn't worry too much - our experts find it likely we won't even notice it.

ANNOTATE
BOOKMARK
HIGHLIGHT

Continue

IN SUMMATION

To sum up our findings--

① A MERE LAYER

The infinite universe we exist in is merely a layer, a waiting state until it is observed, at which point it will collapse into one singular entity (perhaps a thing, perhaps an action, perhaps a choice, we cannot know).

② A STATE OF CONSTANT COLLAPSE

This collapse has already occurred and is indeed occurring constantly, with notions of time and distance irrelevant. Our existence is merely to serve the observation, so therefore the observation is already in play.

③ TRACK & STUDY

We have isolated a test subject, to track and study the nature of the observation-collapse.

④
ONE.
There is only one universe.

AND THERE YOU HAVE IT, GENTLEMEN-- AS REQUESTED, OUR SPECIAL ADVISORY REPORT ON THE PUBLIC STATEMENTS AND GOVERNING THEOLOGY OF THE SINGULARIST MOVEMENT.

ANY QUESTIONS? COMMENTS?

PREPOSTEROUS.

LUDICROUS.

SEXY.

MARKETING!

SORRY.

BUT--BUT YOU'RE TALKING ABOUT THE VERY EXTINCTION OF AN INFINITE MULTIVERSE... YOU'RE TALKING ABOUT US!

AND YOU'RE ACTING LIKE IT ALREADY HAPPENED!

QUITE RIGHT, SIR.

BUT WE'RE STILL ALL HERE.

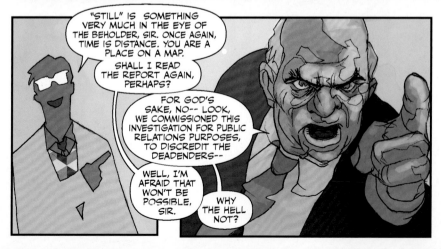

"STILL" IS SOMETHING VERY MUCH IN THE EYE OF THE BEHOLDER, SIR. ONCE AGAIN, TIME IS DISTANCE. YOU ARE A PLACE ON A MAP.

SHALL I READ THE REPORT AGAIN, PERHAPS?

FOR GOD'S SAKE, NO-- LOOK, WE COMMISSIONED THIS INVESTIGATION FOR PUBLIC RELATIONS PURPOSES, TO DISCREDIT THE DEADENDERS--

WELL, I'M AFRAID THAT WON'T BE POSSIBLE, SIR.

WHY THE HELL NOT?

BECAUSE THEY'RE CORRECT, SIR.

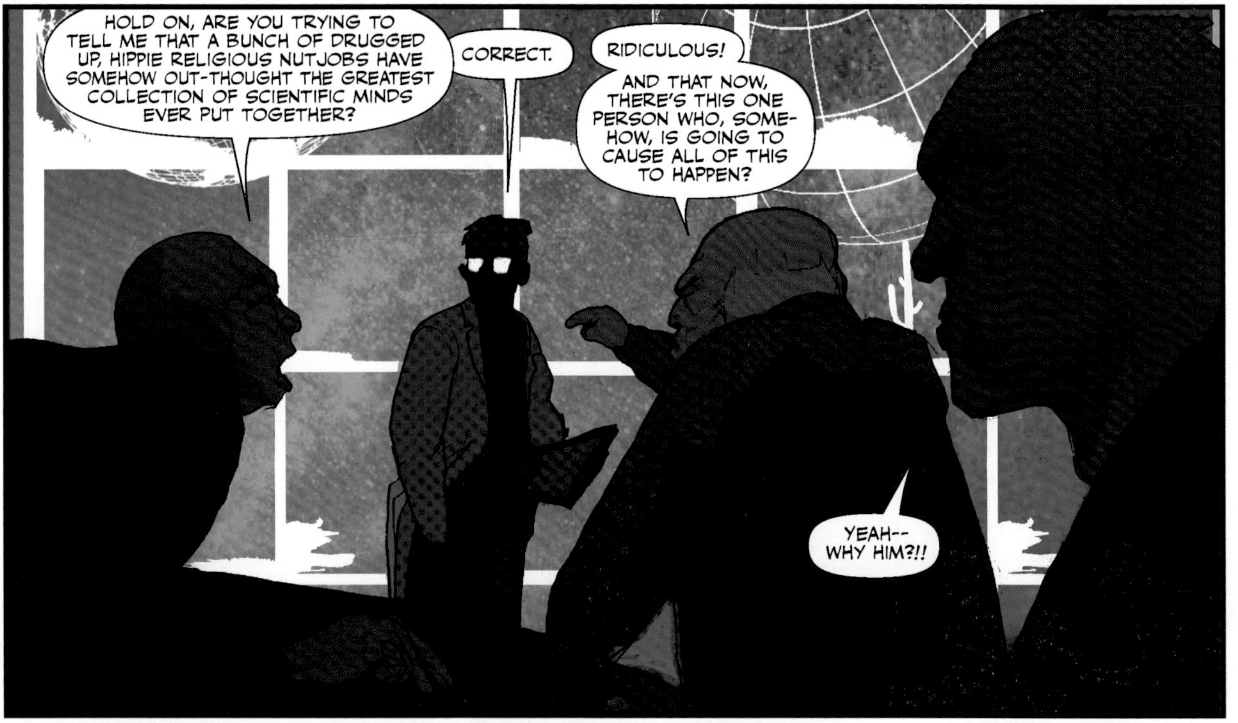
HOLD ON, ARE YOU TRYING TO TELL ME THAT A BUNCH OF DRUGGED UP, HIPPIE RELIGIOUS NUTJOBS HAVE SOMEHOW OUT-THOUGHT THE GREATEST COLLECTION OF SCIENTIFIC MINDS EVER PUT TOGETHER?
CORRECT.
RIDICULOUS!
AND THAT NOW, THERE'S THIS ONE PERSON WHO, SOMEHOW, IS GOING TO CAUSE ALL OF THIS TO HAPPEN?
YEAH-- WHY HIM?!!

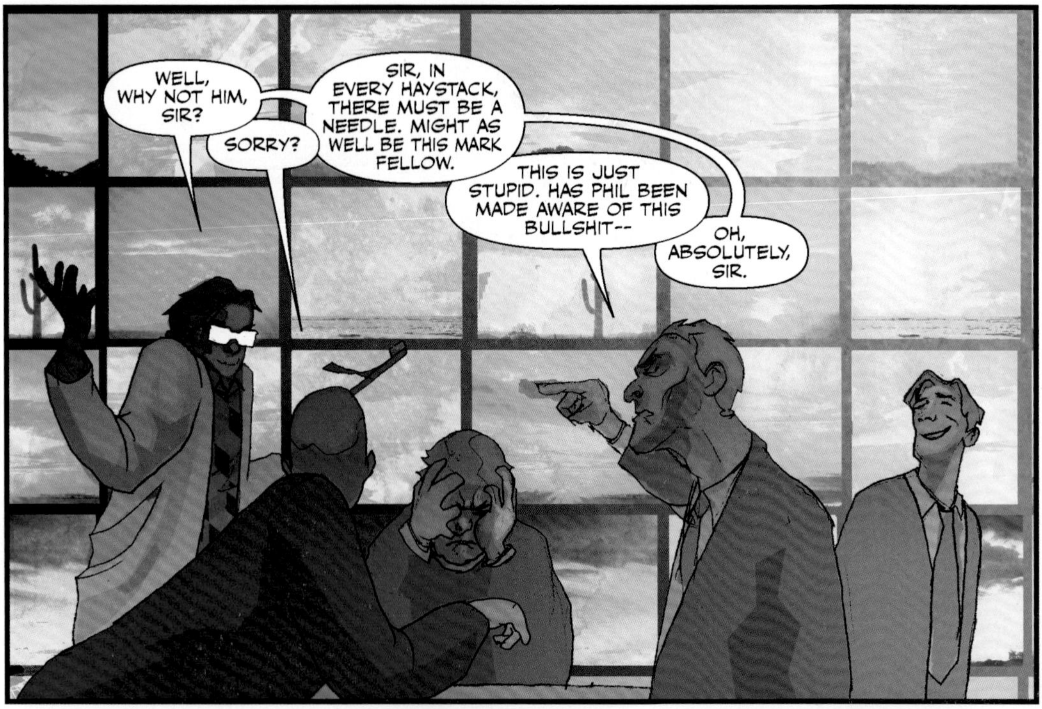
WELL, WHY NOT HIM, SIR?
SORRY?
SIR, IN EVERY HAYSTACK, THERE MUST BE A NEEDLE. MIGHT AS WELL BE THIS MARK FELLOW.
THIS IS JUST STUPID. HAS PHIL BEEN MADE AWARE OF THIS BULLSHIT--
OH, ABSOLUTELY, SIR.

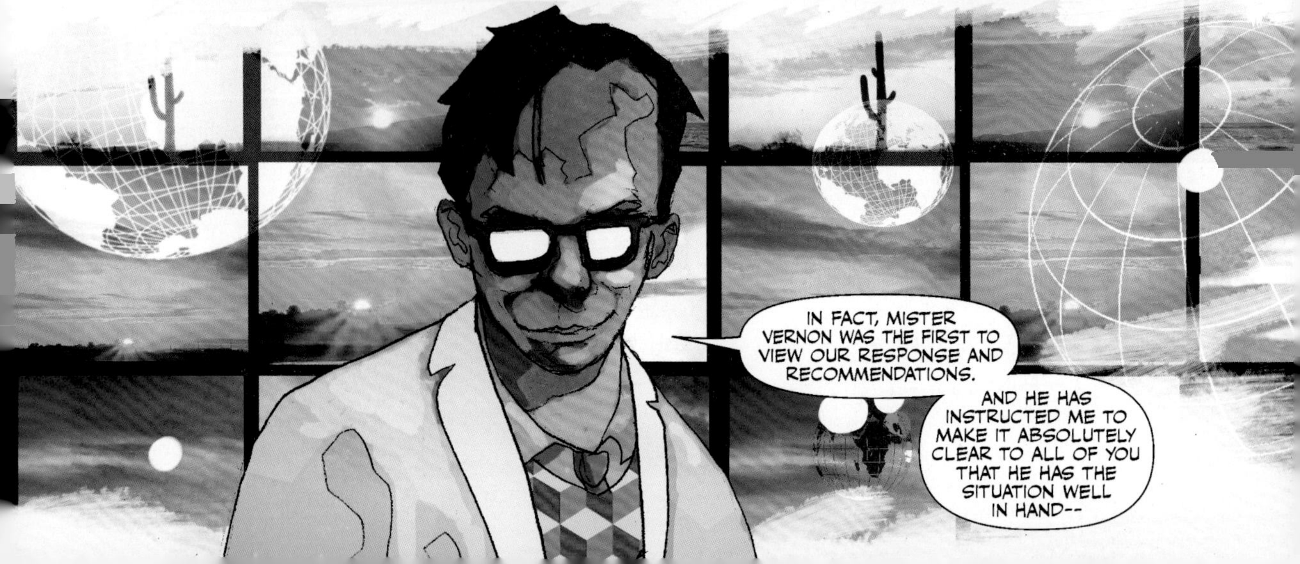
IN FACT, MISTER VERNON WAS THE FIRST TO VIEW OUR RESPONSE AND RECOMMENDATIONS.
AND HE HAS INSTRUCTED ME TO MAKE IT ABSOLUTELY CLEAR TO ALL OF YOU THAT HE HAS THE SITUATION WELL IN HAND--

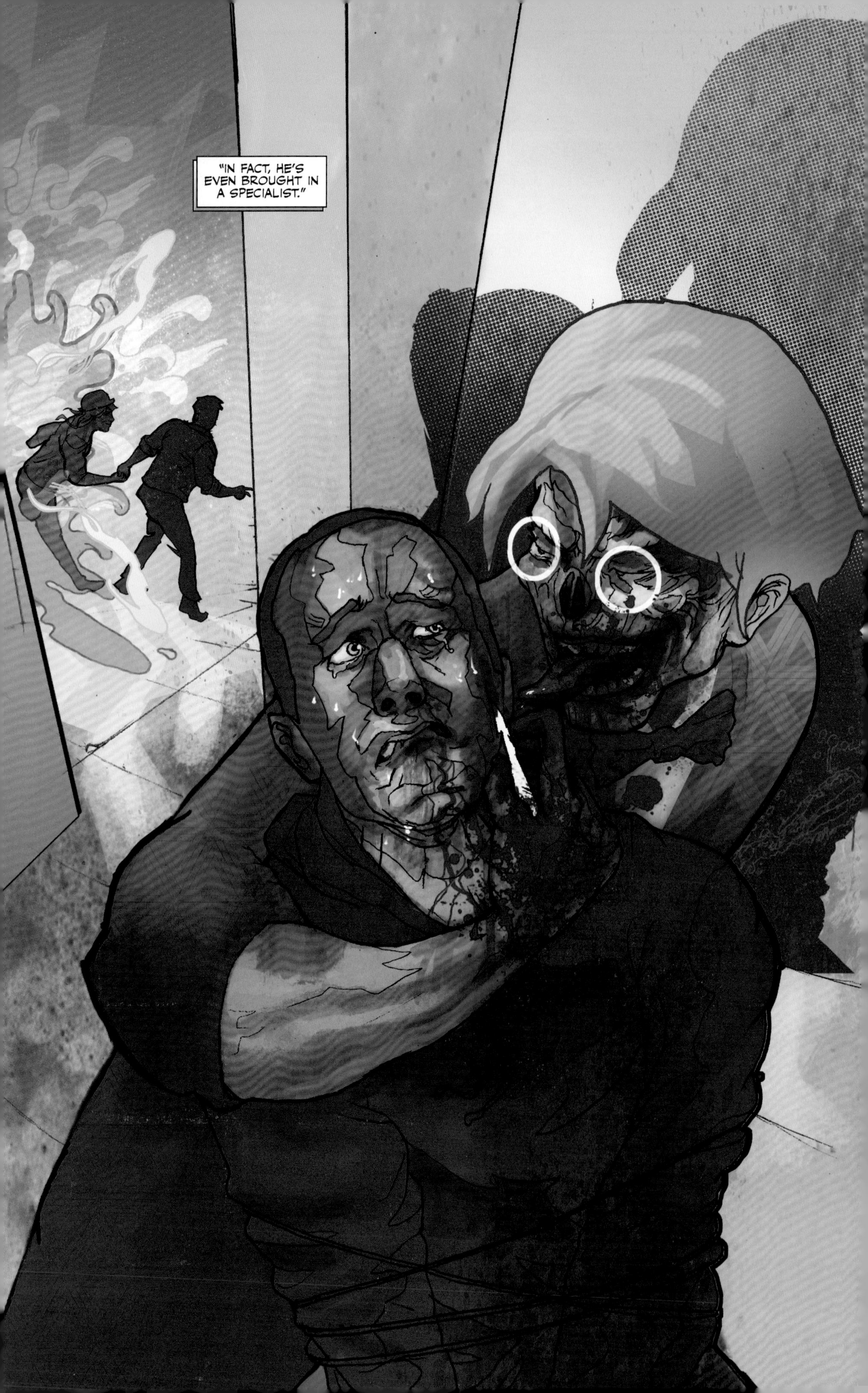
"IN FACT, HE'S EVEN BROUGHT IN A SPECIALIST."

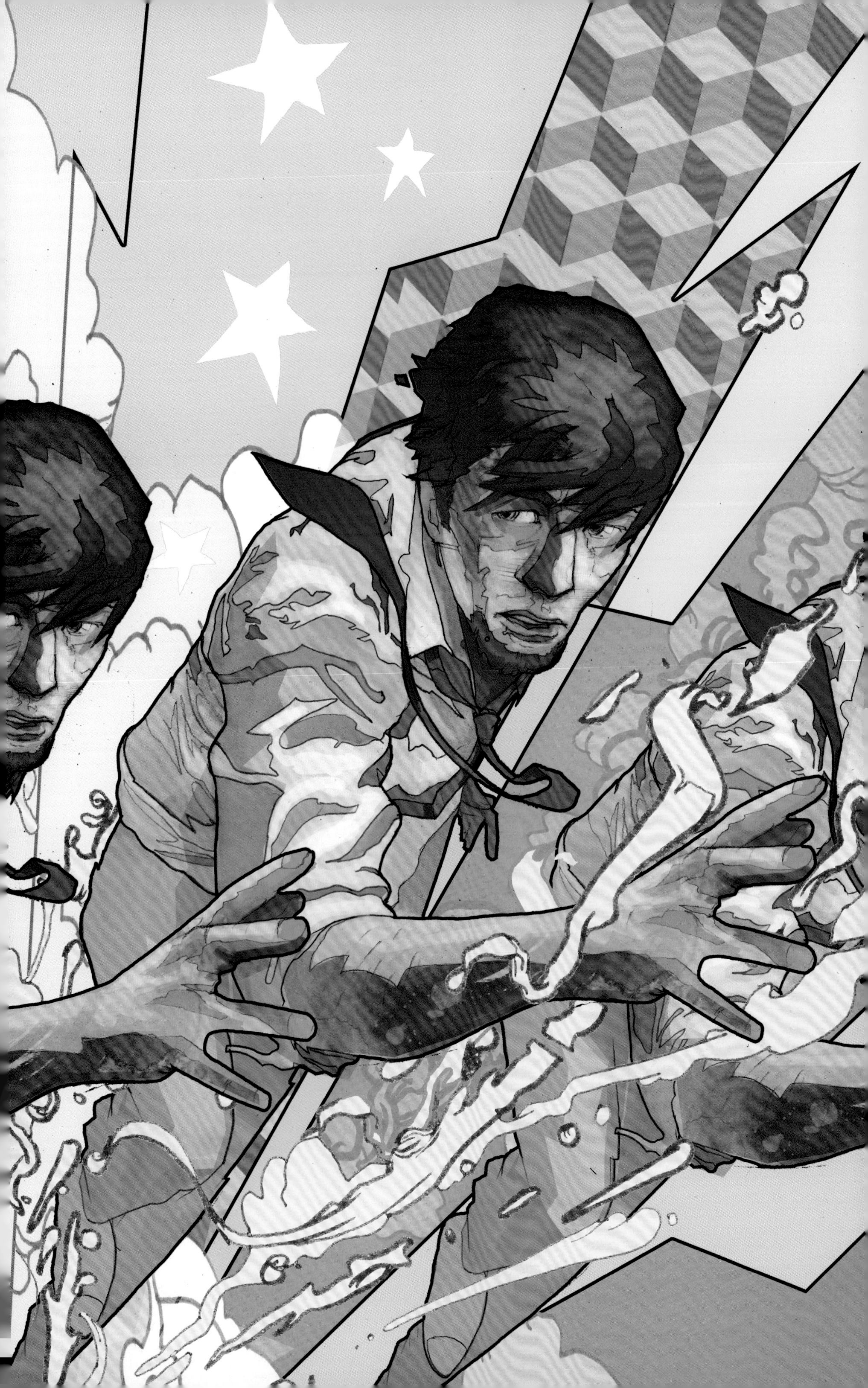

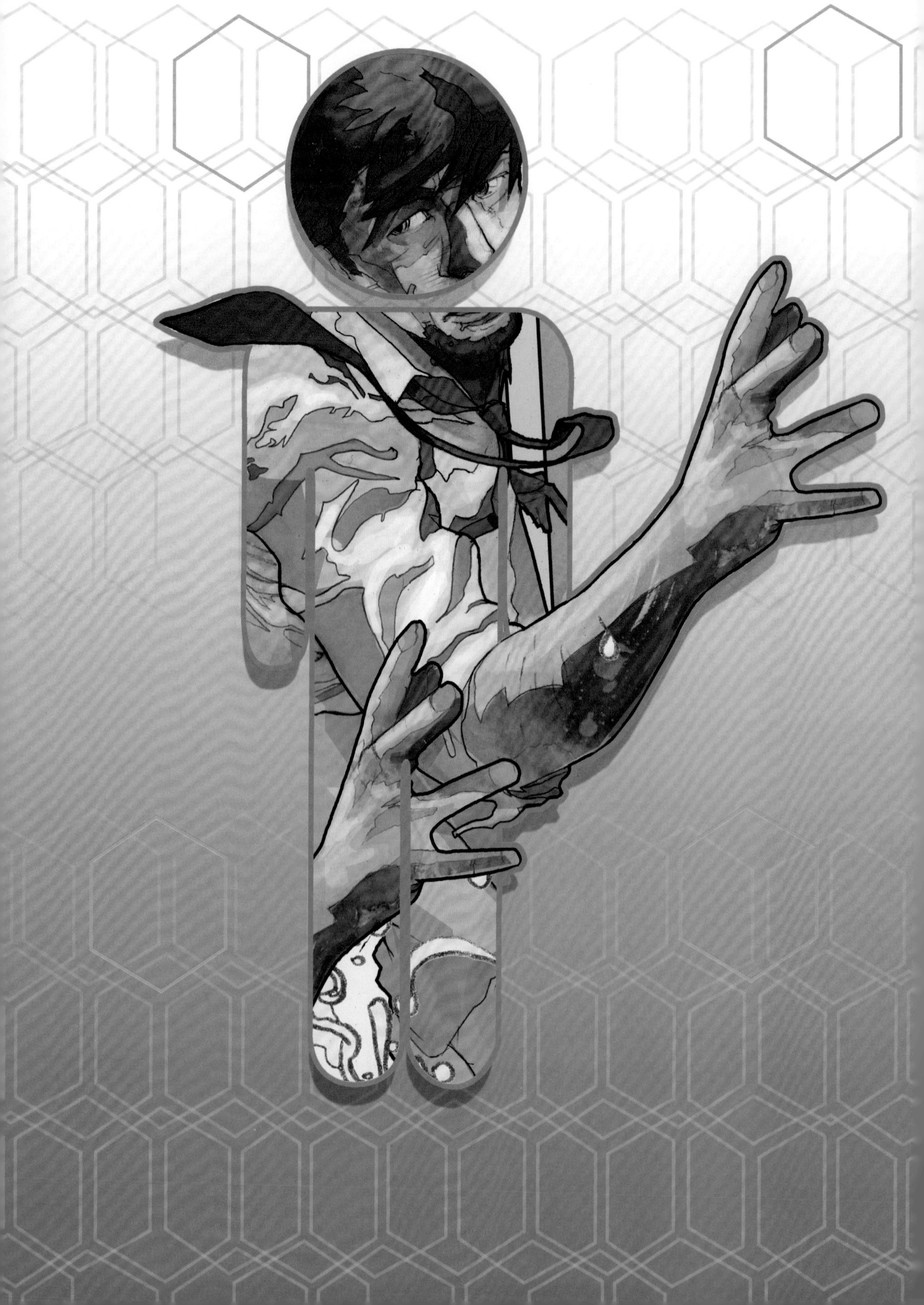

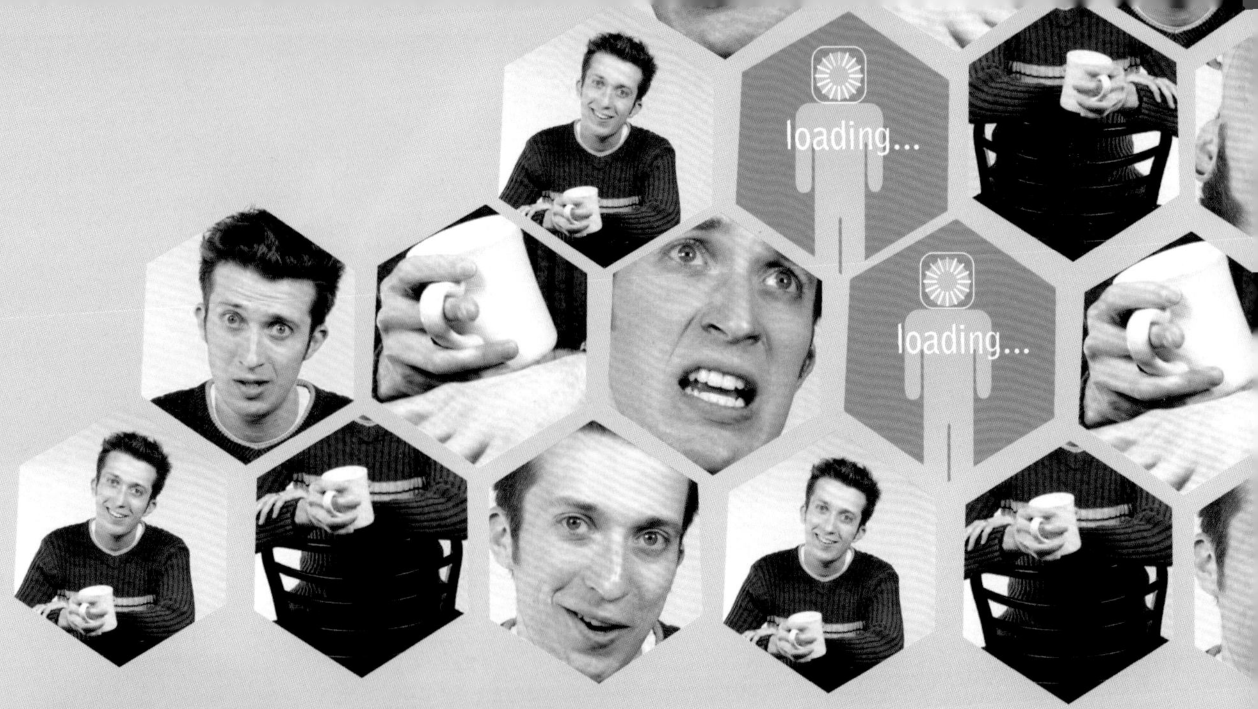
loading...
loading...

THE FOLLOWING IS A PUBLIC SERVICE ANNOUNCEMENT OF THE INFINITE VACATION

loading...

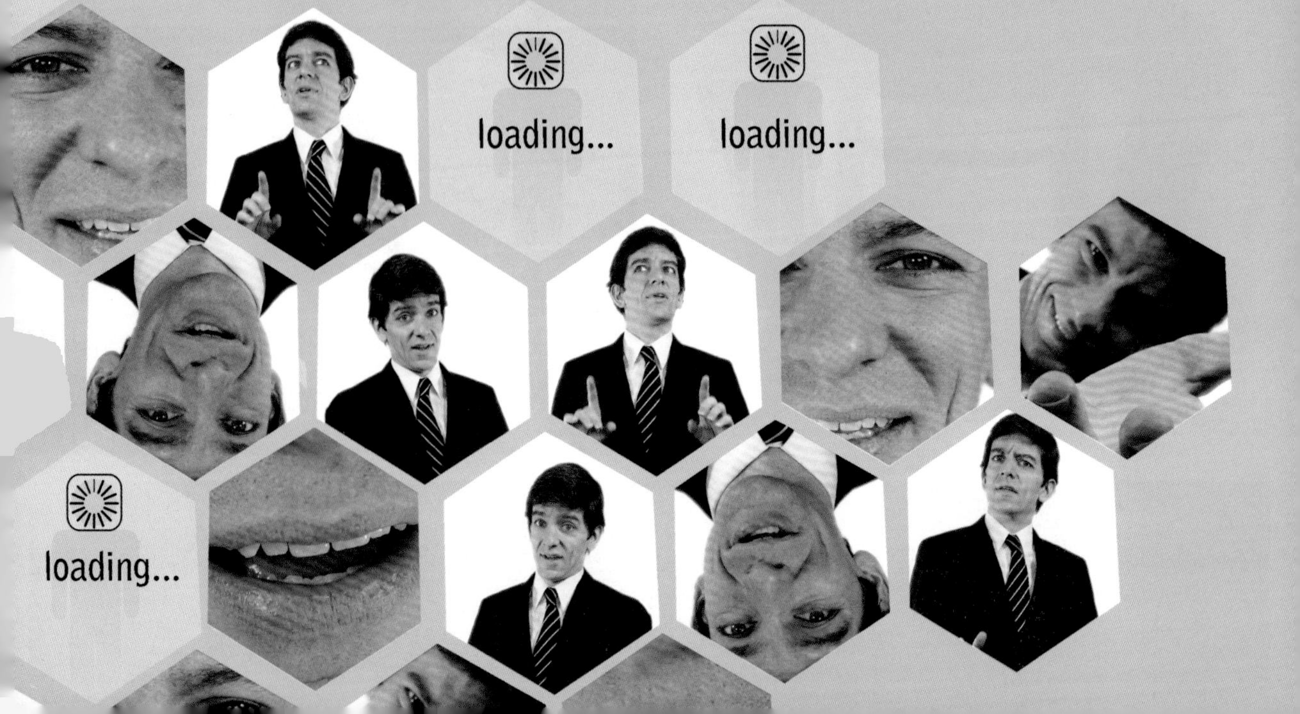
loading...
loading...
loading...

THIS IS A PUBLIC NOTIFICATION OF THE TEMPORAL COMPRESSION OF UNIVERSES DESIGNATED ZONE 10854A960SV29.

AS REQUIRED BY THE SAFER UNIVERSES ACT, PRIVATE MULTIVERSAL TRAVEL ENTITIES ARE EMPOWERED TO COMPRESS--OR BOX, AS IT IS COMMONLY KNOWN-- UNIVERSES DEEMED A THREAT TO OTHERS.

IN THIS PARTICULAR ZONE, HUMAN BEINGS HAVE TAKEN TO CANNIBALISM AS THE PRIMARY SOURCE OF SUSTENANCE, AND RECENTLY, MANY INHABITANTS HAVE TRAVELED INTO OTHER ZONES TO STALK NEW PREY.

AFTER SEVERAL ATTEMPTS TO END THIS ACTIVITY, THE DECISION TO PURSUE BOXING WAS REACHED BY THE PUBLIC-PRIVATE MANY WORLDS COMMISSION'S EMERGING THREATS TASK FORCE.

CESSATION OF ALL ACTIVE LIFE ENGAGEMENT IN THIS ZONE IS EXPECTED WITHIN FOUR HOURS.

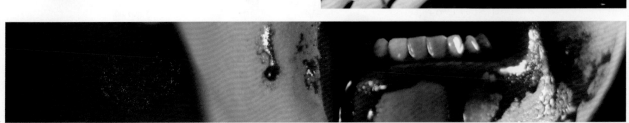

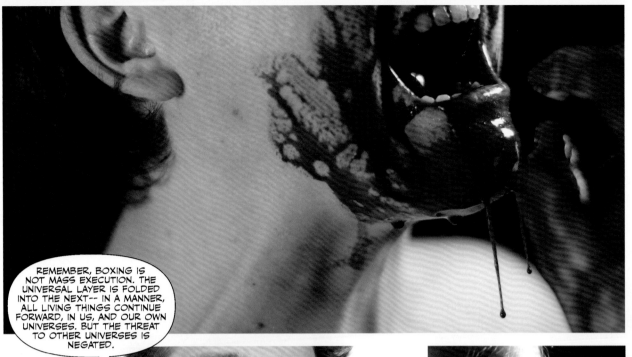

REMEMBER, BOXING IS NOT MASS EXECUTION. THE UNIVERSAL LAYER IS FOLDED INTO THE NEXT-- IN A MANNER, ALL LIVING THINGS CONTINUE FORWARD, IN US, AND OUR OWN UNIVERSES. BUT THE THREAT TO OTHER UNIVERSES IS NEGATED.

IF BOXING WERE NOT UNDERTAKEN, THE UNFORTUNATE REALITY IS THAT AGGRESSIVE, PREDATORY UNIVERSES WOULD CONSISTENTLY ATTACK AND WAGE WAR ON THE MAJORITY OF PEACEFUL, BENIGN SPHERES OF EXISTENCE.

WHILE INFINITY MEANS BEING PRESENTED WITH A WIDER VARIETY OF ACCEPTABLE MORES AND WAYS OF LIFE THAN EVER BEFORE DREAMED POSSIBLE, WE MUST ALL BE FREE TO CHOOSE OUR OWN MANIFOLD PATH.

FREE FROM FEAR. FREE FROM OPPRESSION. TO PROTECT THIS, WE REMAIN COMMITTED TO OUR MULTIVERSAL DEFENSE.

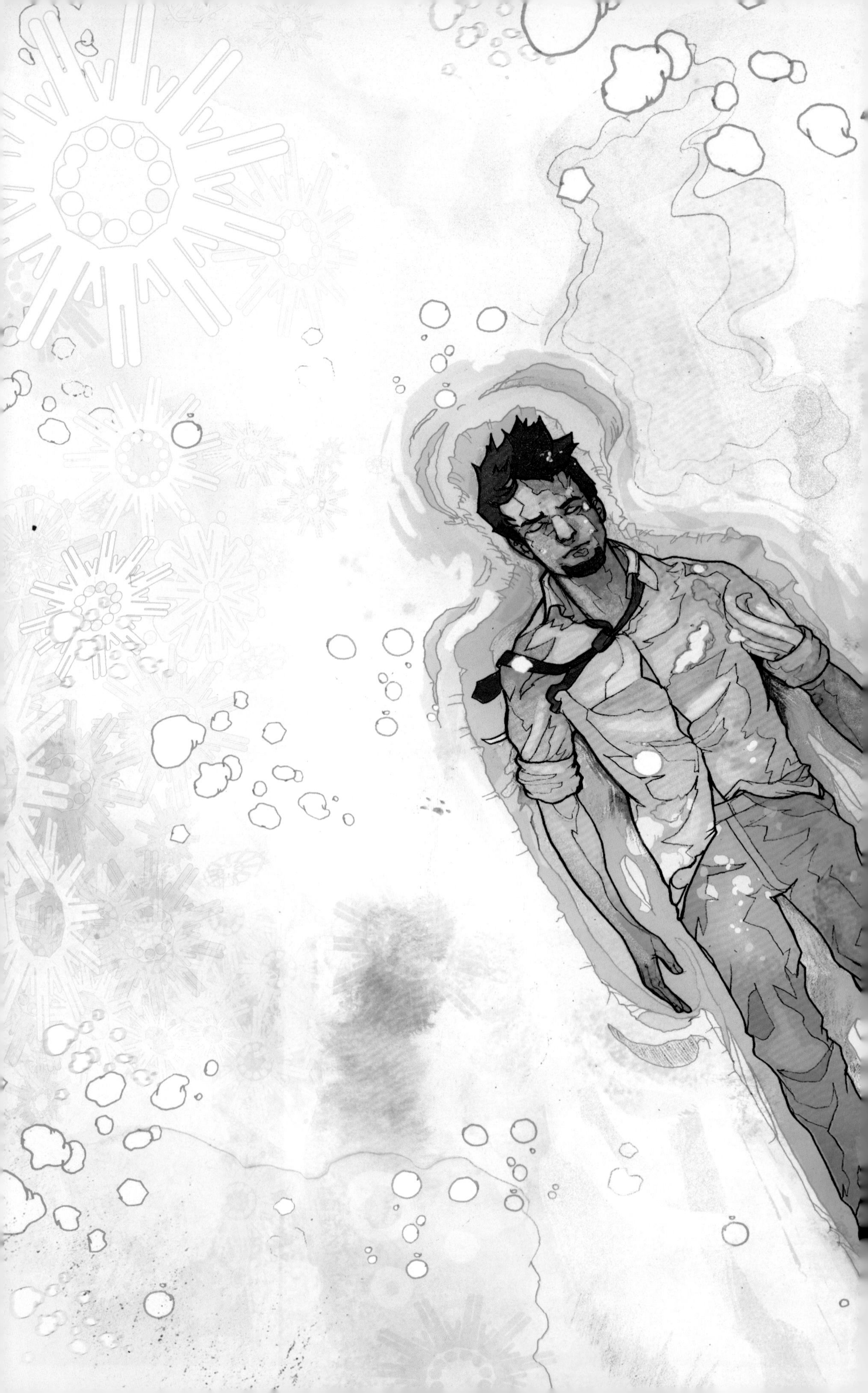

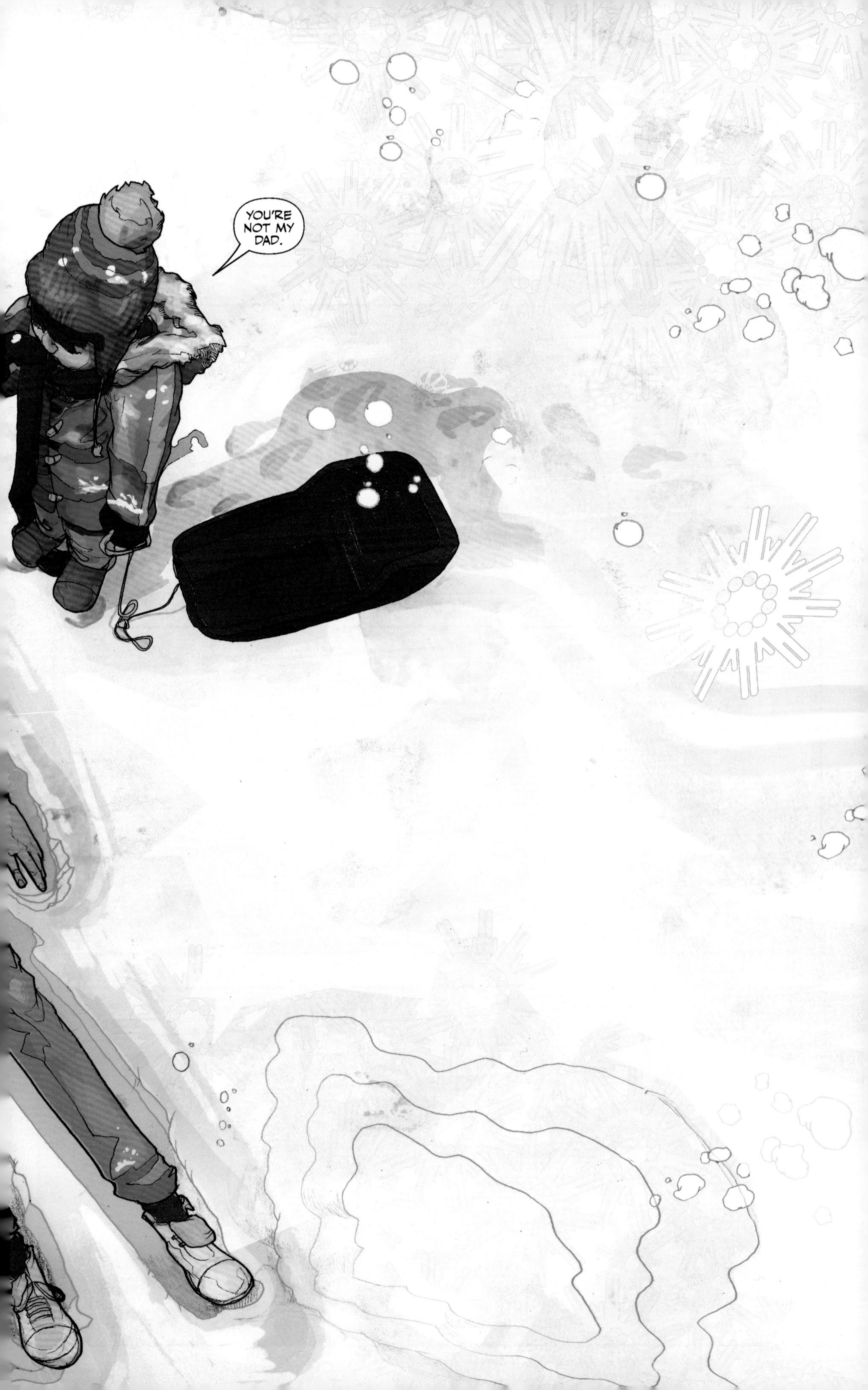
YOU'RE NOT MY DAD.

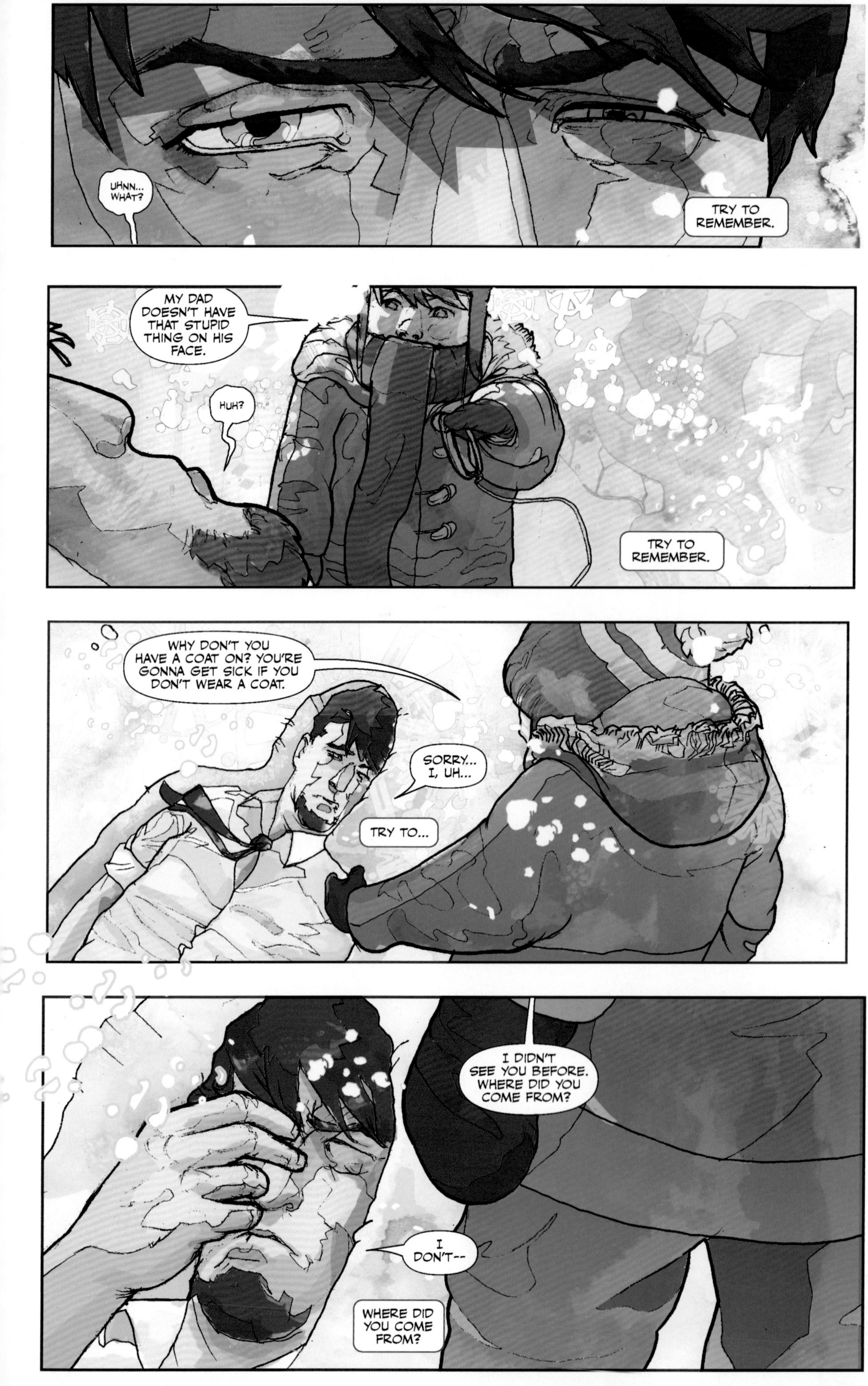
UHNN... WHAT?
TRY TO REMEMBER.
MY DAD DOESN'T HAVE THAT STUPID THING ON HIS FACE.
HUH?
TRY TO REMEMBER.
WHY DON'T YOU HAVE A COAT ON? YOU'RE GONNA GET SICK IF YOU DON'T WEAR A COAT.
SORRY... I, UH...
TRY TO...
I DIDN'T SEE YOU BEFORE. WHERE DID YOU COME FROM?
I DON'T--
WHERE DID YOU COME FROM?

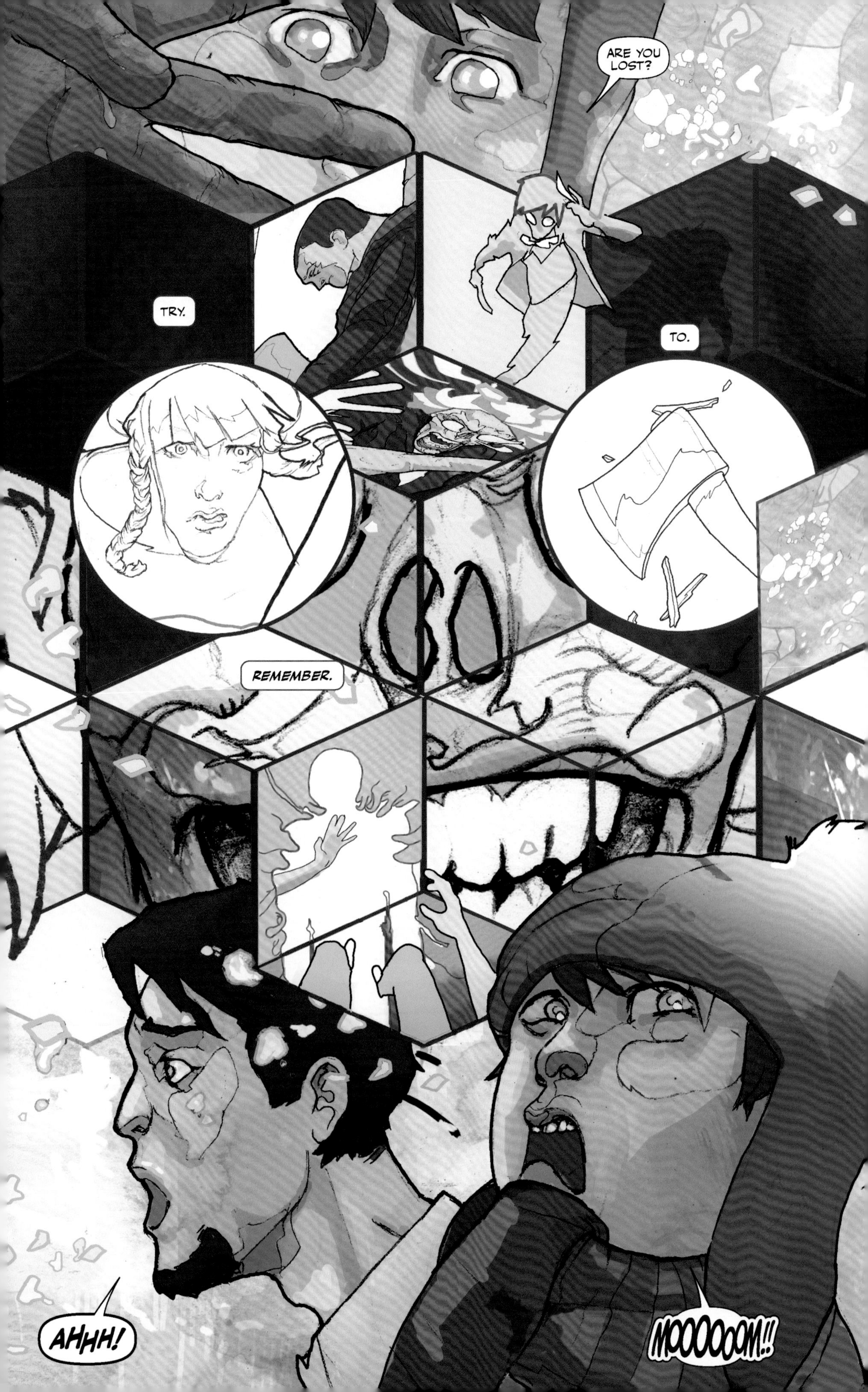
ARE YOU LOST?
TRY.
TO.
REMEMBER.
AHHH!
MOOOOOOM!!

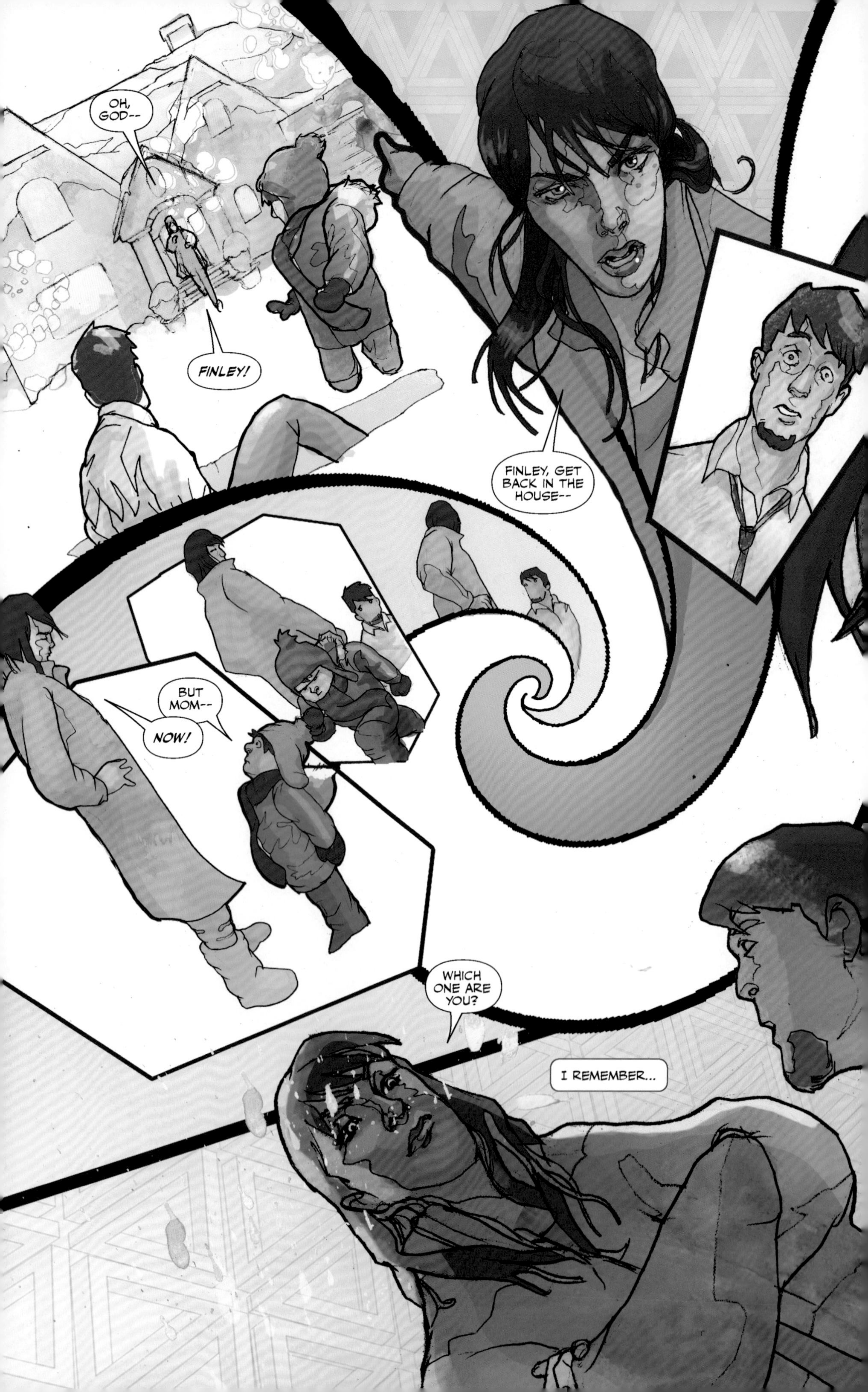
OH, GOD--
FINLEY!
FINLEY, GET BACK IN THE HOUSE--
BUT MOM--
NOW!
WHICH ONE ARE YOU?
I REMEMBER...

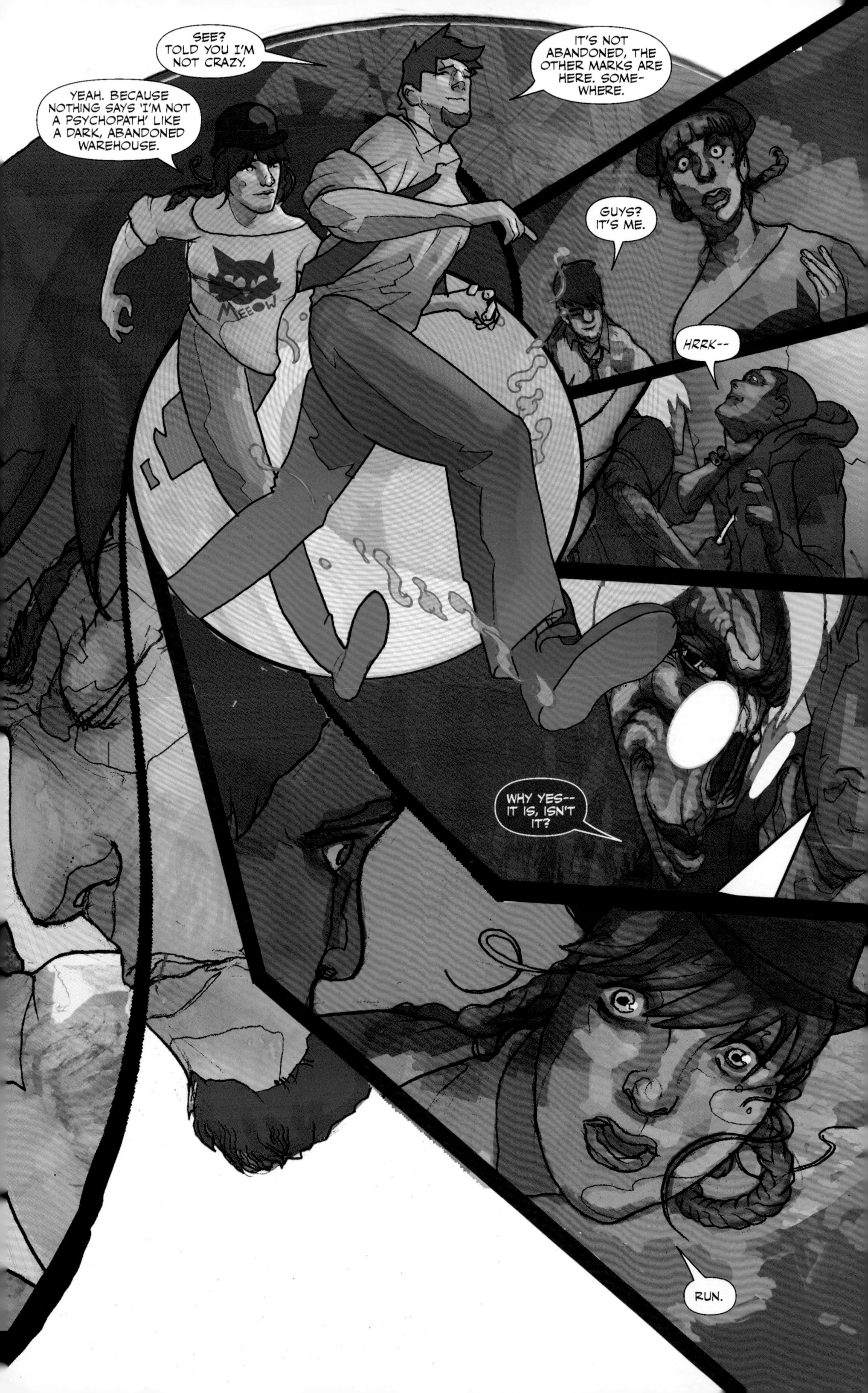
SEE? TOLD YOU I'M NOT CRAZY.
YEAH. BECAUSE NOTHING SAYS 'I'M NOT A PSYCHOPATH' LIKE A DARK, ABANDONED WAREHOUSE.
IT'S NOT ABANDONED, THE OTHER MARKS ARE HERE. SOME-WHERE.
MEEOW
GUYS? IT'S ME.
HRRK--
WHY YES-- IT IS, ISN'T IT?
RUN.

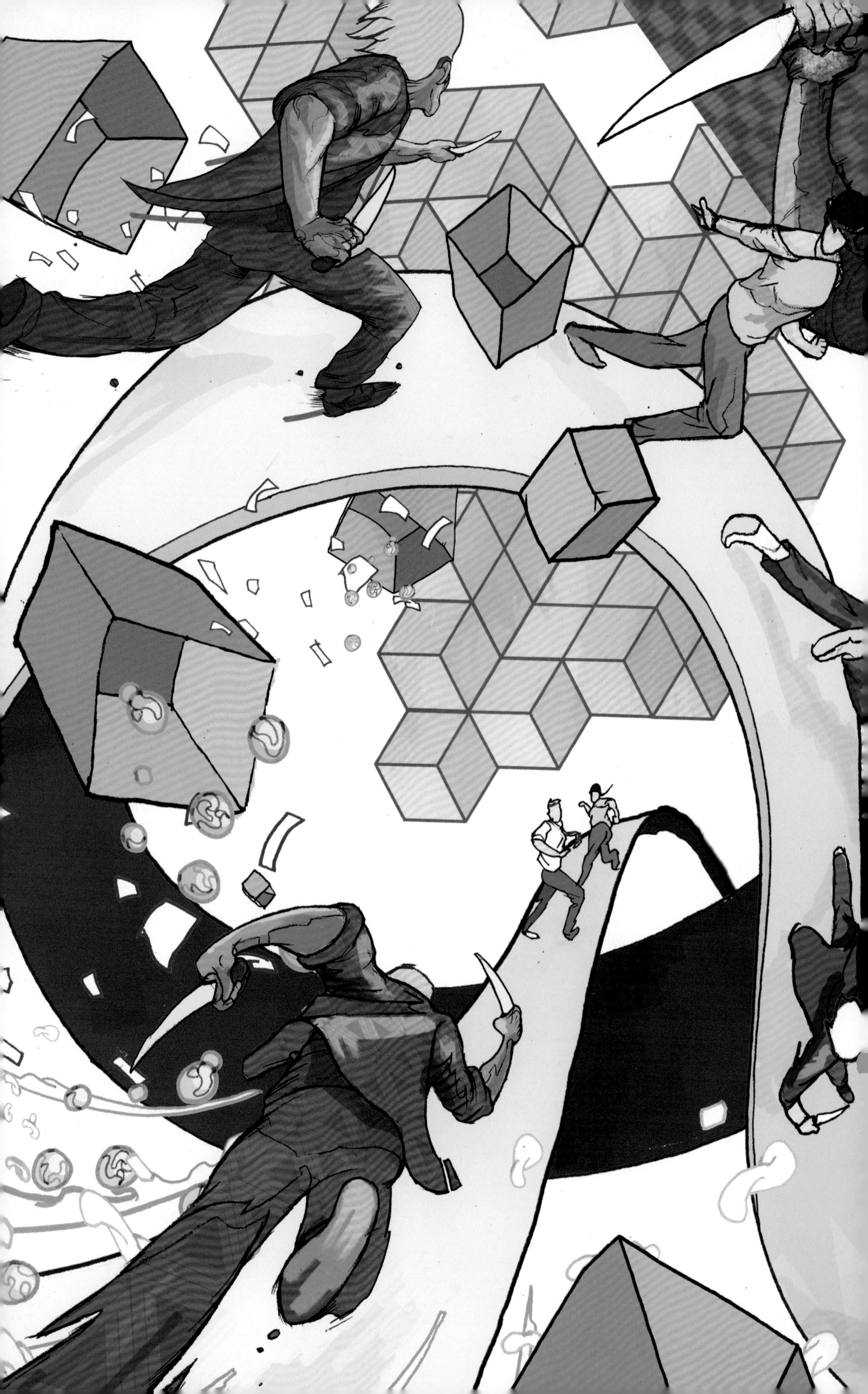

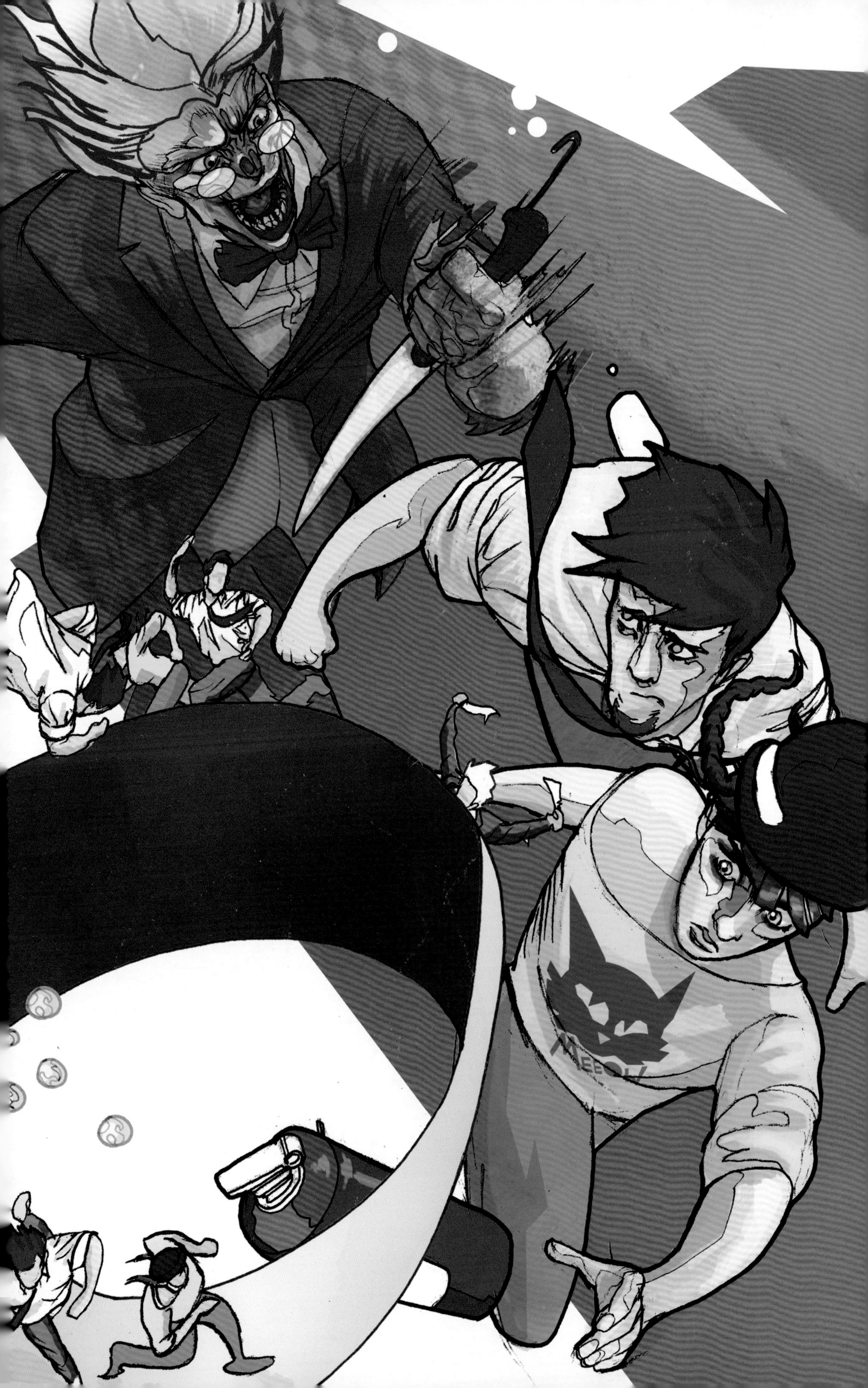
MEEOW

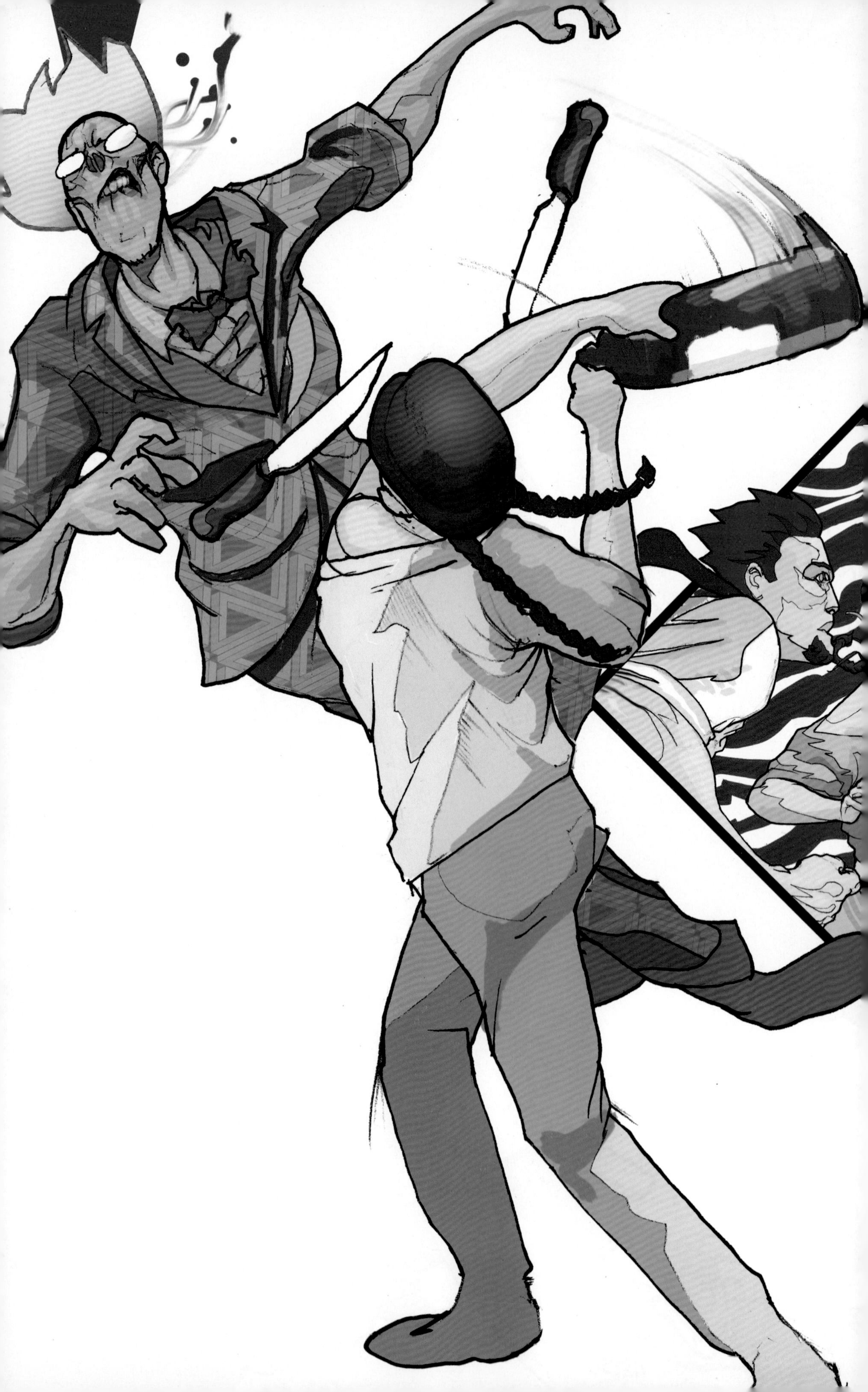

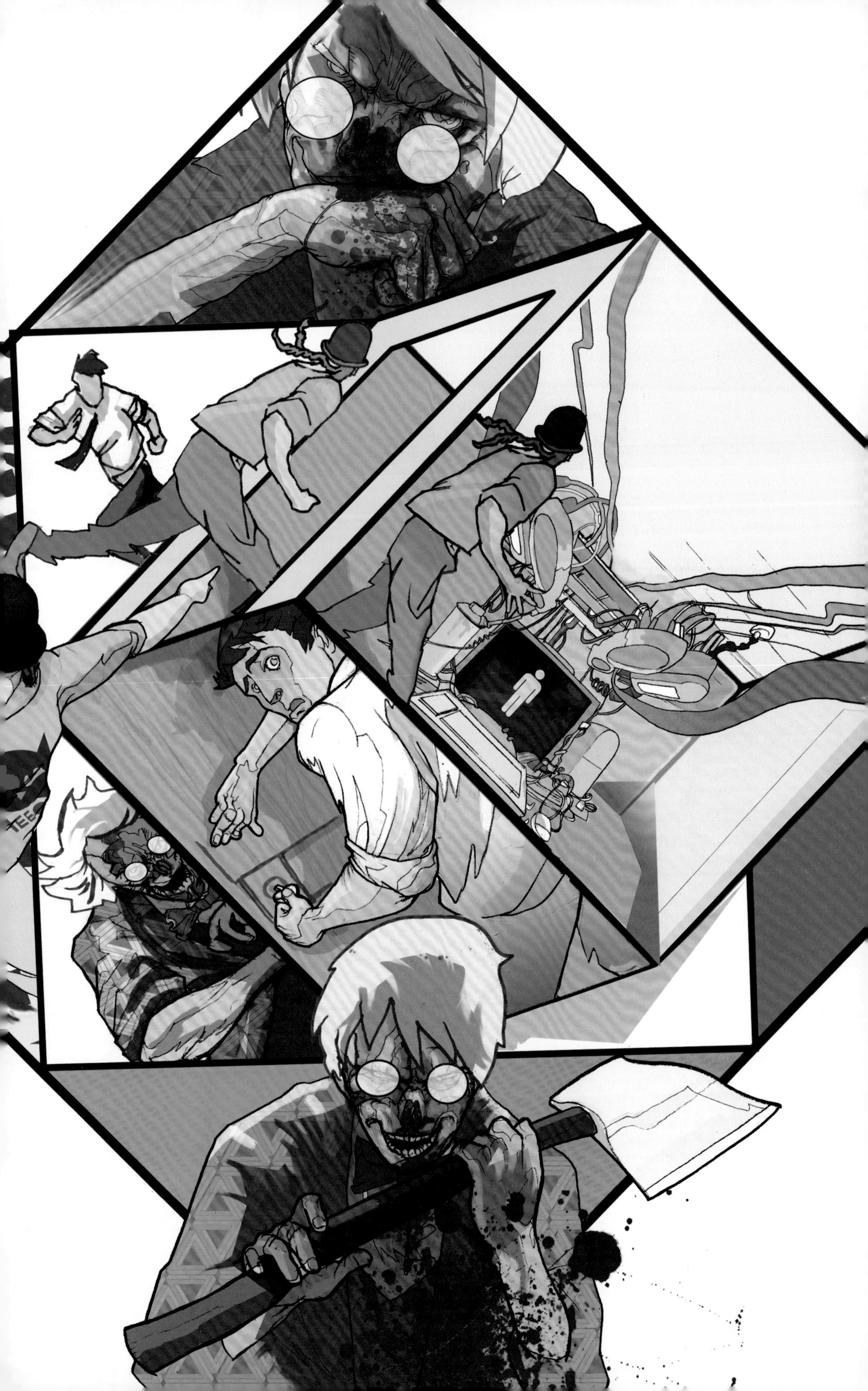

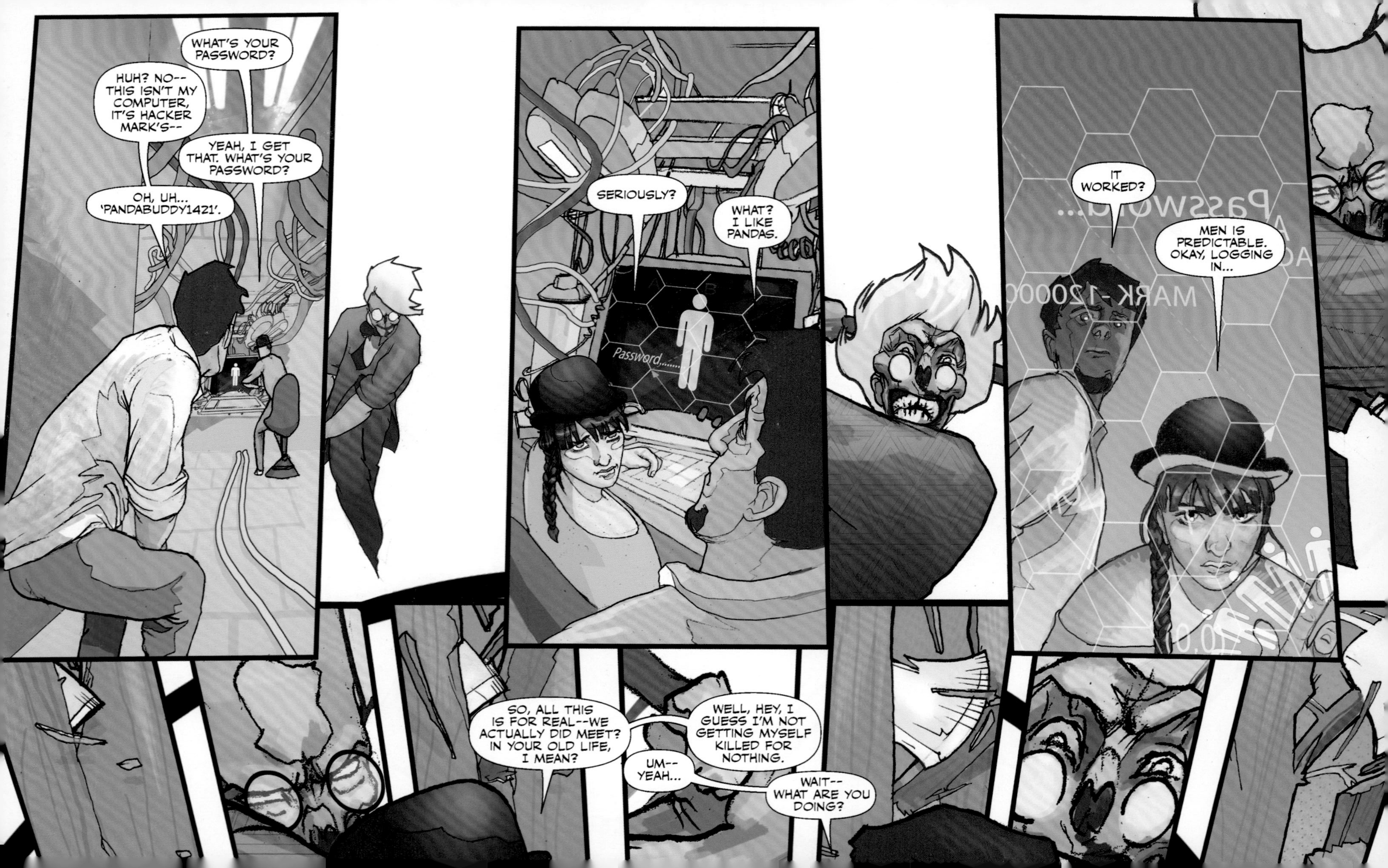
WHAT'S YOUR PASSWORD?
HUH? NO-- THIS ISN'T MY COMPUTER, IT'S HACKER MARK'S--
YEAH, I GET THAT. WHAT'S YOUR PASSWORD?
OH, UH... 'PANDABUDDY1421'.
Password........
SERIOUSLY?
WHAT? I LIKE PANDAS.
IT WORKED?
MEN IS PREDICTABLE. OKAY, LOGGING IN...
MARK-120000
SO, ALL THIS IS FOR REAL--WE ACTUALLY DID MEET? IN YOUR OLD LIFE, I MEAN?
UM-- YEAH...
WELL, HEY, I GUESS I'M NOT GETTING MYSELF KILLED FOR NOTHING.
WAIT-- WHAT ARE YOU DOING?

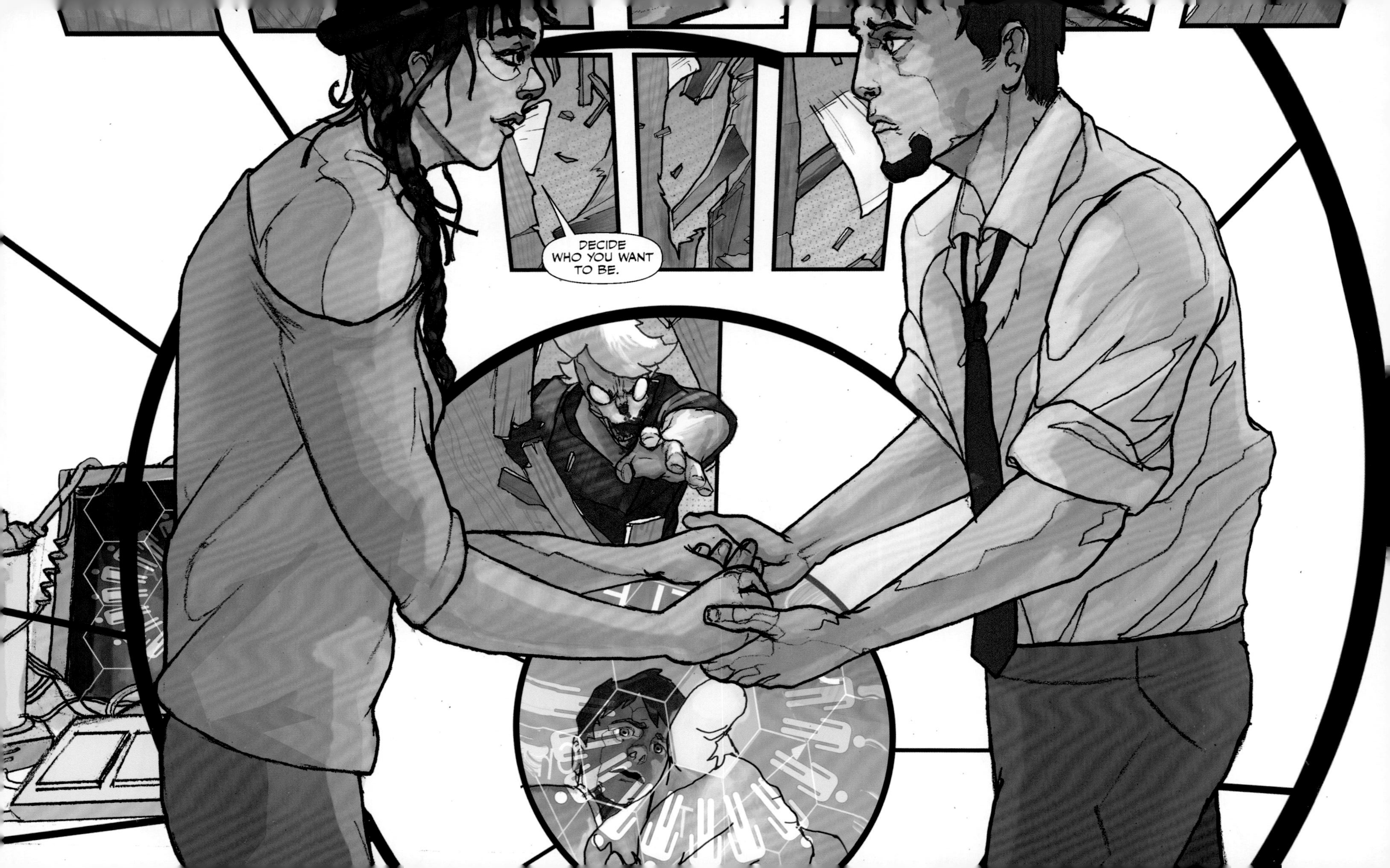
DECIDE WHO YOU WANT TO BE.

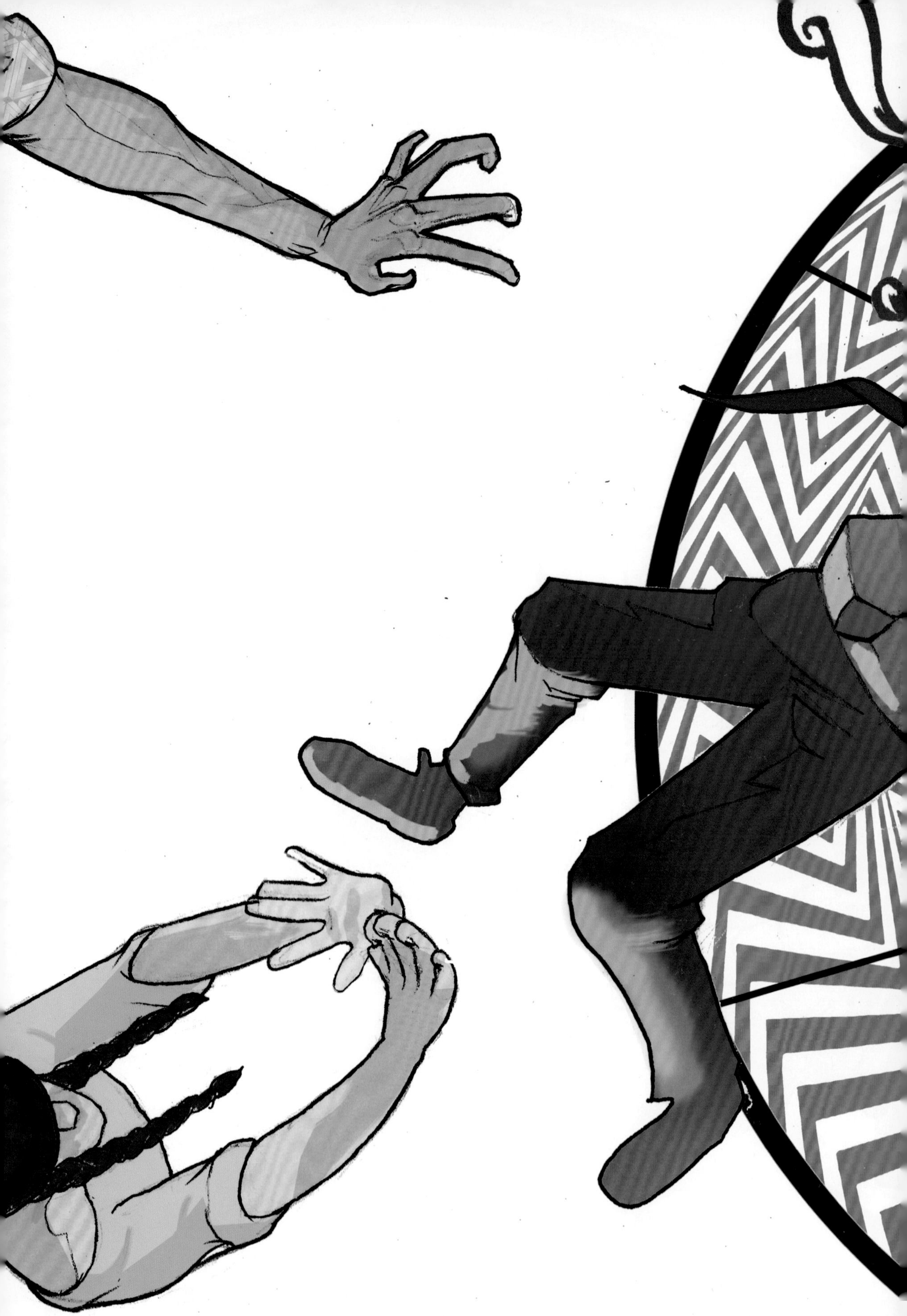

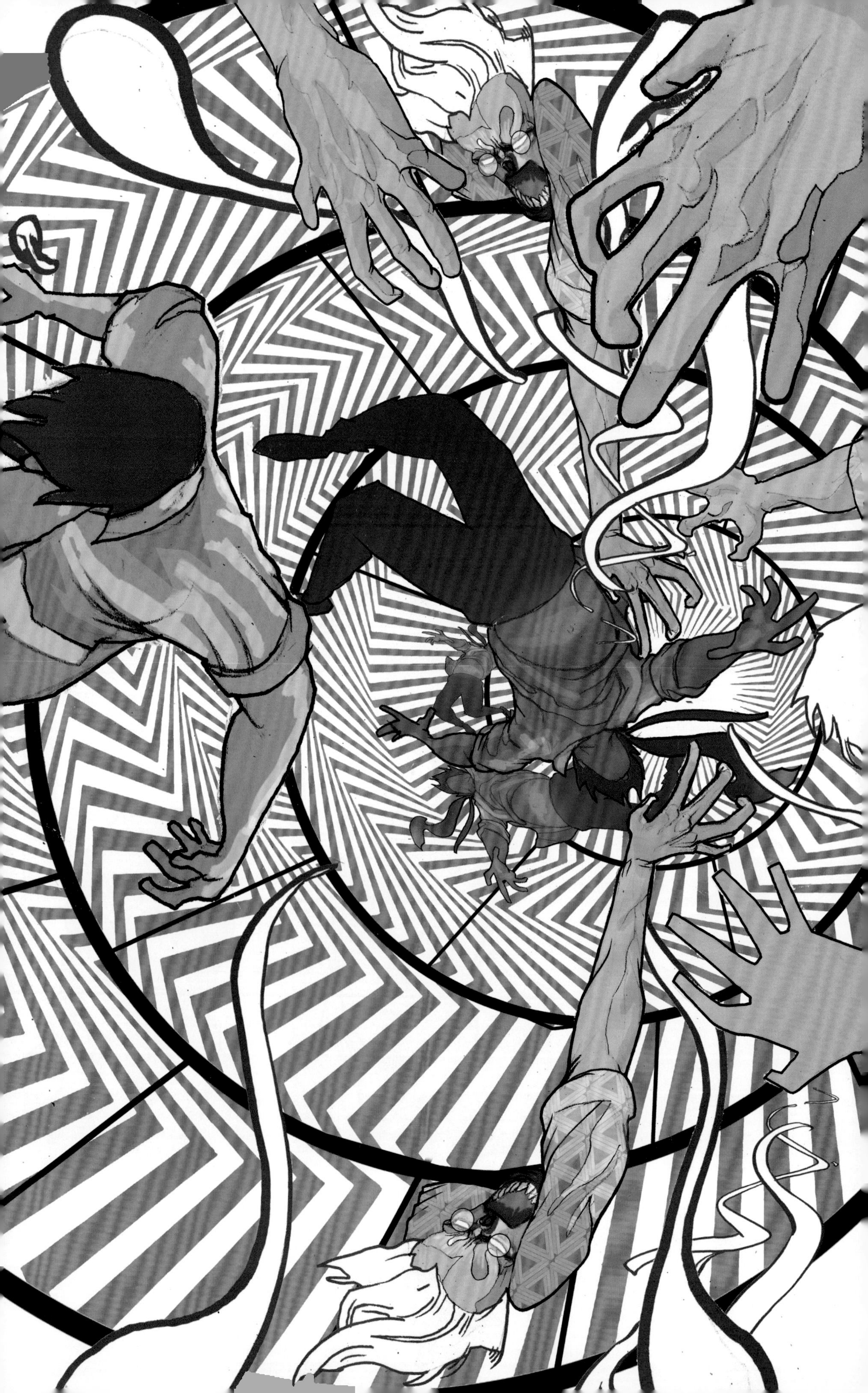

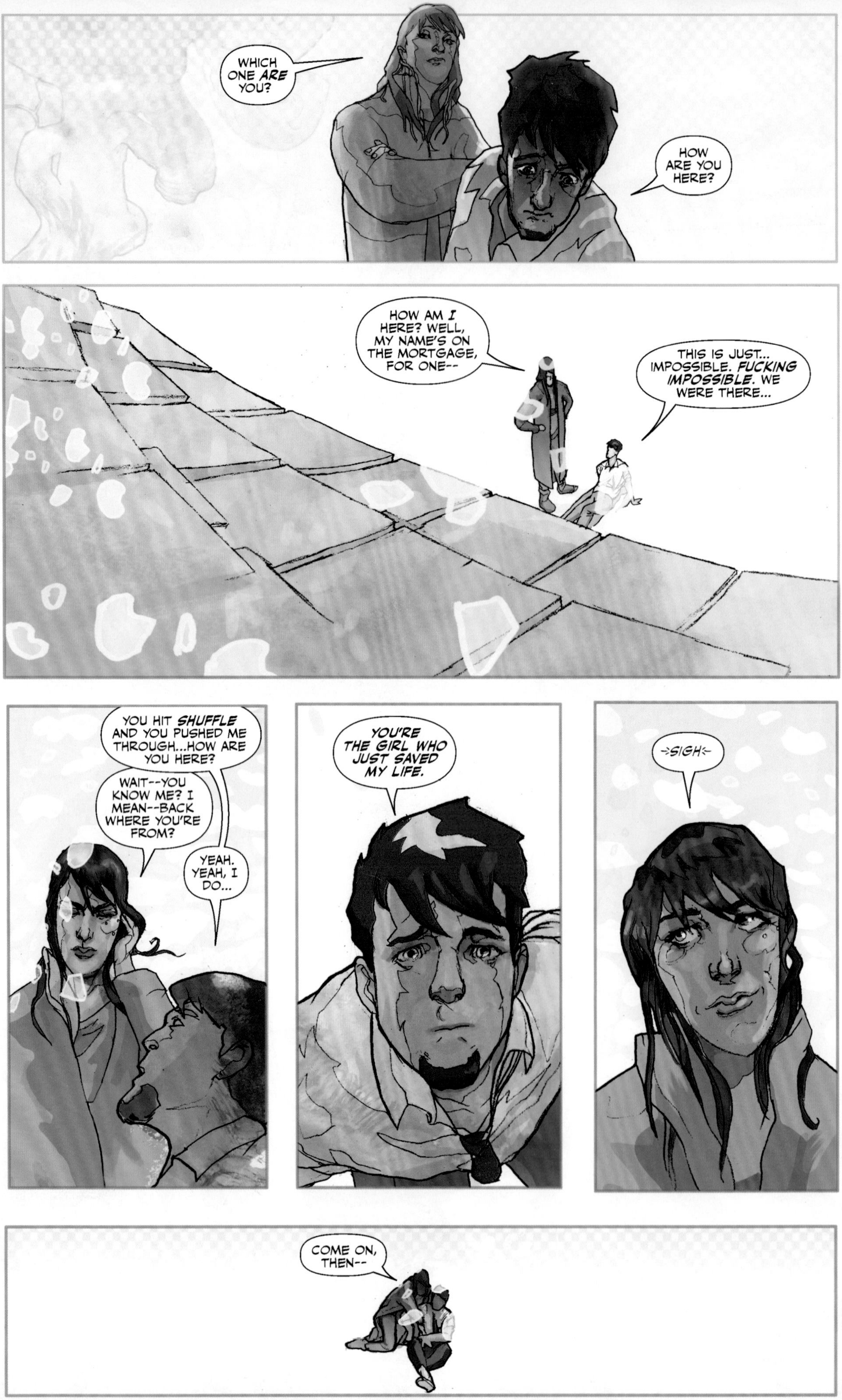
WHICH ONE ARE YOU?
HOW ARE YOU HERE?
HOW AM I HERE? WELL, MY NAME'S ON THE MORTGAGE, FOR ONE--
THIS IS JUST... IMPOSSIBLE. FUCKING IMPOSSIBLE. WE WERE THERE...
YOU HIT SHUFFLE AND YOU PUSHED ME THROUGH...HOW ARE YOU HERE?
WAIT--YOU KNOW ME? I MEAN--BACK WHERE YOU'RE FROM?
YEAH. YEAH, I DO...
YOU'RE THE GIRL WHO JUST SAVED MY LIFE.
-SIGH-
COME ON, THEN--

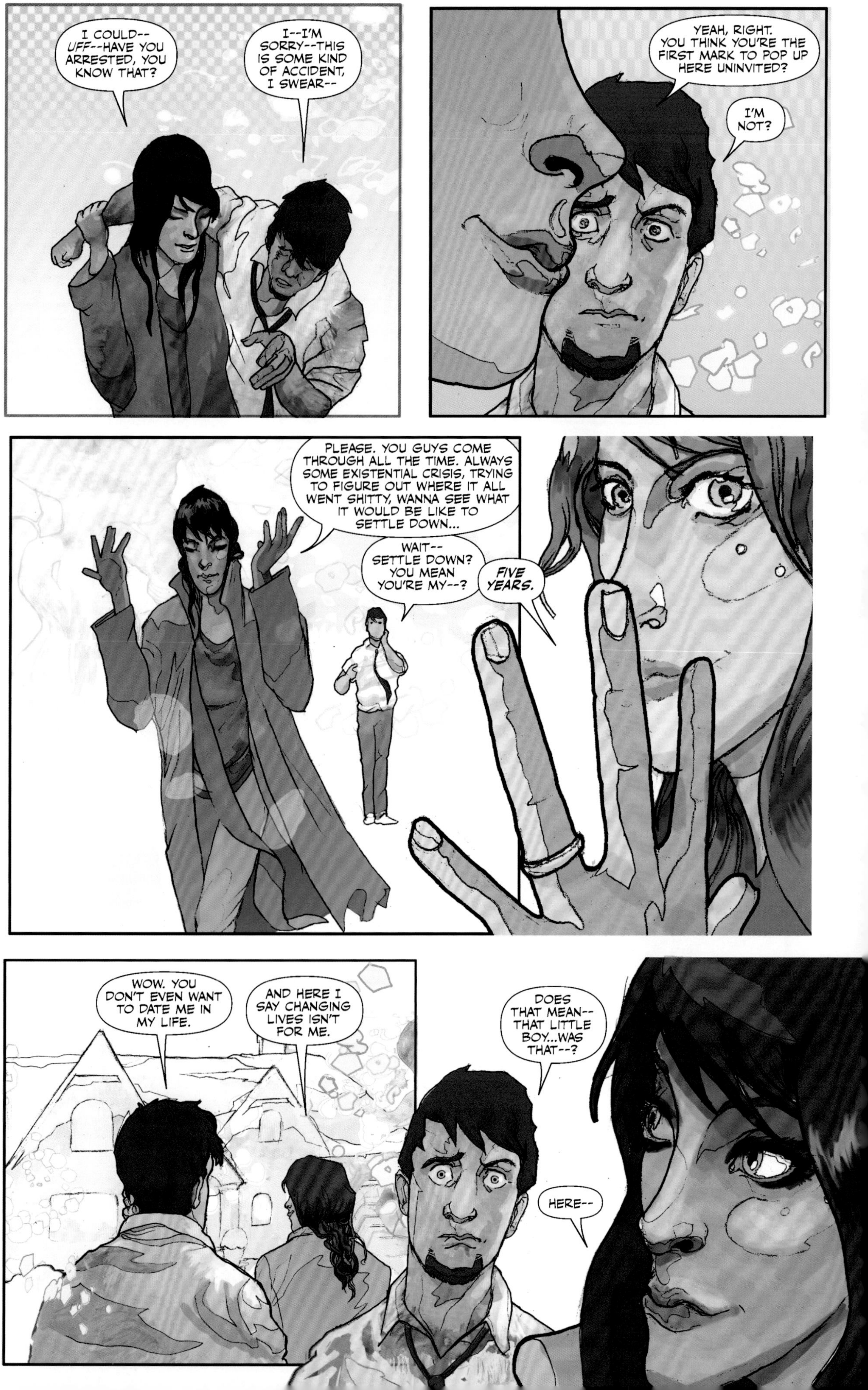

I COULD-- UFF--HAVE YOU ARRESTED, YOU KNOW THAT?
I--I'M SORRY--THIS IS SOME KIND OF ACCIDENT, I SWEAR--
YEAH, RIGHT. YOU THINK YOU'RE THE FIRST MARK TO POP UP HERE UNINVITED?
I'M NOT?
PLEASE. YOU GUYS COME THROUGH ALL THE TIME. ALWAYS SOME EXISTENTIAL CRISIS, TRYING TO FIGURE OUT WHERE IT ALL WENT SHITTY, WANNA SEE WHAT IT WOULD BE LIKE TO SETTLE DOWN...
WAIT-- SETTLE DOWN? YOU MEAN YOU'RE MY--?
FIVE YEARS.
WOW. YOU DON'T EVEN WANT TO DATE ME IN MY LIFE.
AND HERE I SAY CHANGING LIVES ISN'T FOR ME.
DOES THAT MEAN-- THAT LITTLE BOY...WAS THAT--?
HERE--

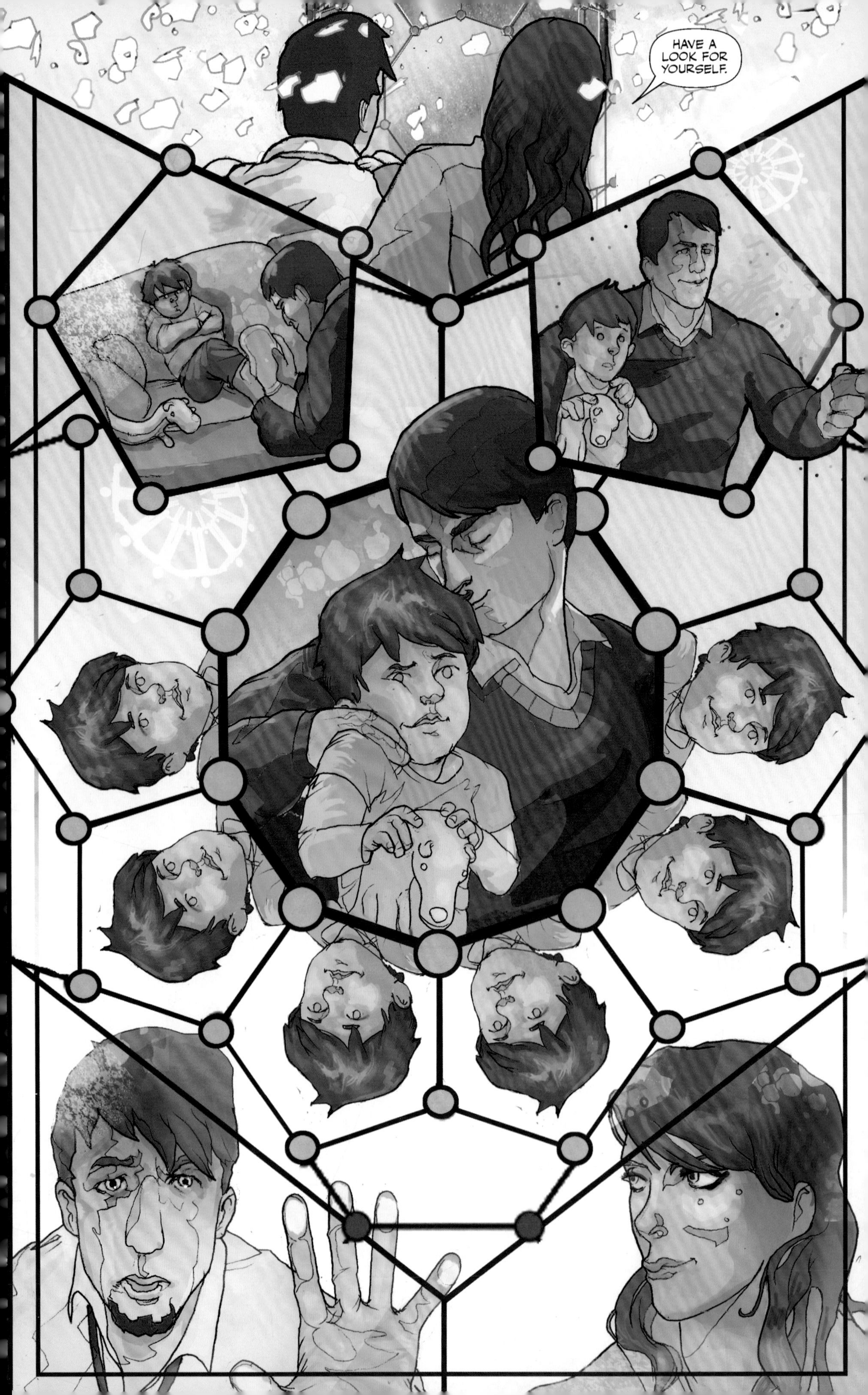
HAVE A LOOK FOR YOURSELF.

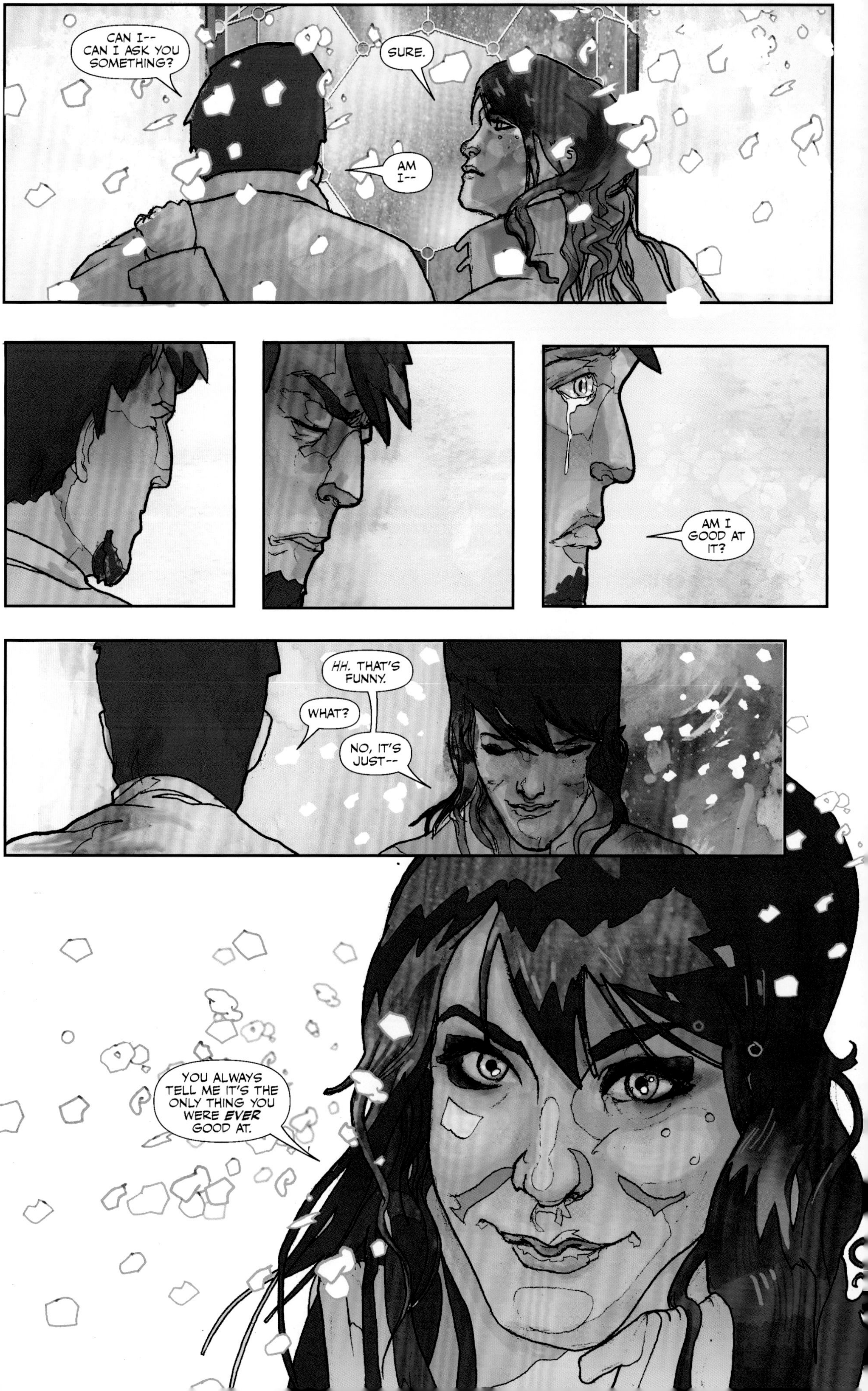
CAN I-- CAN I ASK YOU SOMETHING?
SURE.
AM I--
AM I GOOD AT IT?
HH. THAT'S FUNNY.
WHAT?
NO, IT'S JUST--
YOU ALWAYS TELL ME IT'S THE ONLY THING YOU WERE *EVER* GOOD AT.

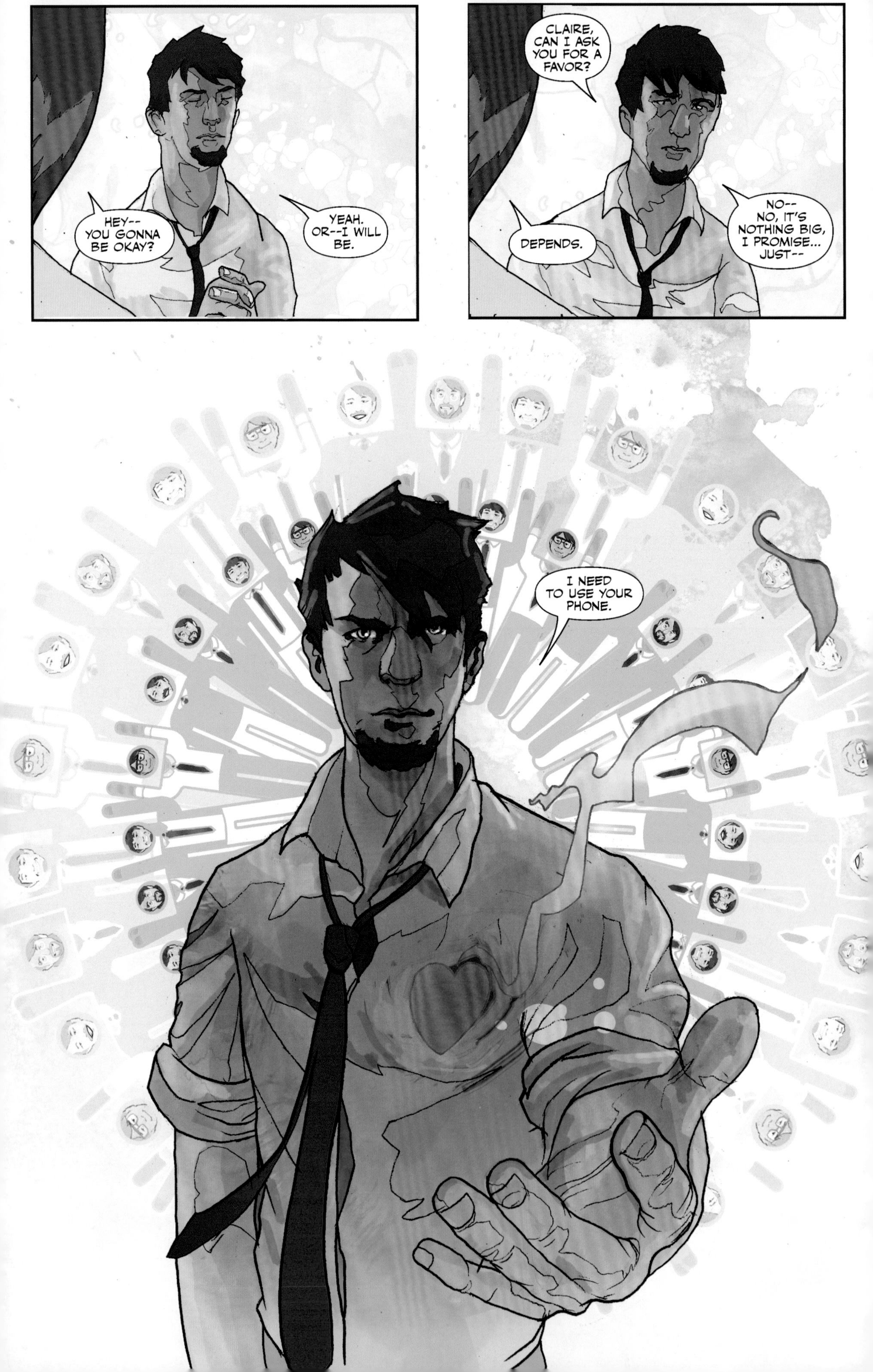
HEY-- YOU GONNA BE OKAY?
YEAH. OR--I WILL BE.
CLAIRE, CAN I ASK YOU FOR A FAVOR?
DEPENDS.
NO-- NO, IT'S NOTHING BIG, I PROMISE... JUST--
I NEED TO USE YOUR PHONE.

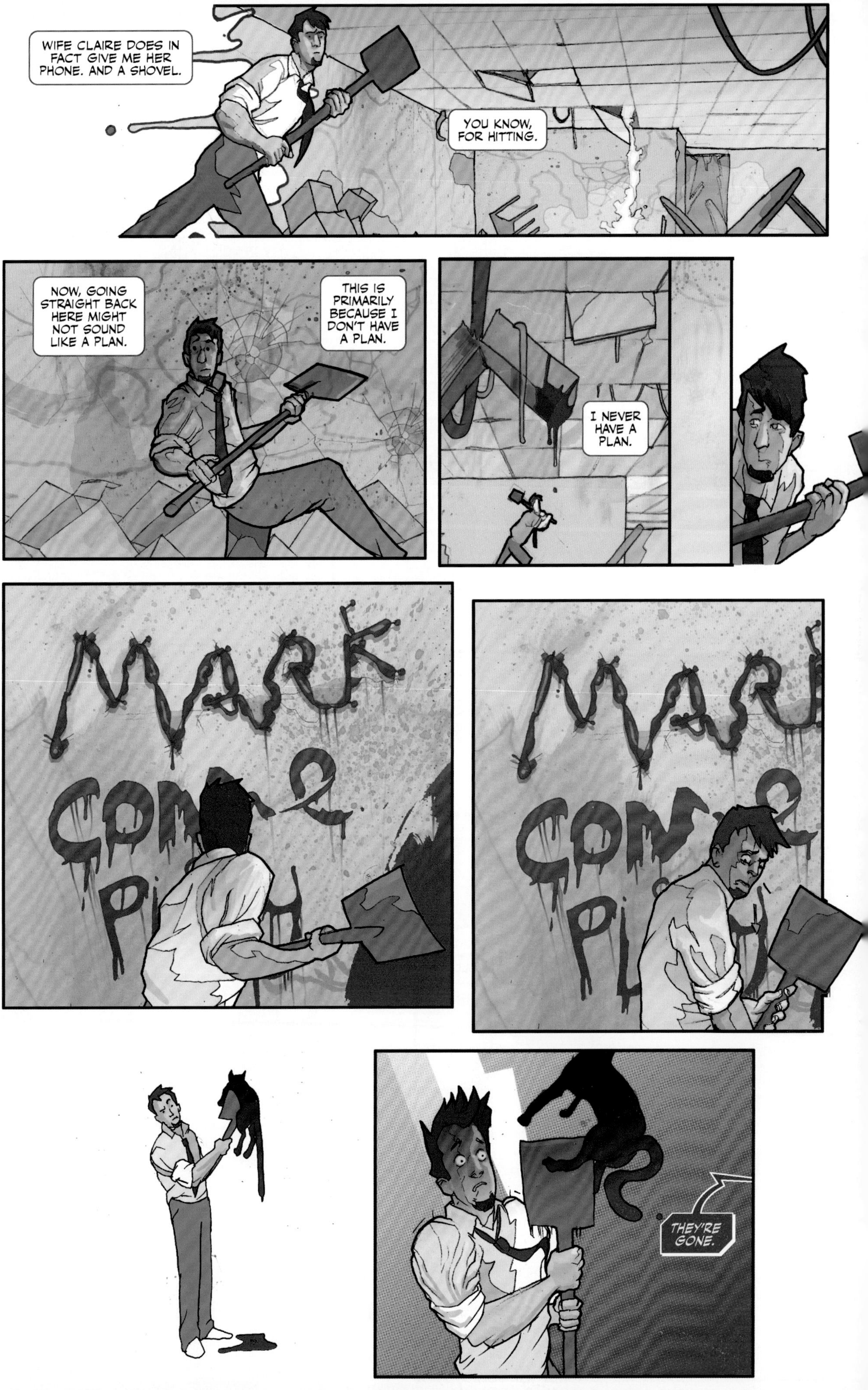
WIFE CLAIRE DOES IN FACT GIVE ME HER PHONE. AND A SHOVEL.
YOU KNOW, FOR HITTING.
NOW, GOING STRAIGHT BACK HERE MIGHT NOT SOUND LIKE A PLAN.
THIS IS PRIMARILY BECAUSE I DON'T HAVE A PLAN.
I NEVER HAVE A PLAN.
MARK
THEY'RE GONE.

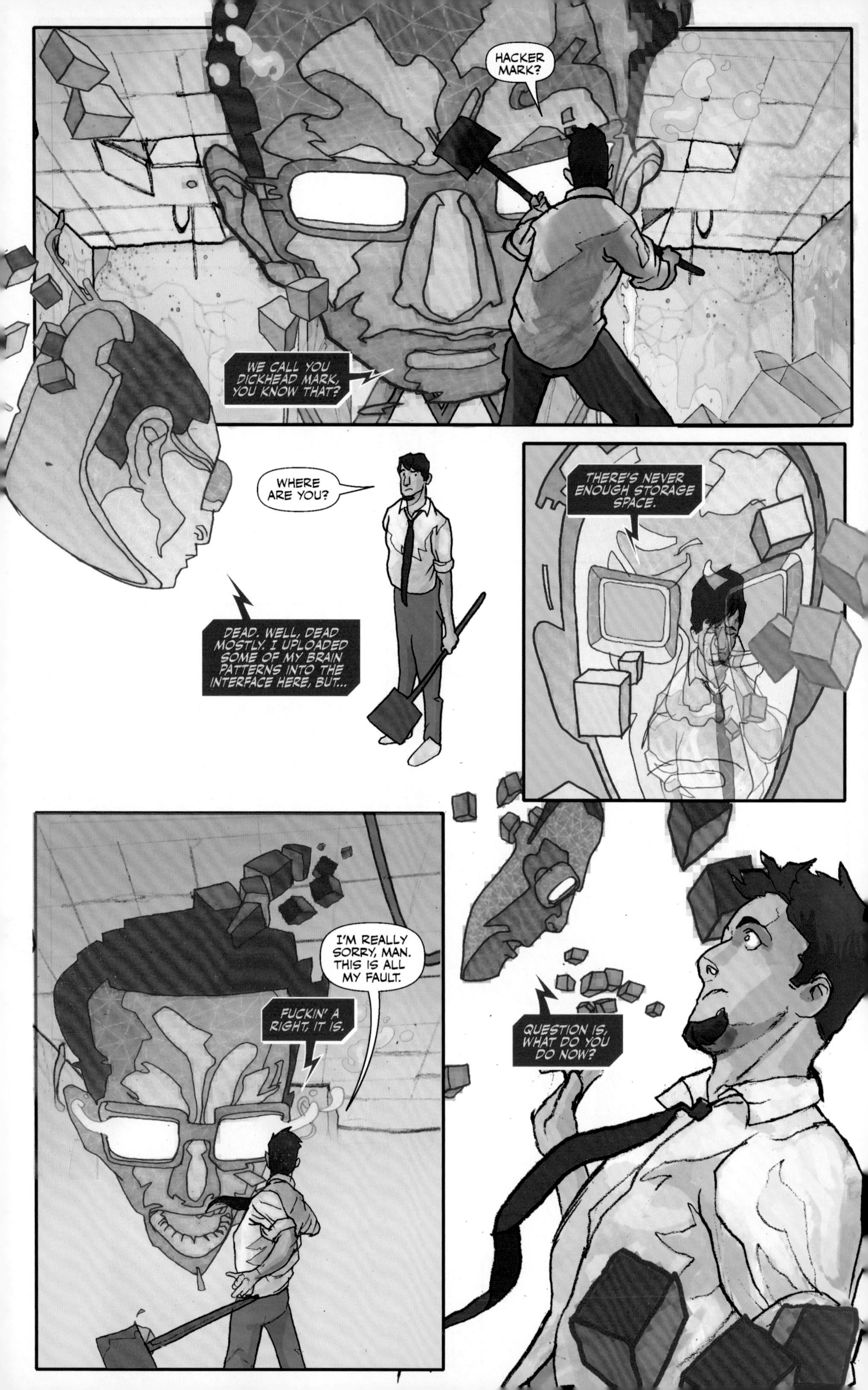

HACKER MARK?
WE CALL YOU DICKHEAD MARK, YOU KNOW THAT?
WHERE ARE YOU?
DEAD. WELL, DEAD MOSTLY. I UPLOADED SOME OF MY BRAIN PATTERNS INTO THE INTERFACE HERE, BUT...
THERE'S NEVER ENOUGH STORAGE SPACE.
I'M REALLY SORRY, MAN. THIS IS ALL MY FAULT.
FUCKIN' A RIGHT, IT IS.
QUESTION IS, WHAT DO YOU DO NOW?

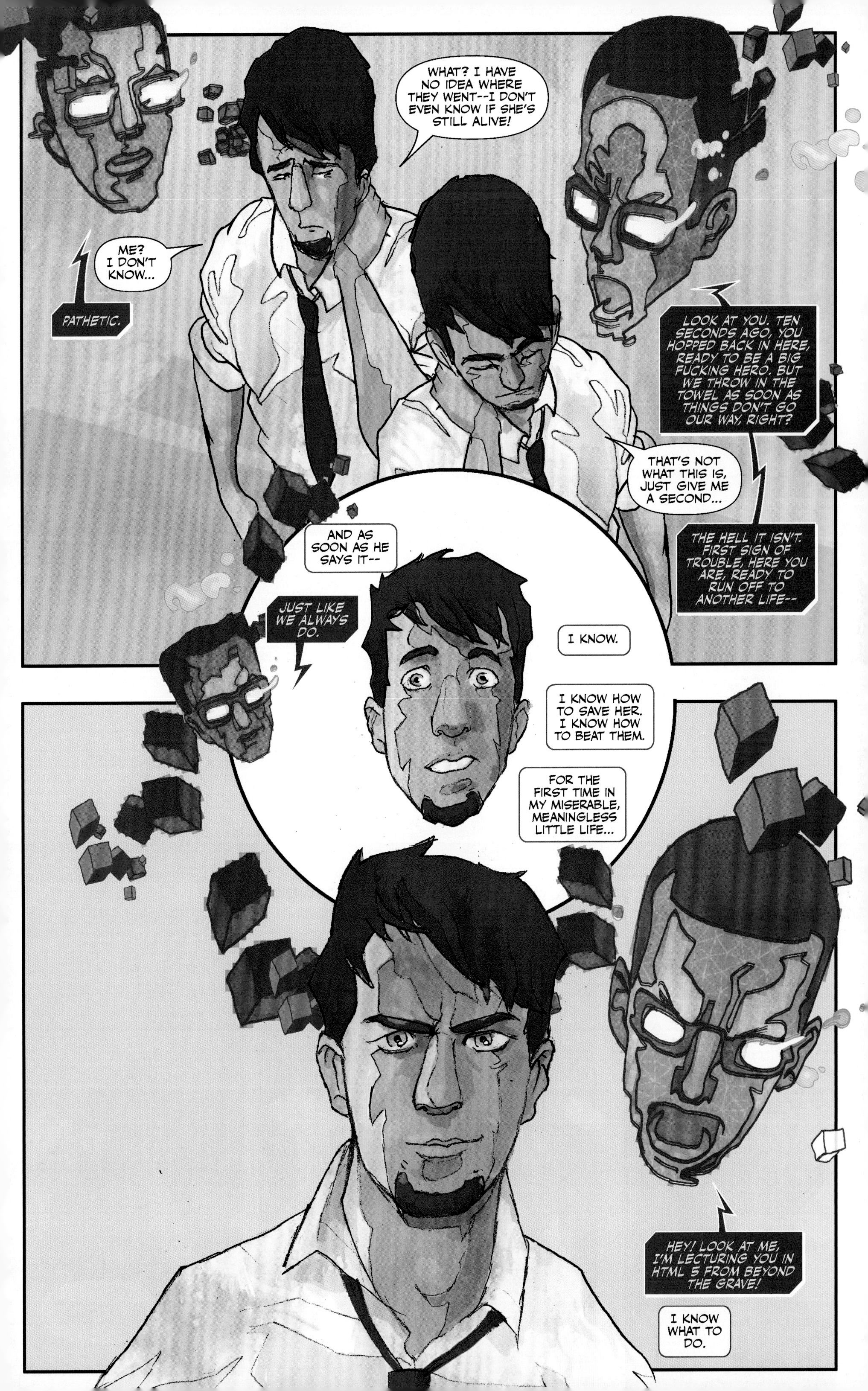
WHAT? I HAVE NO IDEA WHERE THEY WENT--I DON'T EVEN KNOW IF SHE'S STILL ALIVE!
ME? I DON'T KNOW...
PATHETIC.
LOOK AT YOU. TEN SECONDS AGO, YOU HOPPED BACK IN HERE, READY TO BE A BIG FUCKING HERO. BUT WE THROW IN THE TOWEL AS SOON AS THINGS DON'T GO OUR WAY, RIGHT?
THAT'S NOT WHAT THIS IS, JUST GIVE ME A SECOND...
THE HELL IT ISN'T. FIRST SIGN OF TROUBLE, HERE YOU ARE, READY TO RUN OFF TO ANOTHER LIFE--
AND AS SOON AS HE SAYS IT--
JUST LIKE WE ALWAYS DO.
I KNOW.
I KNOW HOW TO SAVE HER. I KNOW HOW TO BEAT THEM.
FOR THE FIRST TIME IN MY MISERABLE, MEANINGLESS LITTLE LIFE...
HEY! LOOK AT ME, I'M LECTURING YOU IN HTML 5 FROM BEYOND THE GRAVE!
I KNOW WHAT TO DO.

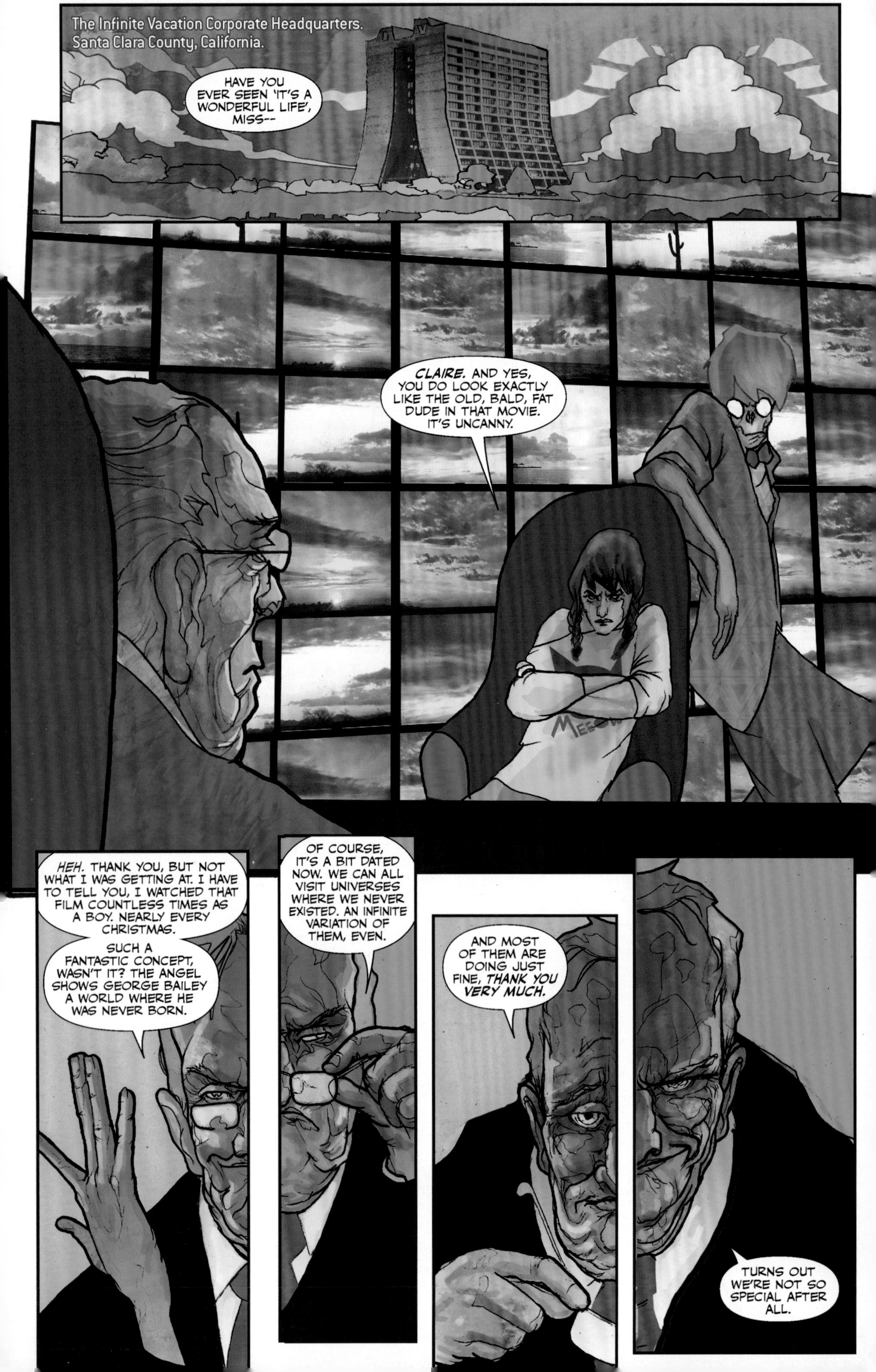

The Infinite Vacation Corporate Headquarters.
Santa Clara County, California.
HAVE YOU EVER SEEN 'IT'S A WONDERFUL LIFE', MISS--
CLAIRE. AND YES, YOU DO LOOK EXACTLY LIKE THE OLD, BALD, FAT DUDE IN THAT MOVIE. IT'S UNCANNY.
MEEOW
HEH. THANK YOU, BUT NOT WHAT I WAS GETTING AT. I HAVE TO TELL YOU, I WATCHED THAT FILM COUNTLESS TIMES AS A BOY. NEARLY EVERY CHRISTMAS.
SUCH A FANTASTIC CONCEPT, WASN'T IT? THE ANGEL SHOWS GEORGE BAILEY A WORLD WHERE HE WAS NEVER BORN.
OF COURSE, IT'S A BIT DATED NOW. WE CAN ALL VISIT UNIVERSES WHERE WE NEVER EXISTED. AN INFINITE VARIATION OF THEM, EVEN.
AND MOST OF THEM ARE DOING JUST FINE, *THANK YOU VERY MUCH.*
TURNS OUT WE'RE NOT SO SPECIAL AFTER ALL.

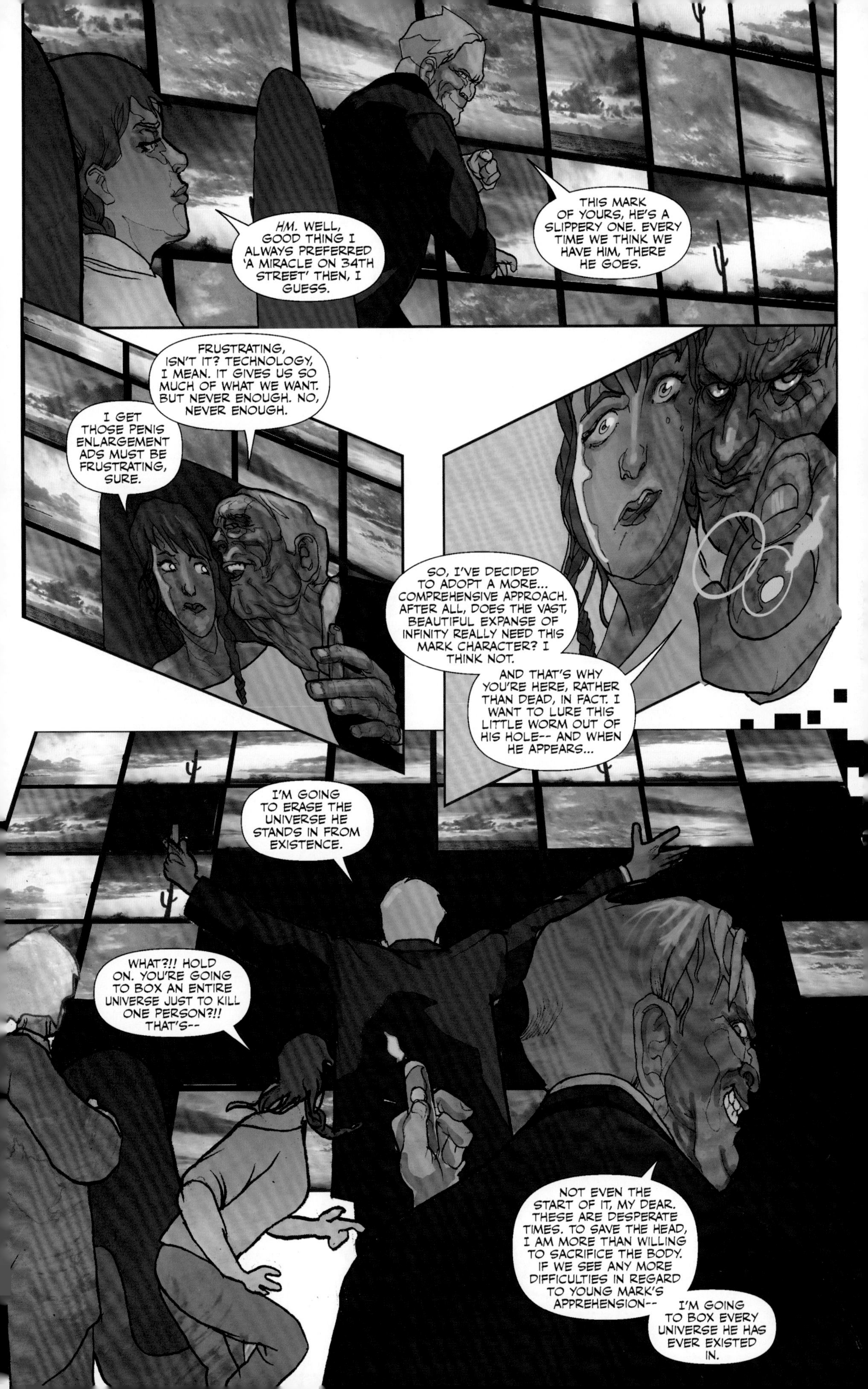
THIS MARK OF YOURS, HE'S A SLIPPERY ONE. EVERY TIME WE THINK WE HAVE HIM, THERE HE GOES.
HM. WELL, GOOD THING I ALWAYS PREFERRED 'A MIRACLE ON 34TH STREET' THEN, I GUESS.
FRUSTRATING, ISN'T IT? TECHNOLOGY, I MEAN. IT GIVES US SO MUCH OF WHAT WE WANT. BUT NEVER ENOUGH. NO, NEVER ENOUGH.
I GET THOSE PENIS ENLARGEMENT ADS MUST BE FRUSTRATING, SURE.
SO, I'VE DECIDED TO ADOPT A MORE... COMPREHENSIVE APPROACH. AFTER ALL, DOES THE VAST, BEAUTIFUL EXPANSE OF INFINITY REALLY NEED THIS MARK CHARACTER? I THINK NOT.
AND THAT'S WHY YOU'RE HERE, RATHER THAN DEAD, IN FACT. I WANT TO LURE THIS LITTLE WORM OUT OF HIS HOLE-- AND WHEN HE APPEARS...
I'M GOING TO ERASE THE UNIVERSE HE STANDS IN FROM EXISTENCE.
WHAT?!! HOLD ON. YOU'RE GOING TO BOX AN ENTIRE UNIVERSE JUST TO KILL ONE PERSON?!! THAT'S--
NOT EVEN THE START OF IT, MY DEAR. THESE ARE DESPERATE TIMES. TO SAVE THE HEAD, I AM MORE THAN WILLING TO SACRIFICE THE BODY. IF WE SEE ANY MORE DIFFICULTIES IN REGARD TO YOUNG MARK'S APPREHENSION--
I'M GOING TO BOX EVERY UNIVERSE HE HAS EVER EXISTED IN.

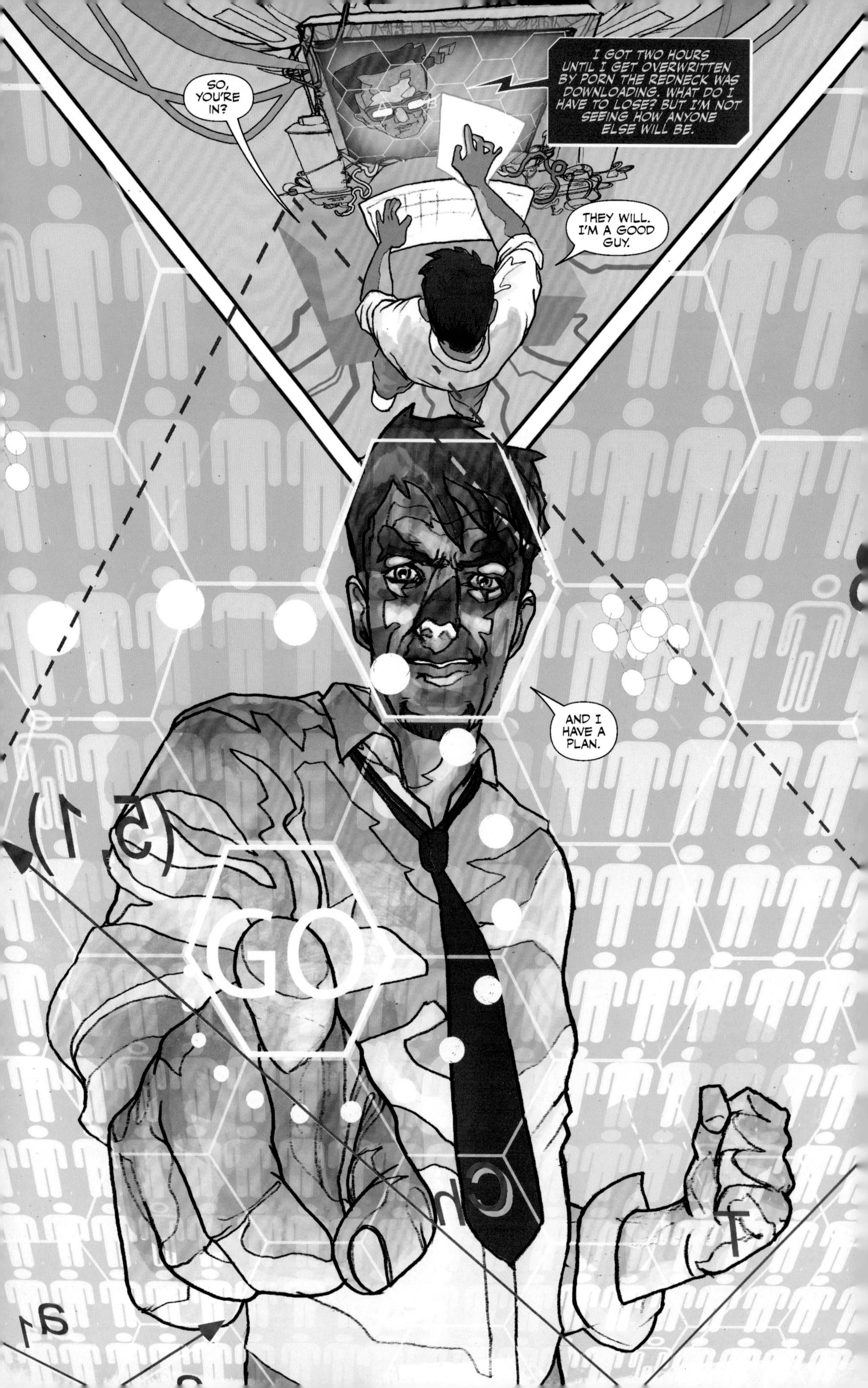
SO, YOU'RE IN?
I GOT TWO HOURS UNTIL I GET OVERWRITTEN BY PORN THE REDNECK WAS DOWNLOADING. WHAT DO I HAVE TO LOSE? BUT I'M NOT SEEING HOW ANYONE ELSE WILL BE.
THEY WILL. I'M A GOOD GUY.
AND I HAVE A PLAN.
GO

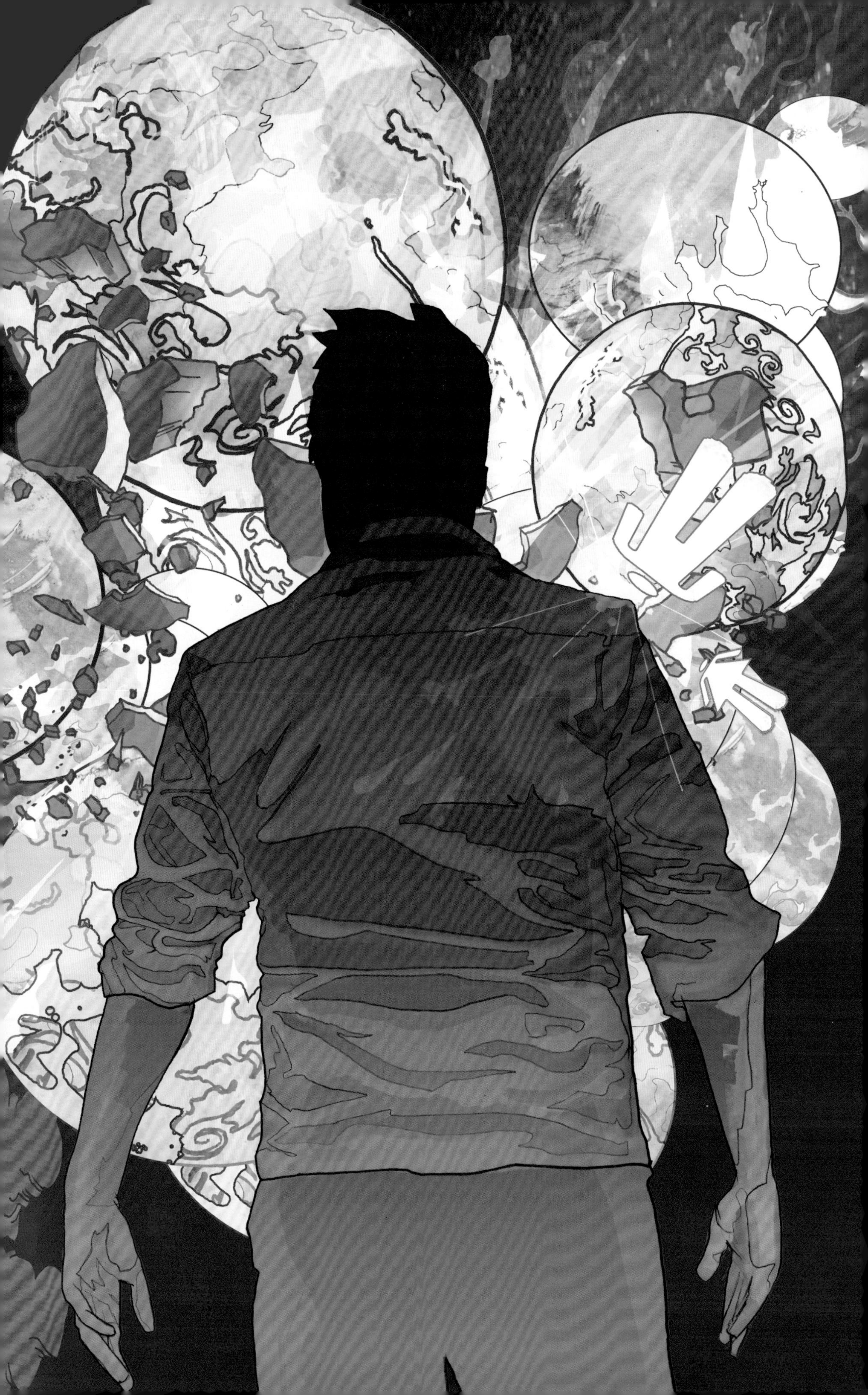

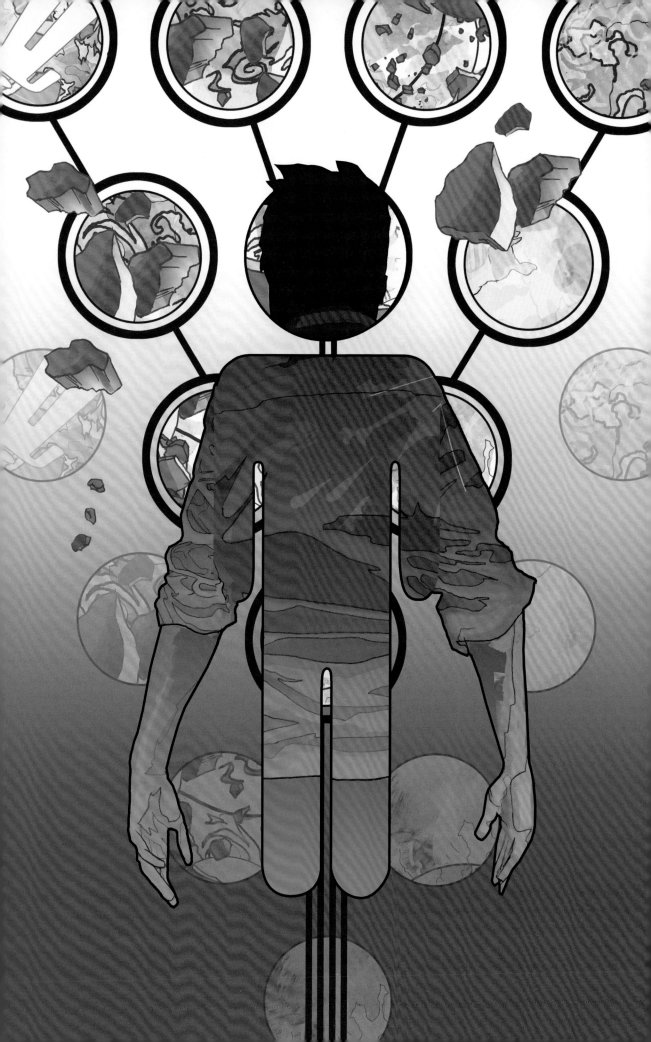

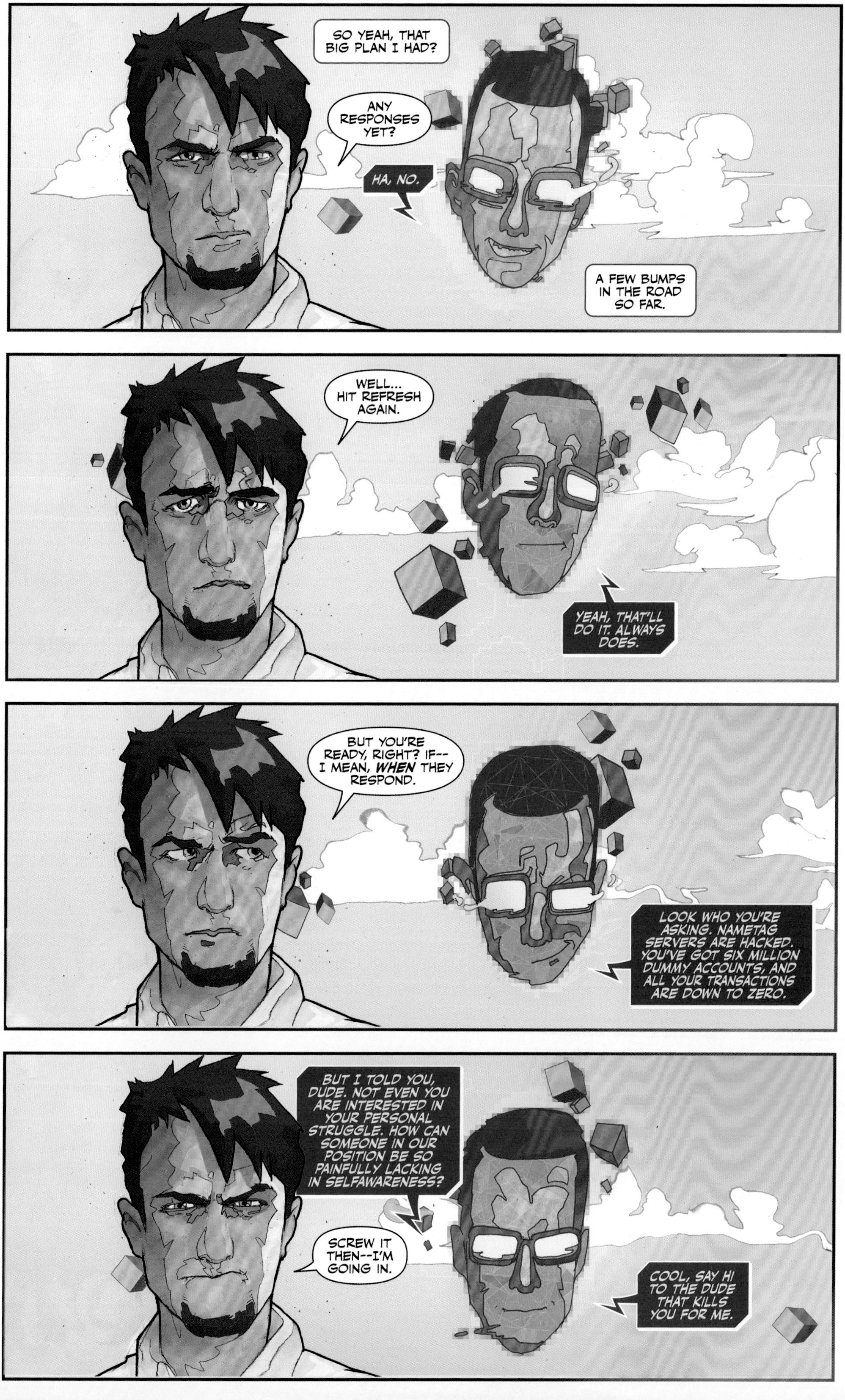
SO YEAH, THAT BIG PLAN I HAD?
ANY RESPONSES YET?
HA, NO.
A FEW BUMPS IN THE ROAD SO FAR.
WELL... HIT REFRESH AGAIN.
YEAH, THAT'LL DO IT. ALWAYS DOES.
BUT YOU'RE READY, RIGHT? IF-- I MEAN, WHEN THEY RESPOND.
LOOK WHO YOU'RE ASKING. NAMETAG SERVERS ARE HACKED. YOU'VE GOT SIX MILLION DUMMY ACCOUNTS, AND ALL YOUR TRANSACTIONS ARE DOWN TO ZERO.
BUT I TOLD YOU, DUDE. NOT EVEN YOU ARE INTERESTED IN YOUR PERSONAL STRUGGLE. HOW CAN SOMEONE IN OUR POSITION BE SO PAINFULLY LACKING IN SELFAWARENESS?
SCREW IT THEN--I'M GOING IN.
COOL, SAY HI TO THE DUDE THAT KILLS YOU FOR ME.

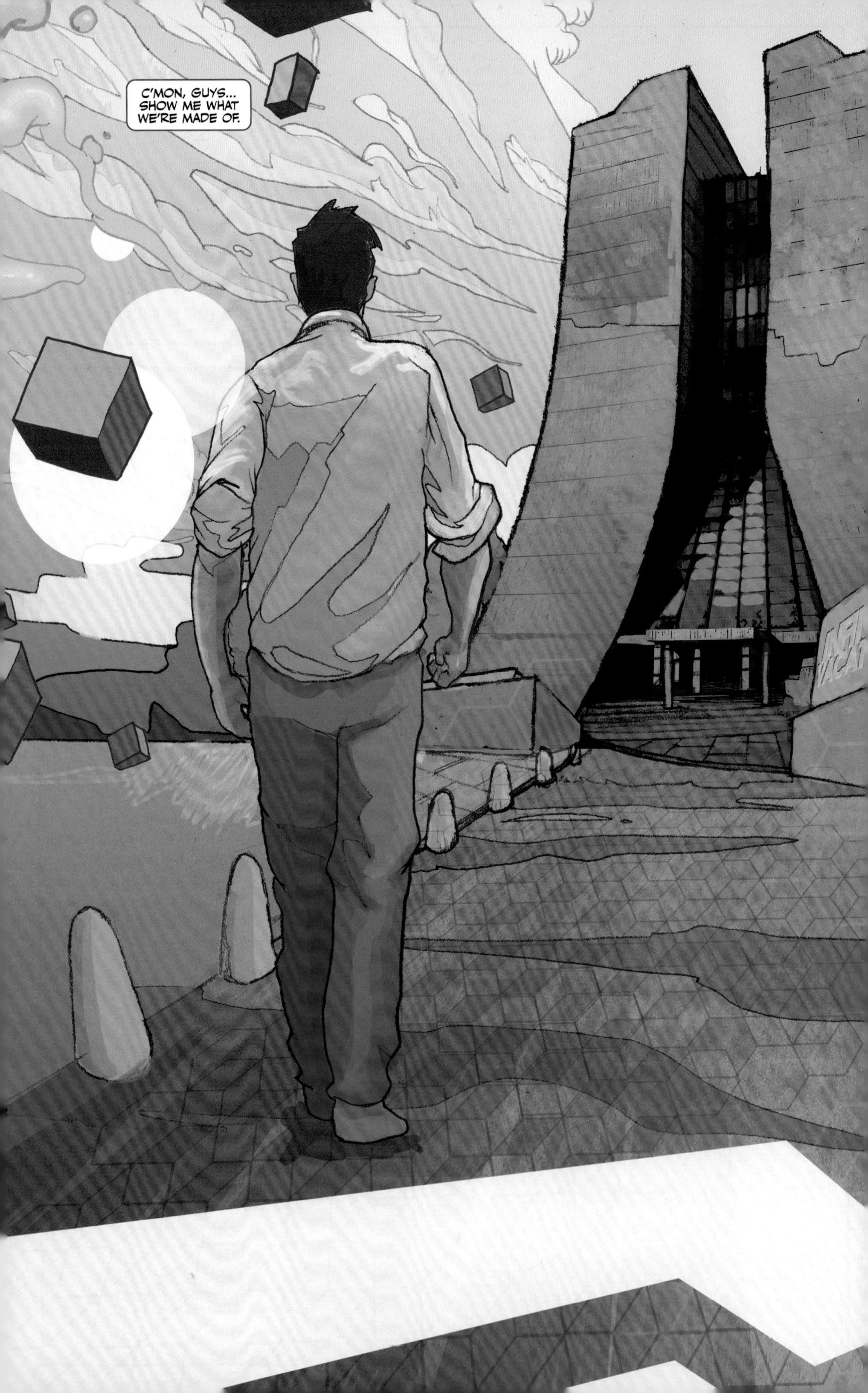
C'MON, GUYS... SHOW ME WHAT WE'RE MADE OF.

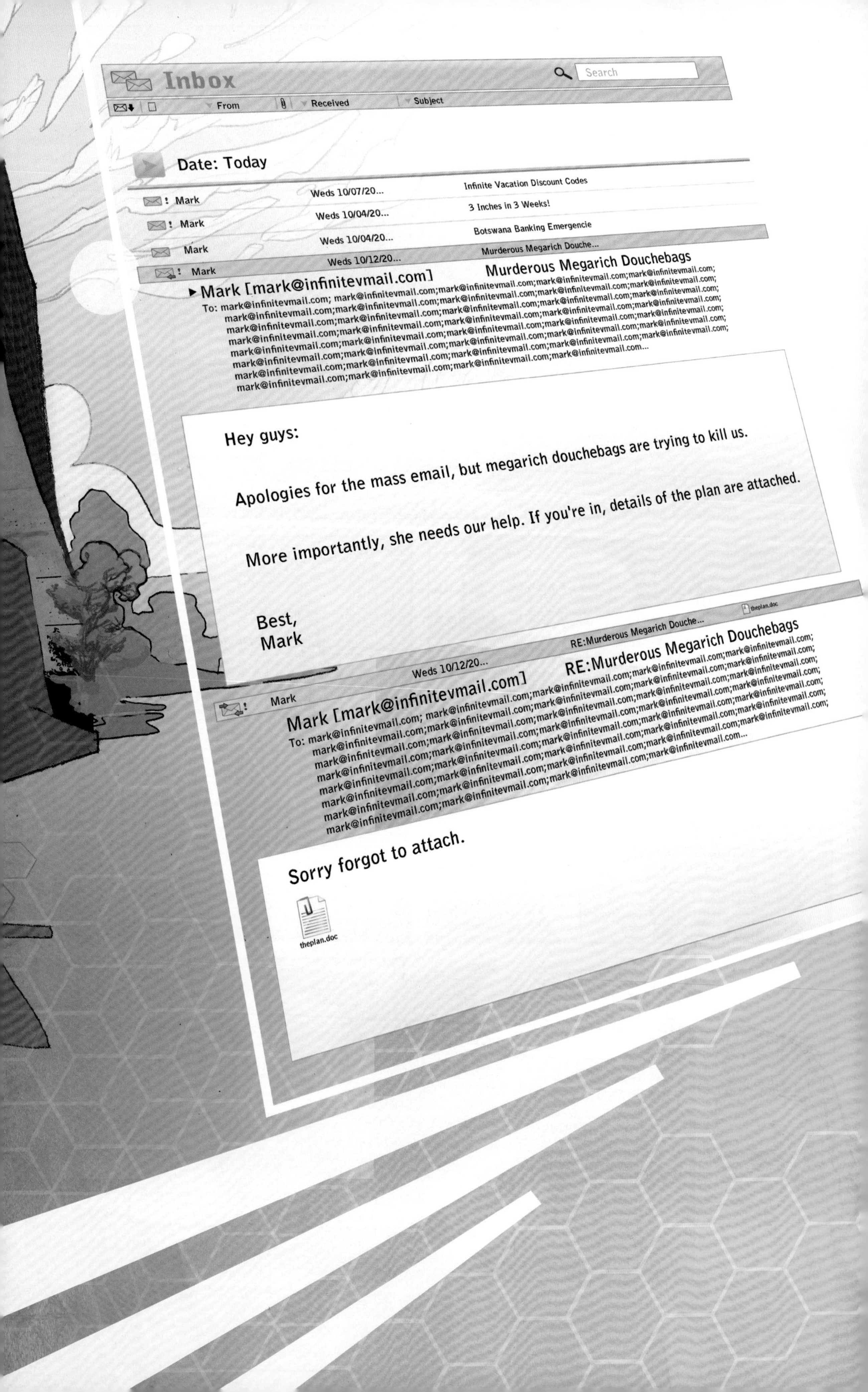
Inbox
Search
From
Received
Subject
Date: Today
Mark
Weds 10/07/20...
Infinite Vacation Discount Codes
Mark
Weds 10/04/20...
3 Inches in 3 Weeks!
Mark
Weds 10/04/20...
Botswana Banking Emergencie
Mark
Weds 10/12/20...
Murderous Megarich Douche...
Mark [mark@infinitevmail.com]
Murderous Megarich Douchebags
To: mark@infinitevmail.com; mark@infinitevmail.com;mark@infinitevmail.com;mark@infinitevmail.com;mark@infinitevmail.com;mark@infinitevmail.com;
mark@infinitevmail.com;mark@infinitevmail.com;mark@infinitevmail.com;mark@infinitevmail.com;mark@infinitevmail.com;mark@infinitevmail.com;
mark@infinitevmail.com;mark@infinitevmail.com;mark@infinitevmail.com;mark@infinitevmail.com;mark@infinitevmail.com;mark@infinitevmail.com;
mark@infinitevmail.com;mark@infinitevmail.com;mark@infinitevmail.com;mark@infinitevmail.com;mark@infinitevmail.com;mark@infinitevmail.com;
mark@infinitevmail.com;mark@infinitevmail.com;mark@infinitevmail.com;mark@infinitevmail.com;mark@infinitevmail.com;mark@infinitevmail.com...
Hey guys:
Apologies for the mass email, but megarich douchebags are trying to kill us.
More importantly, she needs our help. If you're in, details of the plan are attached.
Best,
Mark
theplan.doc
RE:Murderous Megarich Douche...
Mark
Weds 10/12/20...
Mark [mark@infinitevmail.com]
RE:Murderous Megarich Douchebags
To: mark@infinitevmail.com; mark@infinitevmail.com;mark@infinitevmail.com;mark@infinitevmail.com;mark@infinitevmail.com;mark@infinitevmail.com;
mark@infinitevmail.com;mark@infinitevmail.com;mark@infinitevmail.com;mark@infinitevmail.com;mark@infinitevmail.com;mark@infinitevmail.com;
mark@infinitevmail.com;mark@infinitevmail.com;mark@infinitevmail.com;mark@infinitevmail.com;mark@infinitevmail.com;mark@infinitevmail.com;
mark@infinitevmail.com;mark@infinitevmail.com;mark@infinitevmail.com;mark@infinitevmail.com;mark@infinitevmail.com;mark@infinitevmail.com;
mark@infinitevmail.com;mark@infinitevmail.com;mark@infinitevmail.com;mark@infinitevmail.com;mark@infinitevmail.com...
Sorry forgot to attach.
theplan.doc

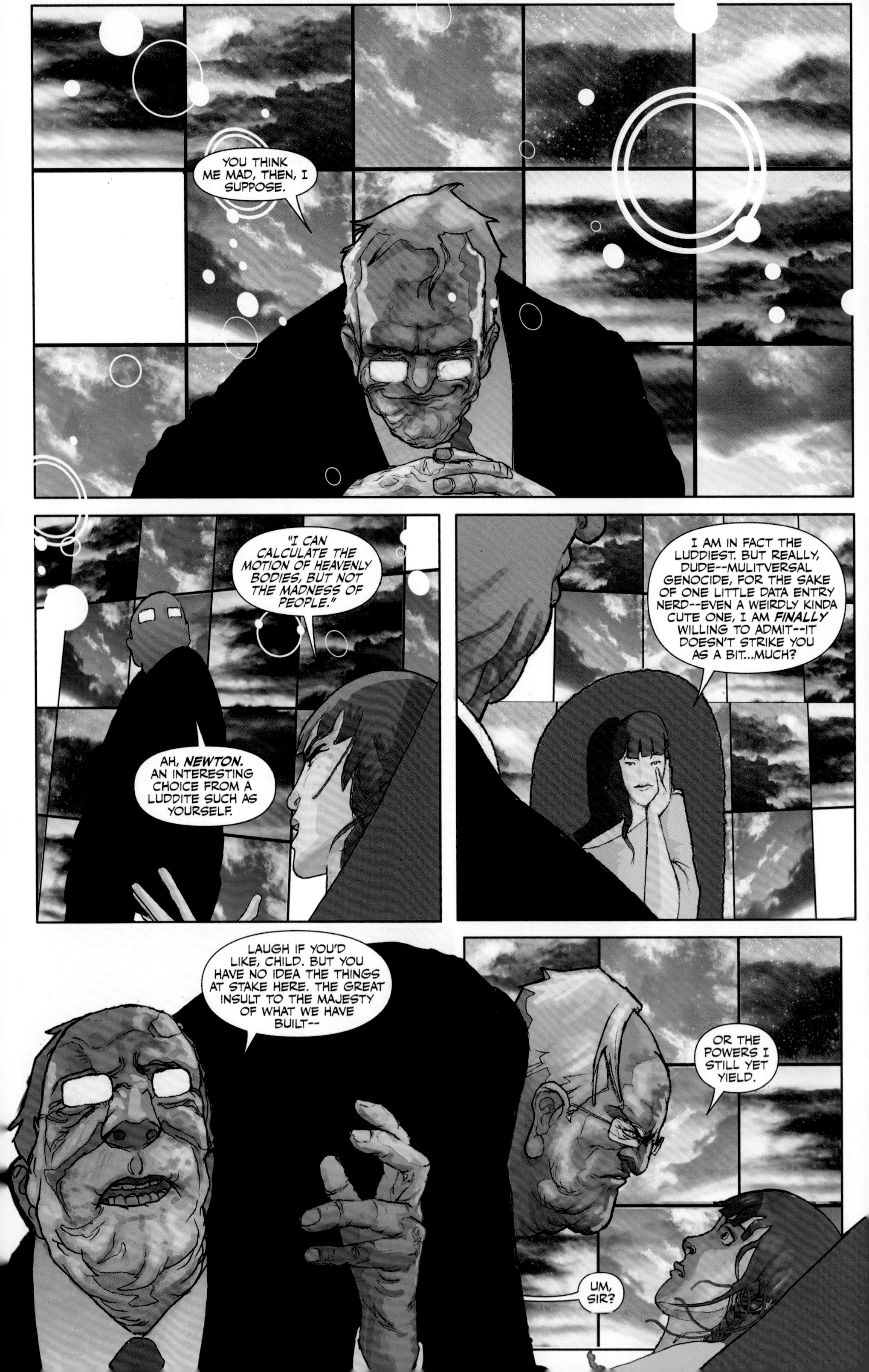
YOU THINK ME MAD, THEN, I SUPPOSE.
"I CAN CALCULATE THE MOTION OF HEAVENLY BODIES, BUT NOT THE MADNESS OF PEOPLE."
AH, NEWTON. AN INTERESTING CHOICE FROM A LUDDITE SUCH AS YOURSELF.
I AM IN FACT THE LUDDIEST. BUT REALLY, DUDE--MULITVERSAL GENOCIDE, FOR THE SAKE OF ONE LITTLE DATA ENTRY NERD--EVEN A WEIRDLY KINDA CUTE ONE, I AM FINALLY WILLING TO ADMIT--IT DOESN'T STRIKE YOU AS A BIT...MUCH?
LAUGH IF YOU'D LIKE, CHILD. BUT YOU HAVE NO IDEA THE THINGS AT STAKE HERE. THE GREAT INSULT TO THE MAJESTY OF WHAT WE HAVE BUILT--
OR THE POWERS I STILL YET YIELD.
UM, SIR?

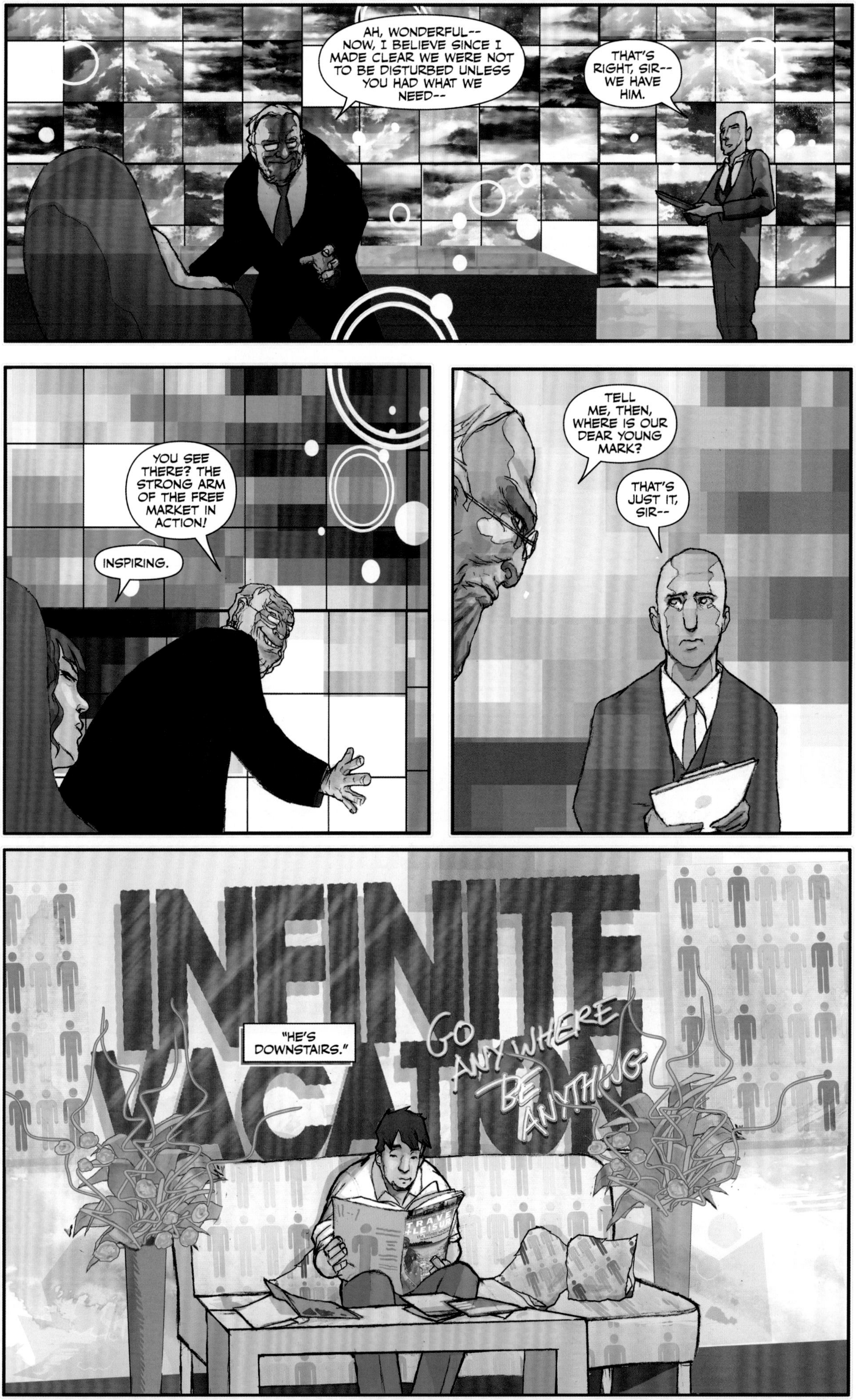

AH, WONDERFUL-- NOW, I BELIEVE SINCE I MADE CLEAR WE WERE NOT TO BE DISTURBED UNLESS YOU HAD WHAT WE NEED--
THAT'S RIGHT, SIR-- WE HAVE HIM.
YOU SEE THERE? THE STRONG ARM OF THE FREE MARKET IN ACTION!
INSPIRING.
TELL ME, THEN, WHERE IS OUR DEAR YOUNG MARK?
THAT'S JUST IT, SIR--
INFINITE VACATION
"HE'S DOWNSTAIRS."
GO ANYWHERE BE ANYTHING

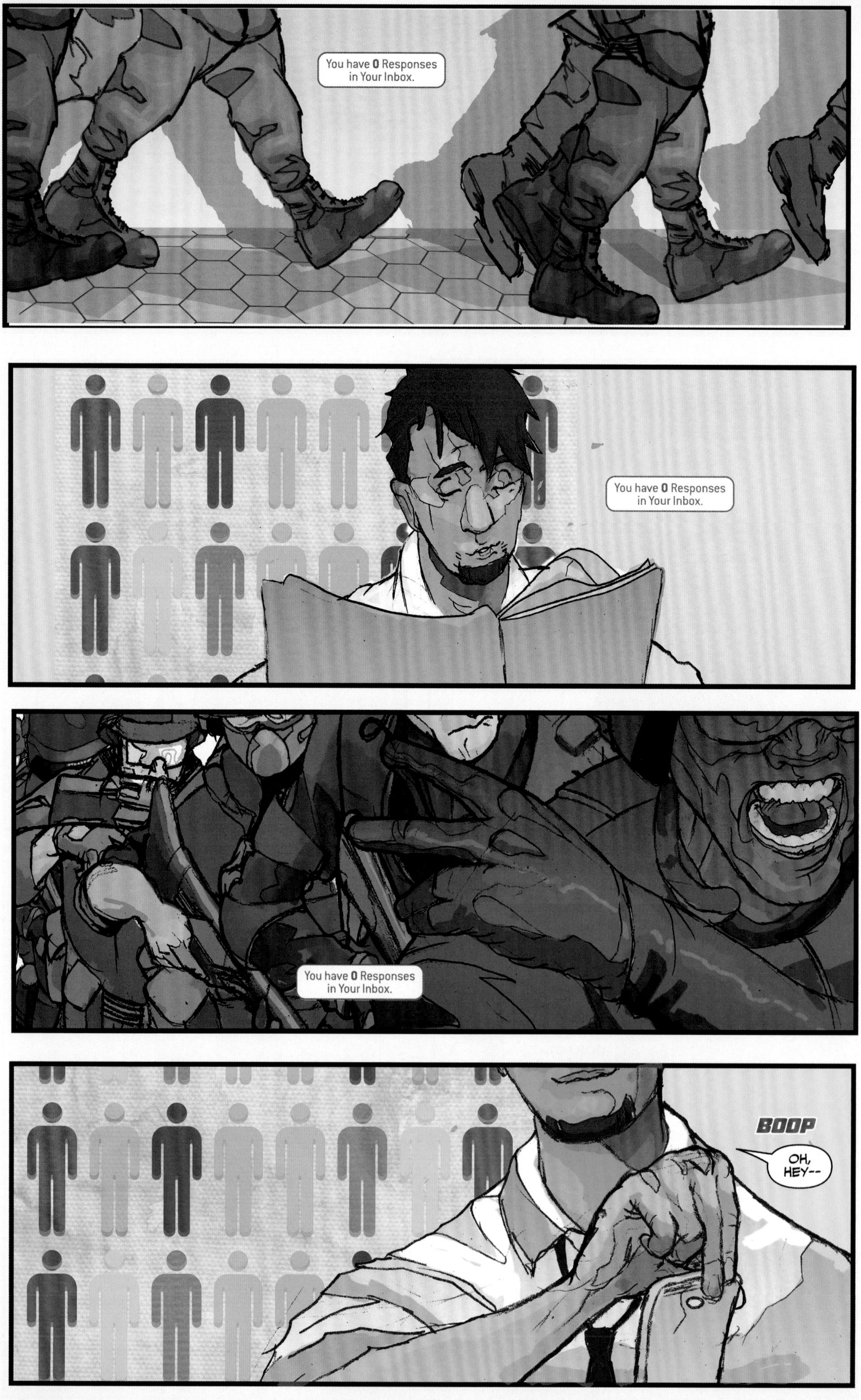
You have 0 Responses in Your Inbox.
You have 0 Responses in Your Inbox.
You have 0 Responses in Your Inbox.
BOOP
OH, HEY--

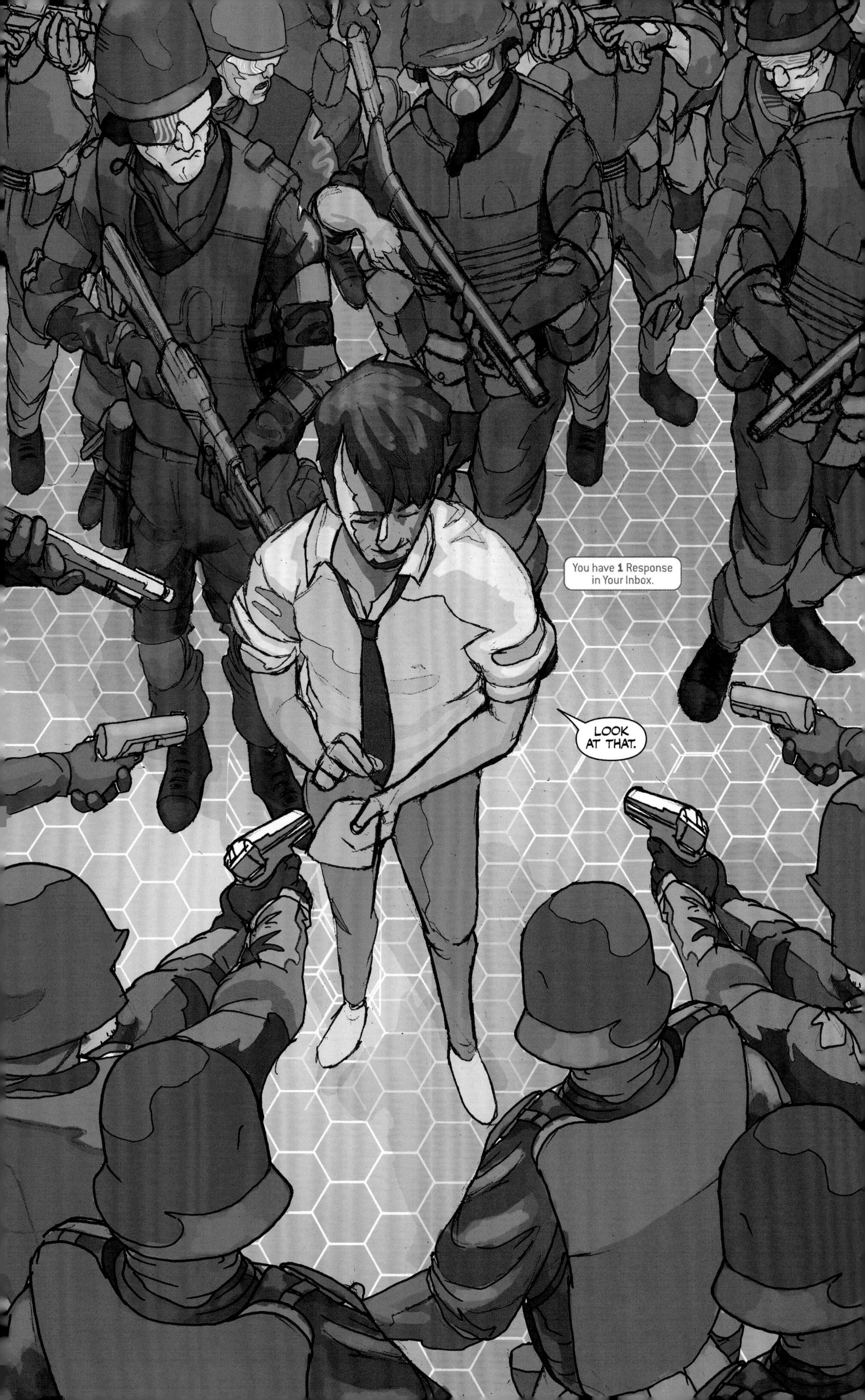
You have 1 Response in Your Inbox.
LOOK AT THAT.

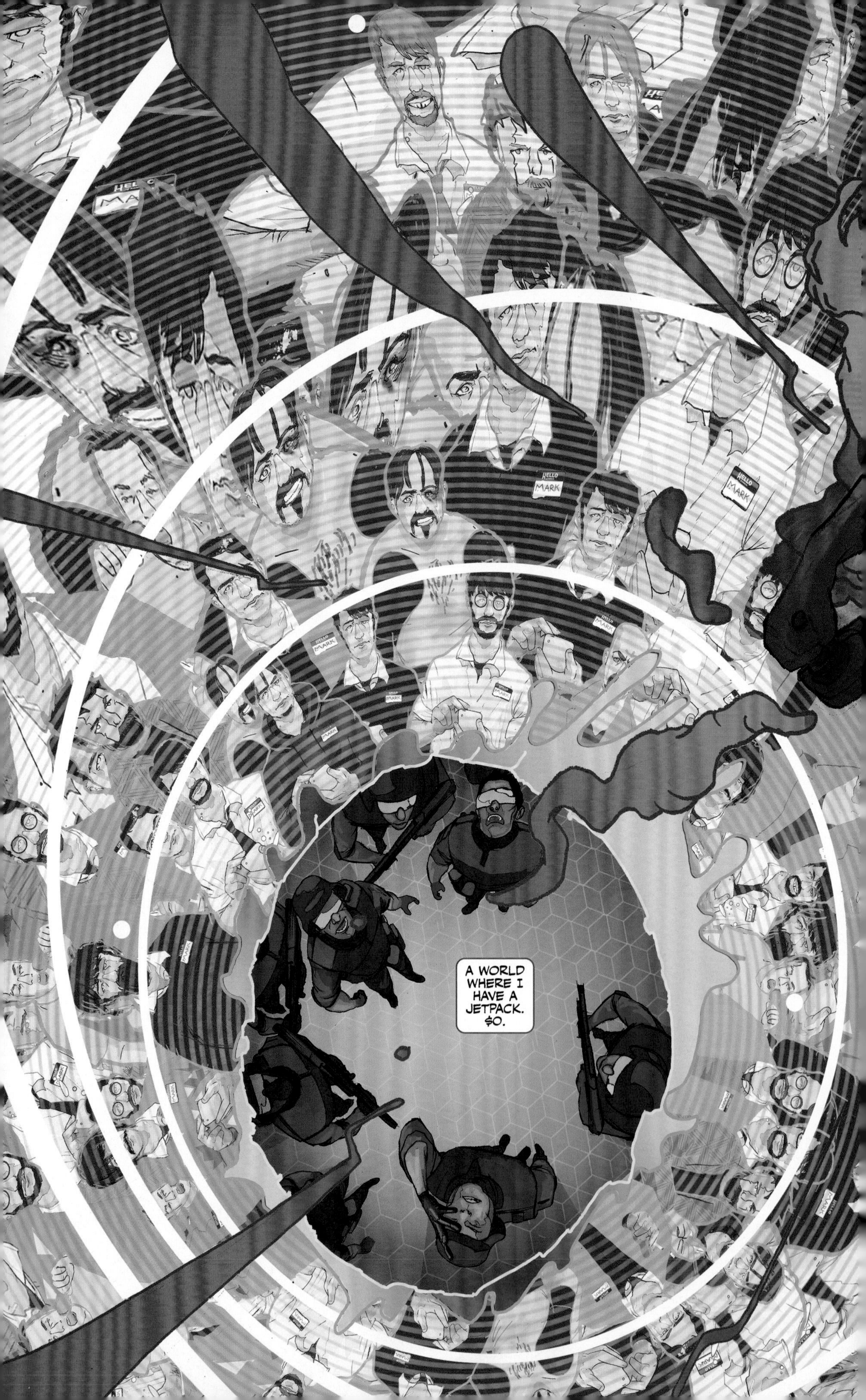
A WORLD WHERE I HAVE A JETPACK. $0.

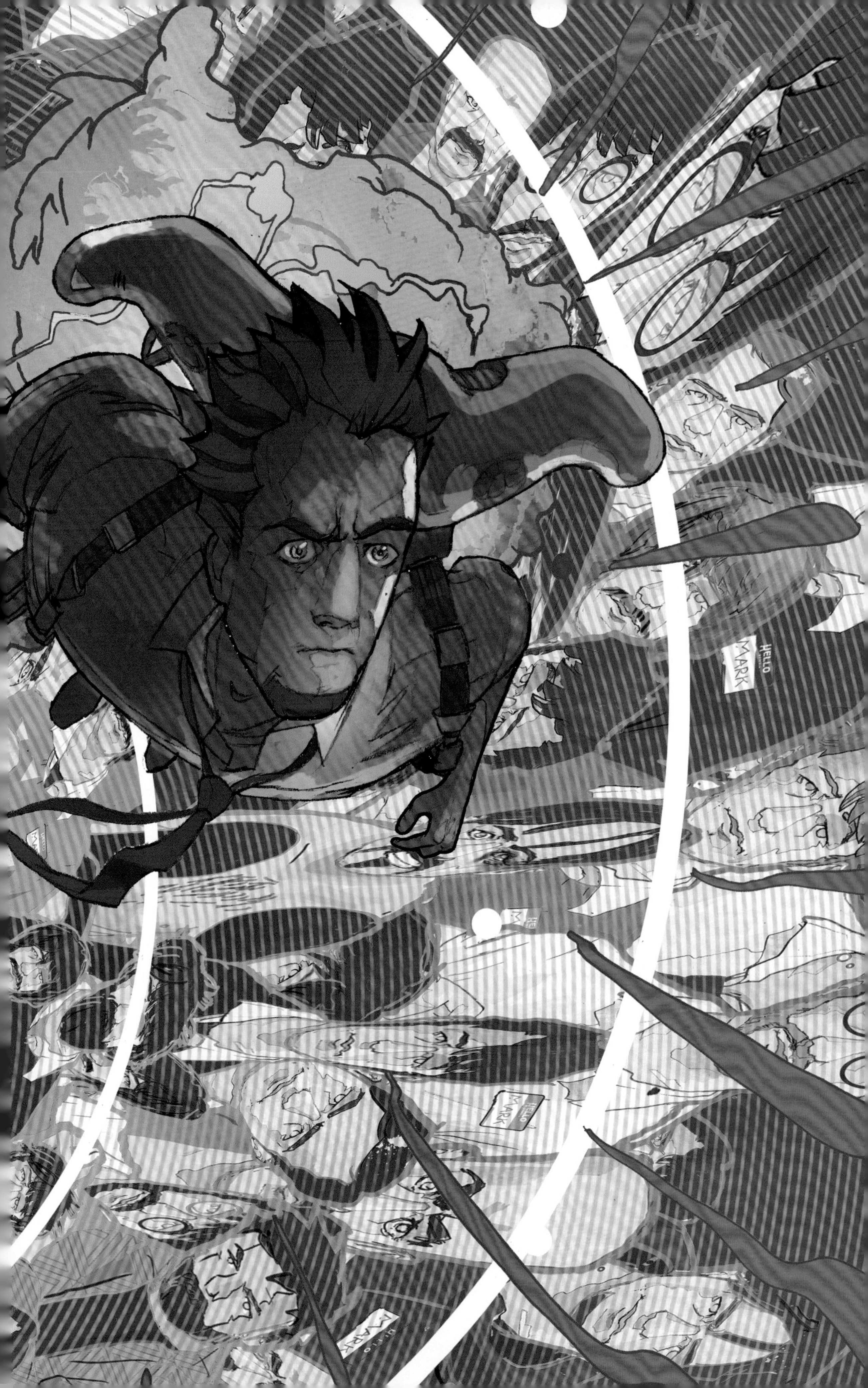
HELLO
MARK
HELLO
MARK

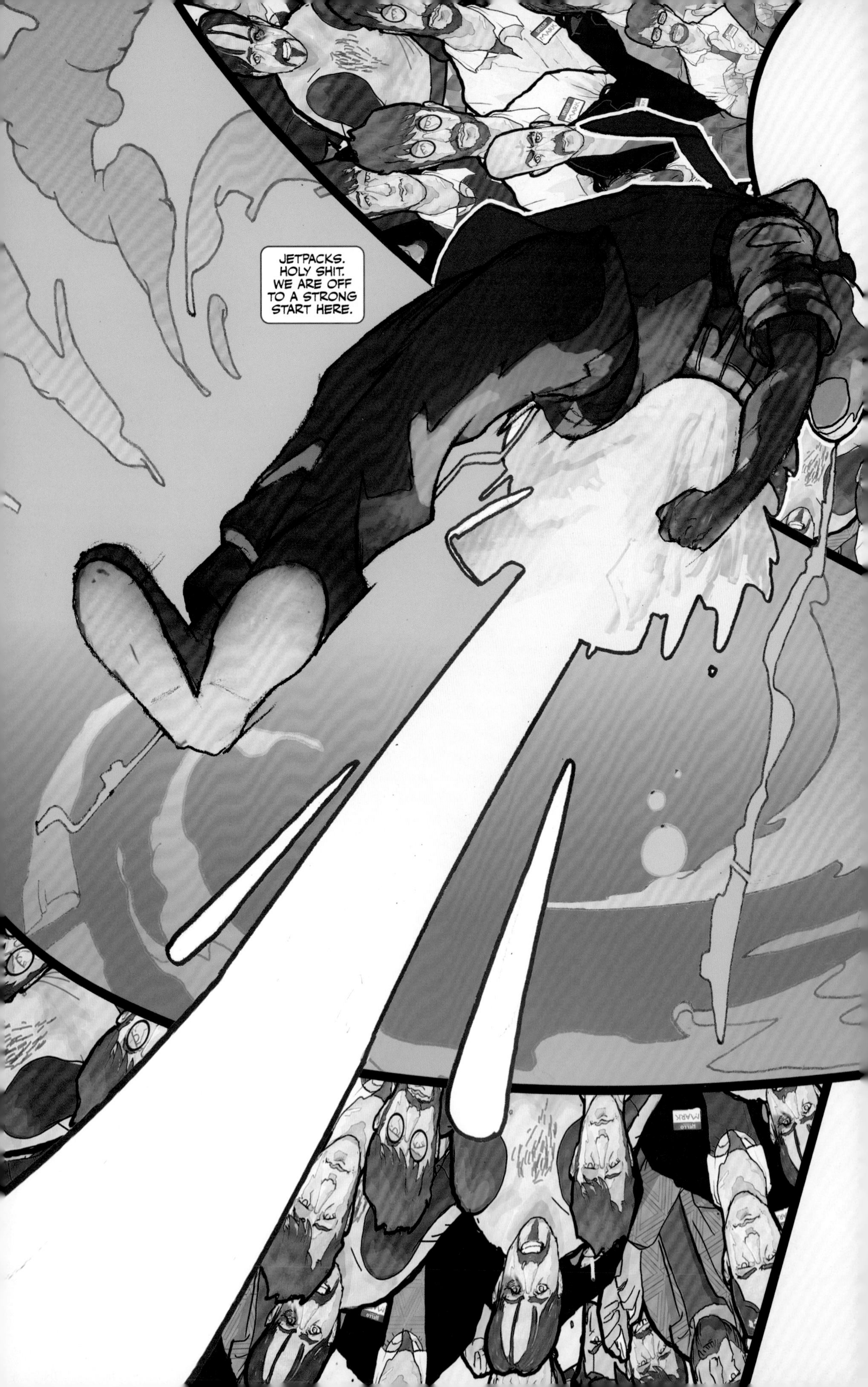
JETPACKS. HOLY SHIT. WE ARE OFF TO A STRONG START HERE.

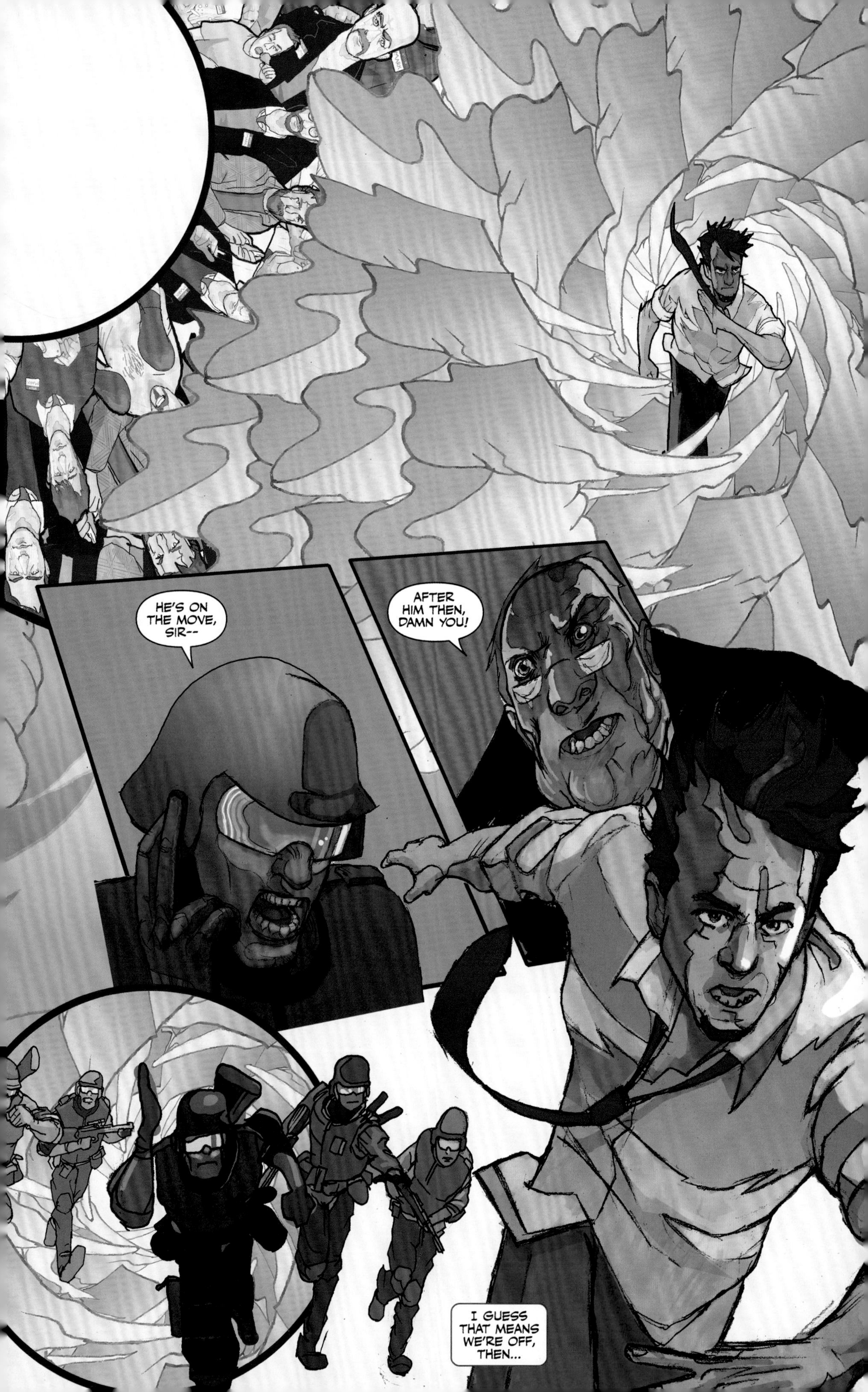
HE'S ON THE MOVE, SIR--
AFTER HIM THEN, DAMN YOU!
I GUESS THAT MEANS WE'RE OFF, THEN...

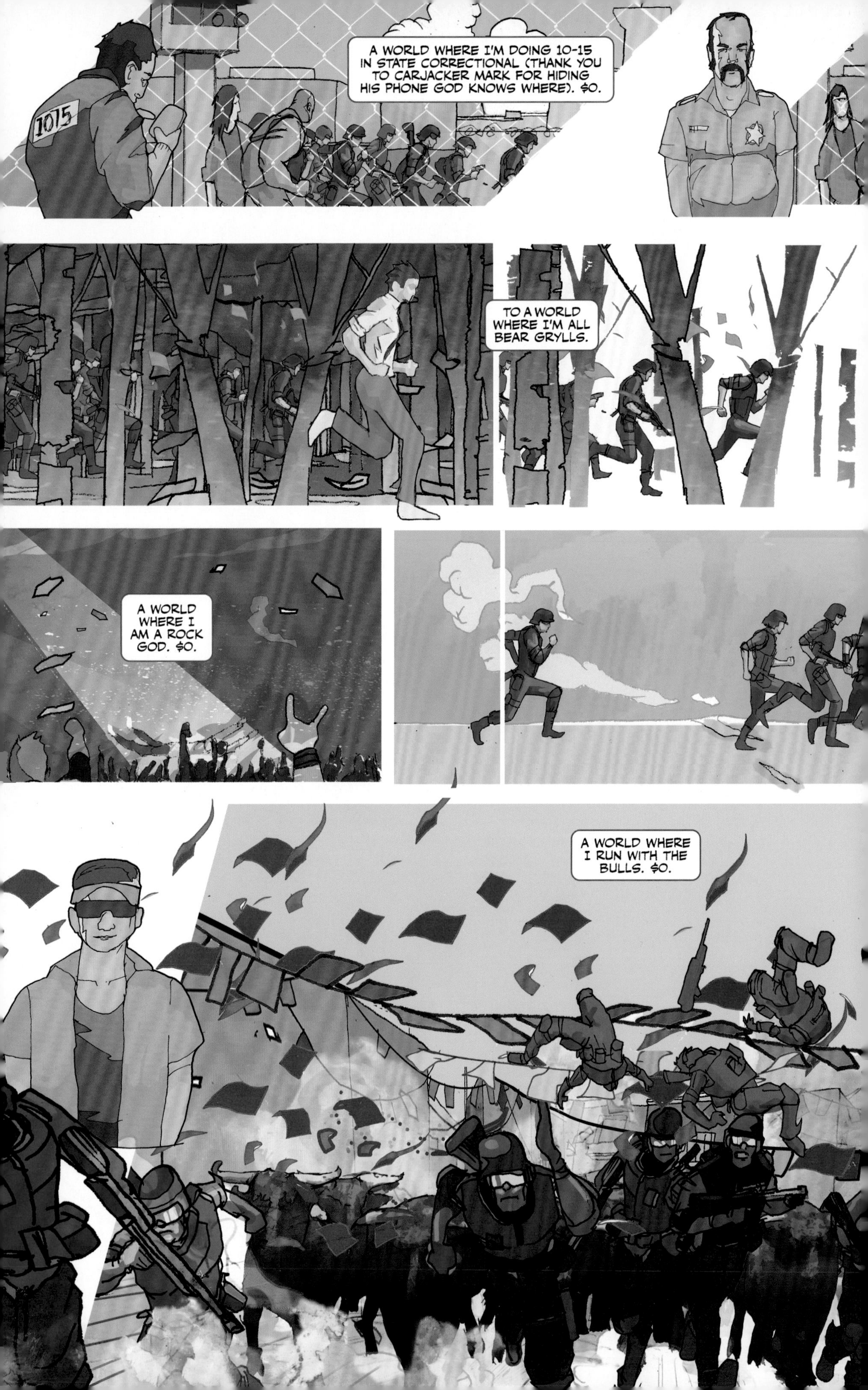
A WORLD WHERE I'M DOING 10-15 IN STATE CORRECTIONAL (THANK YOU TO CARJACKER MARK FOR HIDING HIS PHONE GOD KNOWS WHERE). $0.
1015
TO A WORLD WHERE I'M ALL BEAR GRYLLS.
A WORLD WHERE I AM A ROCK GOD. $0.
A WORLD WHERE I RUN WITH THE BULLS. $0.

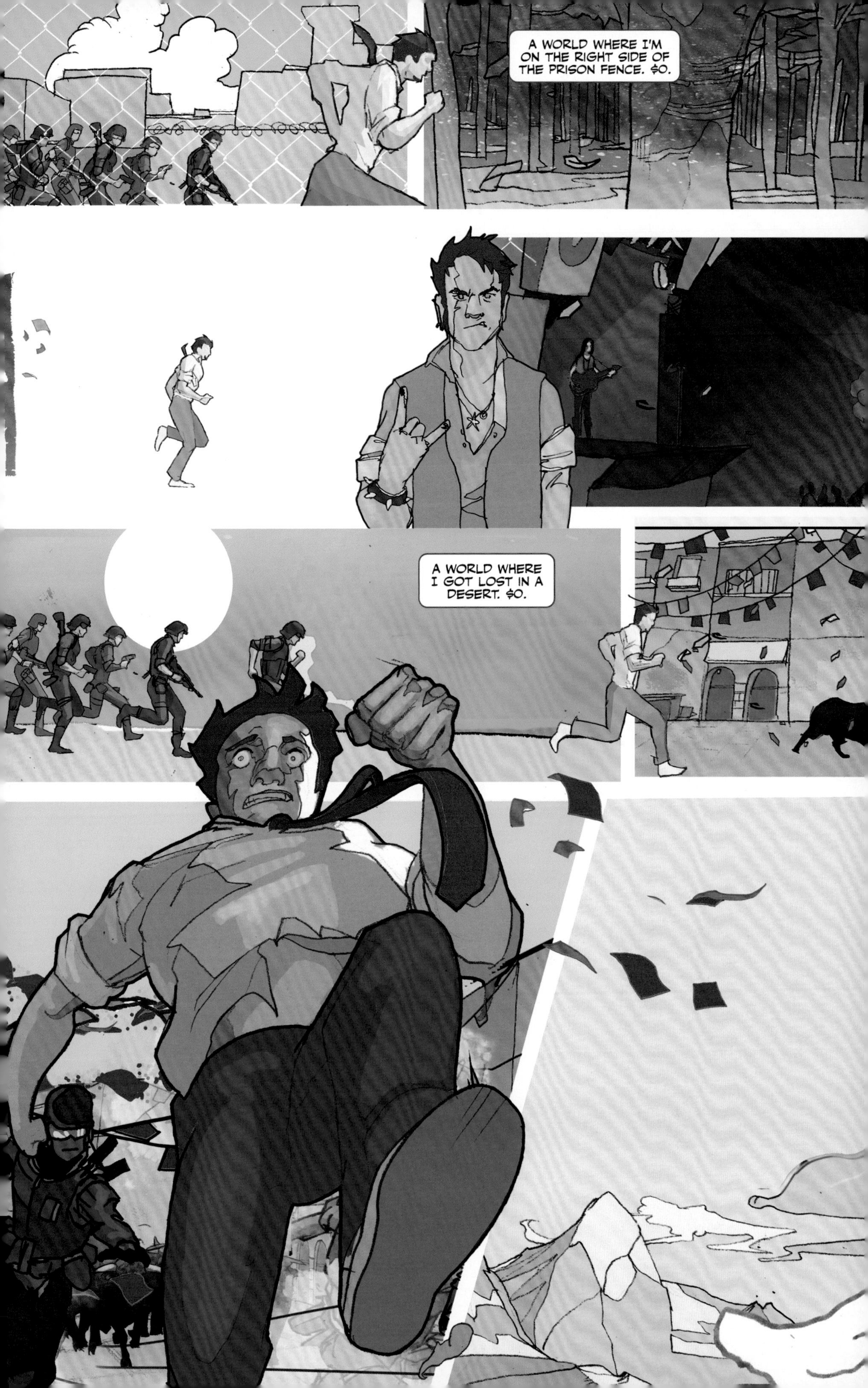
A WORLD WHERE I'M ON THE RIGHT SIDE OF THE PRISON FENCE. $0.
A WORLD WHERE I GOT LOST IN A DESERT. $0.

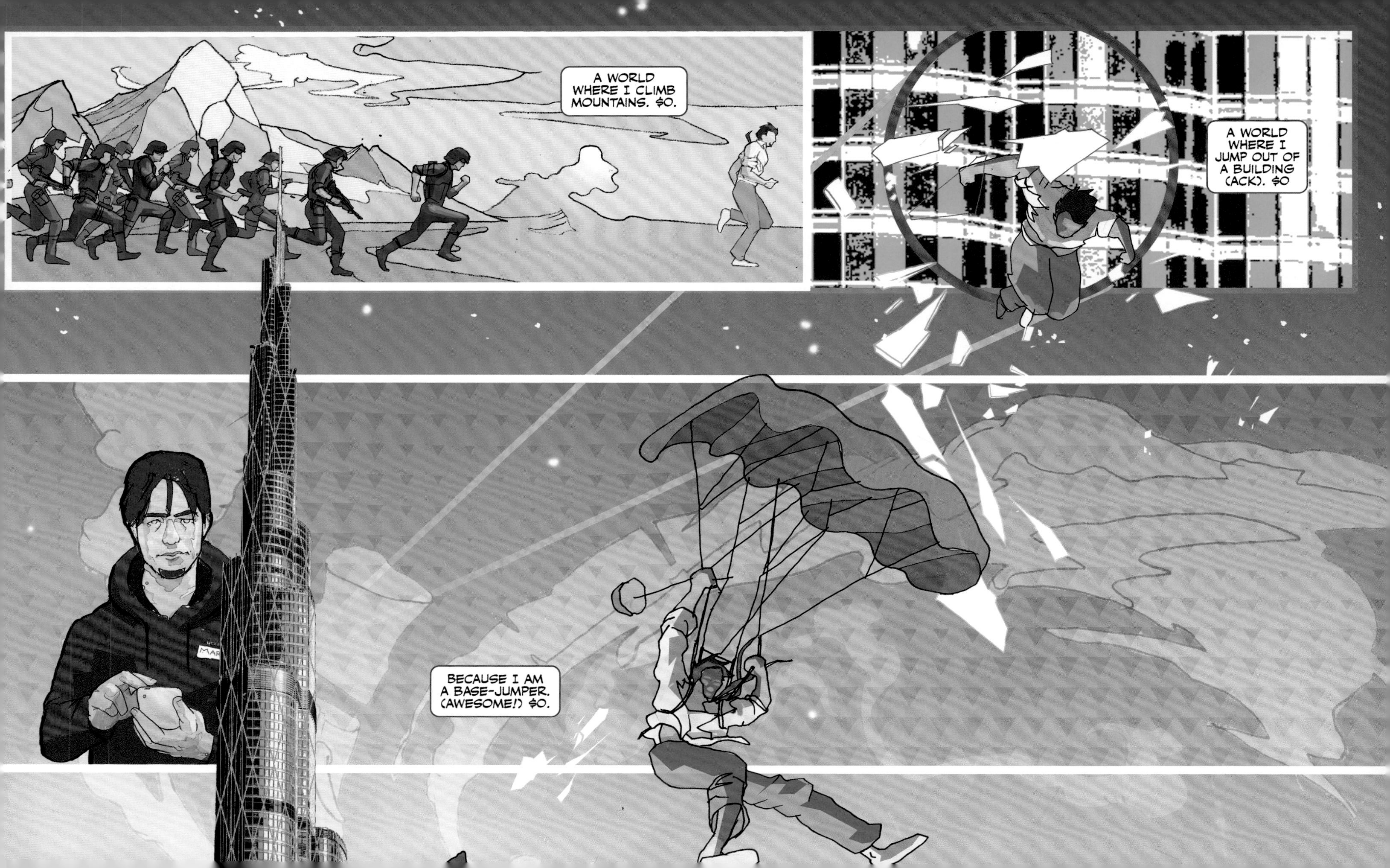
A WORLD WHERE I CLIMB MOUNTAINS. $0.
A WORLD WHERE I JUMP OUT OF A BUILDING (ACK). $0
BECAUSE I AM A BASE-JUMPER. (AWESOME!) $0.

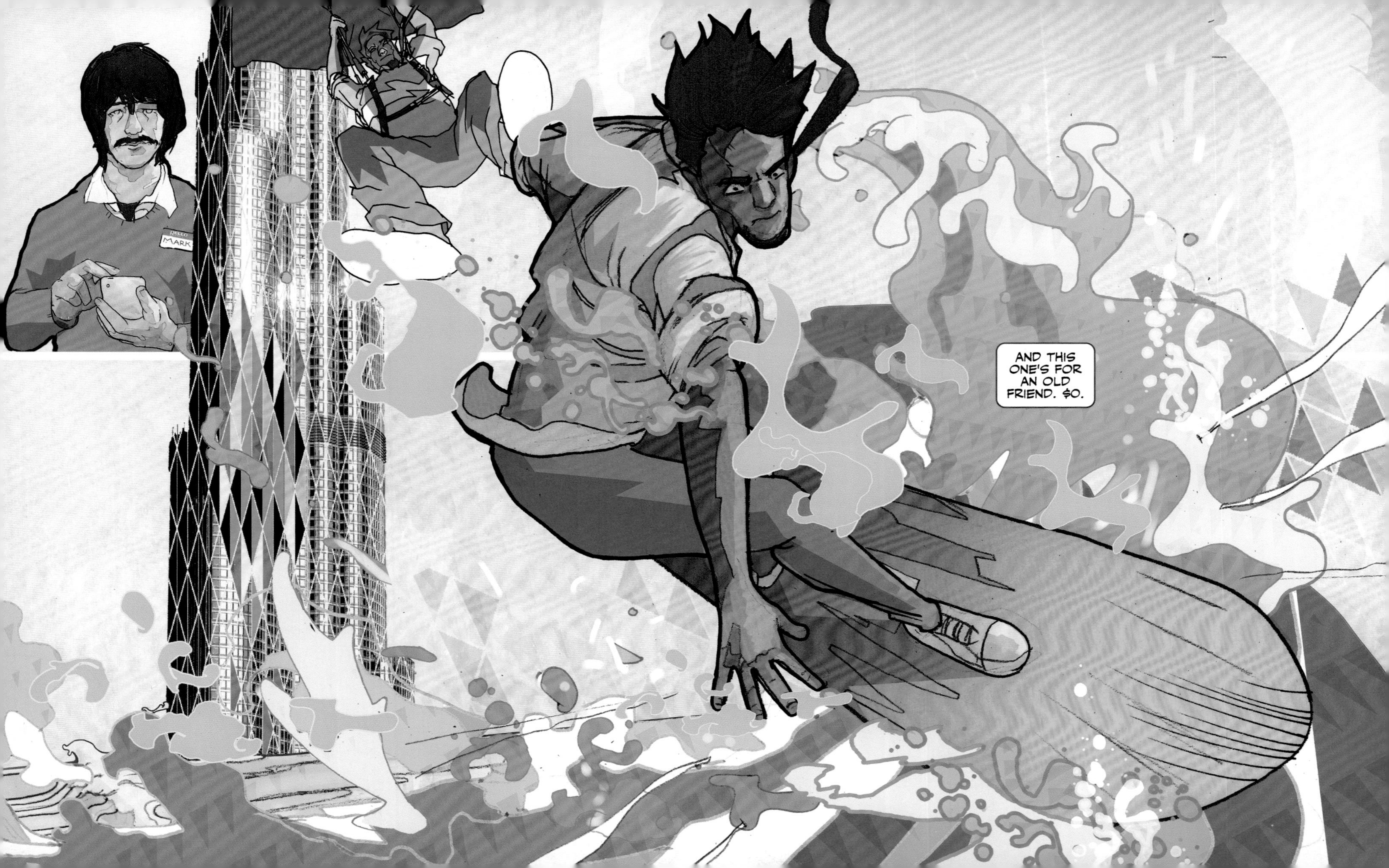
HELLO
MARK
AND THIS ONE'S FOR AN OLD FRIEND. $0.

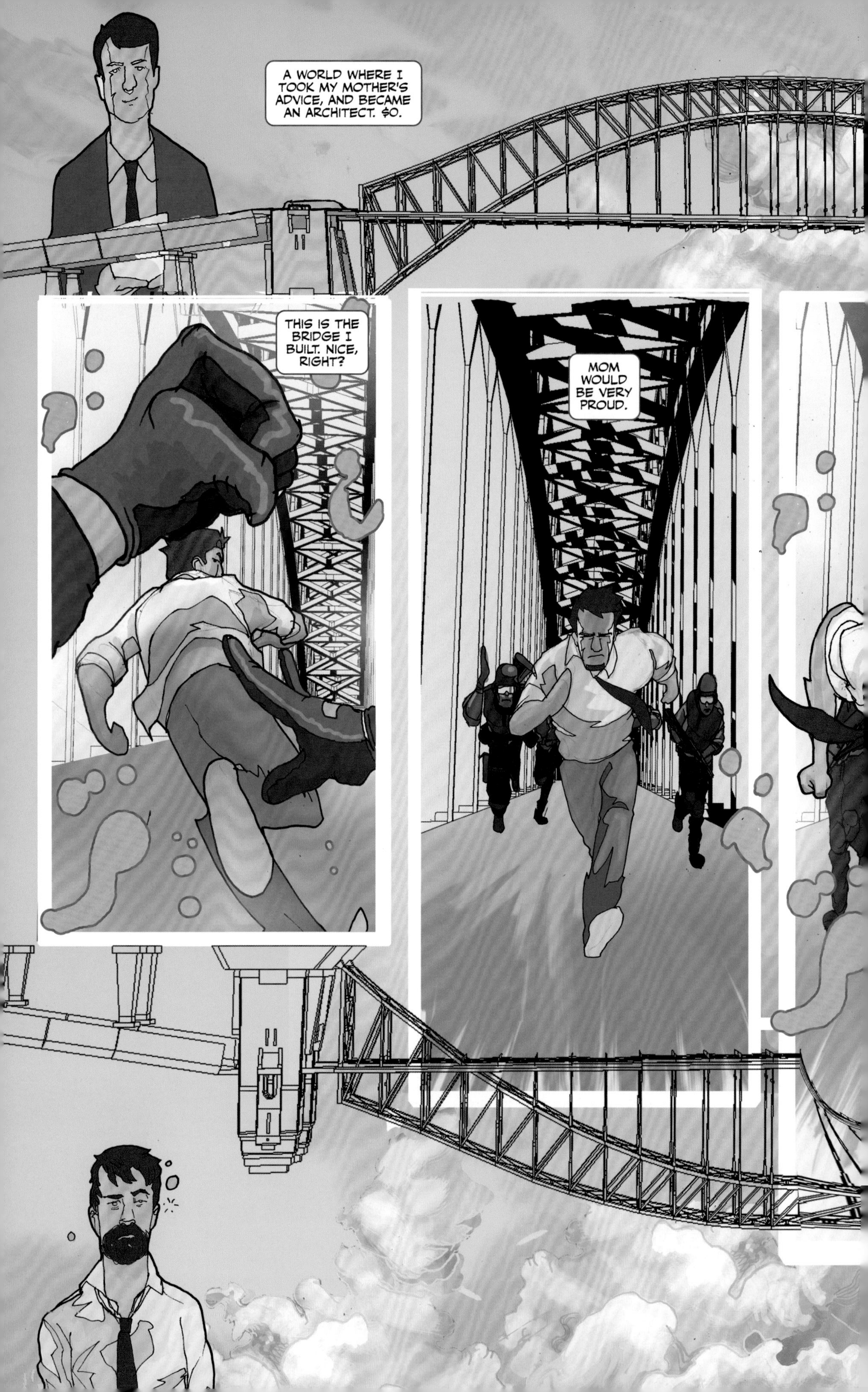
A WORLD WHERE I TOOK MY MOTHER'S ADVICE, AND BECAME AN ARCHITECT. $0.
THIS IS THE BRIDGE I BUILT. NICE, RIGHT?
MOM WOULD BE VERY PROUD.

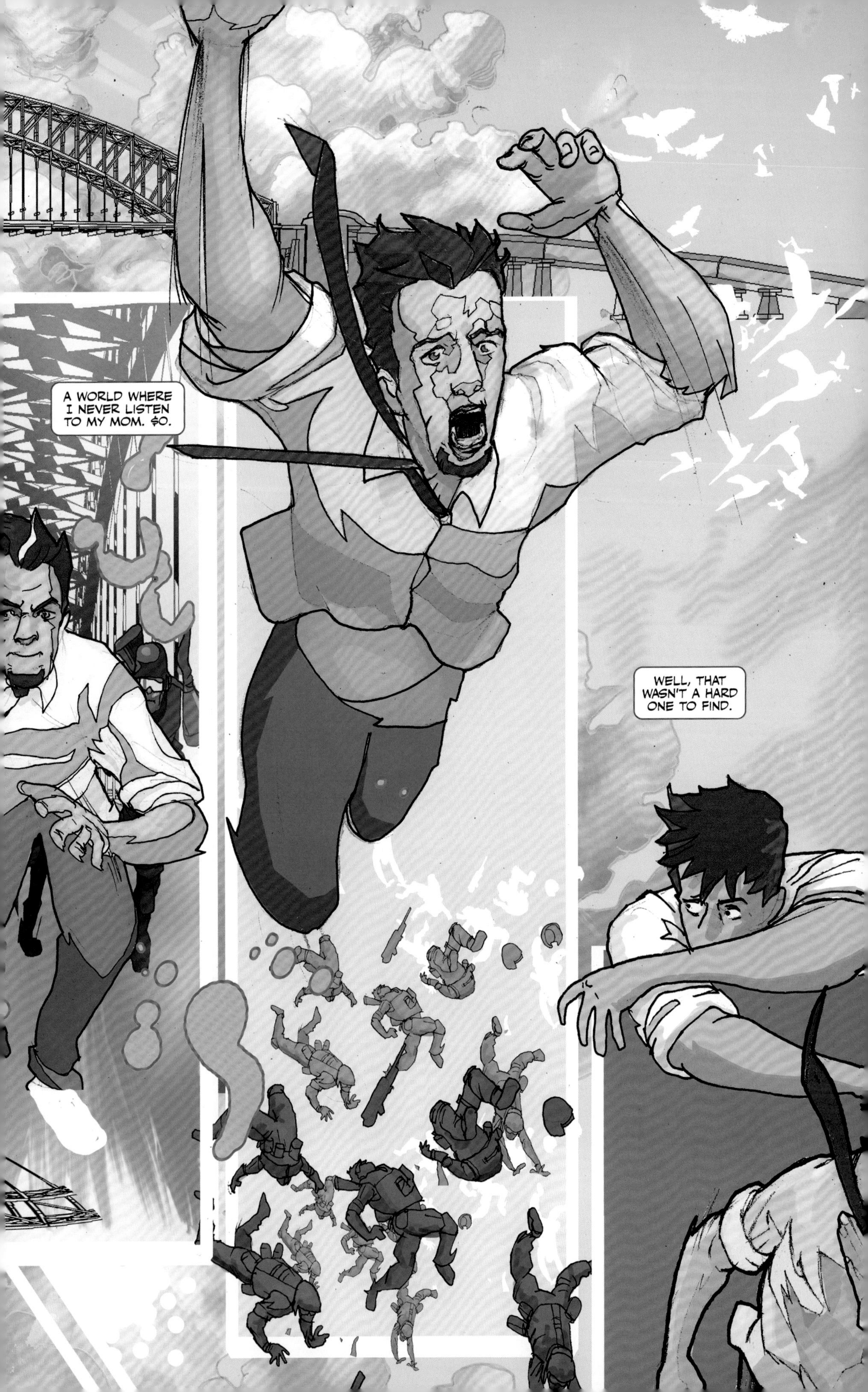
A WORLD WHERE I NEVER LISTEN TO MY MOM. $0.
WELL, THAT WASN'T A HARD ONE TO FIND.

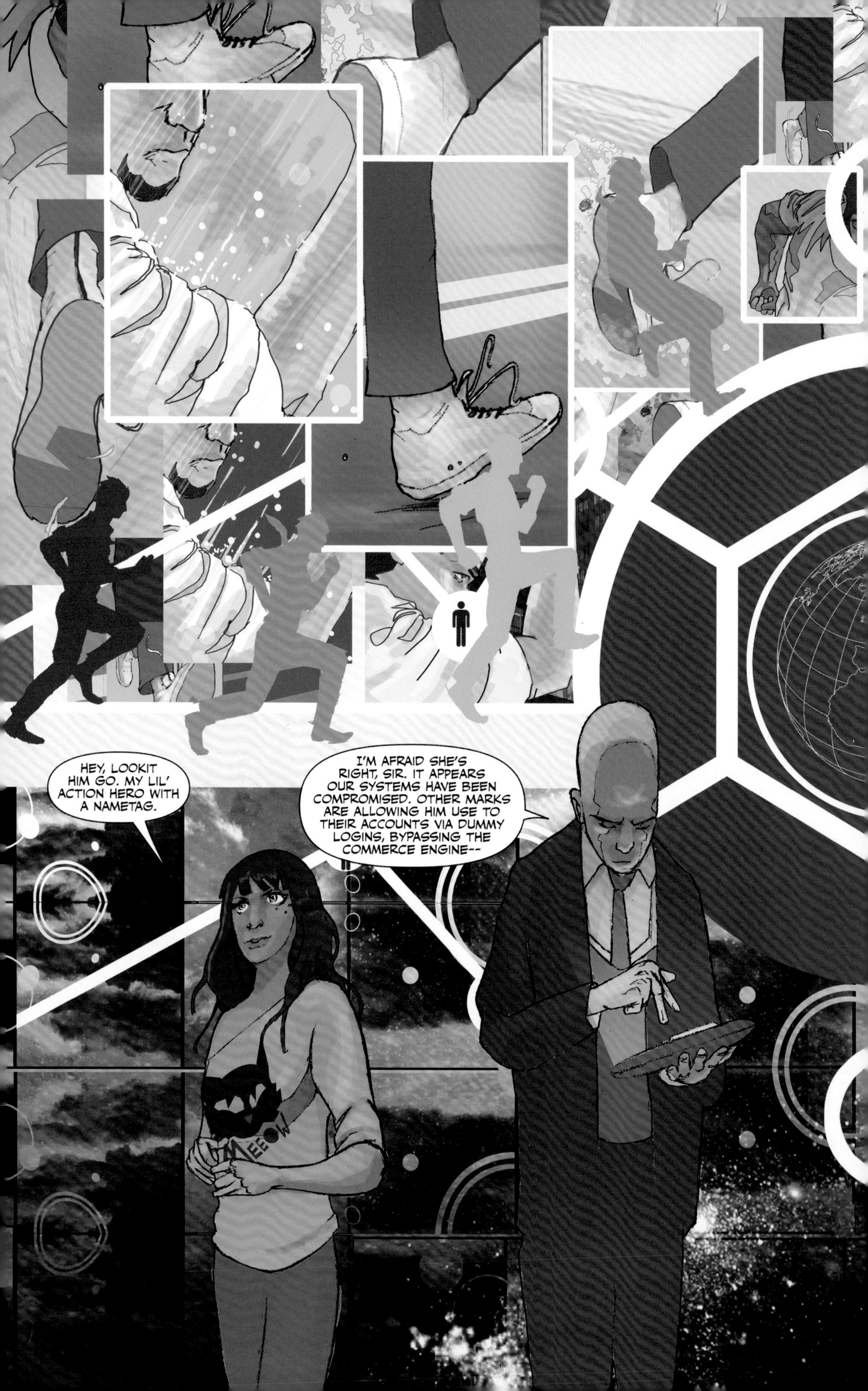
HEY, LOOKIT HIM GO. MY LIL' ACTION HERO WITH A NAMETAG.
I'M AFRAID SHE'S RIGHT, SIR. IT APPEARS OUR SYSTEMS HAVE BEEN COMPROMISED. OTHER MARKS ARE ALLOWING HIM USE TO THEIR ACCOUNTS VIA DUMMY LOGINS, BYPASSING THE COMMERCE ENGINE--
MEEOW

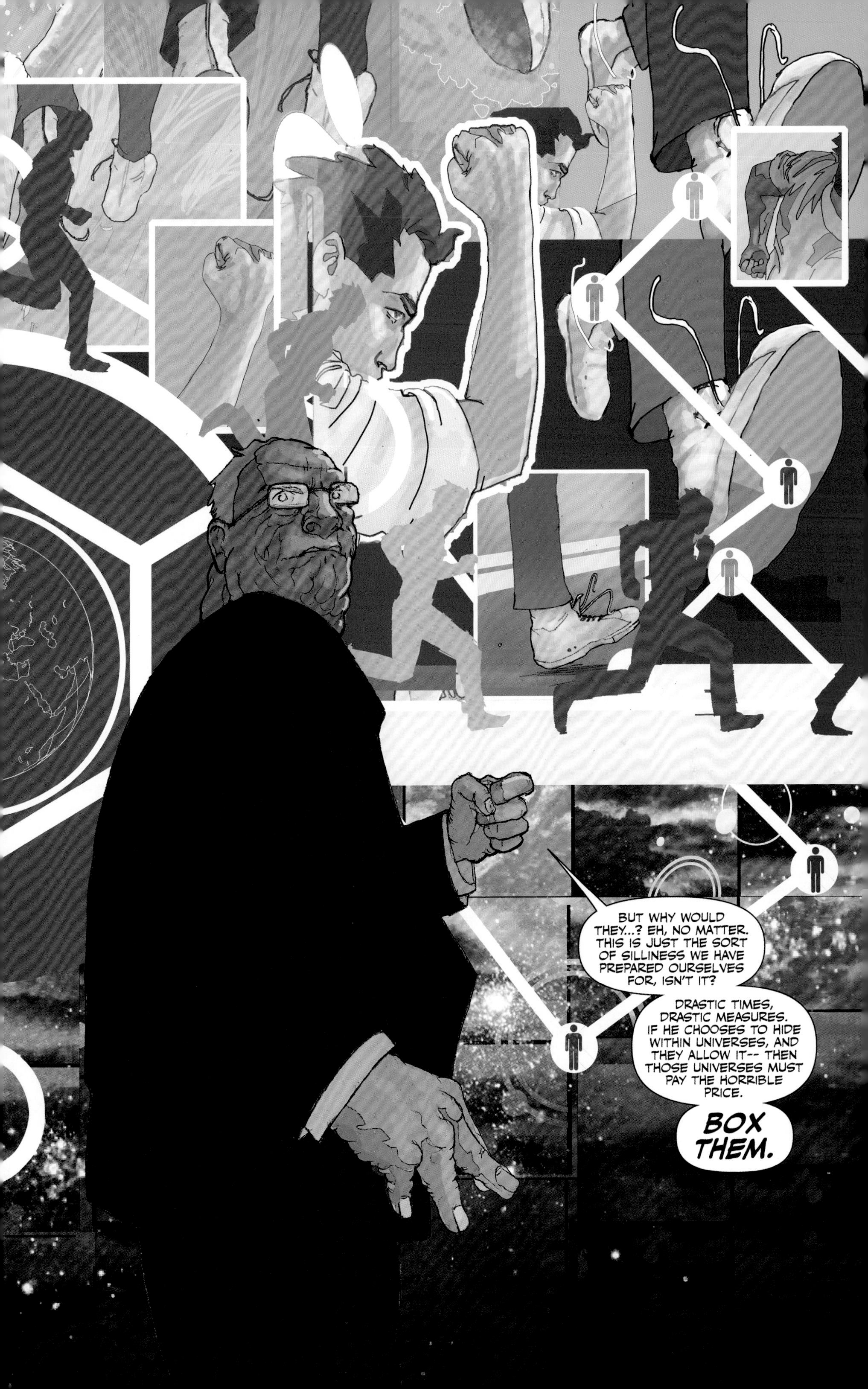
BUT WHY WOULD THEY...? EH, NO MATTER. THIS IS JUST THE SORT OF SILLINESS WE HAVE PREPARED OURSELVES FOR, ISN'T IT?
DRASTIC TIMES, DRASTIC MEASURES. IF HE CHOOSES TO HIDE WITHIN UNIVERSES, AND THEY ALLOW IT-- THEN THOSE UNIVERSES MUST PAY THE HORRIBLE PRICE.
BOX THEM.

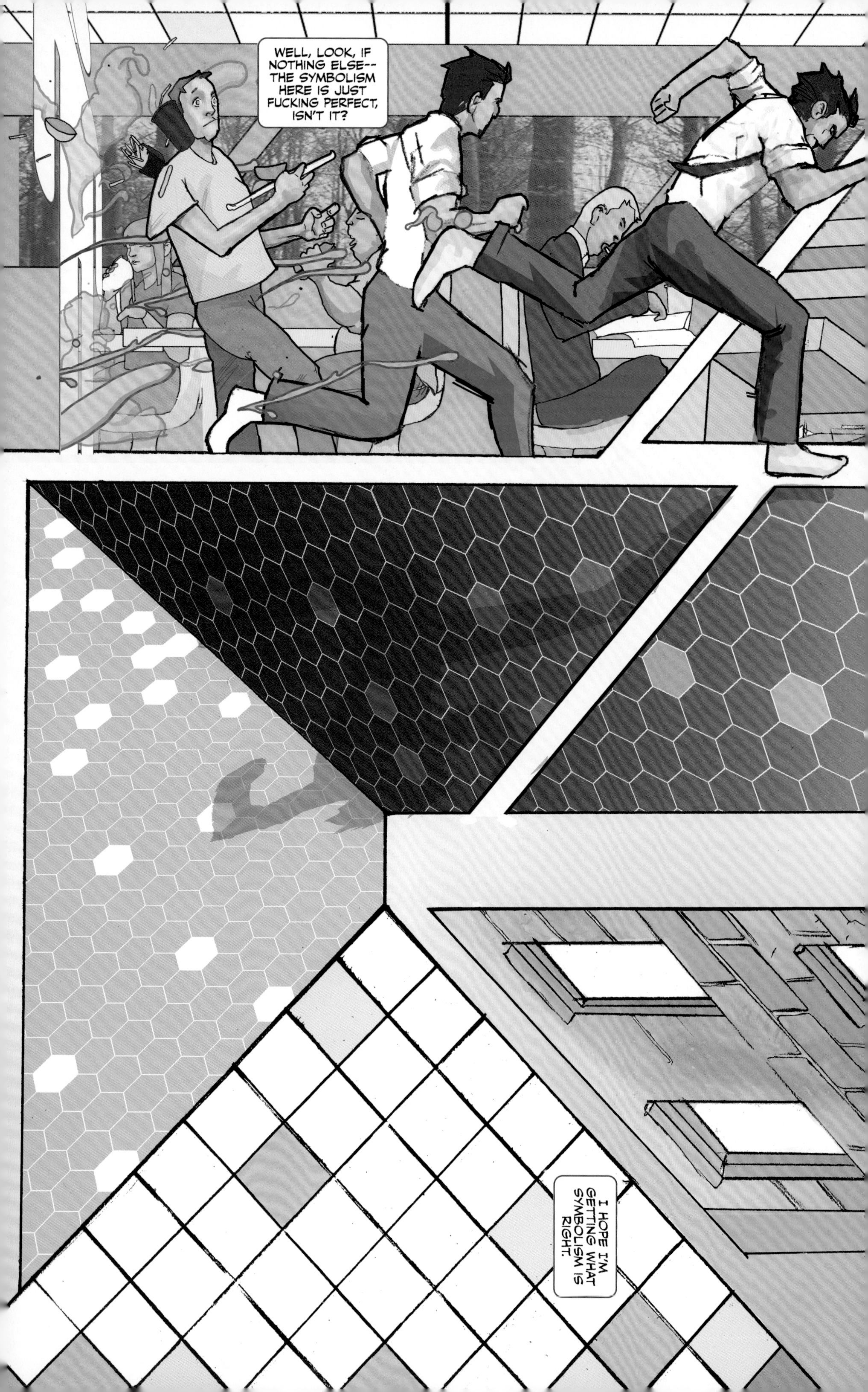
WELL, LOOK, IF NOTHING ELSE-- THE SYMBOLISM HERE IS JUST FUCKING PERFECT, ISN'T IT?
I HOPE I'M GETTING WHAT SYMBOLISM IS RIGHT.

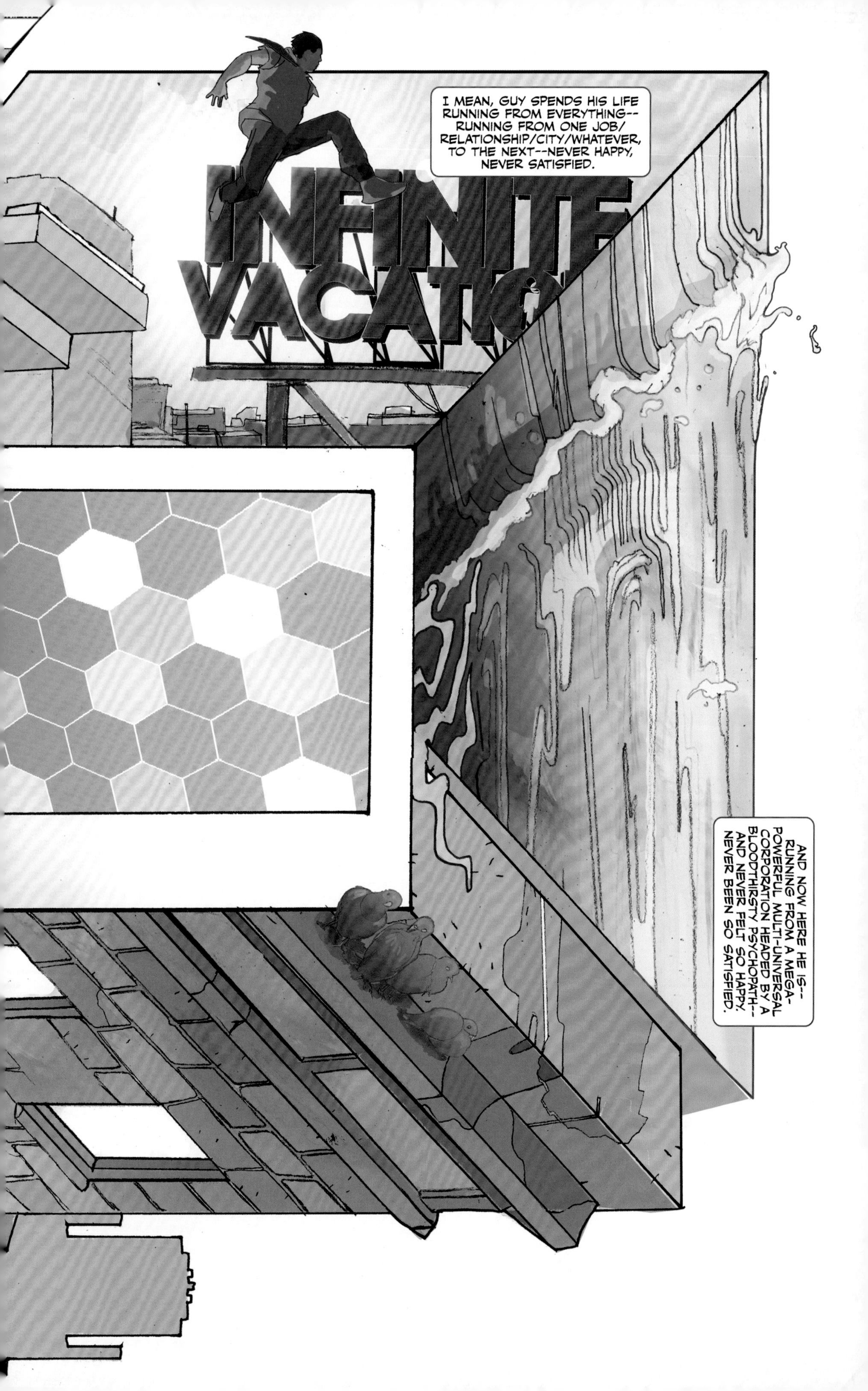

I MEAN, GUY SPENDS HIS LIFE RUNNING FROM EVERYTHING-- RUNNING FROM ONE JOB/ RELATIONSHIP/CITY/WHATEVER, TO THE NEXT--NEVER HAPPY, NEVER SATISFIED.
INFINITE
VACATIO
AND NOW HERE HE IS-- RUNNING FROM A MEGA-POWERFUL MULTI-UNIVERSAL CORPORATION HEADED BY A BLOODTHIRSTY PSYCHOPATH-- AND NEVER FELT SO HAPPY. NEVER BEEN SO SATISFIED.

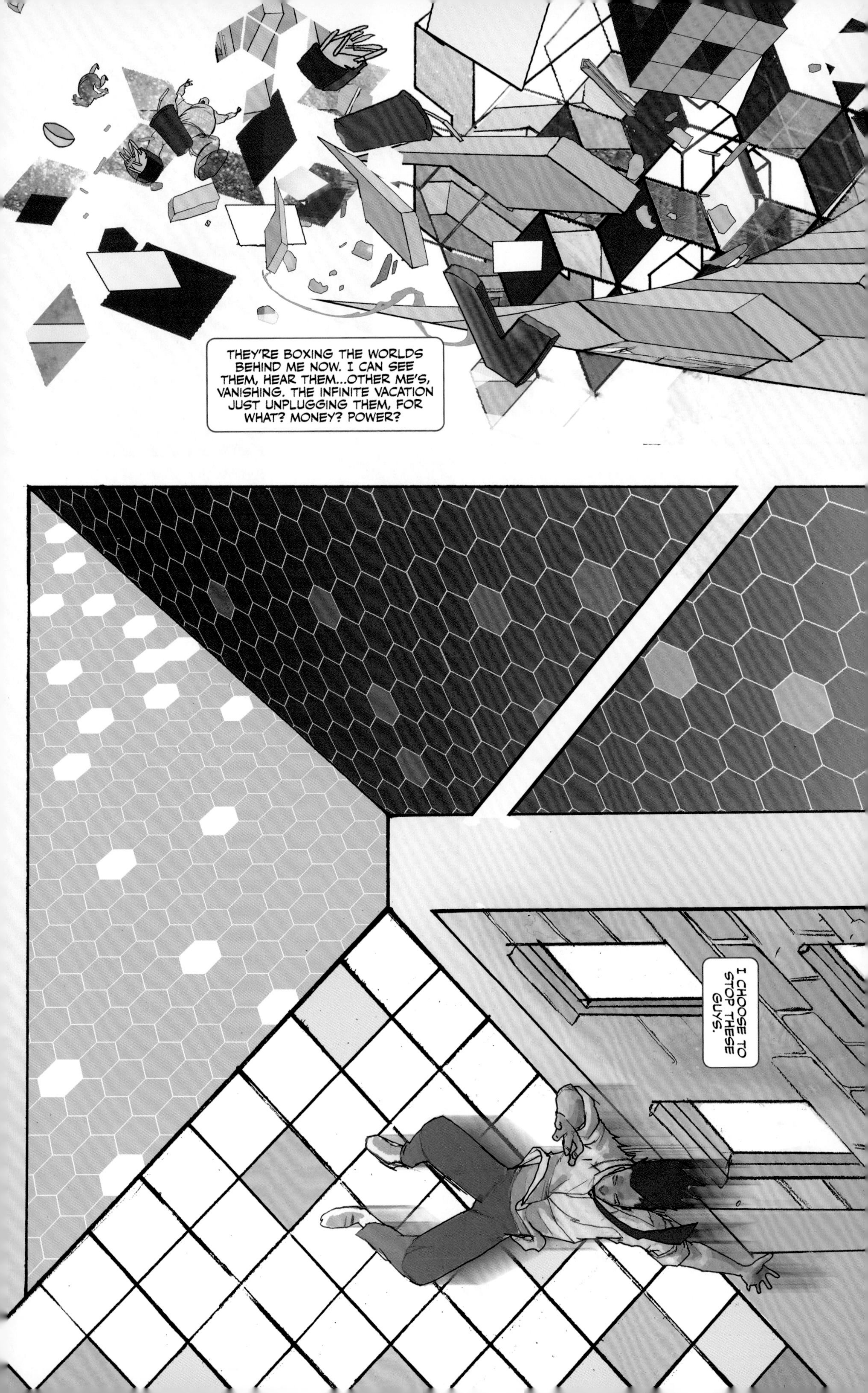
THEY'RE BOXING THE WORLDS BEHIND ME NOW. I CAN SEE THEM, HEAR THEM...OTHER ME'S, VANISHING. THE INFINITE VACATION JUST UNPLUGGING THEM, FOR WHAT? MONEY? POWER?
I CHOOSE TO STOP THESE GUYS.

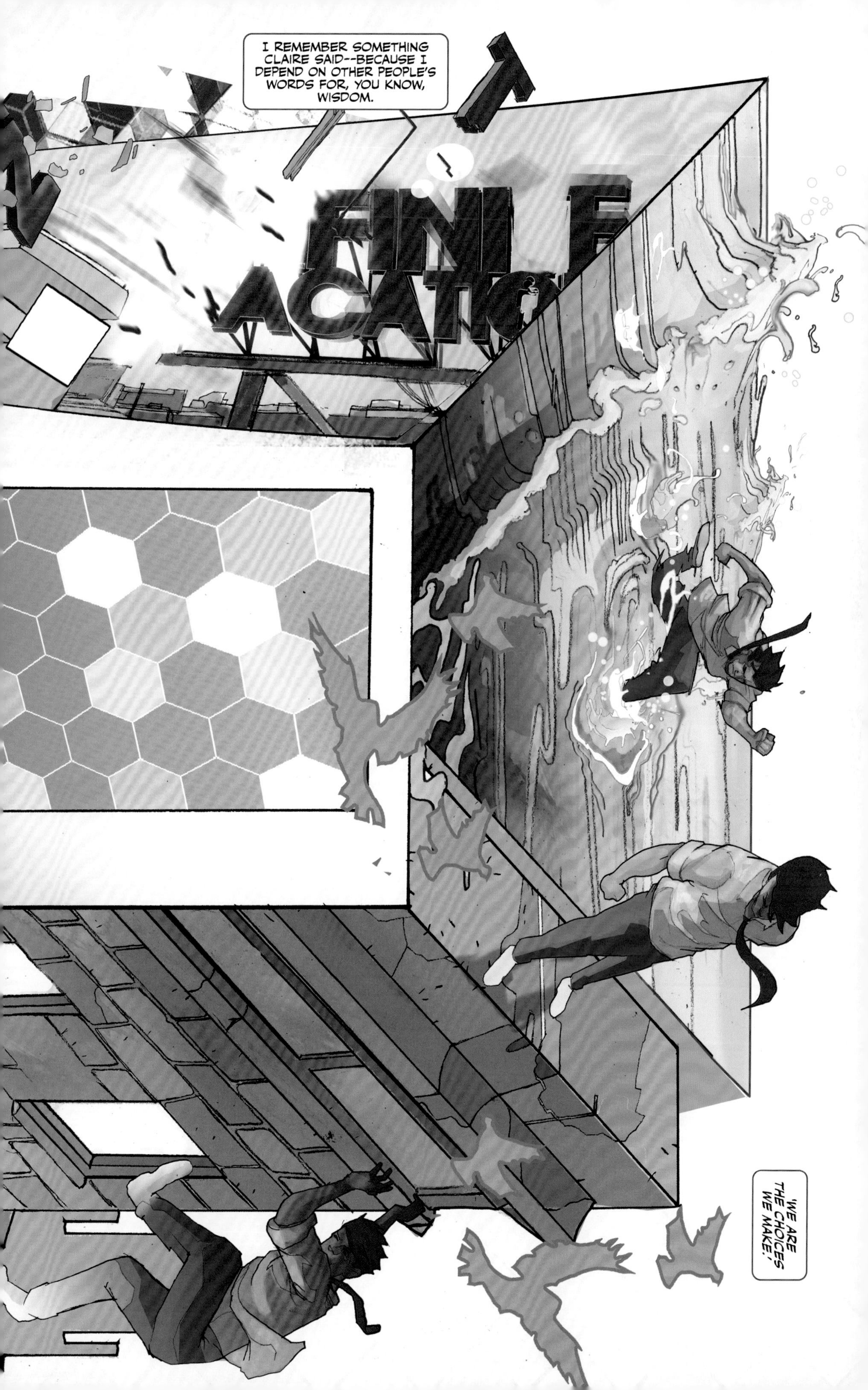
I REMEMBER SOMETHING CLAIRE SAID--BECAUSE I DEPEND ON OTHER PEOPLE'S WORDS FOR, YOU KNOW, WISDOM.
'WE ARE THE CHOICES WE MAKE.'

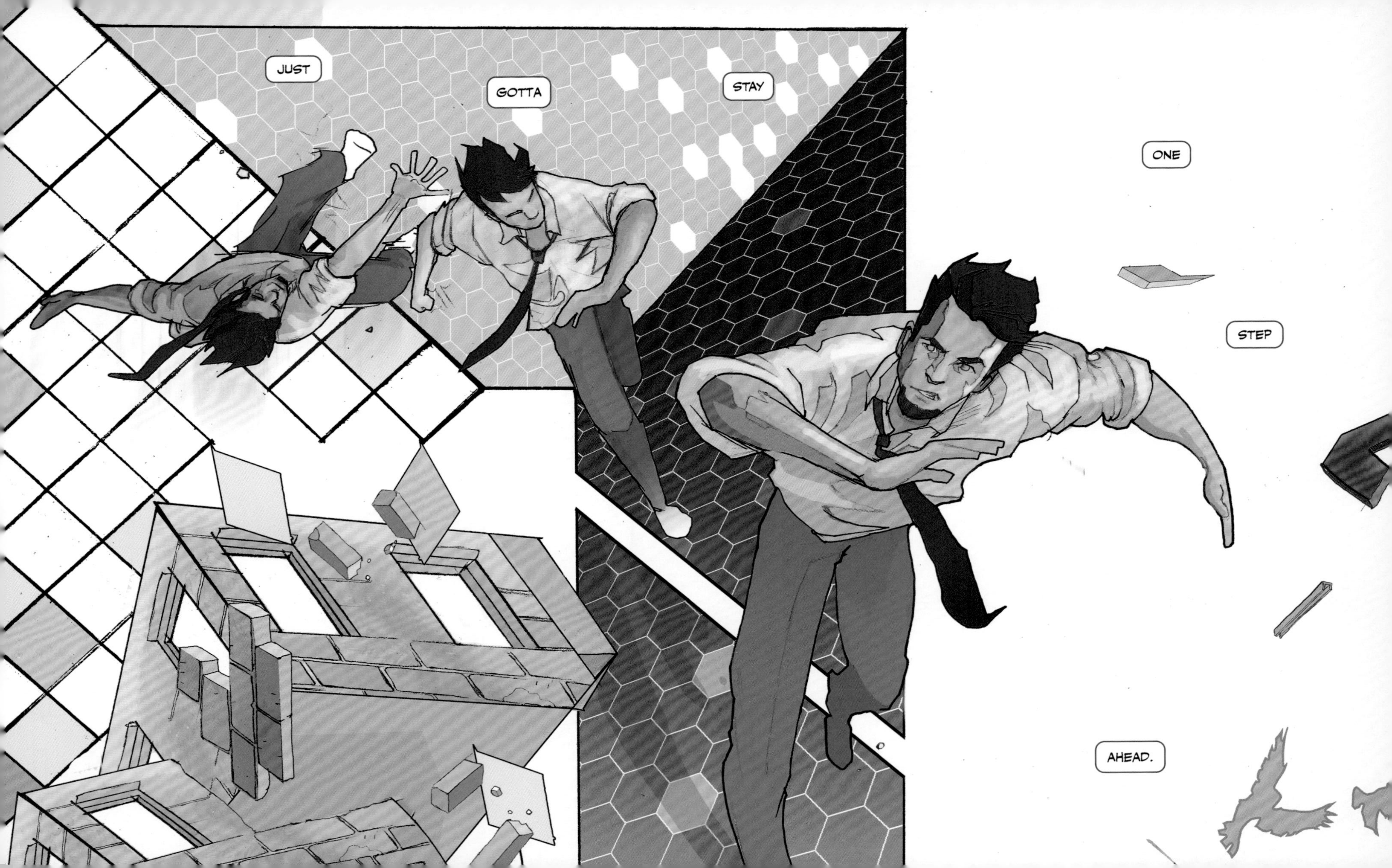
JUST
GOTTA
STAY
ONE
STEP
AHEAD.

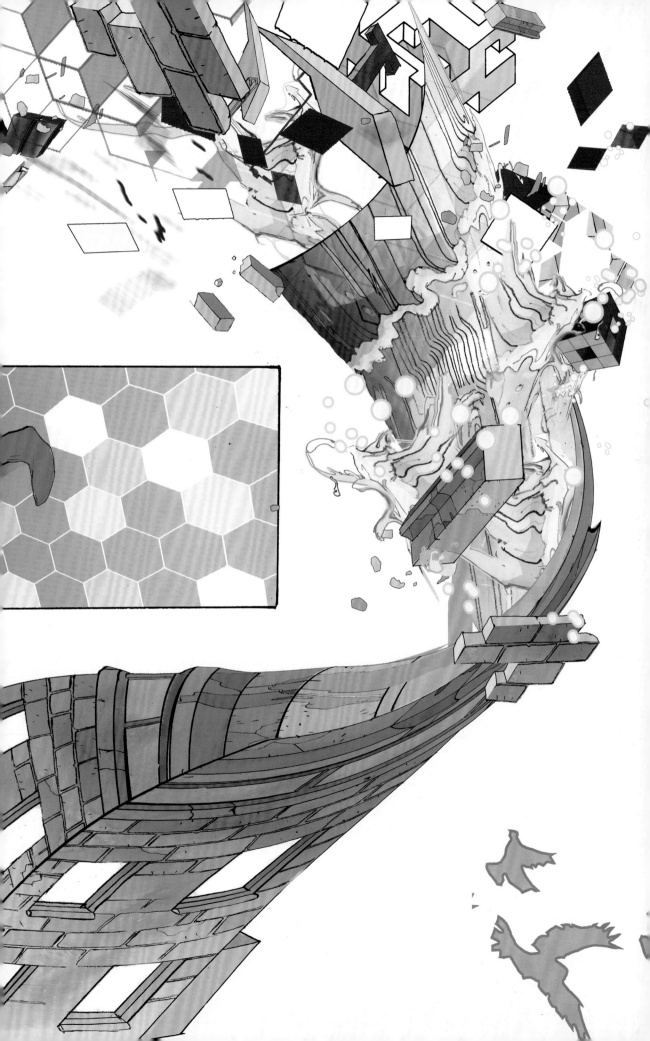

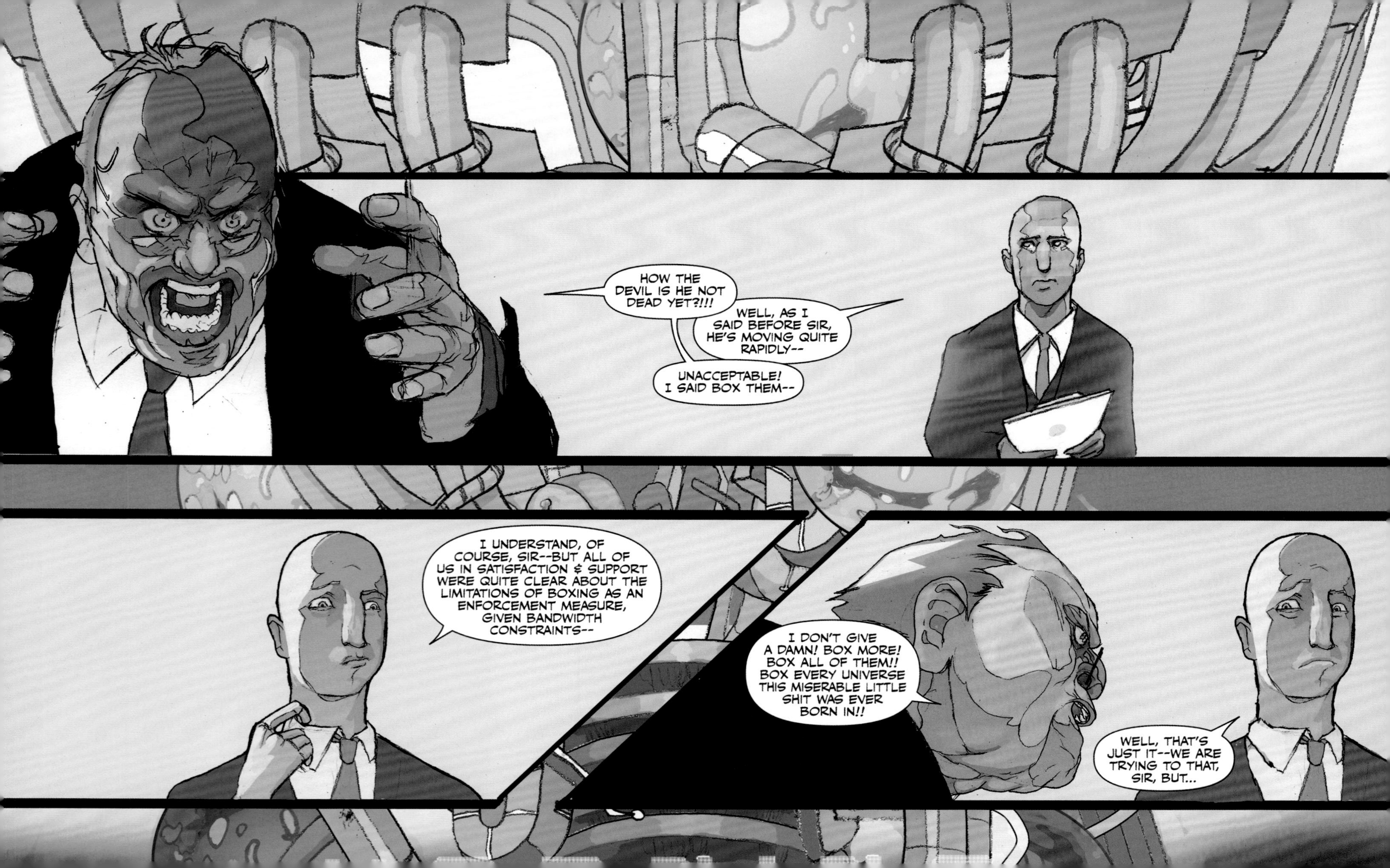
HOW THE DEVIL IS HE NOT DEAD YET?!!!
WELL, AS I SAID BEFORE SIR, HE'S MOVING QUITE RAPIDLY--
UNACCEPTABLE! I SAID BOX THEM--
I UNDERSTAND, OF COURSE, SIR--BUT ALL OF US IN SATISFACTION & SUPPORT WERE QUITE CLEAR ABOUT THE LIMITATIONS OF BOXING AS AN ENFORCEMENT MEASURE, GIVEN BANDWIDTH CONSTRAINTS--
I DON'T GIVE A DAMN! BOX MORE! BOX ALL OF THEM!! BOX EVERY UNIVERSE THIS MISERABLE LITTLE SHIT WAS EVER BORN IN!!
WELL, THAT'S JUST IT--WE ARE TRYING TO THAT, SIR, BUT...

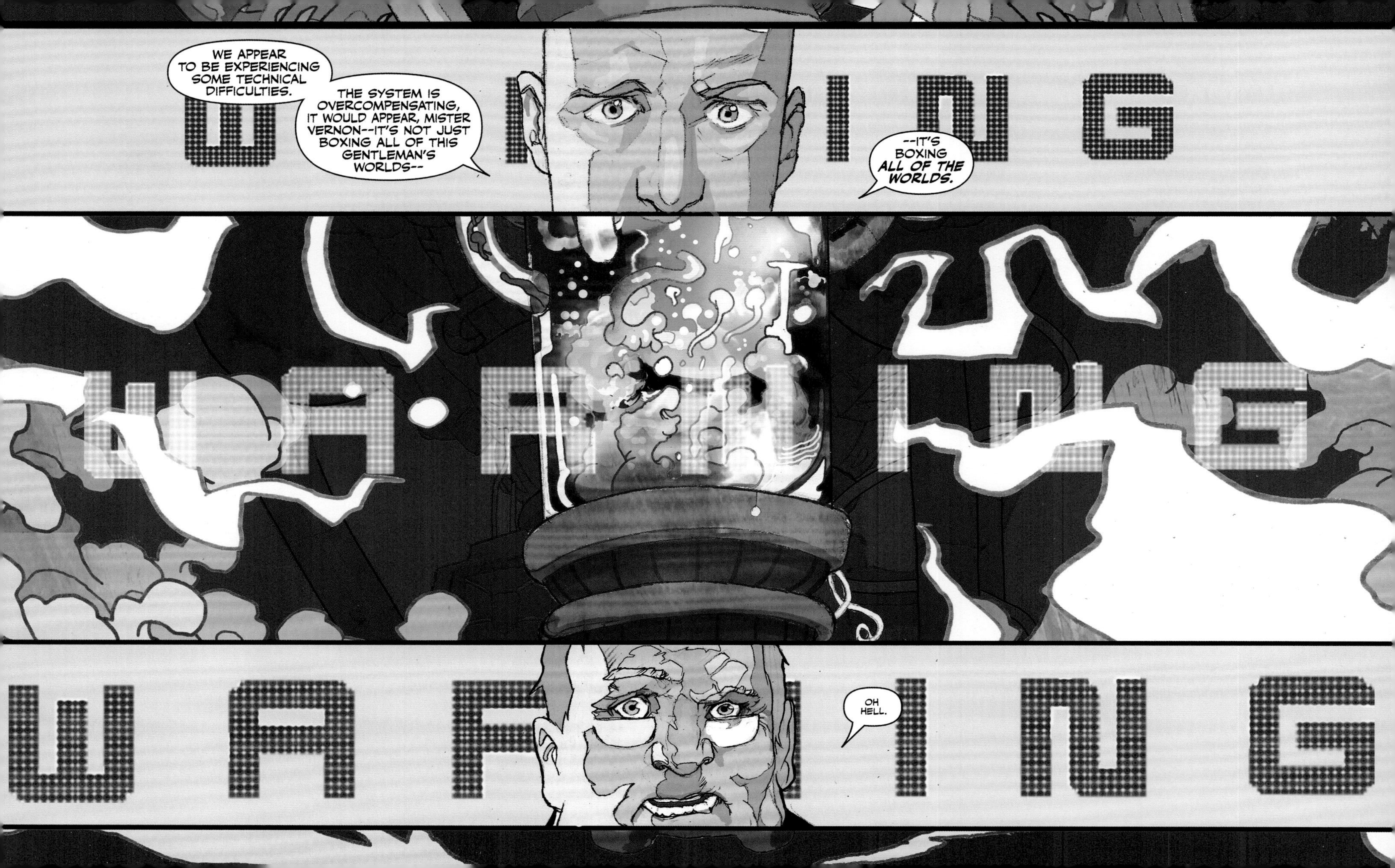
WE APPEAR TO BE EXPERIENCING SOME TECHNICAL DIFFICULTIES.
THE SYSTEM IS OVERCOMPENSATING, IT WOULD APPEAR, MISTER VERNON--IT'S NOT JUST BOXING ALL OF THIS GENTLEMAN'S WORLDS--
--IT'S BOXING *ALL OF THE WORLDS.*
OH HELL.

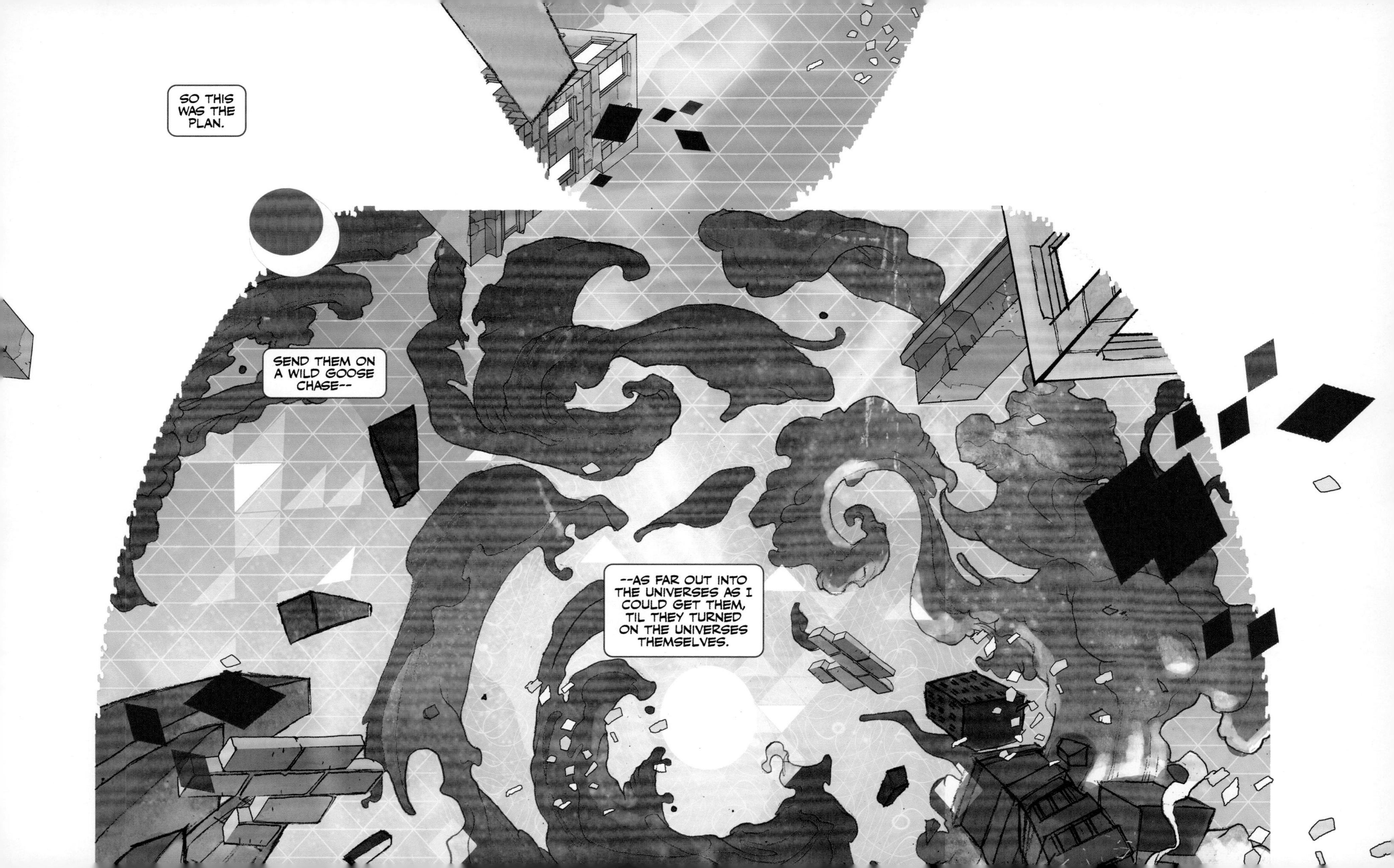
SO THIS WAS THE PLAN.
SEND THEM ON A WILD GOOSE CHASE--
--AS FAR OUT INTO THE UNIVERSES AS I COULD GET THEM, TIL THEY TURNED ON THE UNIVERSES THEMSELVES.

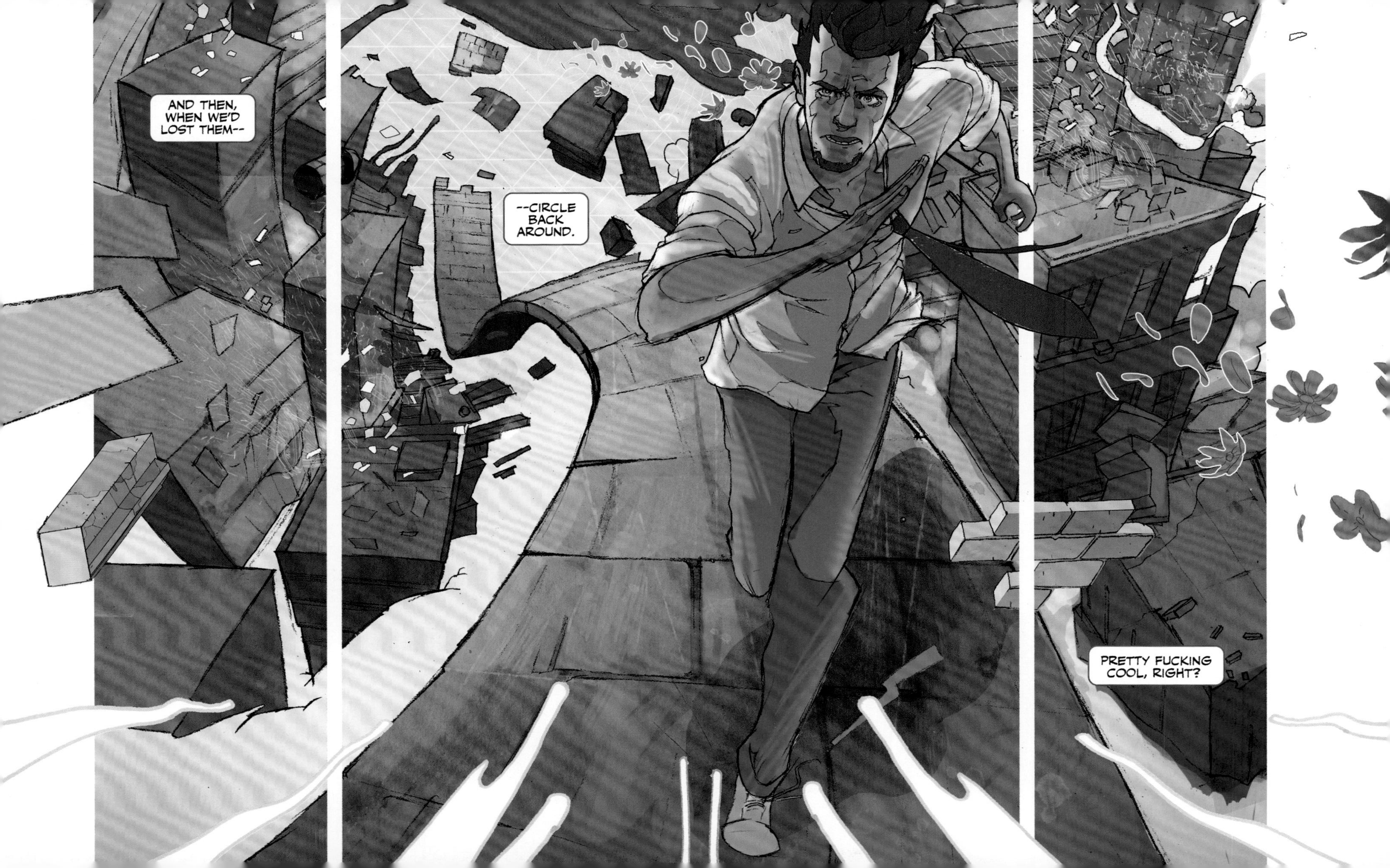
AND THEN, WHEN WE'D LOST THEM--
--CIRCLE BACK AROUND.
PRETTY FUCKING COOL, RIGHT?

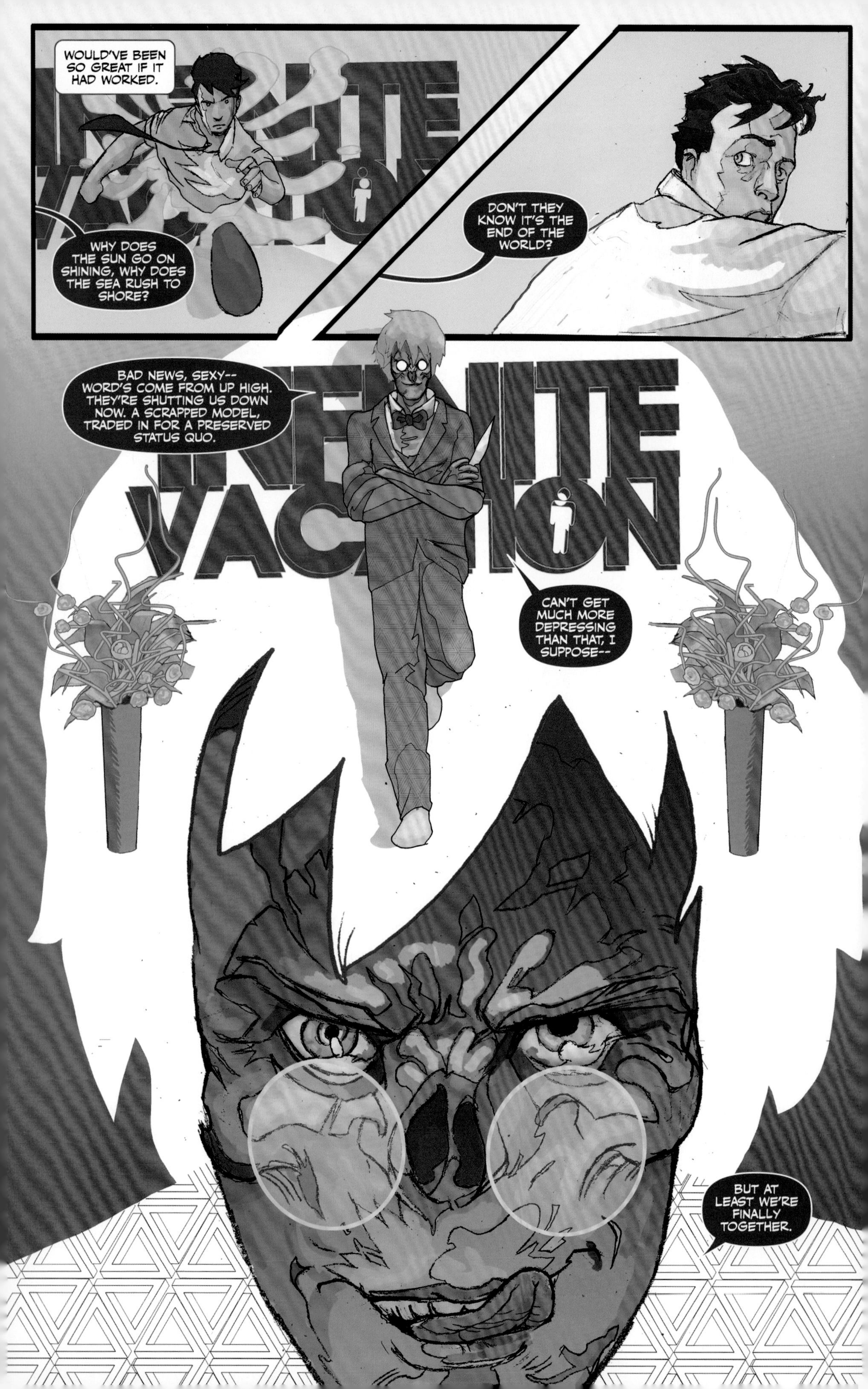
WOULD'VE BEEN SO GREAT IF IT HAD WORKED.
WHY DOES THE SUN GO ON SHINING, WHY DOES THE SEA RUSH TO SHORE?
DON'T THEY KNOW IT'S THE END OF THE WORLD?
BAD NEWS, SEXY-- WORD'S COME FROM UP HIGH. THEY'RE SHUTTING US DOWN NOW. A SCRAPPED MODEL, TRADED IN FOR A PRESERVED STATUS QUO.
INFINITE VACATION
CAN'T GET MUCH MORE DEPRESSING THAN THAT, I SUPPOSE--
BUT AT LEAST WE'RE FINALLY TOGETHER.

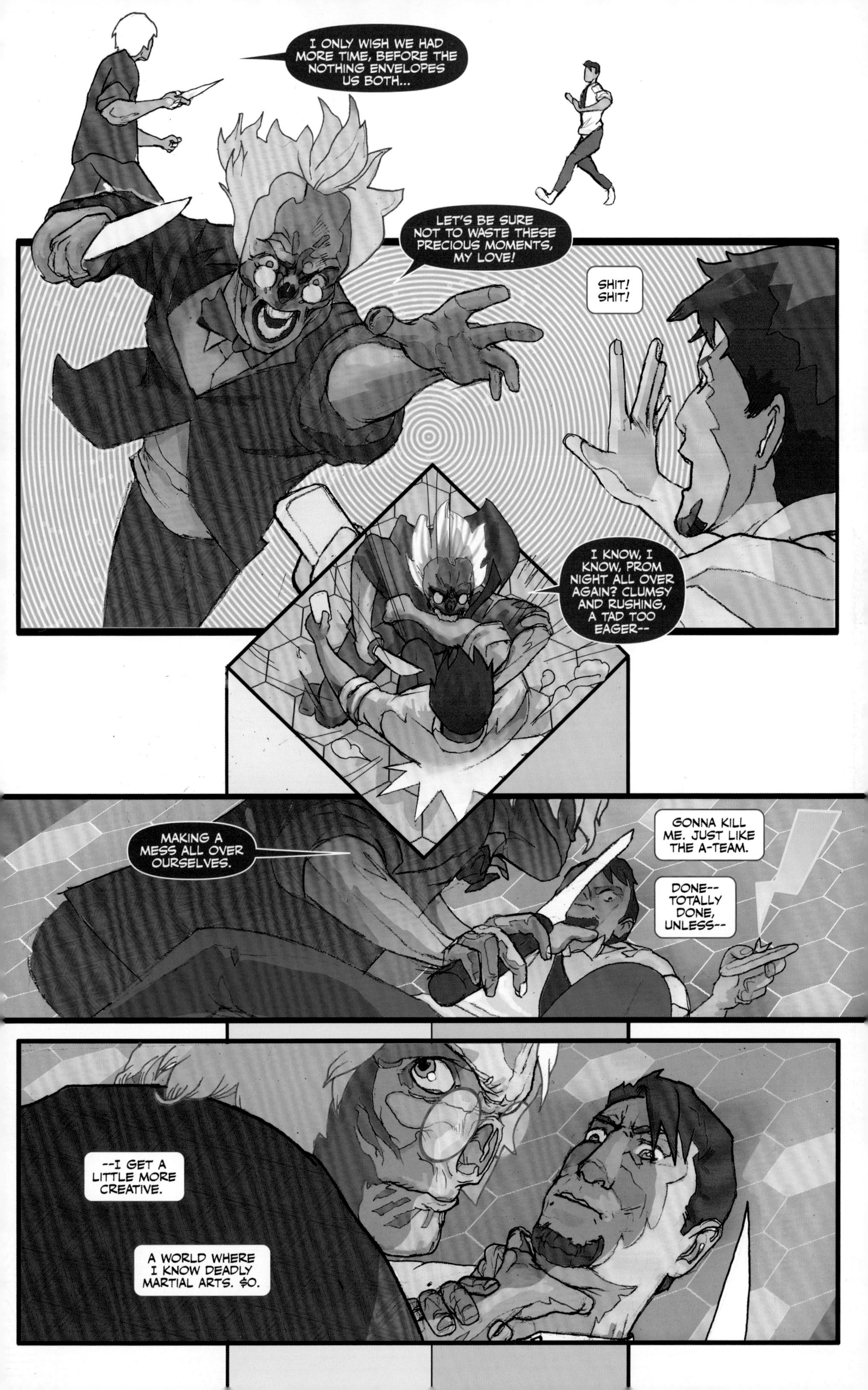
I ONLY WISH WE HAD MORE TIME, BEFORE THE NOTHING ENVELOPES US BOTH...
LET'S BE SURE NOT TO WASTE THESE PRECIOUS MOMENTS, MY LOVE!
SHIT! SHIT!
I KNOW, I KNOW, PROM NIGHT ALL OVER AGAIN? CLUMSY AND RUSHING, A TAD TOO EAGER--
MAKING A MESS ALL OVER OURSELVES.
GONNA KILL ME. JUST LIKE THE A-TEAM.
DONE-- TOTALLY DONE, UNLESS--
--I GET A LITTLE MORE CREATIVE.
A WORLD WHERE I KNOW DEADLY MARTIAL ARTS. $0.

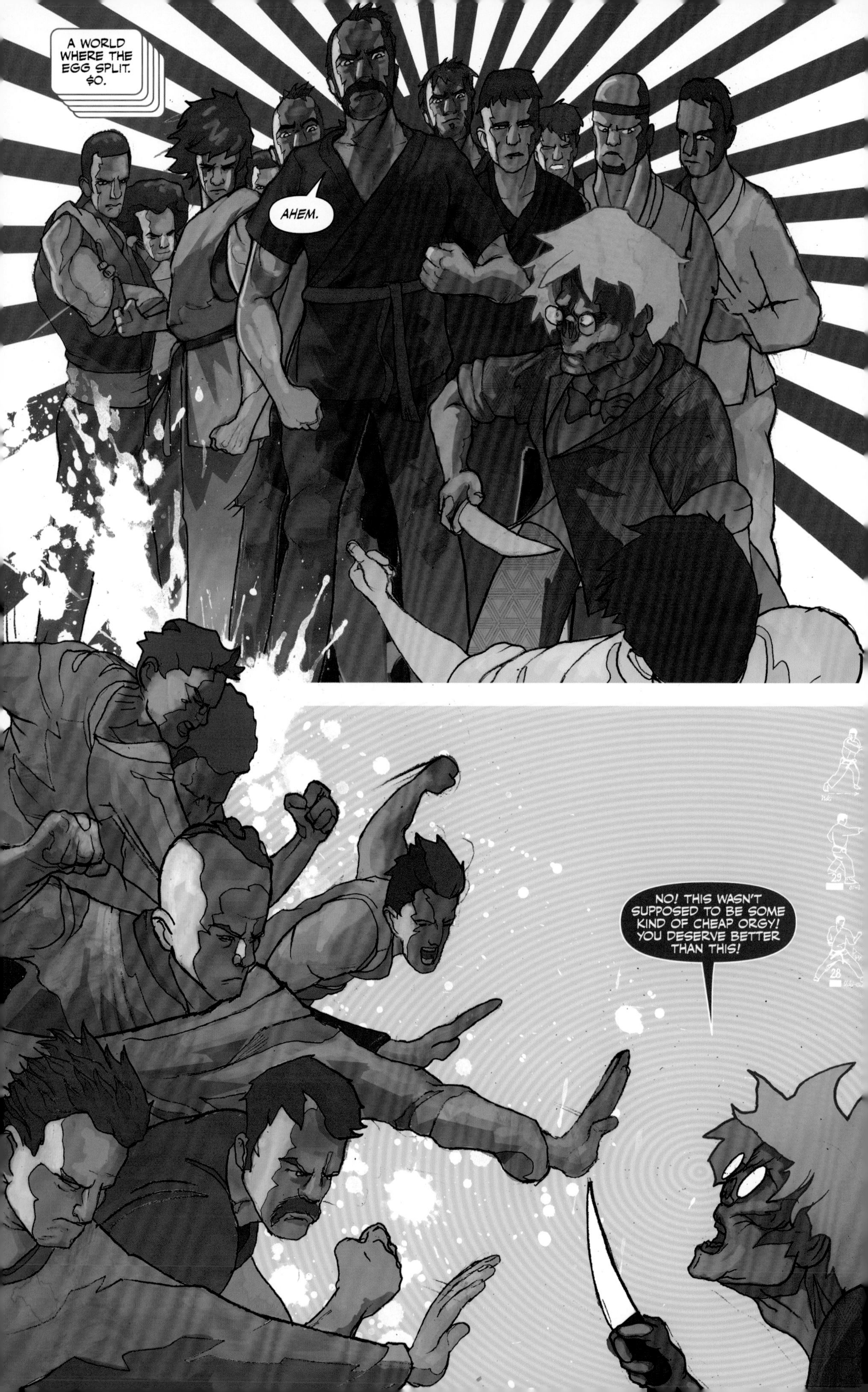
A WORLD WHERE THE EGG SPLIT. $0.
AHEM.
NO! THIS WASN'T SUPPOSED TO BE SOME KIND OF CHEAP ORGY! YOU DESERVE BETTER THAN THIS!

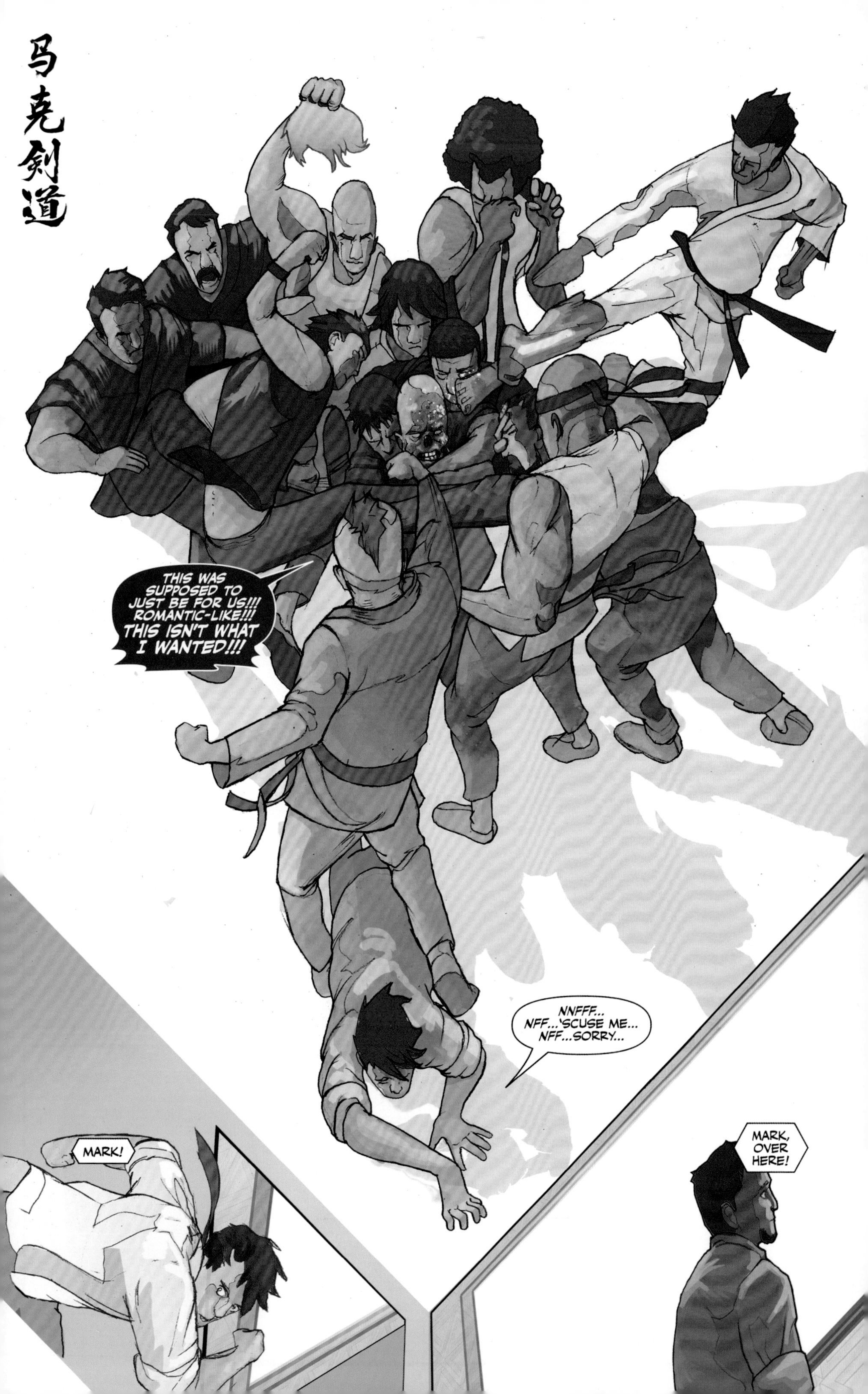
马克剑道
THIS WAS SUPPOSED TO JUST BE FOR US!!! ROMANTIC-LIKE!!! THIS ISN'T WHAT I WANTED!!!
NNFFF... NFF...'SCUSE ME... NFF...SORRY...
MARK!
MARK, OVER HERE!

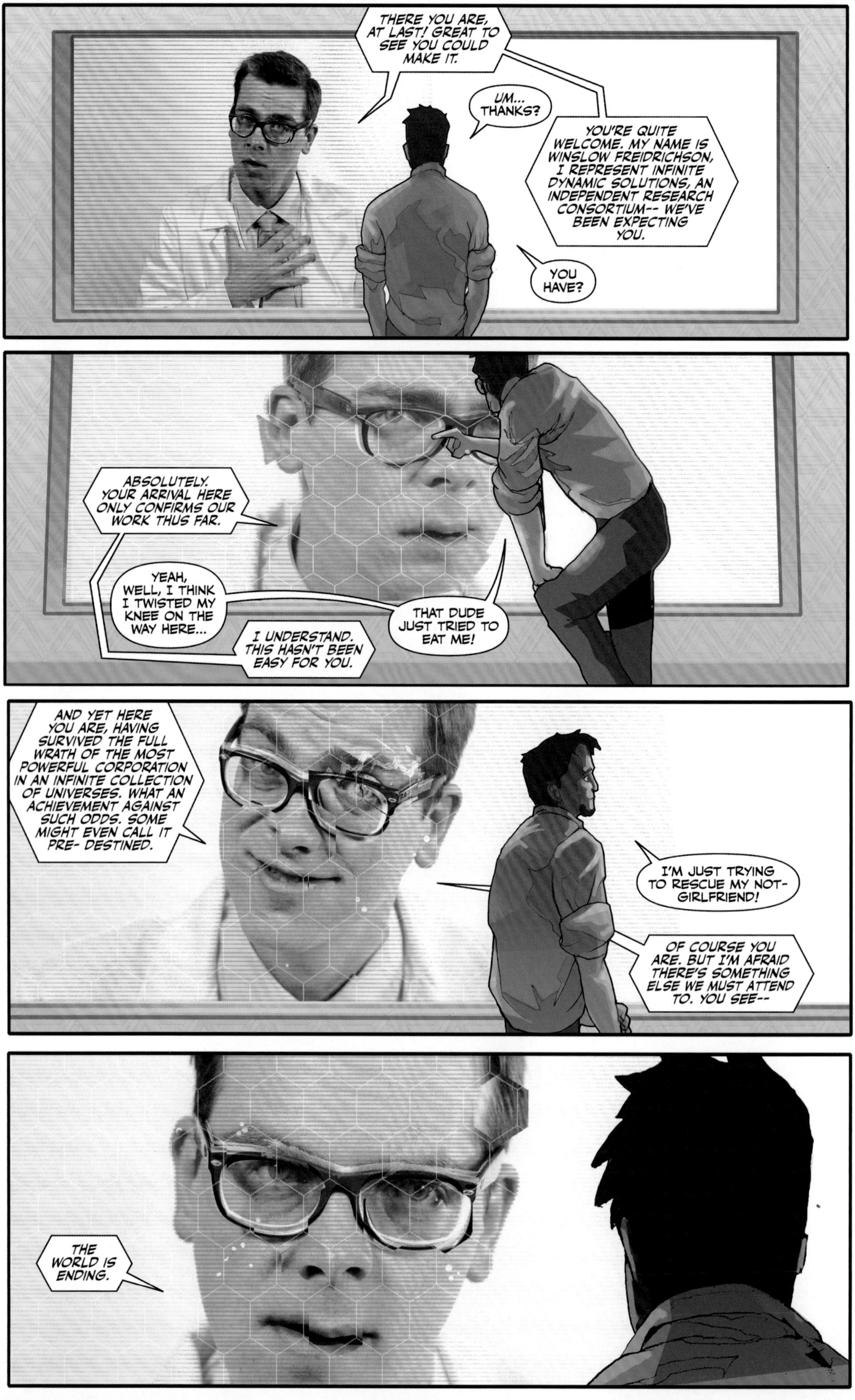
THERE YOU ARE, AT LAST! GREAT TO SEE YOU COULD MAKE IT.
UM... THANKS?
YOU'RE QUITE WELCOME. MY NAME IS WINSLOW FREIDRICHSON, I REPRESENT INFINITE DYNAMIC SOLUTIONS, AN INDEPENDENT RESEARCH CONSORTIUM-- WE'VE BEEN EXPECTING YOU.
YOU HAVE?
ABSOLUTELY. YOUR ARRIVAL HERE ONLY CONFIRMS OUR WORK THUS FAR.
THAT DUDE JUST TRIED TO EAT ME!
YEAH, WELL, I THINK I TWISTED MY KNEE ON THE WAY HERE...
I UNDERSTAND. THIS HASN'T BEEN EASY FOR YOU.
AND YET HERE YOU ARE, HAVING SURVIVED THE FULL WRATH OF THE MOST POWERFUL CORPORATION IN AN INFINITE COLLECTION OF UNIVERSES. WHAT AN ACHIEVEMENT AGAINST SUCH ODDS. SOME MIGHT EVEN CALL IT PRE- DESTINED.
I'M JUST TRYING TO RESCUE MY NOT-GIRLFRIEND!
OF COURSE YOU ARE. BUT I'M AFRAID THERE'S SOMETHING ELSE WE MUST ATTEND TO. YOU SEE--
THE WORLD IS ENDING.

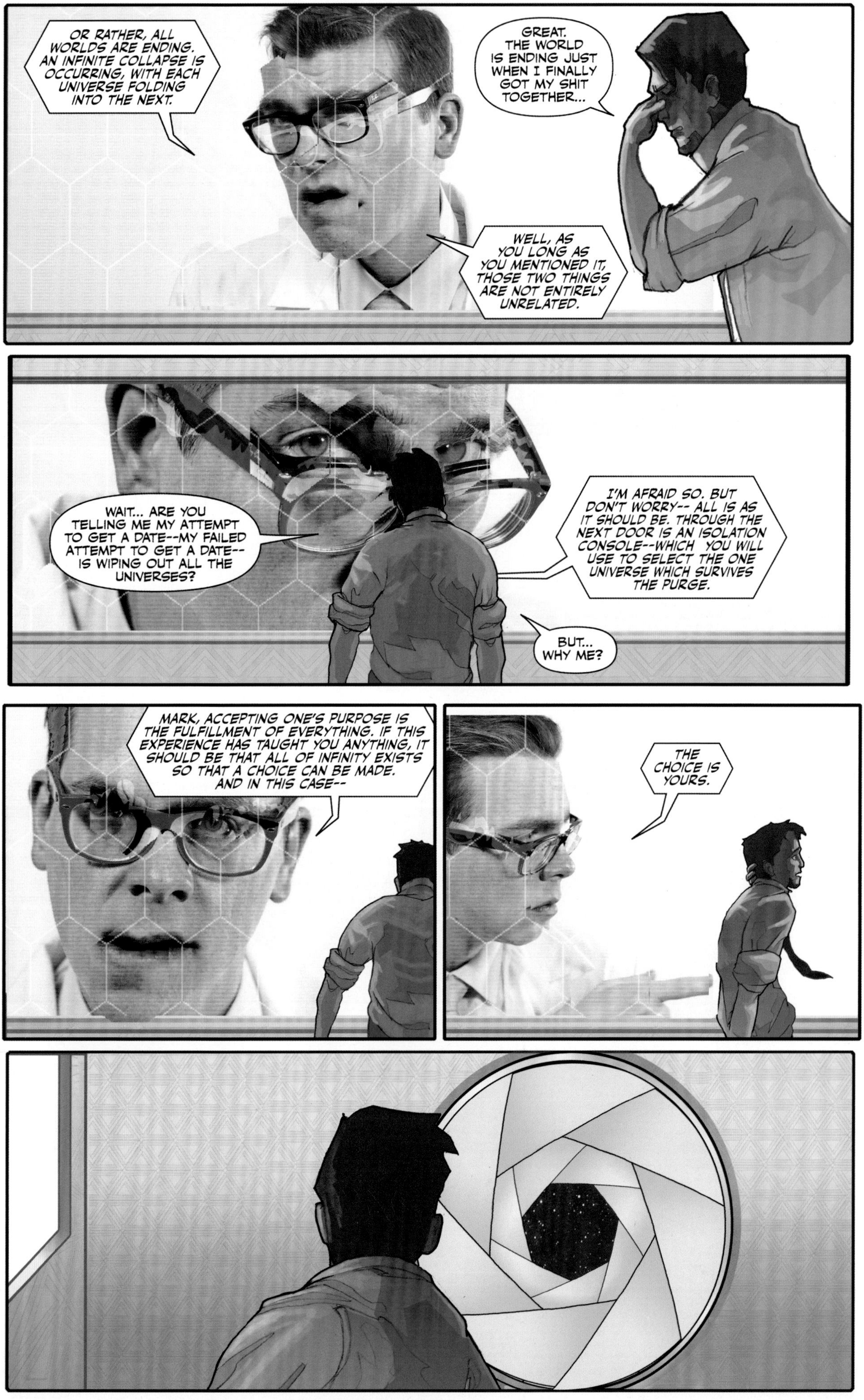
OR RATHER, ALL WORLDS ARE ENDING. AN INFINITE COLLAPSE IS OCCURRING, WITH EACH UNIVERSE FOLDING INTO THE NEXT.
GREAT. THE WORLD IS ENDING JUST WHEN I FINALLY GOT MY SHIT TOGETHER...
WELL, AS YOU LONG AS YOU MENTIONED IT, THOSE TWO THINGS ARE NOT ENTIRELY UNRELATED.
WAIT... ARE YOU TELLING ME MY ATTEMPT TO GET A DATE--MY FAILED ATTEMPT TO GET A DATE--IS WIPING OUT ALL THE UNIVERSES?
I'M AFRAID SO. BUT DON'T WORRY-- ALL IS AS IT SHOULD BE. THROUGH THE NEXT DOOR IS AN ISOLATION CONSOLE--WHICH YOU WILL USE TO SELECT THE ONE UNIVERSE WHICH SURVIVES THE PURGE.
BUT... WHY ME?
MARK, ACCEPTING ONE'S PURPOSE IS THE FULFILLMENT OF EVERYTHING. IF THIS EXPERIENCE HAS TAUGHT YOU ANYTHING, IT SHOULD BE THAT ALL OF INFINITY EXISTS SO THAT A CHOICE CAN BE MADE. AND IN THIS CASE--
THE CHOICE IS YOURS.

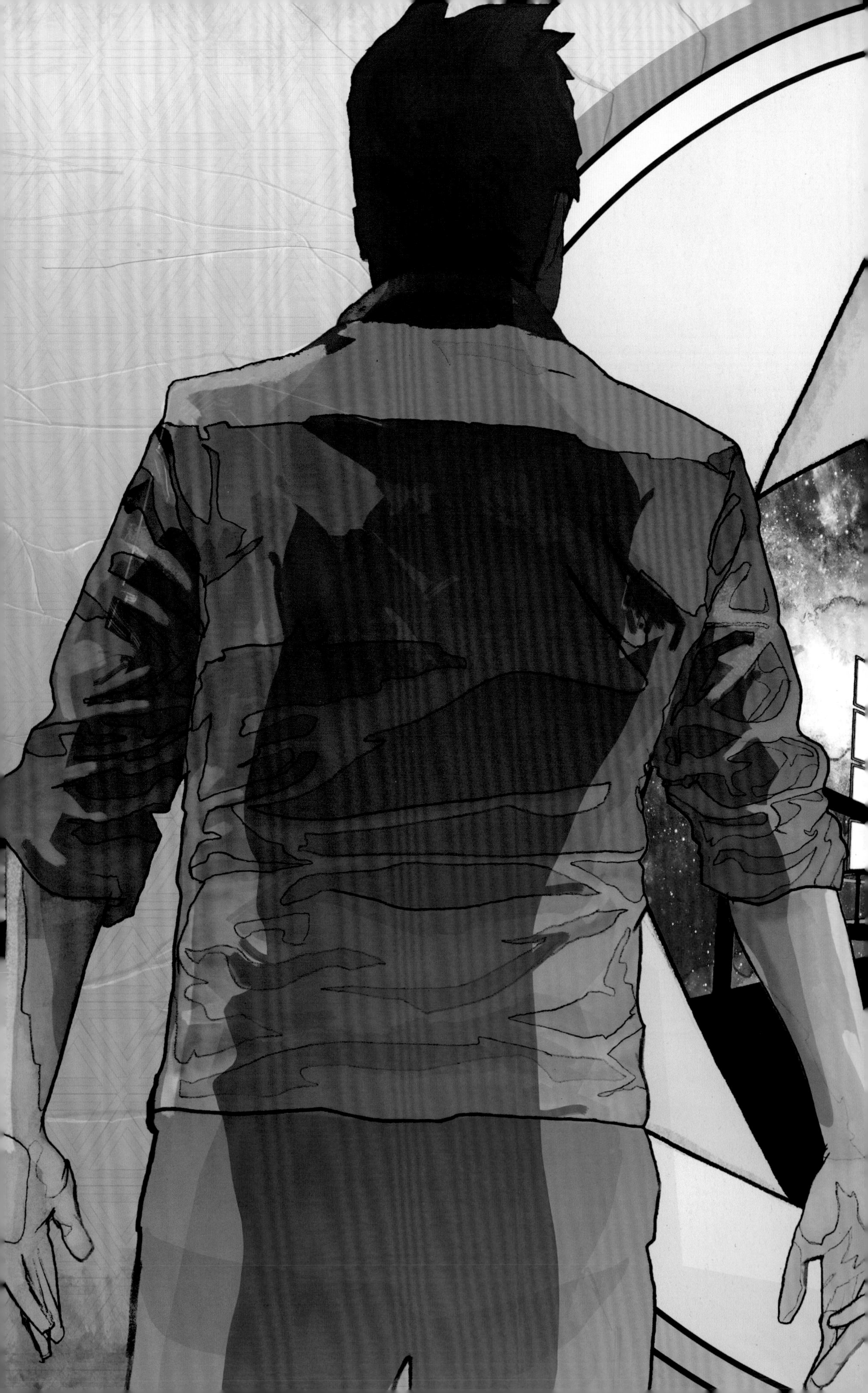

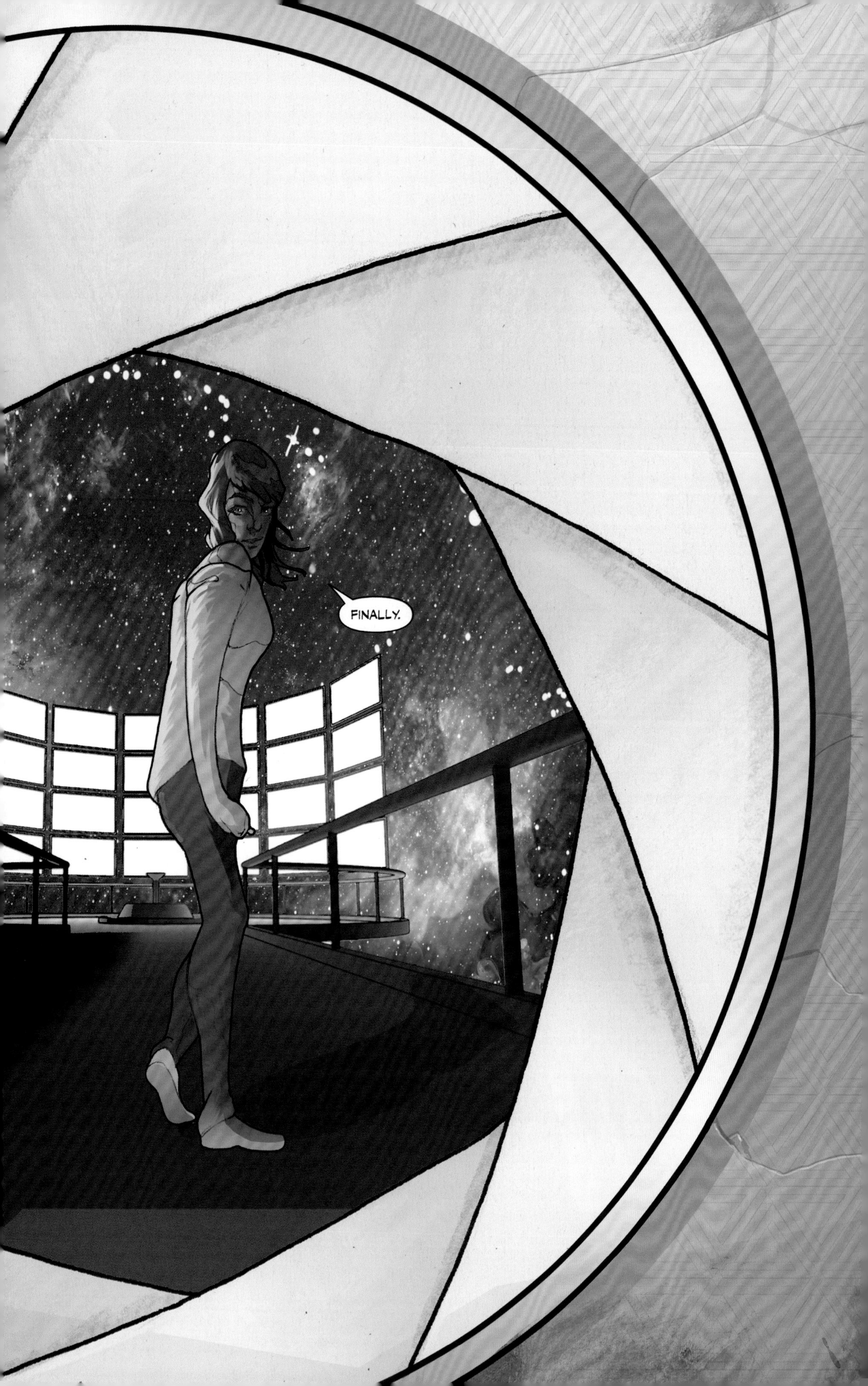
FINALLY.

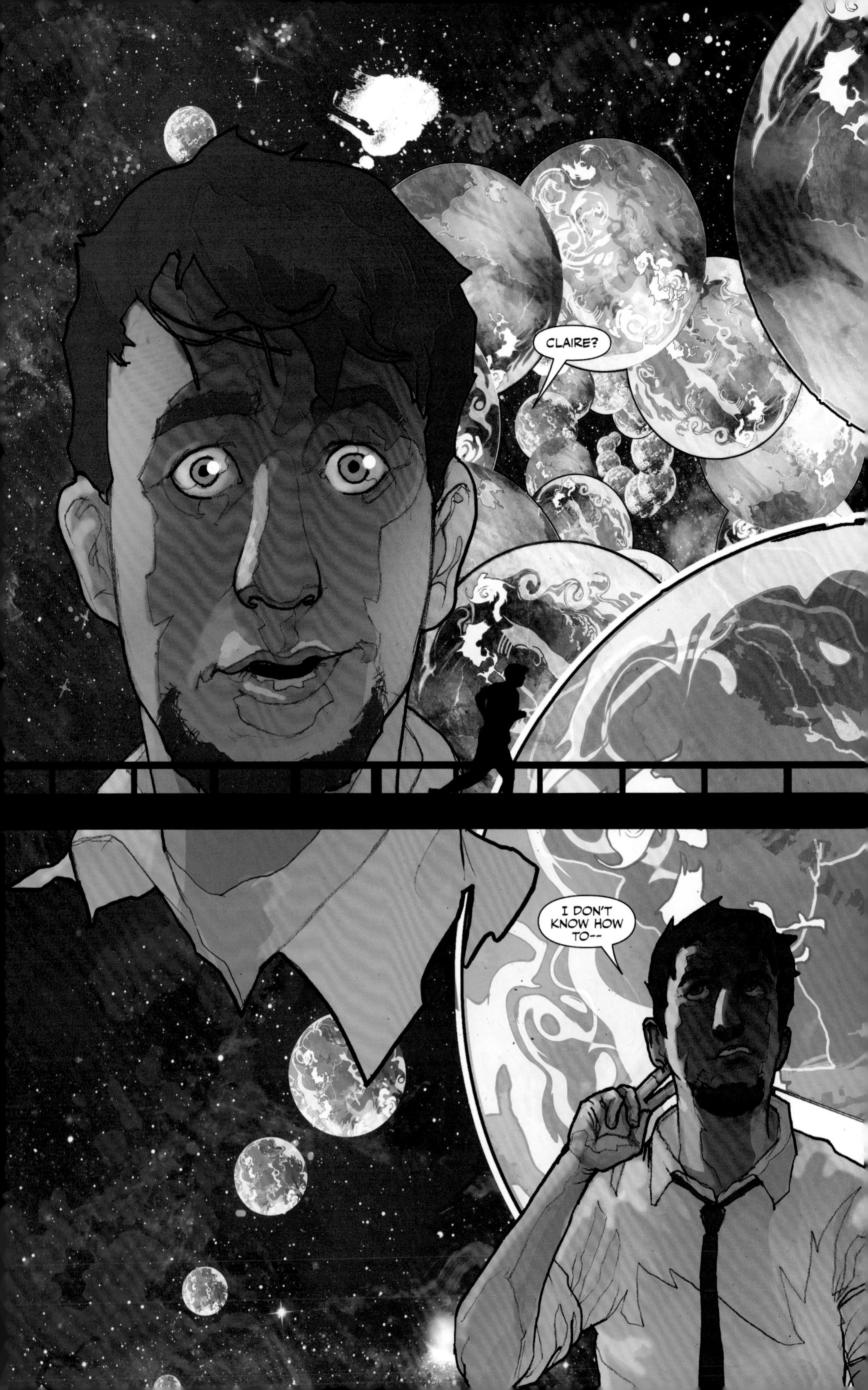
CLAIRE?
I DON'T KNOW HOW TO--

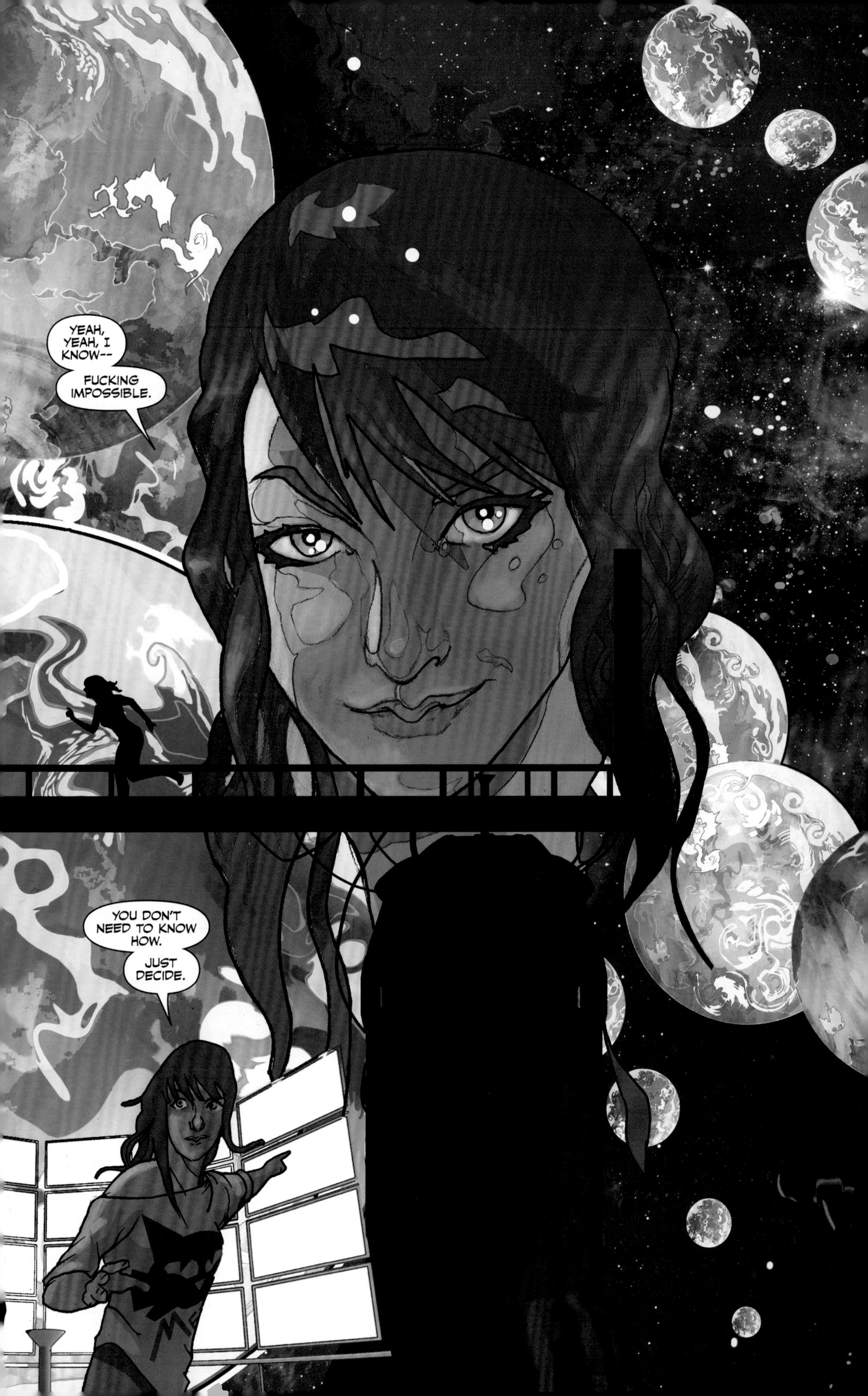
YEAH, YEAH, I KNOW--
FUCKING IMPOSSIBLE.
YOU DON'T NEED TO KNOW HOW.
JUST DECIDE.

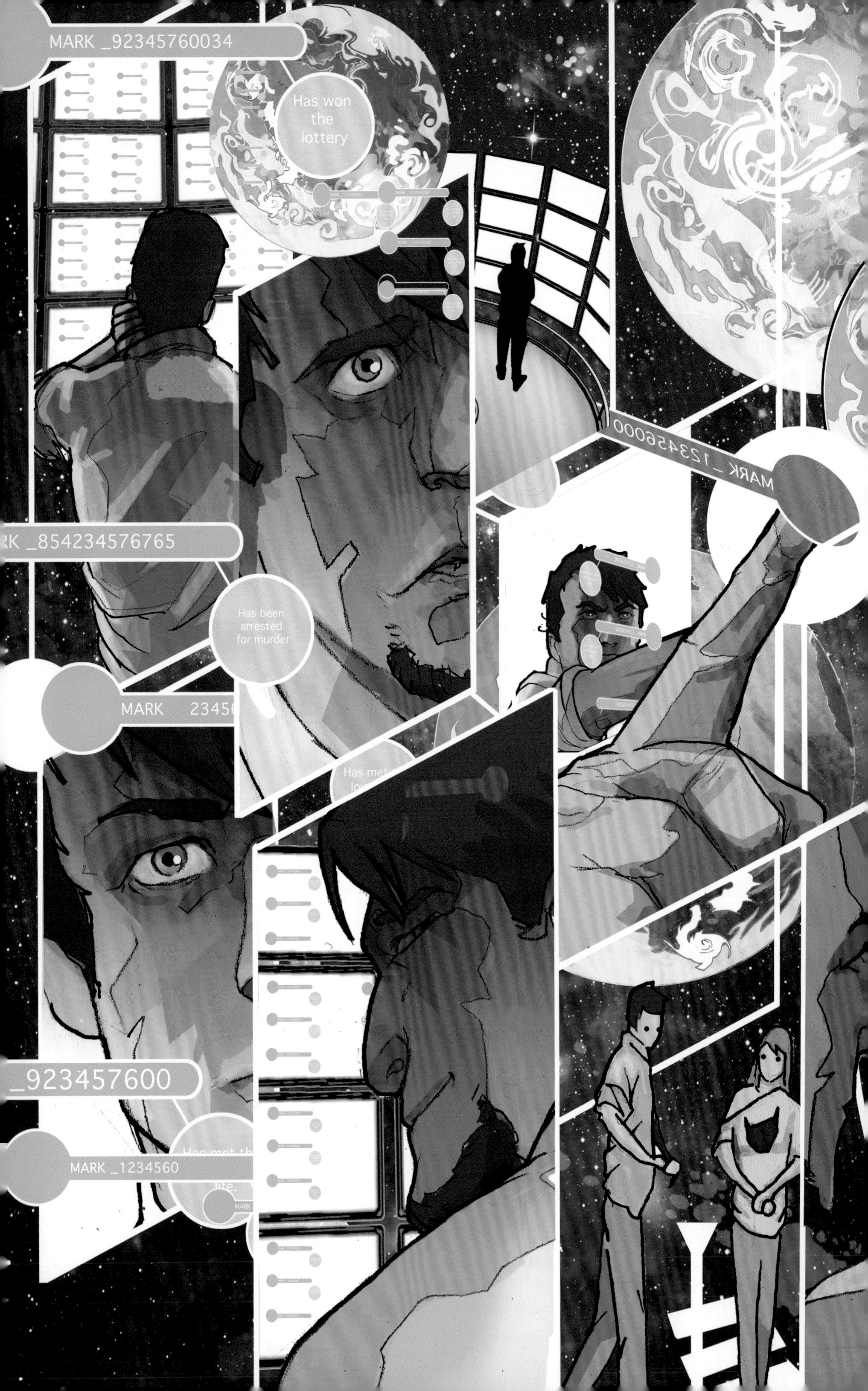
MARK _92345760034
Has won the lottery
RK _854234576765
Has been arrested for murder
MARK _123456000
_923457600
MARK _1234560

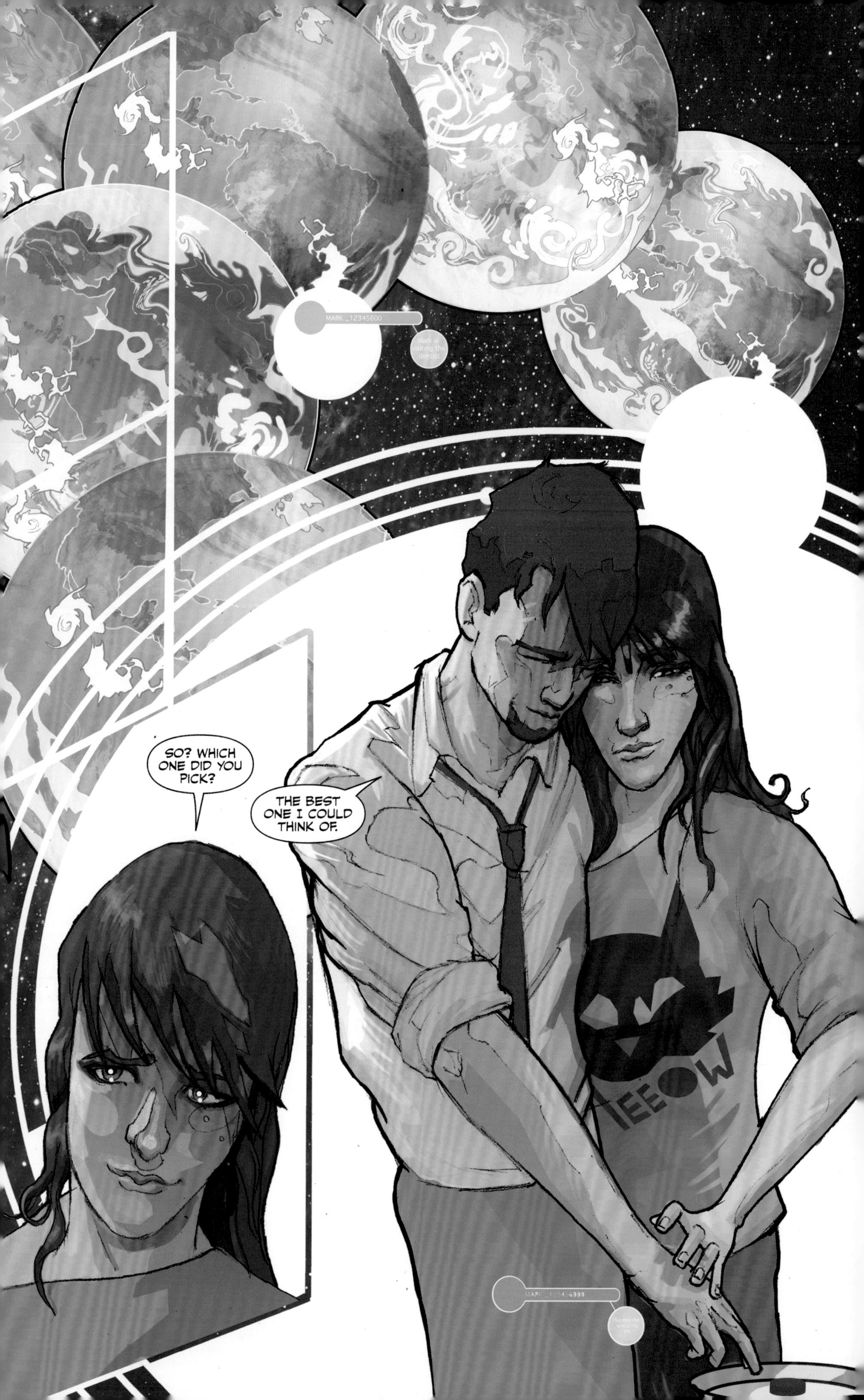
MARK _12345600
Mark is visiting the dentist
SO? WHICH ONE DID YOU PICK?
THE BEST ONE I COULD THINK OF.

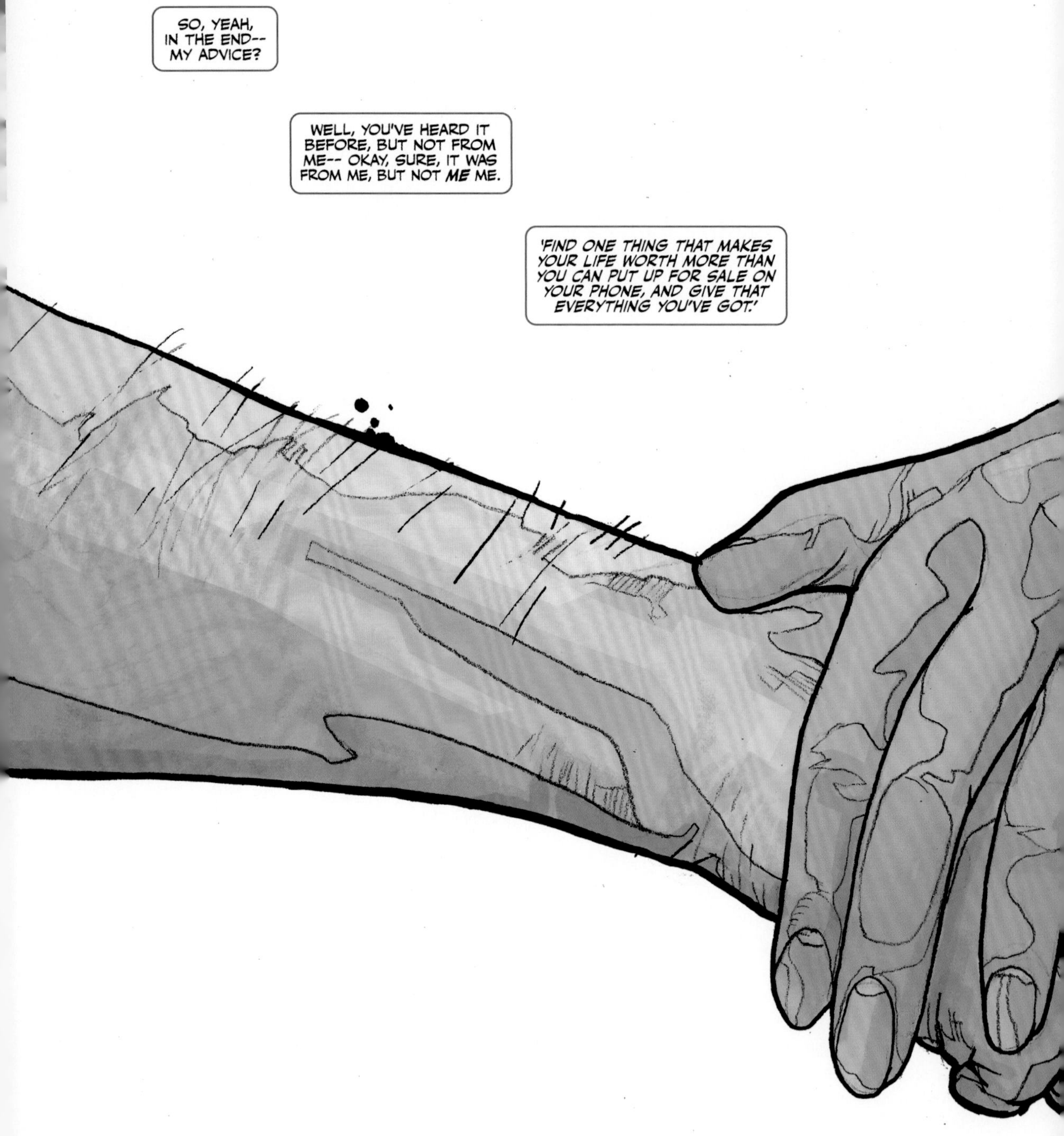
SO, YEAH, IN THE END-- MY ADVICE?
WELL, YOU'VE HEARD IT BEFORE, BUT NOT FROM ME-- OKAY, SURE, IT WAS FROM ME, BUT NOT *ME* ME.
'FIND ONE THING THAT MAKES YOUR LIFE WORTH MORE THAN YOU CAN PUT UP FOR SALE ON YOUR PHONE, AND GIVE THAT EVERYTHING YOU'VE GOT.'

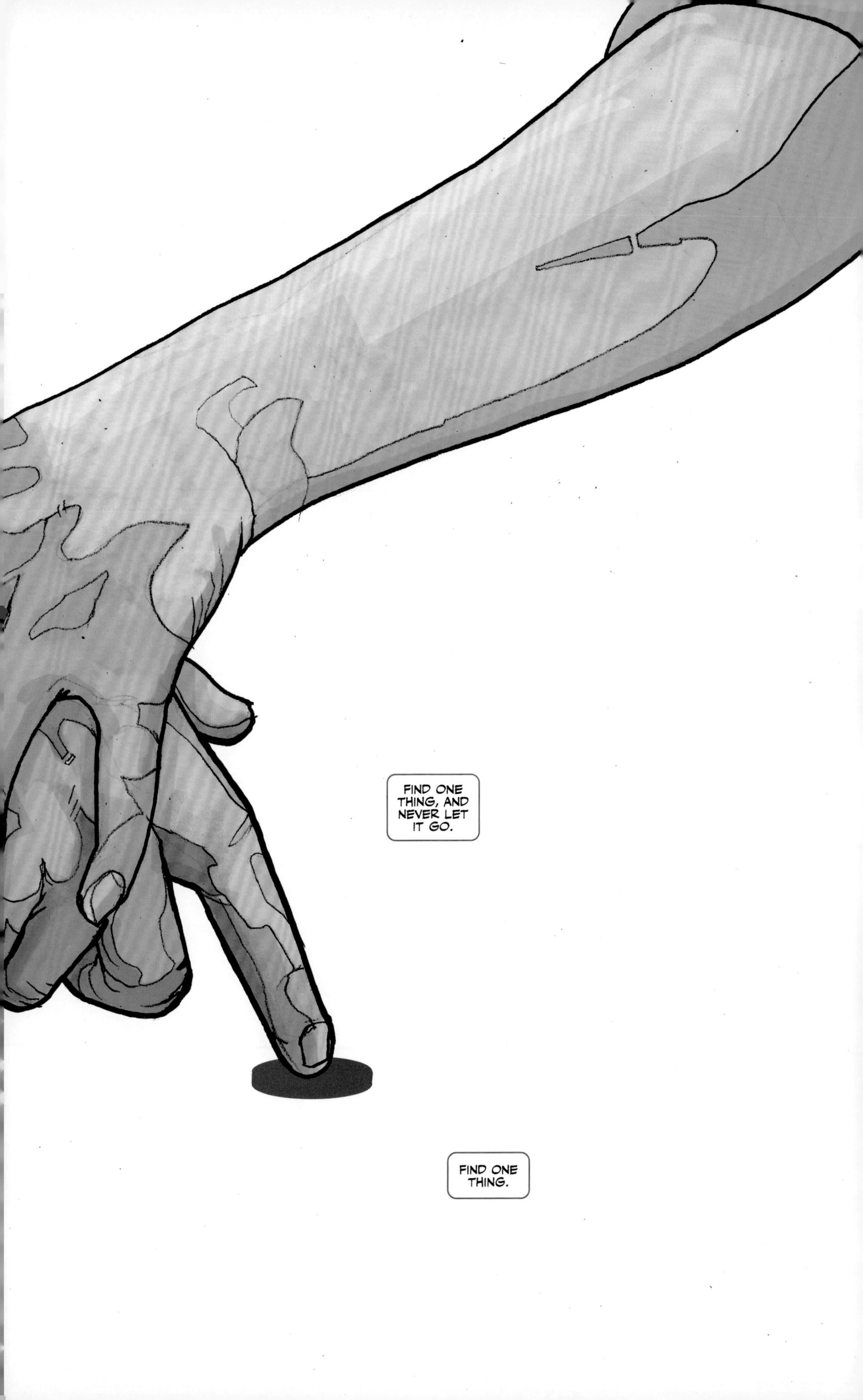
FIND ONE THING, AND NEVER LET IT GO.
FIND ONE THING.

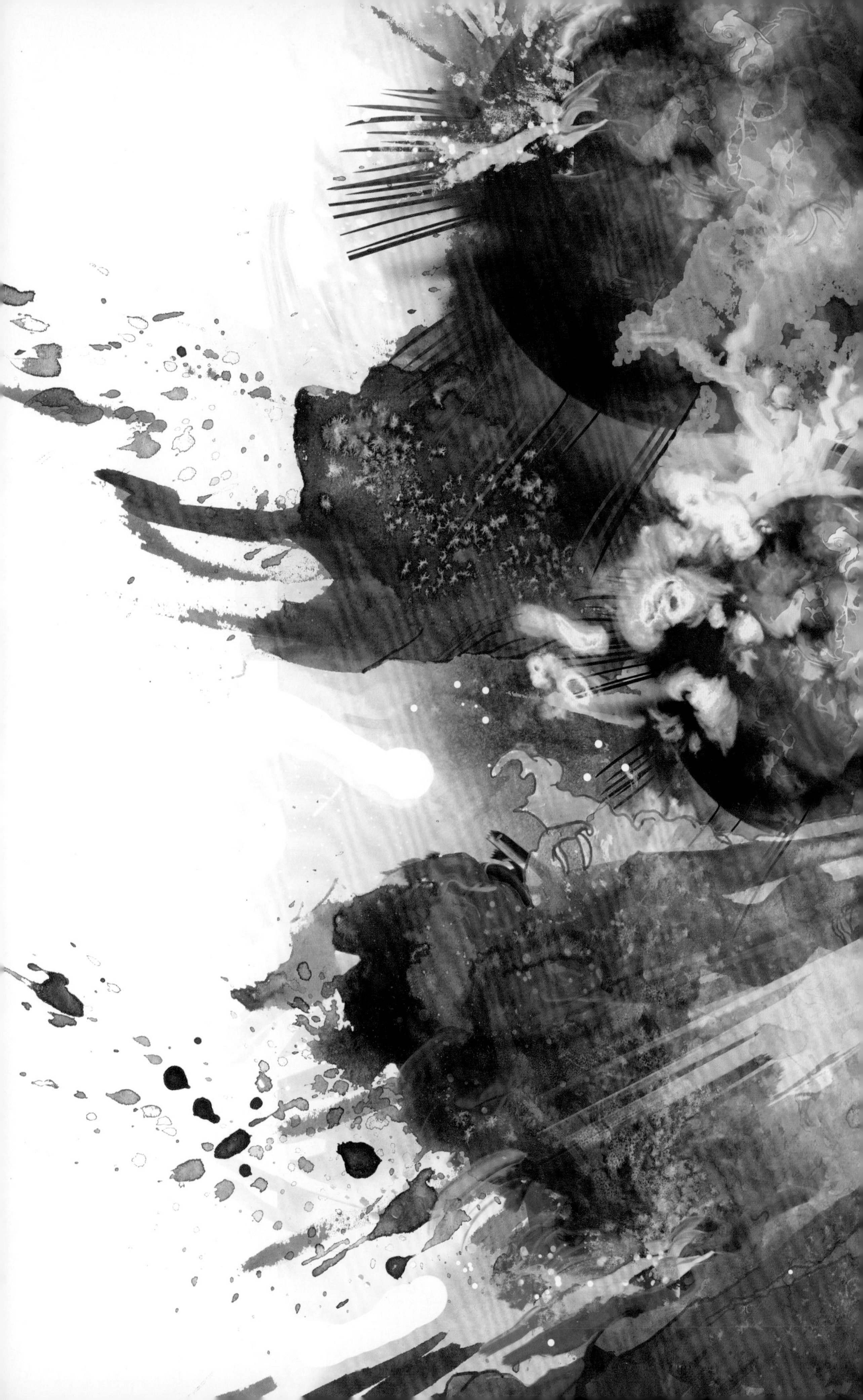

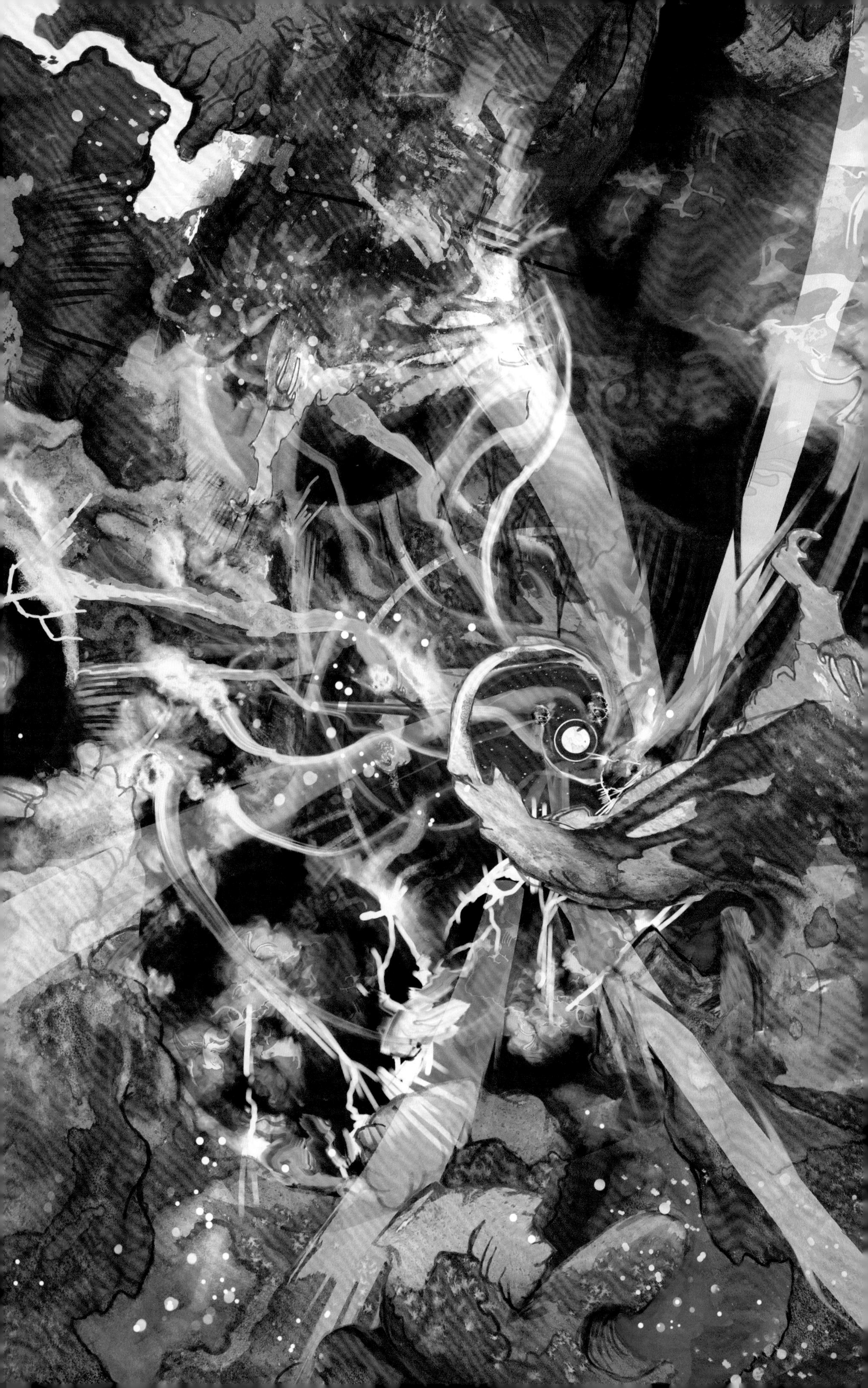

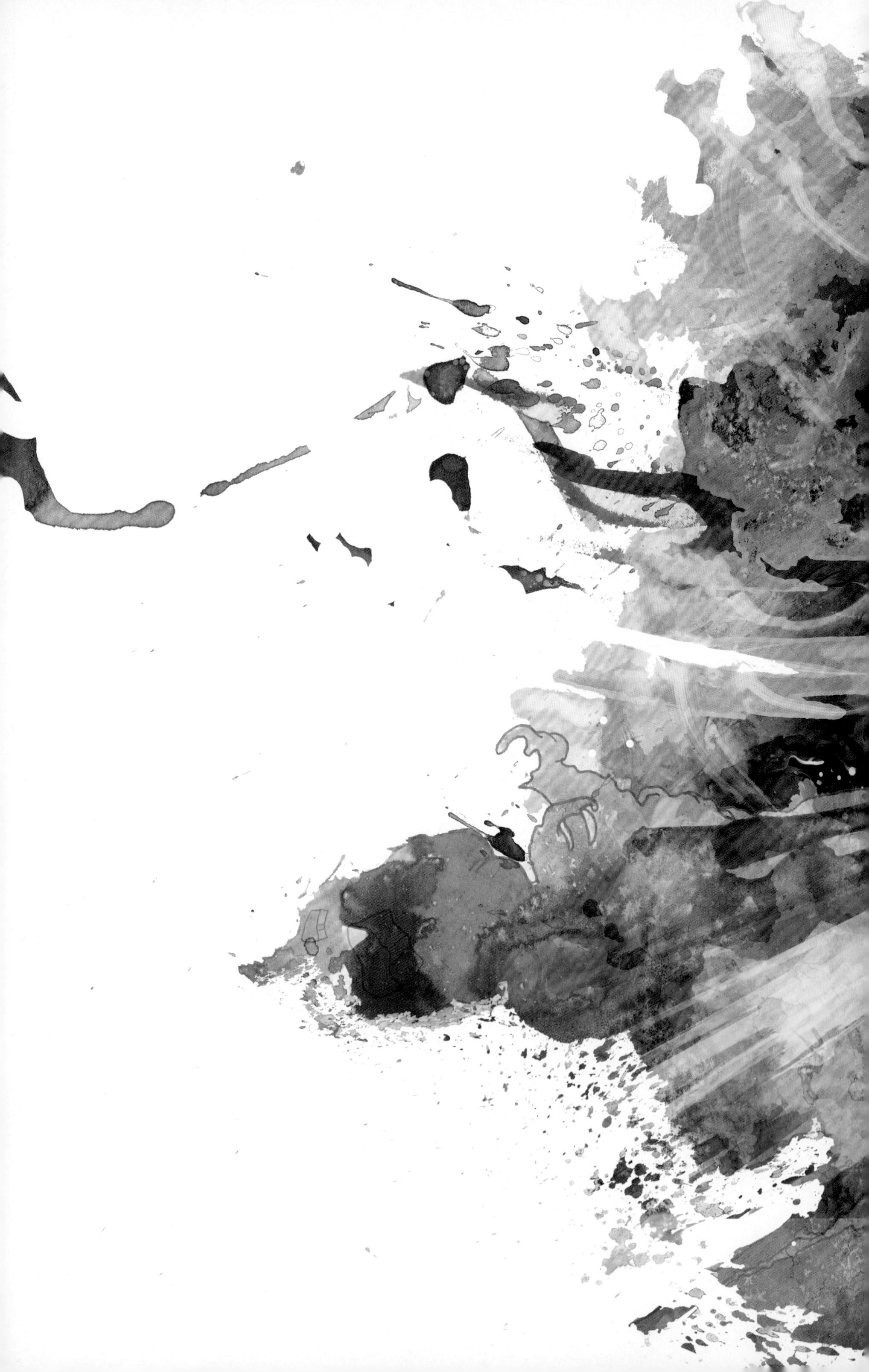

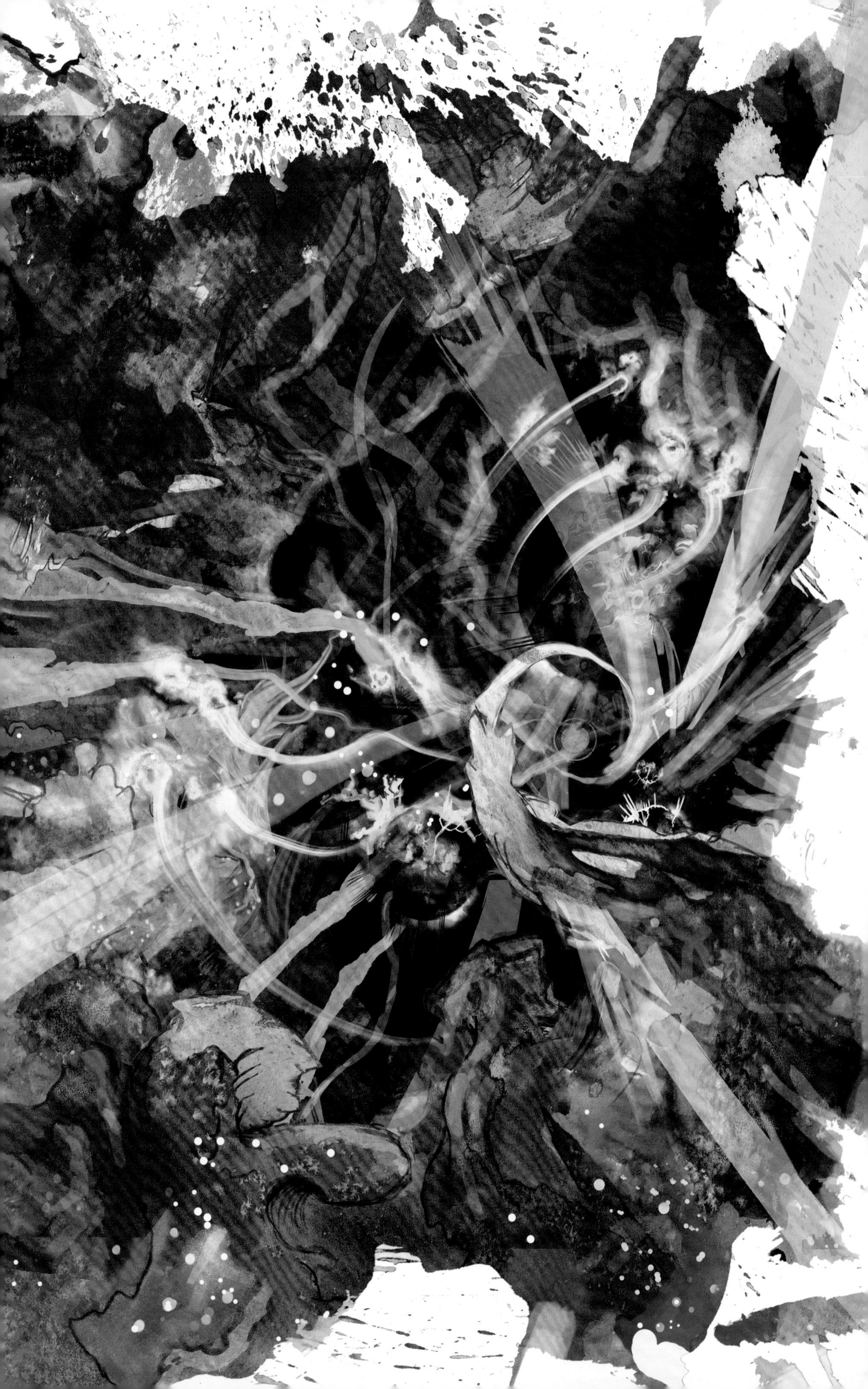

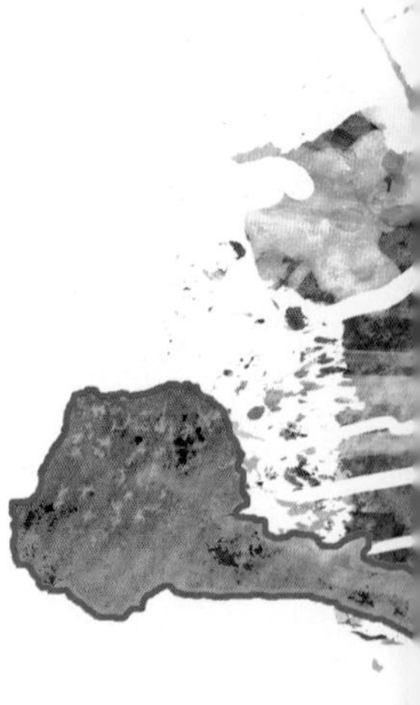

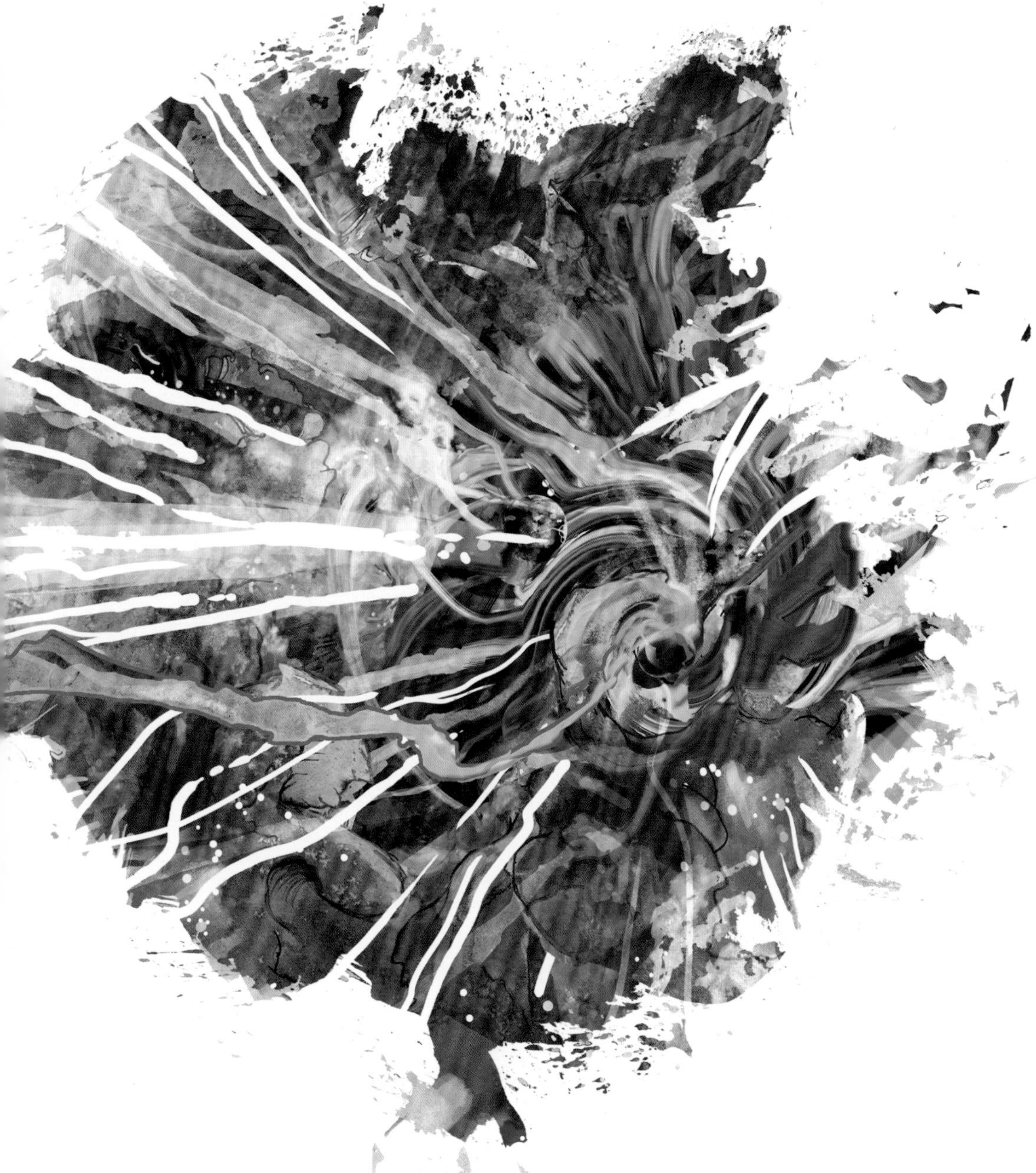

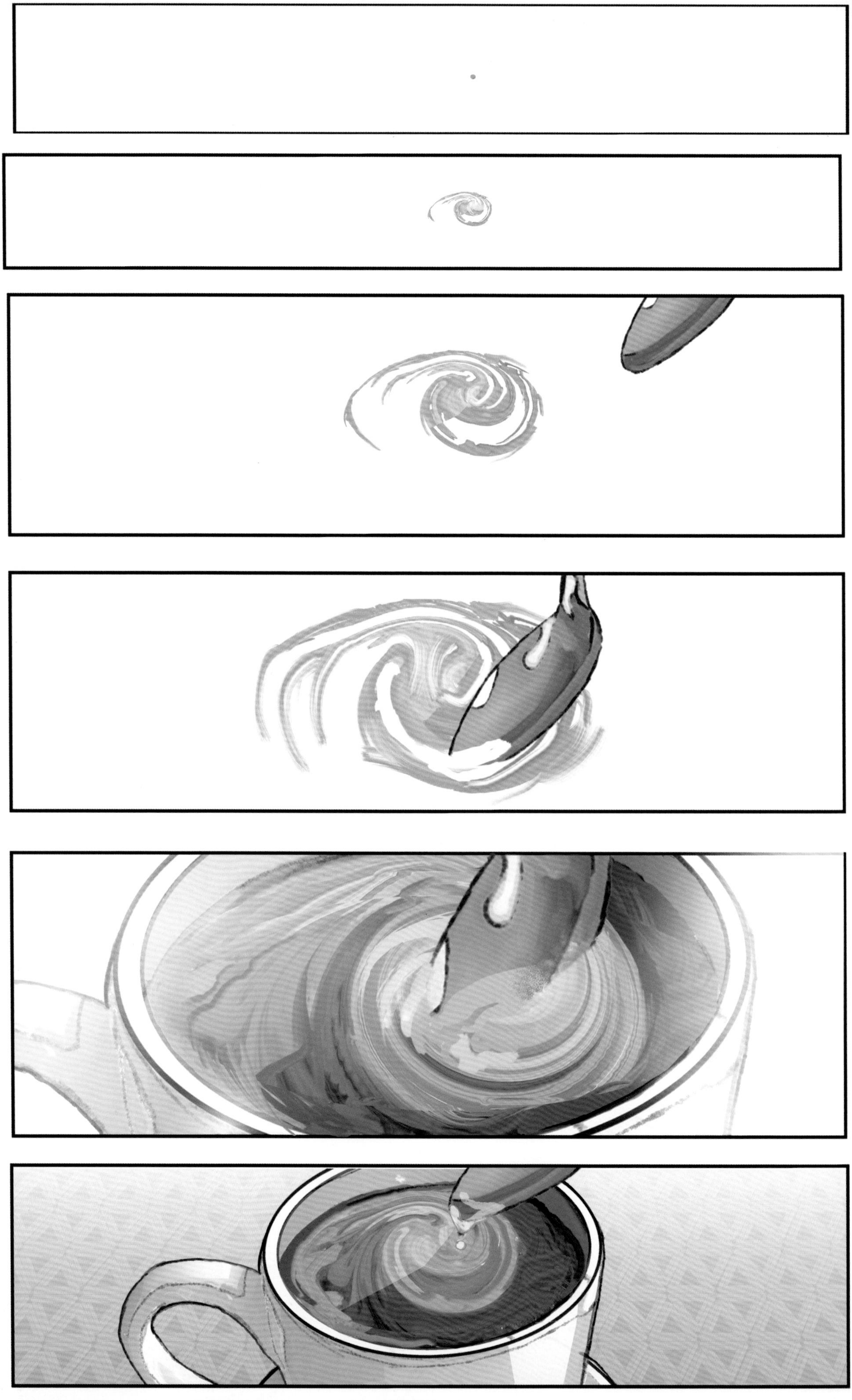

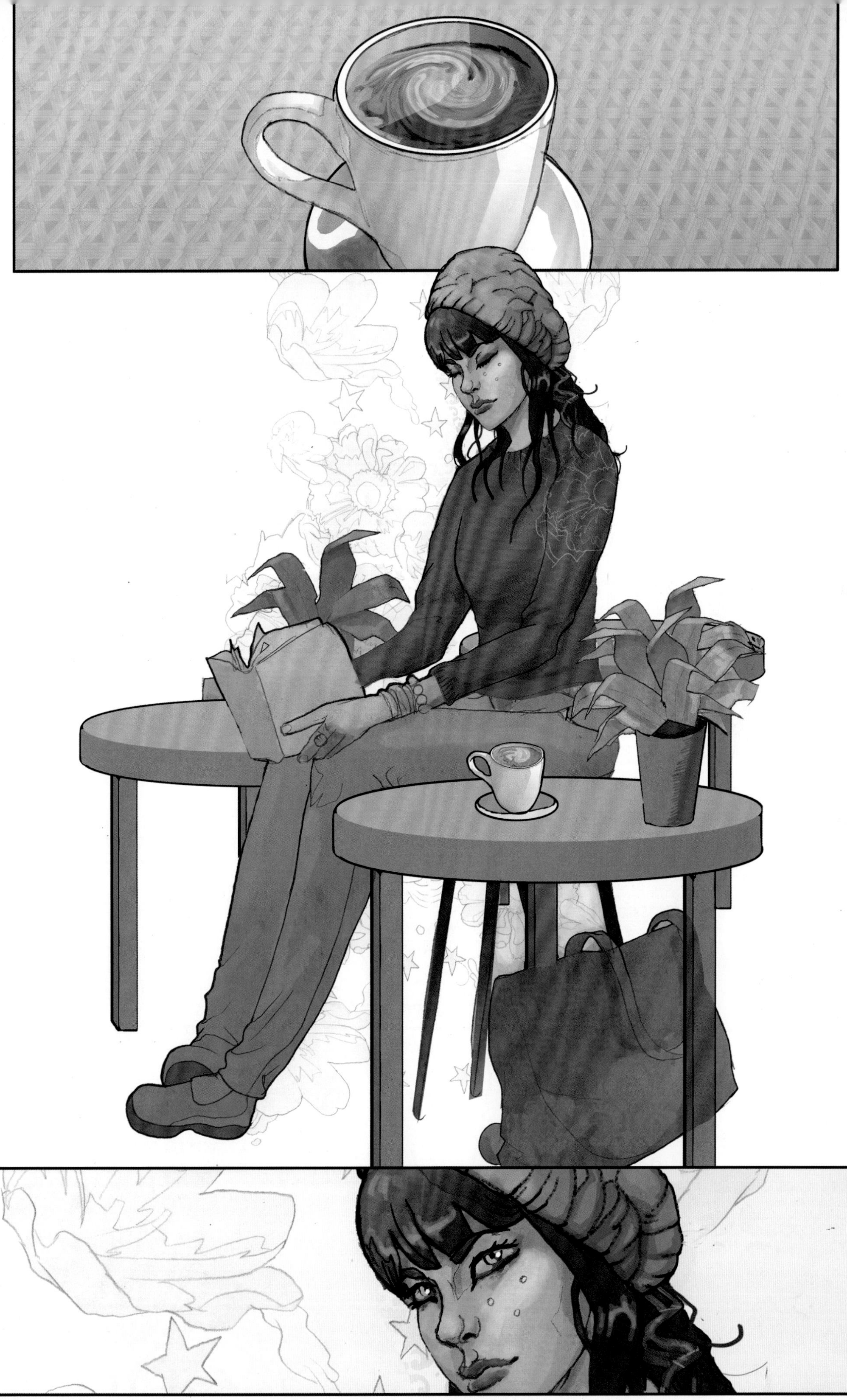

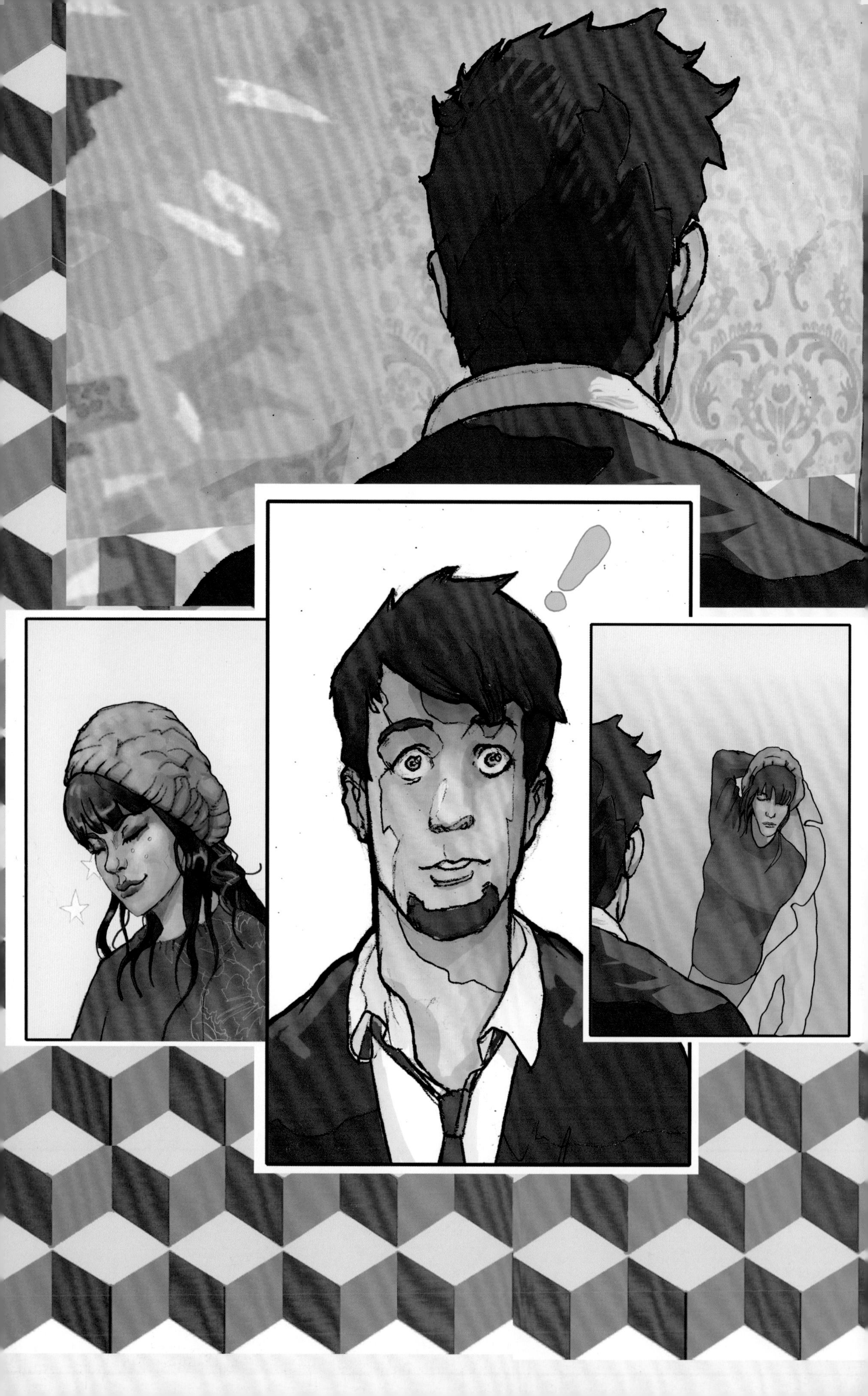
!

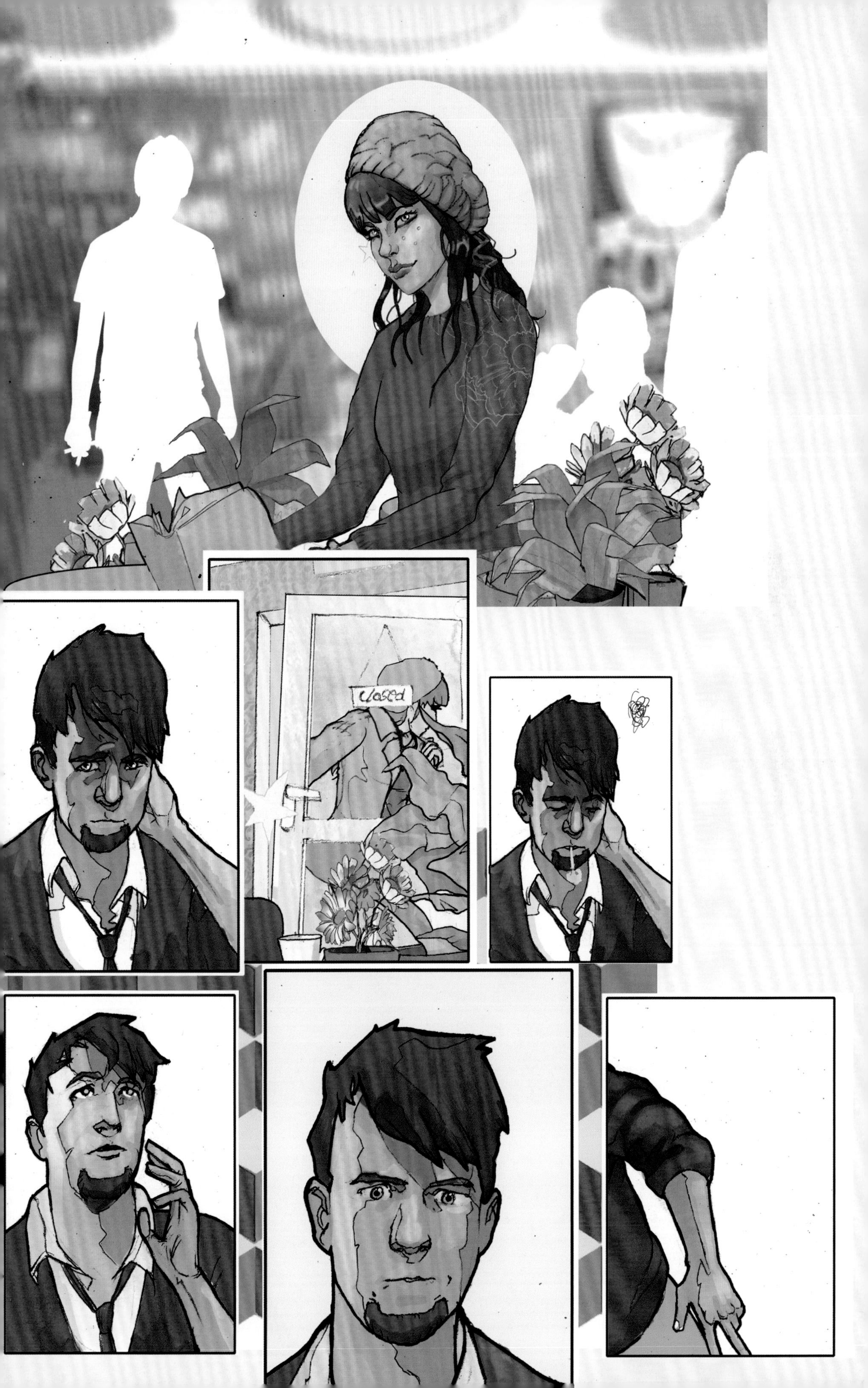
Closed

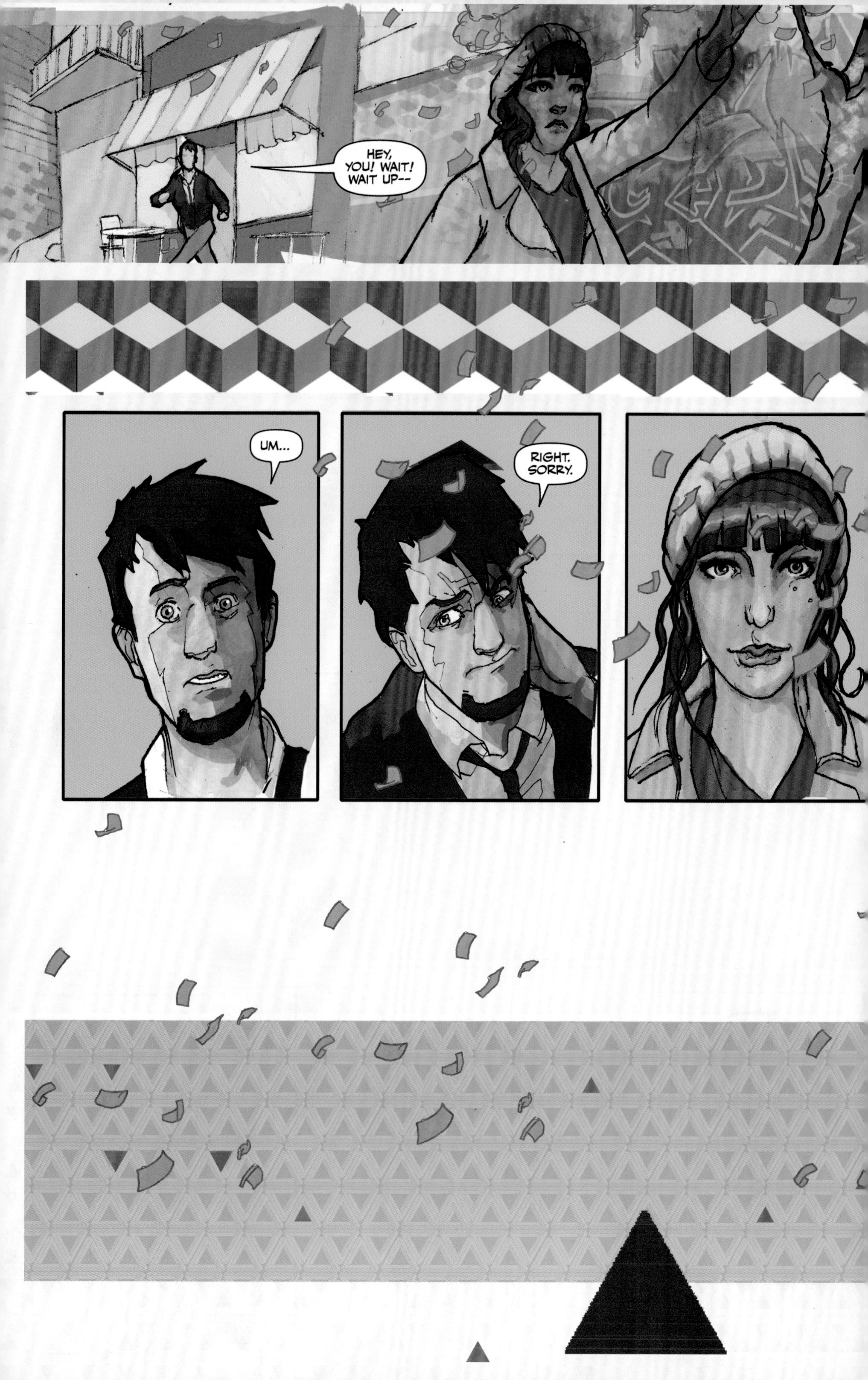
HEY, YOU! WAIT! WAIT UP--
UM...
RIGHT. SORRY.

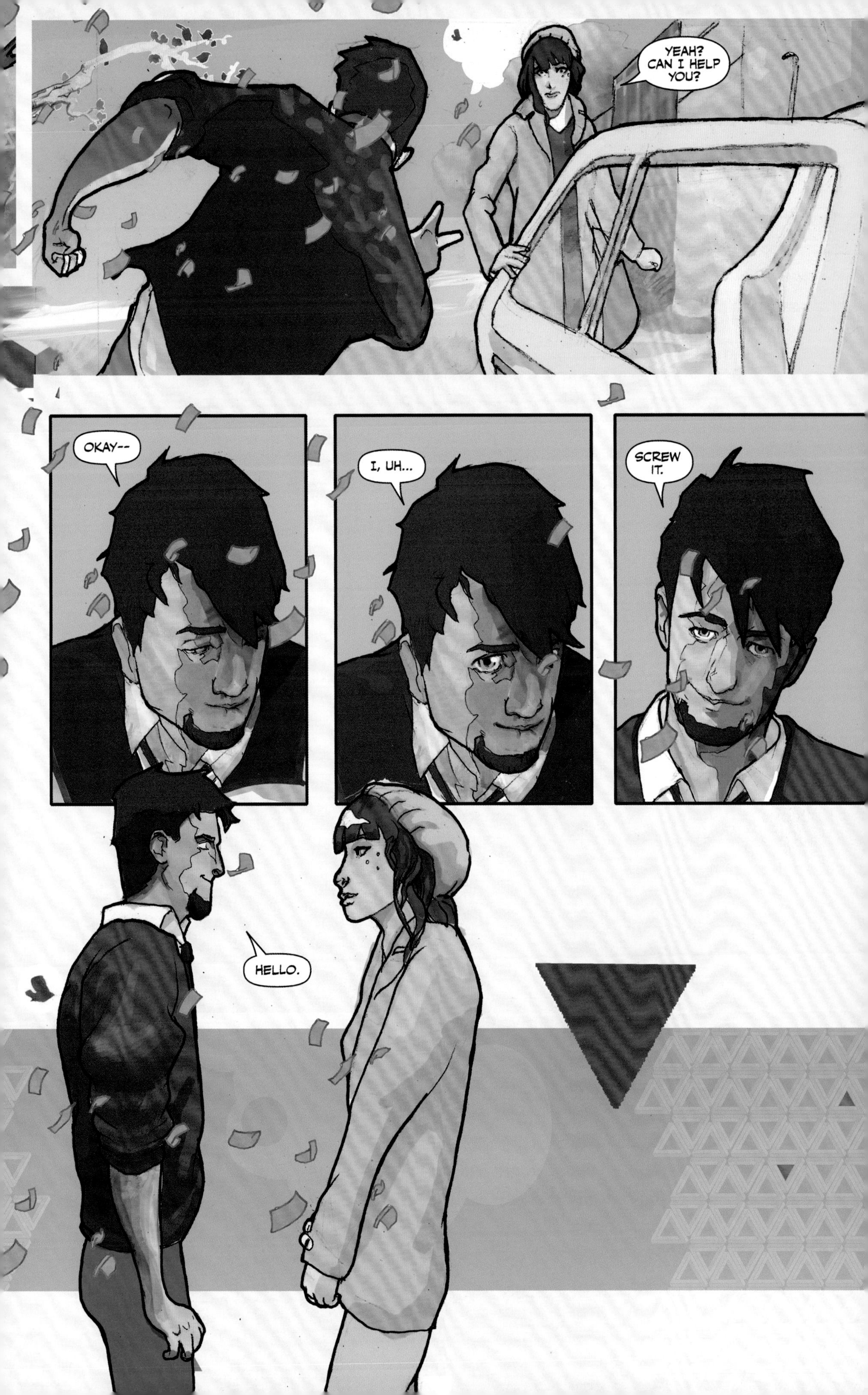
YEAH? CAN I HELP YOU?
OKAY--
I, UH...
SCREW IT.
HELLO.

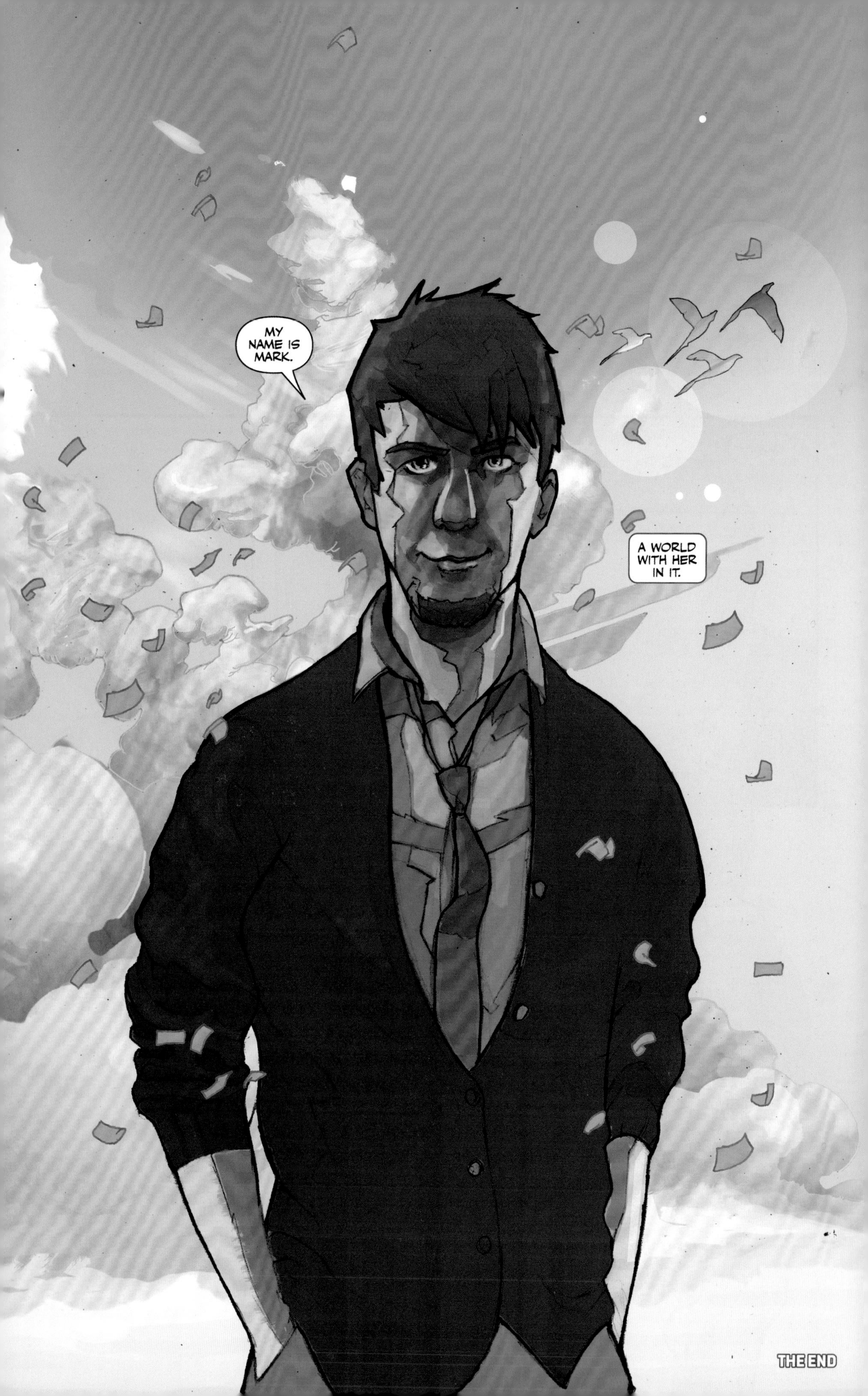
MY NAME IS MARK.
A WORLD WITH HER IN IT.
THE END

PACKING FOR VACTION

THE INFINITE PROCESS

AND THE ART OF CREATION WITH CHRISTIAN WARD

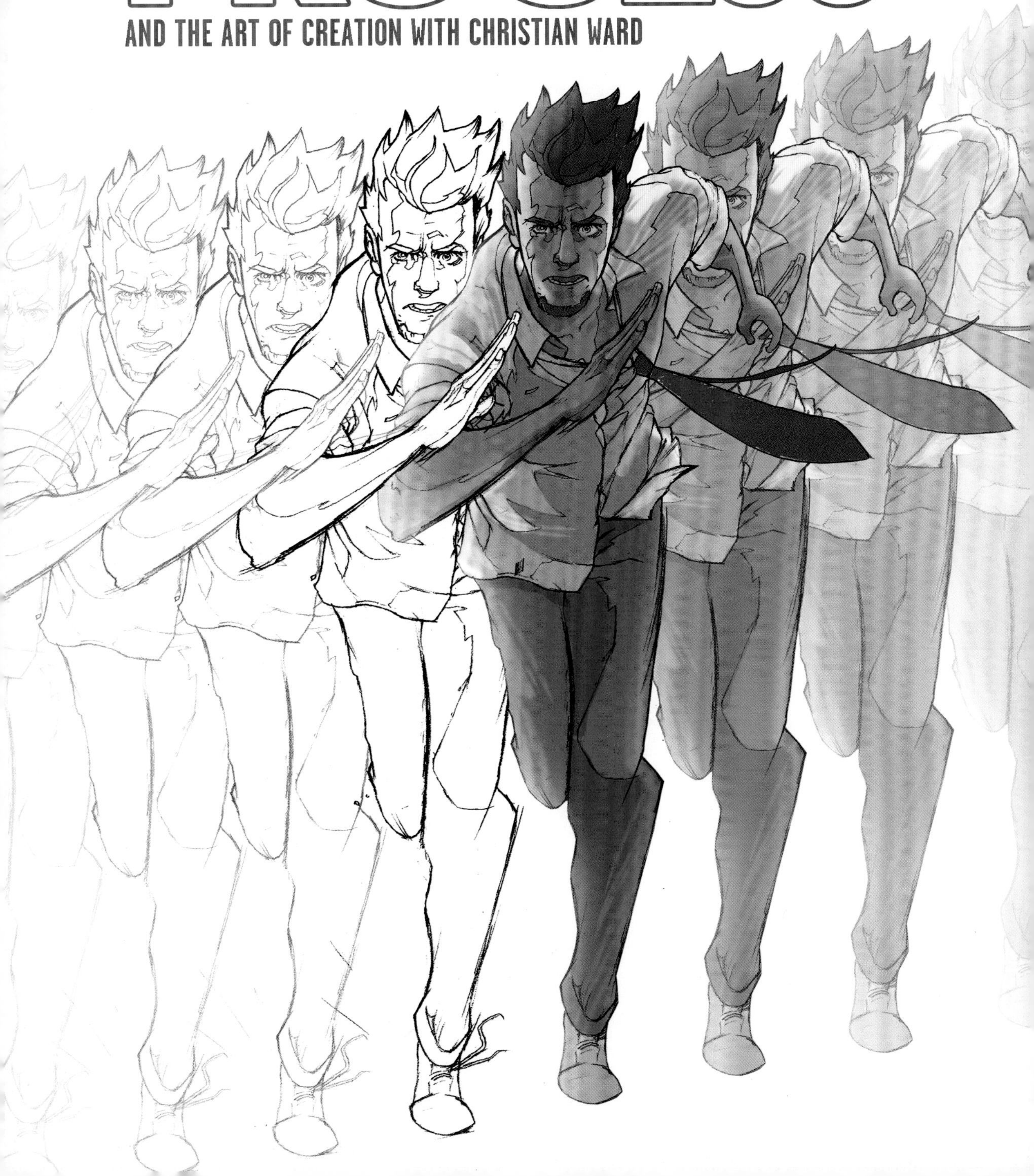

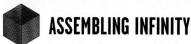

ASSEMBLING INFINITY

I draw the characters and backgrounds separately. This step of the process allows for greater compositional control should I alter the page design.

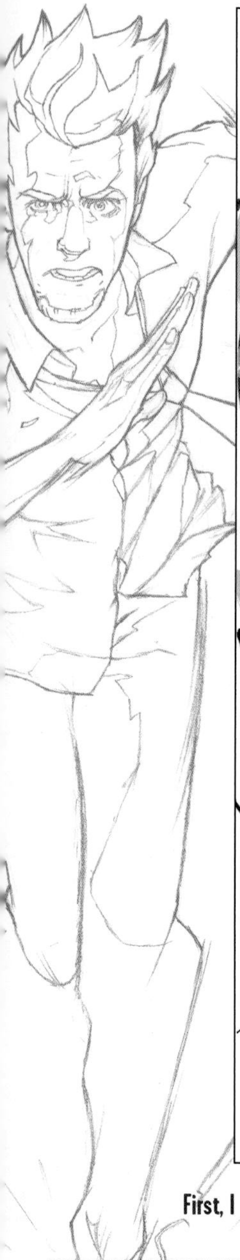

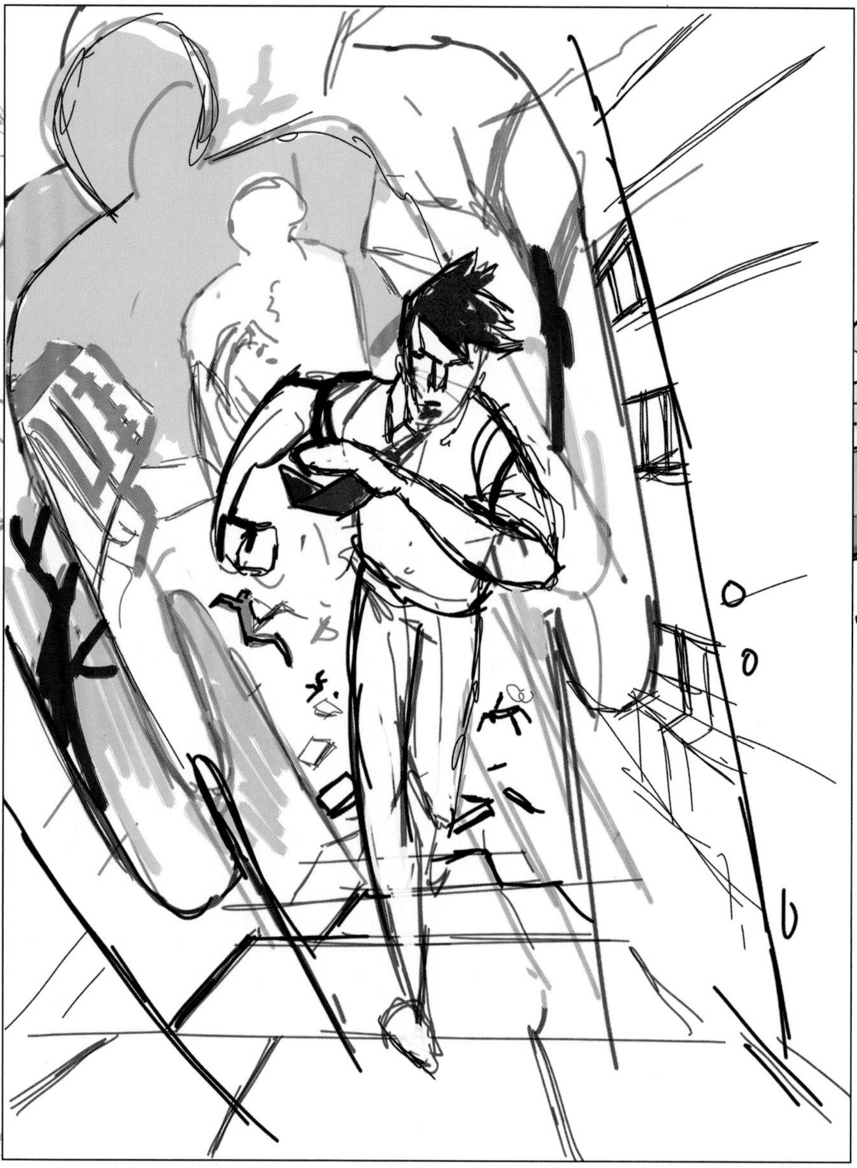

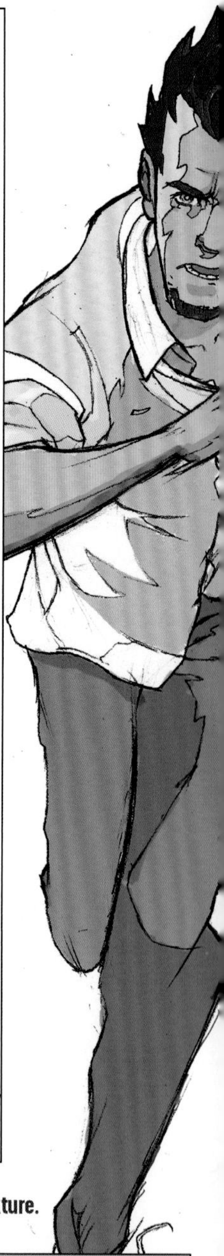

First, I sketch a quick digital mock-up of the page, then I'll paint the colour flats before adding tone and texture.

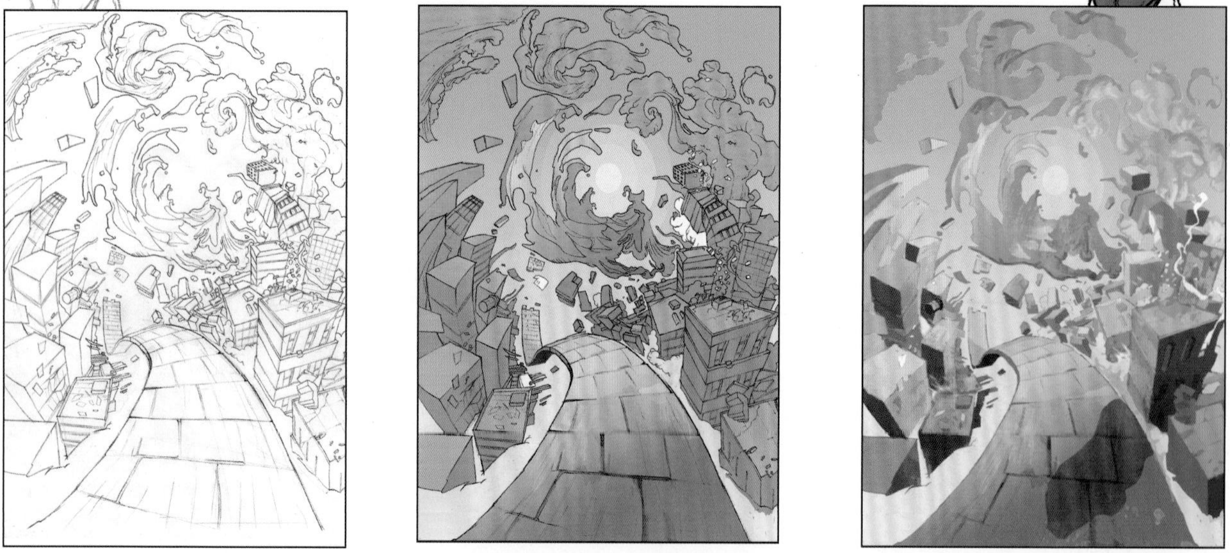

ASSEMBLING INFINITY

I draw the characters and backgrounds separately. This step of the process allows for greater compositional control should I alter the page design.

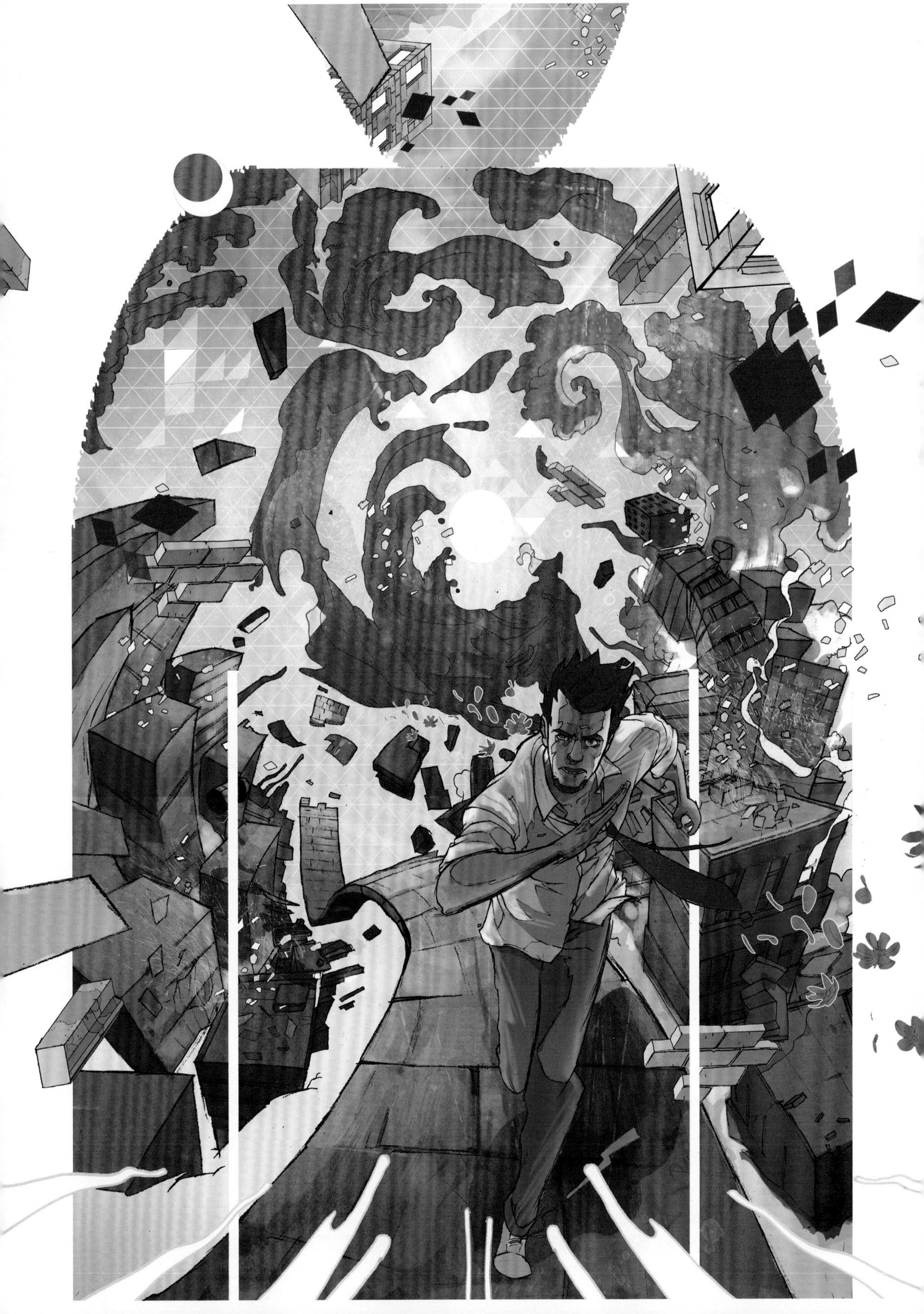

LIGHTING THE FUSE

Despite using some digital painting I still draw all the pencils by hand these are later 'ink' in Photoshop.

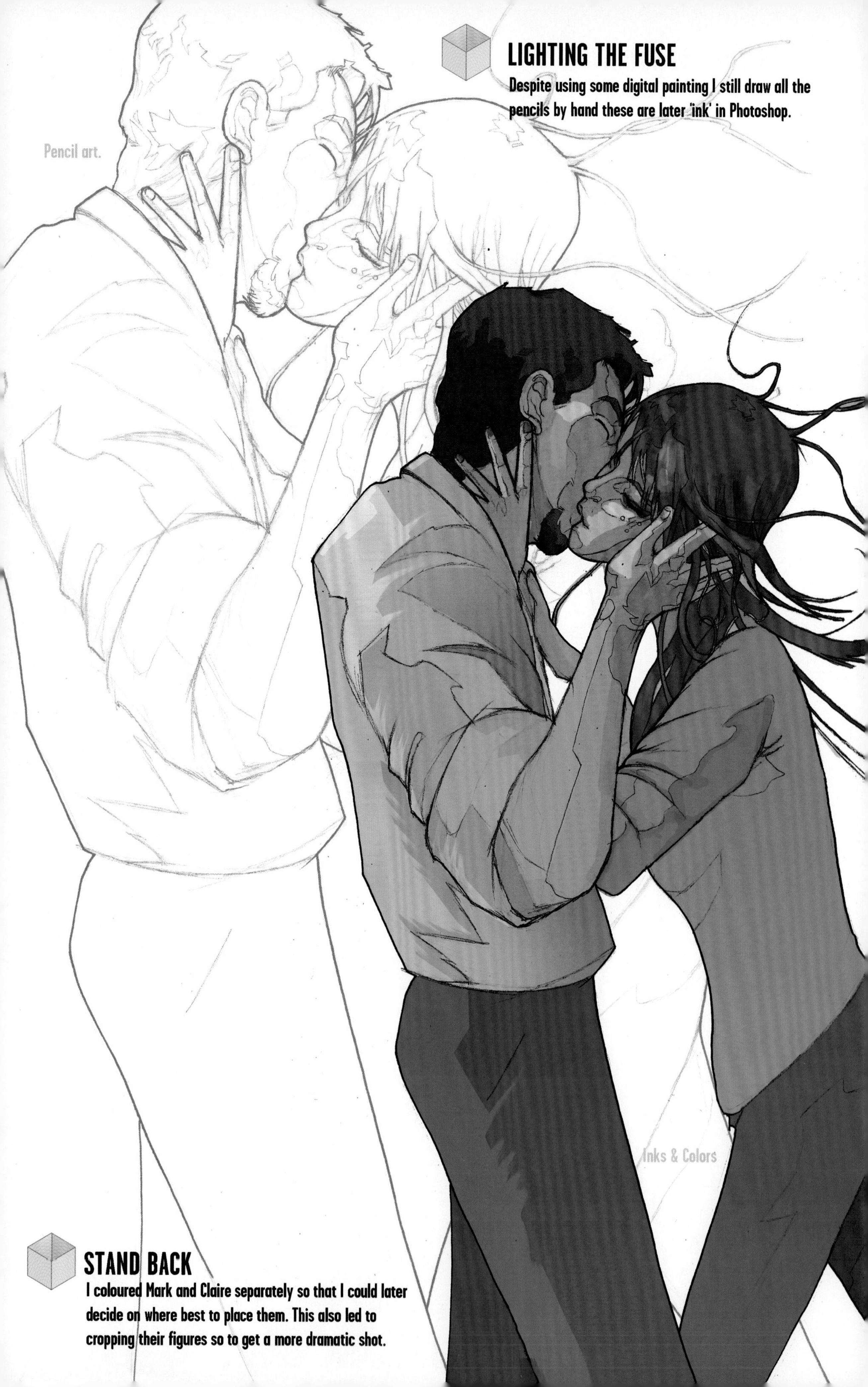
Pencil art.
Inks & Colors

STAND BACK

I coloured Mark and Claire separately so that I could later decide on where best to place them. This also led to cropping their figures so to get a more dramatic shot.

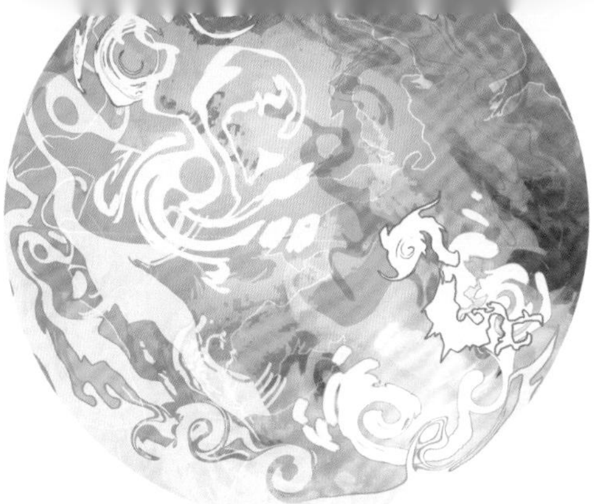

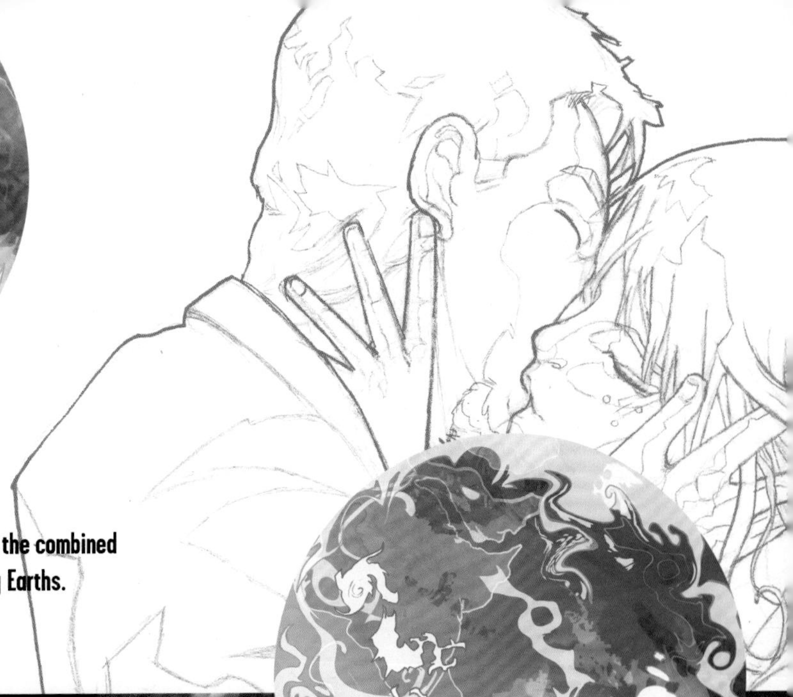

SHIELD YOUR EYES

To create the backdrop, I painted digitally over the combined watercolour paintings then added the exploding Earths.

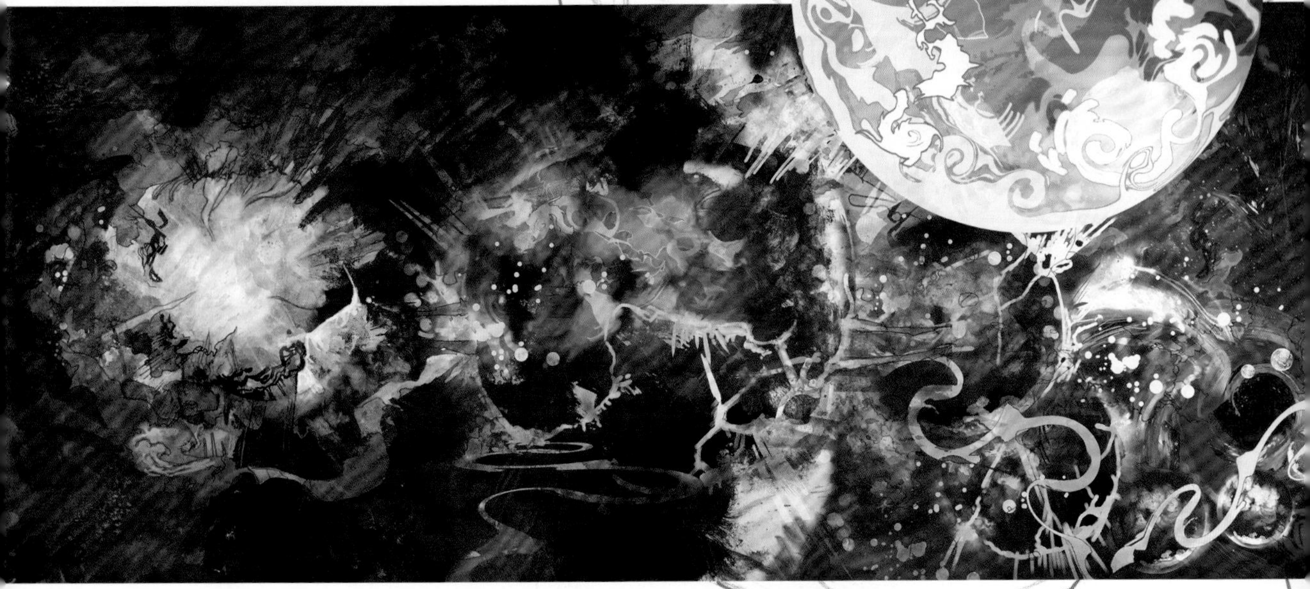

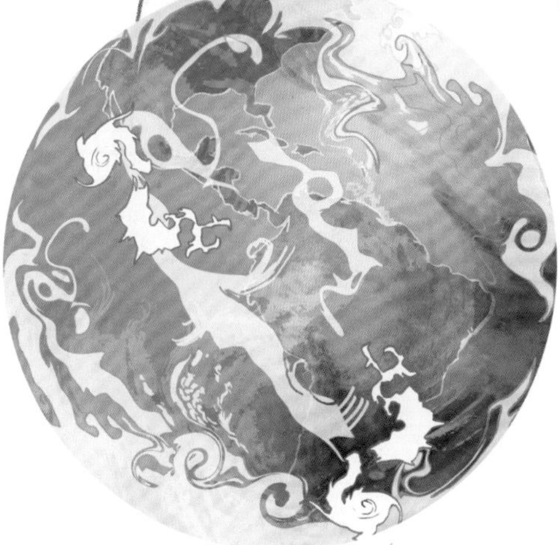

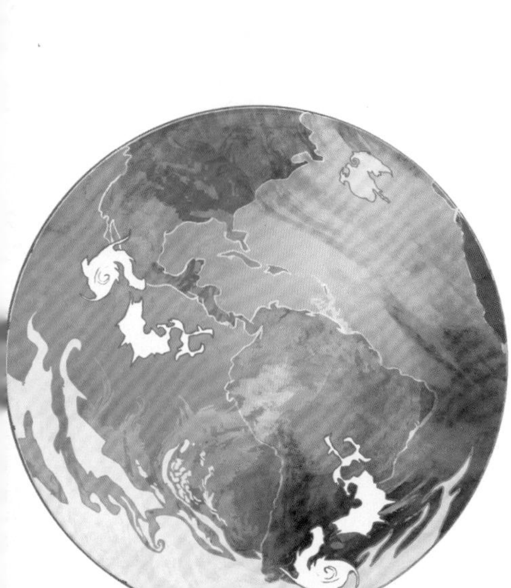

...AS THE UNIVERSE EXPLODES

Each Earth was painted separately - before finishing them off digitally. I used these globes on several of the final spreads before digitally adding the exploding effects.

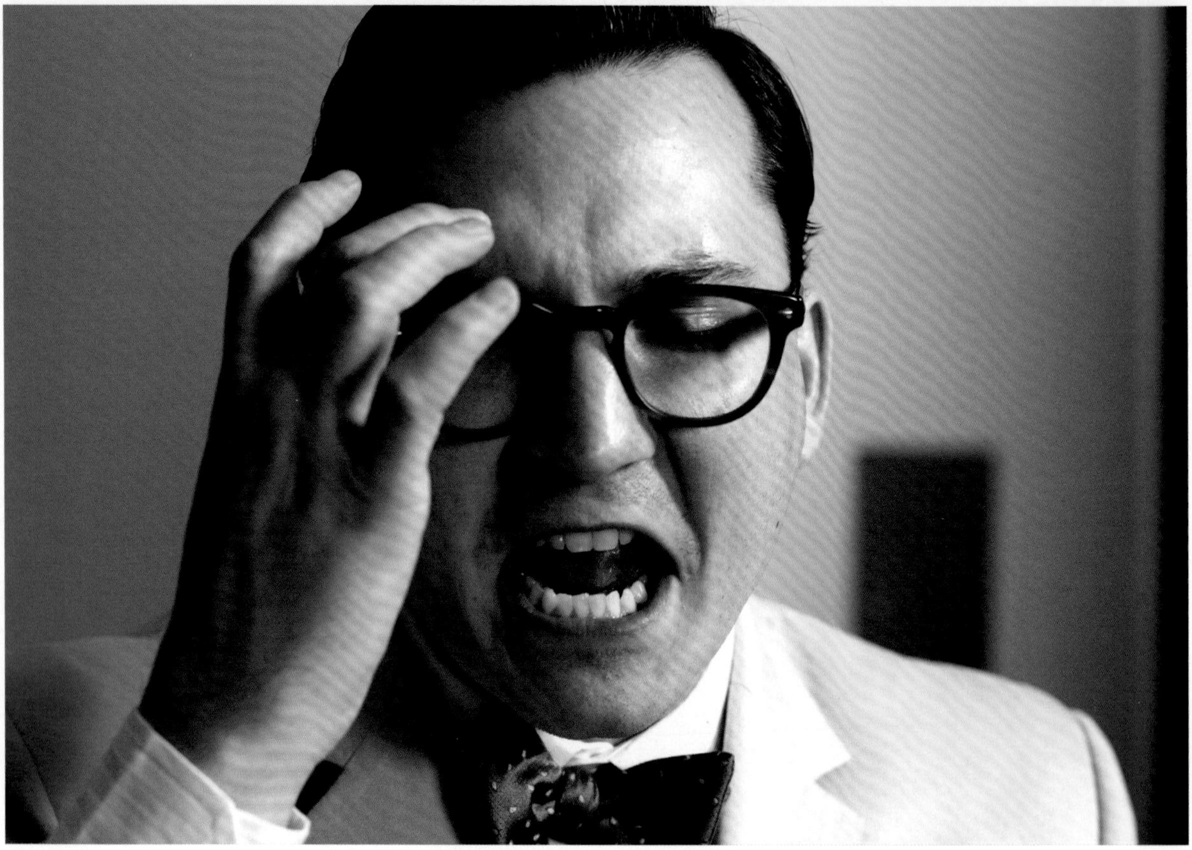

INFINITE IMAGERY: VACATION PHOTOS
BY KENDALL BRUNS

ABOVE: LEE RUSSELL GETS EXPRESSIVE AS THE INIFINITE VACATION'S DIRECTOR OF MARKET DEVELOPMENT, BRUCE WHEELER.

BELOW: FOCUSING IS EASIER WITH STILL DICE.

LOWER LEFT: TOM SOSZKO POSING AS HUGH.

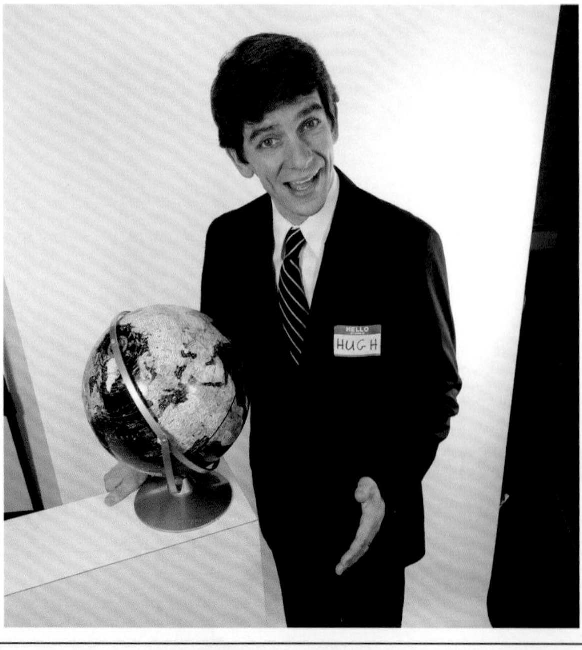
HELLO
HUGH

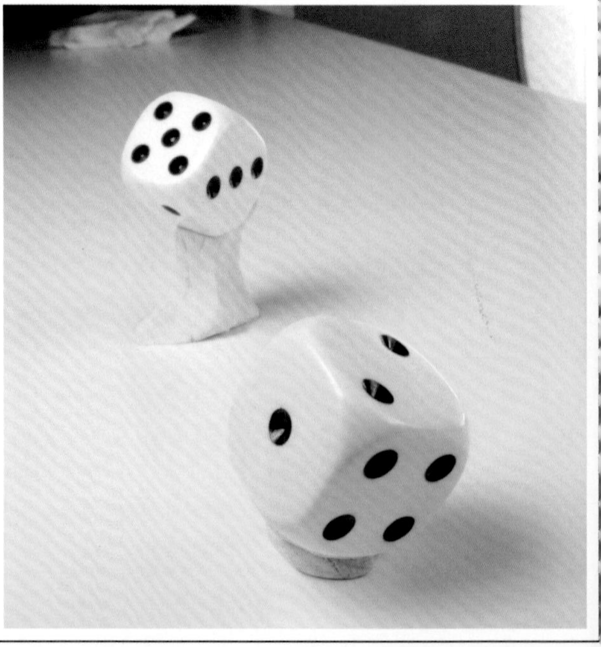

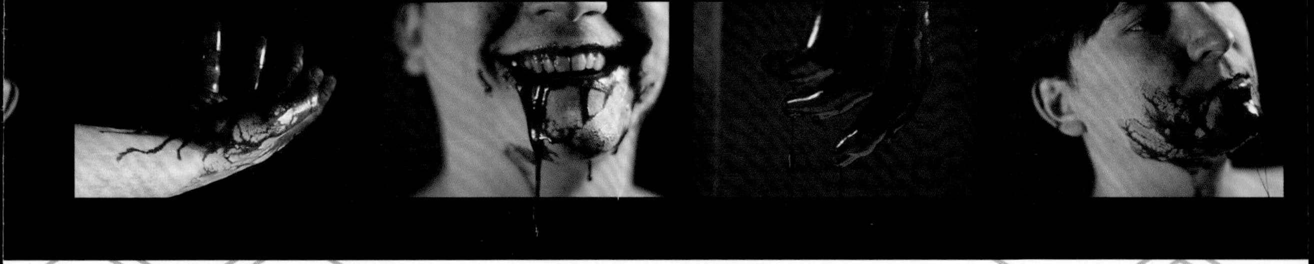

ABOVE: LEE RUSSELL HAS SOME BLOODY FUN AS A CANNIBAL.

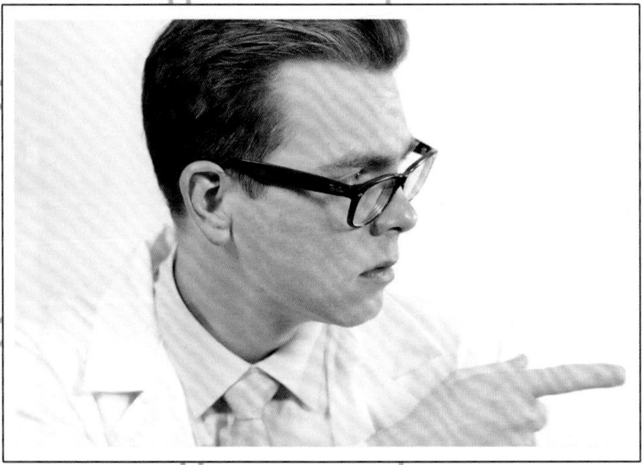

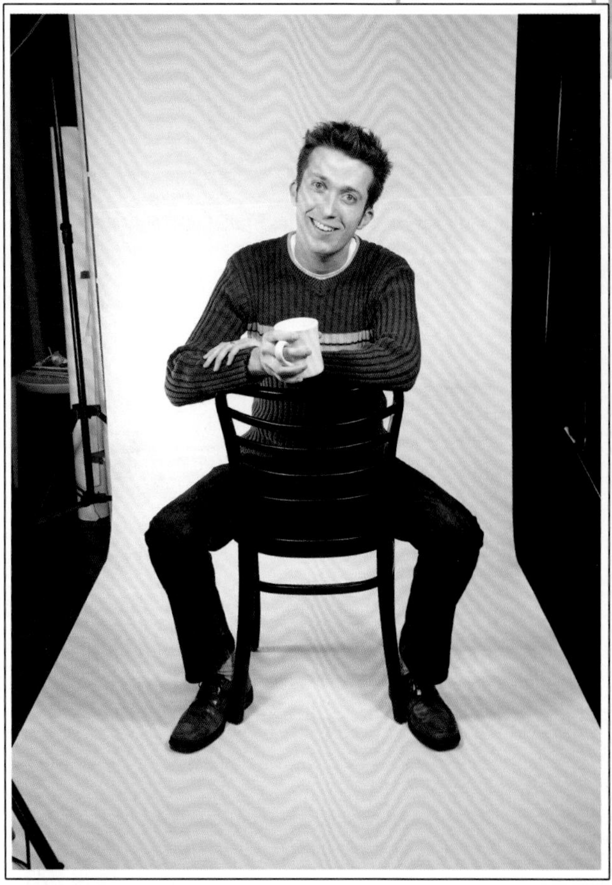

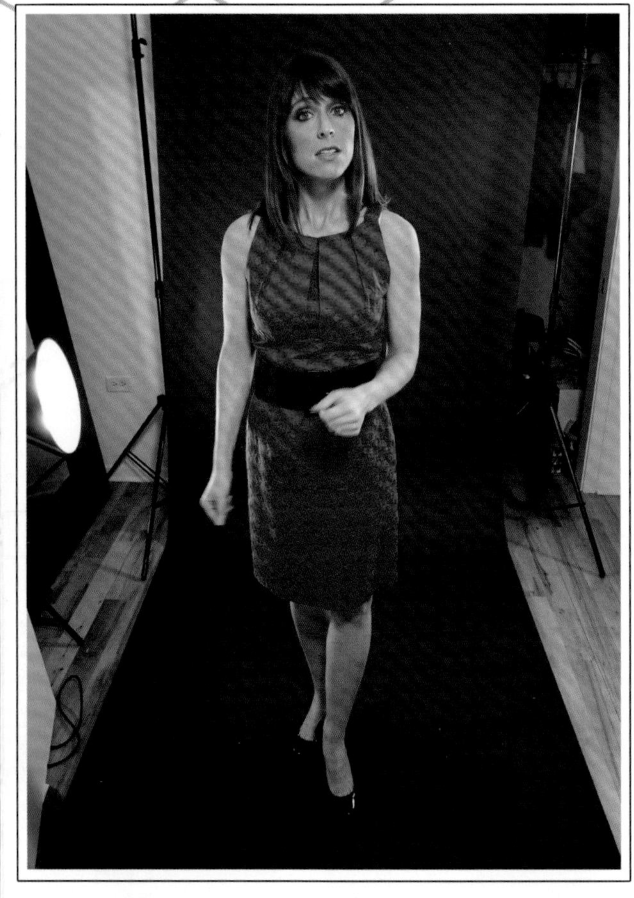

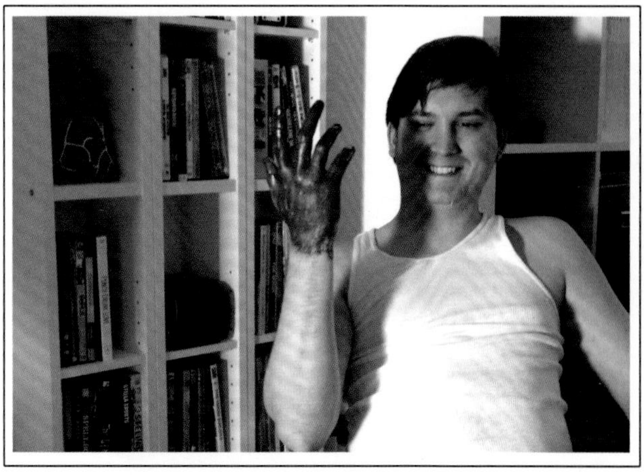

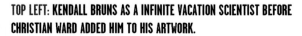

TOP LEFT: KENDALL BRUNS AS A INFINITE VACATION SCIENTIST BEFORE CHRISTIAN WARD ADDED HIM TO HIS ARTWORK.

ABOVE: ASHLEY BUSH IN HER BEST NEWS CORRESPONDENT POSE.

TOP RIGHT: DAVE URLAKIS DOES SOME DAMAGE CONTROL, EXPLAINING WHY BOXING IS "NOT MASS EXECUTION".

ABOVE: FAKE BLOOD MAKES LEE A HAPPY BOY.

ALL PHOTOGRAPHS TAKEN IN CHICAGO, IL 2010-2012

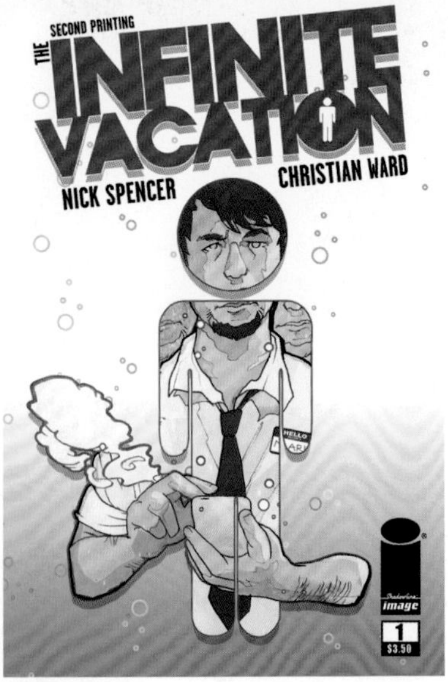
SECOND PRINTING
THE INFINITE VACATION
NICK SPENCER
CHRISTIAN WARD
image
1
$3.50

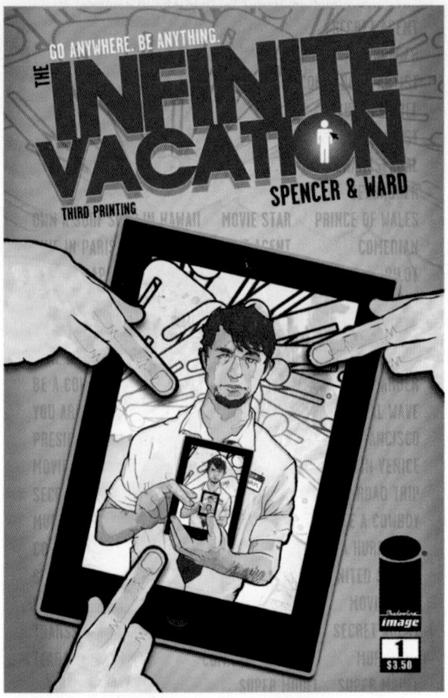
GO ANYWHERE. BE ANYTHING.
THE INFINITE VACATION
SPENCER & WARD
THIRD PRINTING
MOVIE STAR
PRINCE OF WALES
image
1
$3.50

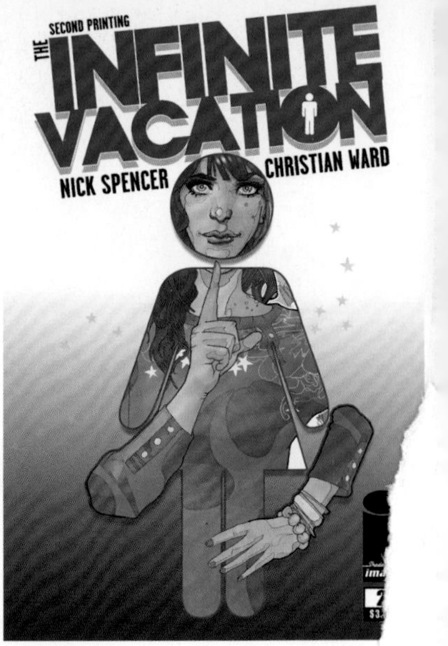
SECOND PRINTING
THE INFINITE VACATION
NICK SPENCER
CHRISTIAN WARD

When Infinite Vacation demand rose, additional printings were requried and multiple covers were conceived.

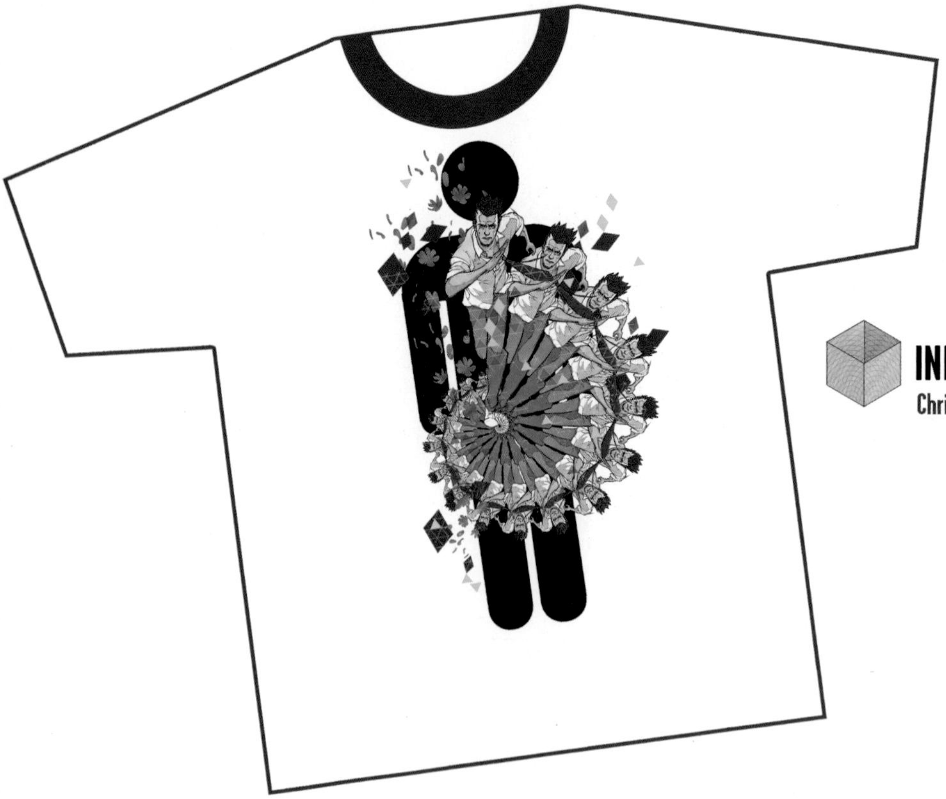

INFINITE POSSIBILITES

Christian's T-Shirt design.

Prior to the launch of the series, these magazine cover 'web-ads' highlighted the Infinite Vacation on Comic Book Resources.

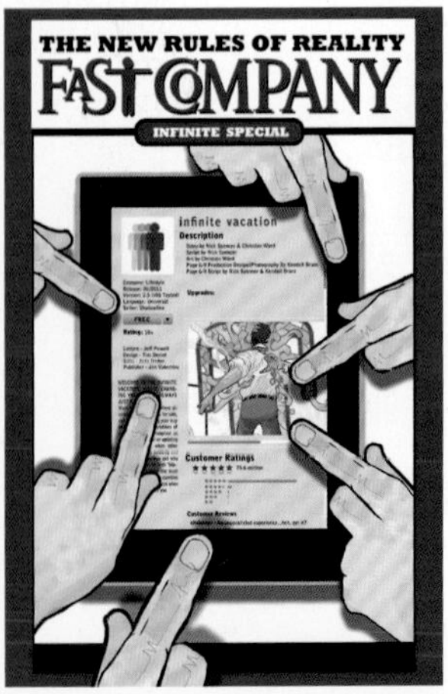
THE NEW RULES OF REALITY
FAST COMPANY
INFINITE SPECIAL
infinite vacation
Description
Customer Ratings

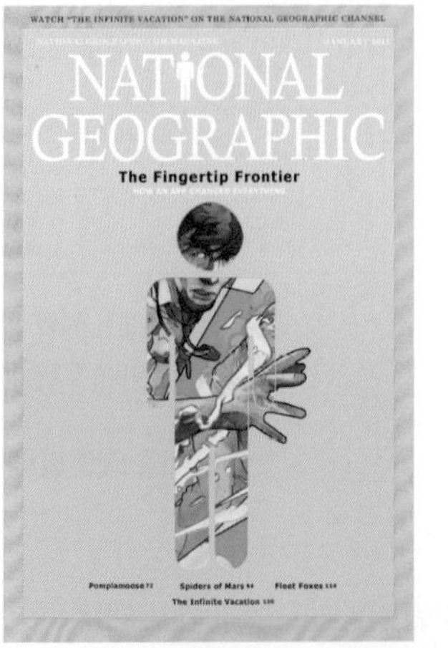
WATCH "THE INFINITE VACATION" ON THE NATIONAL GEOGRAPHIC CHANNEL
NATIONAL GEOGRAPHIC
The Fingertip Frontier
Pomplamoose
Spiders of Mars
Fleet Foxes
The Infinite Vacation

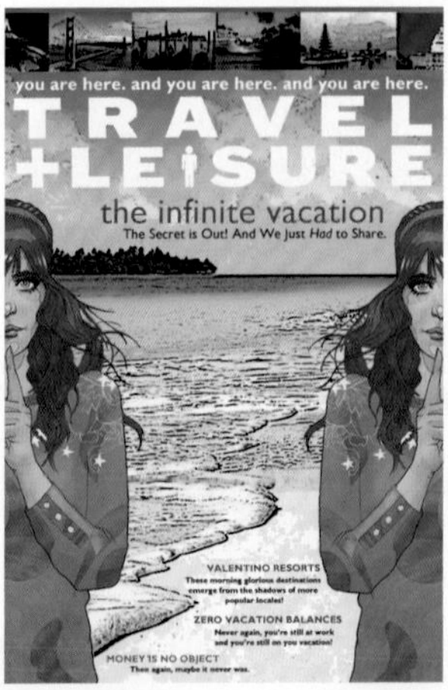
you are here. and you are here. and you are here.
TRAVEL +LEISURE
the infinite vacation
The Secret is Out! And We Just Had to Share.
VALENTINO RESORTS
ZERO VACATION BALANCES
MONEY IS NO OBJECT

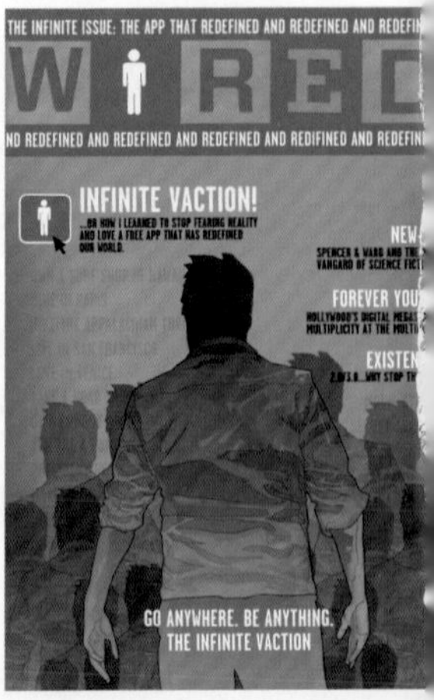
THE INFINITE ISSUE: THE APP THAT REDEFINED AND REDEFINED AND REDEFIN
WIRED
INFINITE VACTION!
FOREVER YOU
GO ANYWHERE. BE ANYTHING.
THE INFINITE VACTION

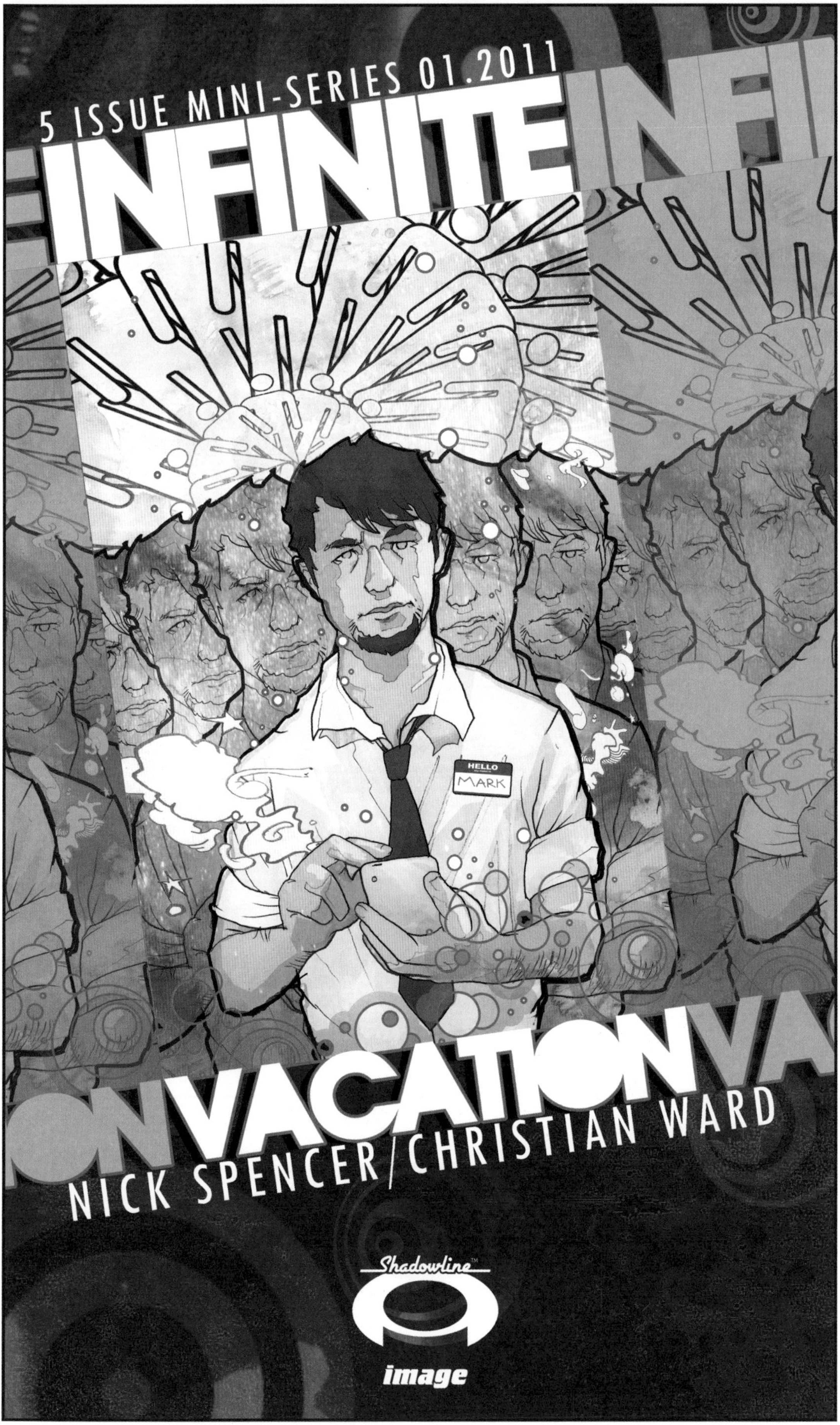
5 ISSUE MINI-SERIES 01.2011
INFINITE
HELLO
MARK
VACATION
NICK SPENCER/CHRISTIAN WARD
Shadowline
image

The first glimpse of Infinite Vacation came in the form of this promotional print distributed exclusively at conventions prior to the release of the first issue.

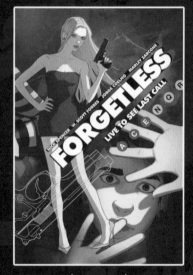

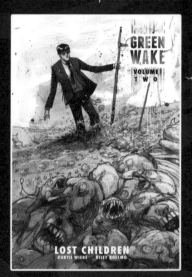